MULTI-TEXTUAL CONSTITUTIONS OF THE WORLD

In this eye-opening study of the world's constitutions, scholars explain the creation, operation, revision, and replacement of multi-textual constitutions – a ubiquitous but woefully understudied constitutional form that is ever-present in many countries of the world but as-yet underappreciated in constitutional studies.

Constitutions are commonly said to be either 'written' or 'unwritten.' This distinction has long been the cornerstone of constitutional studies. Multi-Textual Constitutions of the World presents an alternative view: all constitutions are simultaneously written and unwritten, consisting of unwritten norms, practices, and principles on the one hand, and of written rules on the other.

Given that all constitutions consist of both written and unwritten elements, the conventional distinction between 'written' and 'unwritten' constitutions should be discarded once and for all because it obscures the actual form and content of constitutions. This book lights the path to a better distinction that more correctly reflects the key difference among constitutions: some constitutions consist of one authoritative document while others consist of more than one authoritative document.

Drawing from every major region of the world and featuring expert analysis from outstanding scholars, this book demonstrates that constitutions are better distinguished according to whether they are uni-textual or multi-textual.

Multi-Textual Constitutions of the World

Edited by Richard Albert

• HART •
OXFORD • LONDON • NEW YORK • NEW DELHI • SYDNEY

HART PUBLISHING
Bloomsbury Publishing Plc
Kemp House, Chawley Park, Cumnor Hill, Oxford, OX2 9PH, UK
1385 Broadway, New York, NY 10018, USA
Bloomsbury Publishing Ireland Limited, 29 Earlsfort Terrace, Dublin 2, D02 AY28, Ireland

HART PUBLISHING, the Hart/Stag logo, BLOOMSBURY and the Diana logo are trademarks of Bloomsbury Publishing Plc
First published in Great Britain 2026

1

A catalogue record for this book is available from the British Library.

A catalogue record for this book is available from the Library of Congress.

Library of Congress Control Number: 2026030538

ISBN: HB: 978-1-5099-8069-7
ePDF: 978-1-5099-8071-0
ePub: 978-1-5099-8070-3

Typeset by Lumina Datamatics Ltd

For product safety related questions contact productsafety@bloomsbury.com

To find out more about our authors and books visit www.hartpublishing.co.uk. Here you will find extracts, author information, details of forthcoming events and the option to sign up for our newsletters.

For Ran Hirschl,
who believed in me before I believed in myself

CONTENTS

ACKNOWLEDGEMENTS

I will never be able to repay the debt I have accumulated to my teachers. In Canada, Haiti, the United Kingdom and the United States, my teachers gave me so much of their care, knowledge, and inspiration – all without expecting anything in return, except that I do my honest best.

I continue to have excellent teachers today. My colleagues teach me through their scholarship, their lectures, and our personal interactions in our offices, at conferences, on the phone, and online. And my students teach me with their questions and comments, both in and out of the classroom.

I am especially grateful to my dear friends who have contributed chapters to this book. Their insights and analysis have helped me see constitutions more clearly and completely with the benefit of their rich comparative reflections. I thank them for devoting their time and energies to developing truly excellent chapters for this book which I hope will become a source of pride for them.

My sincere and enthusiastic thanks also to Hart for the opportunity to publish this book with them. Thank you to Kate Whetter, Linda Goss, Sasha Jawed, Verity Stuart, Claire Banyard and the entire team with whom I have had the honour of working for several years now, hopefully with many more to come.

Richard Albert
Austin

CONTRIBUTORS

Richard Albert holds the Hines H. Baker and Thelma Kelley Baker Chair in Law at the University of Texas at Austin, United States.

Toma Birmontienė, formerly a Justice of the Constitutional Court of the Republic of Lithuania, is Full Professor at the Institute of Public Law at the Law School of Mykolas Romeris University, Lithuania.

Dolunay Bulut is a Post-Doctoral Scholar in the School of Government & Public Policy at the University of Arizona, United States.

Leigha C Crout is an Assistant Professor of Law at DePaul University College of Law and a non-resident fellow at the Neukom Center for the Rule of Law at Stanford Law School, United States.

Bruno Santos Cunha is a State Attorney and Professor of Constitutional Law based in Recife, Brazil.

Laura-Stella Enonchong is a Reader in Law at the School of Oriental and African Studies, University of London, United Kingdom.

Natalie Fox is an Adjunct Professor in the Chair in Comparative Constitutional Law of Jagiellonian University in Kraków, Poland.

Masahiko Kinoshita is a Professor at Kobe University Graduate School of Law in Japan.

Konrad Lachmayer is Vice-Dean of Research as well as Professor for Public Law, European Law, and Foundations of Law at Sigmund Freud University in Vienna, Austria.

Mary Liston is an Associate Professor at the Peter A. Allard School of Law, University of British Columbia, Canada.

Oleksandr Marusiak is a Senior Research Fellow at Scientific Research Institute of State Building and Local Government of the National Academy of Law Sciences in Kharkiv, Ukraine.

Jolita Miliuvienė is the Parliamentary Ombudsperson of the Republic of Lithuania and an Associate Professor at the Institute of Public Law at the Law School of Mykolas Romeris University, Lithuania.

Jaime Olaiz-González is Professor of Constitutional Theory, International Law, and American Jurisprudence at Universidad Panamericana Law School in Mexico City, Mexico.

Amal Sethi is an Assistant Professor of Public Law at the University of Leicester, United Kingdom.

Introduction – Are There Any Uni-Textual Constitutions in the World?

RICHARD ALBERT

When we picture the US Constitution in our minds, most of us see a single, unified, supreme document that codifies the highest law in the land. This is no surprise, given that we have all been taught either in school or in popular culture that the Constitution exists in a single 'canonical constitutional master-text'.[1] The Constitution is presented to us like this in all aspects of our daily lives, in every part of the world, whether on television or the Internet, including the website of the congressionally chartered National Constitution Center. The Constitution is also represented in this way in casebooks and pocket-sized versions of the Constitution sold by government institutions, for example the US House of Representatives and the US Citizenship and Immigration Services, or sold by private organisations such as the American Civil Liberties Union and the Federalist Society. The single-documentary physical form of the Constitution is ubiquitous in our minds because it is ubiquitous all around us.

In 2025, for the first time ever, the entire US Constitution was showcased to the world on public display in the rotunda of the National Archives in Washington, DC. This historic exhibit revealed that the Constitution is not what we have long believed it to be. It is not the single self-contained document we have grown accustomed to seeing in law and society. This extraordinary presentation taught us that the thing we call 'the US Constitution' consists of a bundle of separate documents. These documents include the four-page founding document, signed in 1787 by the delegates at the Philadelphia Convention; the single-page Bill of Rights, which engrosses all ten amendments enacted simultaneously in 1791; and 17 resolutions certifying the remaining amendments to the Constitution. Contrary to our conventional understanding of the Constitution, none of the 27 amendments to the Constitution has ever been inscribed to the end of the original parchment on which the Constitution was written. Constitutional amendments have instead been enacted separately as self-standing documents that are each physically disconnected from the founding document that continues to govern the country over two centuries since its enactment. Far from being only a single document,

[1] J Gardner, *Law as a Leap of Faith: Essays on Law in General* (Oxford University Press, 2021) 90.

then, the Constitution comprises at least 19 documents. Each possesses the same elevated special status as the highest laws in the land.

The standard account of the unitary form of the US Constitution is therefore incorrect. This discovery raises a question that must be asked: can there be any unitary constitutions in the world if the paradigmatically uni-textual US Constitution is not in fact one lone canonical document?

I. Forms of Writtenness

For far too long we have begun introductory courses in constitutional law with a misleading binary classification of constitutions: they are either written or unwritten. One observer has commented that 'one of the most traditional points of departure in the study of constitutions has been to classify them according to whether they are "written" or "unwritten."'[2] Another has described written constitutions as 'the norm' and unwritten constitutions as 'the rare exception.'[3] Still another has remarked wryly that 'once upon a time some unknown humorist divided constitutions into written and unwritten, and since then text-book after text-book has taken his classification seriously.'[4] Even Albert Venn Dicey accepted the distinction between written and unwritten constitutions.[5] It has been the most foundational teaching in the study of constitutions.

According to this traditional contrast, written constitutions exist on parchment in documentary form, while unwritten constitutions are intangible sets of invisible rules consisting of norms, principles, and practices that sustain the constitutional order without entrenchment in written word.[6] For instance, the Constitution of the United Kingdom is ordinarily distinguished from others in the world precisely because it is understood to be one of a few examples of a constitution that is 'unwritten.' Yet the most learned constitutional scholars know it is incorrect to describe the UK Constitution in this way. The UK Constitution does indeed consist of unwritten constitutional norms, but so much of what comprises 'the Constitution of the UK' is written down somewhere: Magna Carta, the Acts of Union, the Bill of Rights, the Statute of Westminster, for instance. These keystone documents are only some of the many written components of the UK Constitution.

[2] See M Foley, *The Silence of Constitutions: Gaps, 'Abeyances' and Political Temperament in the Maintenance of Government* (Routledge, 1989) 3.

[3] See P Craig, 'Written and Unwritten Constitutions: The Modality of Change' in S Bookman et al (eds), *Pragmatism, Principle, and Power in Common Law Constitutional Systems* (Intersentia, 2022) 263, 263.

[4] HW Horwill, *The Usages of the American Constitution* (Oxford University Press, 1925) 1.

[5] AV Dicey, *Introduction to the Study of the Law of the Constitution*, 3rd edn (Macmillan, 1889) 3–6.

[6] See eg WJ Cocker, *The Government of the United States* (Harper & Brothers, 1889) 55; L Hudson Holt, *The Elementary Principles of Modern Government* (Macmillan, 1923) 26; JA Jameson, *A Treatise on Constitutional Conventions; Their History, Powers, and Modes of Proceeding*, 4th edn (Callaghan, 1887) 77.

This comparative shorthand between written and unwritten constitutions has been pedagogically convenient but it has obscured the main structural difference among the constitutions of the world. That deeper and more consequential distinction is not about the writtenness of constitutions, because all constitutions are in some way written down, and all constitutions consist of unwritten rules.[7] The key difference among constitutions is whether they are uni-textual or multi-textual, namely whether what we call 'the constitution' is understood to reside in a single authoritative document or in a plurality of documents that have a special status.

In this book on multi-textual constitutions of the world, the contributors disrupt the conventional narrative about the standard form of constitutions. The chapters in this book show that constitutions are not always solitary texts. Many constitutions all over the world are complex constitutional ecosystems that consist of authoritative documents adopted at different moments, often by different actors, frequently in response to crisis, necessity, or transition, and bound together by a shared claim to supremacy. Constitutional systems around the globe are therefore often better understood as compound, layered, and plural in the documents that comprise them. Many constitutions self-consciously recognise their own multiplicity by expressly acknowledging the constitutional status of documents promulgated by official actors engaged in constitution-making or -changing, enacted by legislative enactments via basic laws or constitutional statutes, or elevated to the highest law of the land by interpretation or practice. We should appreciate and recognise the prevalence of multi-textual constitutions because they are a common design of world constitutions. Even the US Constitution – the longtime paradigmatic expositor of a uni-textual constitution – is multi-textual.

Multi-textual constitutions exist all around the world, but they are often incorrectly labelled *unwritten* constitutions. Think of the Constitutions of Israel and New Zealand, both grouped with the United Kingdom as having an unwritten constitution. These constitutions are better understood as multi-textual. There are many other constitutions that are multi-textual insofar as they consist of multiple documents of equal authority in either law or society, or both. In this book, experts from around the world explain how their own multi-textual constitutions function. The contributors are scholars and jurists. They are diverse in their countries of birth and residence, institutional affiliation, and seniority. This outstanding group of authors also includes several early-career scholars, and in the aggregate the contributors consist of seven women and six men. The result is a groundbreaking study that covers jurisdictions in Africa, America, Asia, and Europe, namely Afghanistan, Austria, Brazil, Canada, Cameroon, China, Japan, Lithuania, Mexico, Poland, Turkey, and Ukraine. Focusing on these jurisdictions has the advantage of diversifying the comparators that are traditionally used in

[7] See J Pek, 'Things Better Left Unwritten? Constitutional Text and the Rule of Law' (2008) 83 *New York University Law Review* 1979, 1981.

comparative constitutional studies. Too few comparative studies in English focus on these countries, though Brazil, Canada, and Poland are popular comparators, albeit not for their constitutional form. In addition to extending our knowledge of multi-textuality, the chapters in this book invite scholars to learn about understudied jurisdictions.

II. Defining Multi-Textuality

There are three core features of multi-textual constitutions: multiplicity, asynchrony, and shared supremacy. By definition, a multi-textual constitution comprises a plurality of constitutional documents. In jurisdictions governed by a multi-textual constitution, there is no single canonical document to which we can point as 'the constitution'. There are instead several documents that together amount to what is called 'the constitution' in that particular jurisdiction. A multi-textual constitution may consist of two co-equal documents or tens or even hundreds of separate but equal constitutional enactments. Whether there are two or 200 texts is of no significance for defining multi-textuality: as long as there is more than one document known as 'the constitution,' that jurisdiction fulfils the first criterion in the tripartite test for multi-textuality. The multi-textual Constitution of New Zealand, for instance, consists of the Constitution Act 1986, the New Zealand Bill of Rights Act 1990, the Electoral Act 1993, the Public Finance Act 1989, and the Treaty of Waitangi, among many other texts recognised as part of the written components of the constitution.[8] This reflects the common feature of multiplicity in multi-textual constitutions.

The second distinguishing legal feature of multi-textual constitutions is asynchrony. The various documents of higher law in a multi-textual jurisdiction are not necessarily adopted at the same moment. They may alternatively be adopted as separate enactments over the life of a constitutional state. There is no defined interval at which separate enactments may come into force, nor are there rules requiring a specific sequence of enactment. These higher laws are enacted serially when they are adopted, according to no particular schedule, as driven by the needs and forces of the time. The founding 1787 US Constitution and subsequent amendments enacted in the more than two centuries since then illustrate the asynchrony of multi-textual constitutions.

The third basic legal feature of multi-textual constitutions is shared supremacy. To understand this feature, we must begin with its converse. In the standard operation of a uni-textual constitution, the single document known as the constitution stands above all other domestic laws. This constitutional document is supreme, and all other laws are inferior to it. This is a model of exclusive supremacy: in the constitutional hierarchy of uni-textual regimes, there is one single

[8] MSR Palmer and DR Knight, *The Constitution of New Zealand: A Contextual Analysis* (Hart Publishing, 2022) 1.

authoritative document of higher law. As a consequence of this exclusive supremacy in a uni-textual regime, a law is invalid to the extent of any inconsistency with this lone higher law.

Constitutions operate differently in multi-textual regimes. Unlike the model of exclusive supremacy in uni-textual regimes, multi-textual regimes adhere to a model of shared supremacy under which there is more than one higher law at the summit of the constitutional pyramid. In multi-textual regimes, the multiple documents of higher law are by default situated at the same elevated level of constitutional superiority. These higher laws at the summit of the constitutional order share supremacy under law. None automatically trumps another, unlike in a uni-textual regime in which one supreme document occupies the entire field of higher law. In Sweden, for example, the Constitution consists of four fundamental laws, each equally supreme: the Instrument of Government, which details the form of government; the Act of Succession, which regulates succession to the throne; the Freedom of the Press Act, which pertains to the right to disseminate and acquire information; and the Fundamental Law on Freedom of Expression, which protects new forms of media. Their shared supremacy in the Swedish legal order makes them prevail over any other laws that are or become inconsistent with them.

Shared supremacy entails a form of entrenchment, either legal or political. Absent exceptional circumstances, what makes a constitutional document legally entrenched is its immunity from ordinary repeal without recourse to special procedures or thresholds of constitutional reform.[9] For instance, a set of laws could not be regarded as constitutionally supreme if it were susceptible to revision or replacement by the same procedure or threshold used to revise or replace laws that are not regarded as constitutionally supreme. The exceptional circumstances where shared supremacy does not entail legal entrenchment involve jurisdictions where legal documents have become politically entrenched: they are regarded as constitutionally special but nonetheless technically remain revisable or replaceable by ordinary legislative means.[10] The Constitution of the United Kingdom is a useful jurisdiction to illustrate this point. The Constitution does not codify special procedures for constitutional reform, but it operates nonetheless as a hierarchical legal regime insofar as it consists of both ordinary statutes and constitutional statutes. These constitutional statutes do not arise by special procedures; they derive their status instead from their special treatment in politics.[11] They are therefore not legally entrenched against parliamentary repeal or revision, but rather politically entrenched in constitutional politics.

[9] NW Barber, 'Why Entrench?' (2016) 14 *International Journal of Constitutional Law* 325, 325.
[10] ibid 327–28.
[11] See F Ahmed and A Perry, 'Constitutional Statutes' (2017) 37 *Oxford Journal of Legal Studies* 461, 464–65.

III. Origins and Pathways of Multi-Textuality

Multi-textual constitutions emerge in different ways. Sometimes the multi-textual character of a constitution is designed consciously from the beginning. At other times, multi-textuality is the unplanned consequence of legal, political, social evolution and contingency. Often, design and evolution intermingle in a fascinating combination of planning and happenstance. The point here is plain: multi-textuality has no single point of origin.

Consider the intentional creation of a multi-textual constitution. Three models prevail: authorisation, conditionality, and enumeration. These three models represent deliberate design choices at the moment of constitution-making to institutionalise multi-textuality, whether by referencing and incorporating existing documents, reserving space for future documents, or enumerating a menu of constitutional instruments as jointly supreme. In the first model – the multi-textual constitution-making model of authorisation – the founding constitutional document makes clear that additional documents of higher law may be adopted in the future. Italy, for example, authorised the creation of additional constitutional documents in its 1947 Constitution. Constitutional laws may be enacted using a complex procedure requiring their approval in both chambers of the national legislature in two consecutive votes separated by no fewer than three months, followed by a referendum if it is requested either by one-fifth of the members of one chamber of the legislature, or by 500,000 voters, or by five Regional Councils. These constitutional laws have a status equal to each other, to all amendments, and also to the founding document.

The second model of multi-textual constitution-making is conditionality. It is similar to the model of authorisation, only it includes explicit limitations on what kinds of documents may be enacted in the future. The critical feature of this second model of multi-textual constitution-making is the requirement that any new constitutional documents of equal status that may be created to form part of 'the constitution' must remain consistent with the founding document. In Azerbaijan, for example, constitutional laws may be enacted on the condition that they 'shall not contradict the main text of the Constitution,' a reference to the 1995 Constitution in which the authorisation appears. When enacted, they exist and operate as new, self-standing constitutional documents. Yet they are not treated as sub-constitutional nor formally inferior to the founding constitutional document. They are treated as higher laws that share supremacy with the 1995 constitutional text.

The third model of multi-textual constitution-making is a formal model of enumeration. It exists in Lithuania, whose post-independence Constitution of 1992 was adopted as a higher law for a new beginning. The designers of the Constitution indicated in this founding text that their constitution includes more than just the 1992 document. They specified that it includes additional documents of higher law, each of which is enumerated in the 1992 document as additional and equal parts of the Constitution: (1) the Constitutional Law

'On the State of Lithuania' of 11 February 1991; (2) the Constitutional Act 'On the Non-Alignment of the Republic of Lithuania to Post-Soviet Eastern Unions' of 8 June 1992; and (3) the Law 'On the Procedure for the Entry into Force of the Constitution of the Republic of Lithuania' of 25 October 1992. Today, the Lithuanian Constitution enumerates one additional document with the same constitutional status: the Constitutional Act 'On Membership of the Republic of Lithuania in the European Union' of 13 July 2004. Just like the other four documents that comprise the Lithuanian Constitution, this new Constitutional Act is treated as an equal-in-force addition to the founding document enacted into law in 1992. This model of formal enumeration makes clear what has constitutional status.

Multi-textuality can arise also by evolution in at least three ways: formal amendment, political practice, and judicial interpretation. When reformers amend their constitution, they may choose to edit the actual text of the founding document, and to maintain the constitution as one single document. Reformers may alternatively choose to codify and formalise a constitutional reform in its own separate, self-standing document of higher law that exists detached from the founding document. In that case, all of those many texts would be understood as jointly comprising what is regarded in that jurisdiction as 'the constitution.' We can understand this constitutional activity as a pluralisation of constitutional texts. It is one origin of multi-textuality by evolution. An additional path to multi-textuality is by judicial interpretation. In the course of constitutional litigation, judges may confer constitutional status upon documents that have not previously been regarded as 'constitutional.' When a judge designates a given document as 'constitutional,' that document attains a status equal to what is recognised in the jurisdiction as 'the constitution.'

In addition to a constitution's evolution from uni-textual to multi-textual by constitutional amendment and judicial interpretation, the pluralisation of constitutional texts can occur by political practice in the course of the law-making process. Imagine, for example, that a legislature enacts an ordinary law with a simple majority. In the normal course of affairs, that law would be changeable, even repealable, by a simple legislative majority. We would regard that law as legally subordinate to the constitution. But how would we regard that law if the legislature decides later to use the more difficult constitutional amendment procedure – not the ordinary legislative procedure – to make revisions to that law? We might then conclude that the legislature has determined that the law possesses a special 'constitutional' status that it has acquired sometime between its enactment as an ordinary law and its amendment as a higher law. We would then count that document as a constitutional law that sits alongside the founding document as comprising the constitution of that jurisdiction. In summary, multi-textual constitutions may accordingly be created by intentional design at the founding or by unforeseen evolution after the enactment of the constitution through constitutional amendment, political practice, and judicial interpretation.

IV. In this Volume

The chapters in this book each focus on multi-textual constitutions in a specific jurisdiction around the world. They explain how the constitution became multi-textual in its design, identification, or operation. The chapters also highlight some strengths and shortcomings of multi-textual constitutions. The book opens in chapter one with a puzzle: Japan's post-war Constitution has never once been amended, making it at least uni-textual in theory, yet in actuality it is better described as something else. In his chapter titled 'Multi-Textual Constitutions in Japan: History, Functions, and Operations', Masahiko Kinoshita explores Japanese constitutional history and finds that Japanese Constitutions have never strictly conformed either to the model of a uni-textual constitution, nor have they fulfilled the three criteria of multi-textual constitutions, namely multiplicity, asynchrony, and shared supremacy. Under the constitutional regime that preceded the current constitution, the Meiji Constitution shared constitutional supremacy with the Imperial House Law. Then, in the transition from the Meiji Constitution to the current 1946 Constitution under Allied occupation, the Potsdam Declaration and directives issues by the Supreme Commander for the Allied Powers operated as super-constitutional norms. Now, under the 1946 Constitution, the narrow scope of constitutional rules and their relatively weak supremacy have elevated the status of certain statutes in Japan's constitutional order. Kinoshita shows that some form of multi-textuality has therefore been evident at every step in Japan's constitutional history.

In chapter two, Laura-Stella Enonchong examines 'Multi-Textuality and Incrementalism in Cameroon's Democratic Transition'. Enonchong employs the phenomenon of multi-textual constitutions to explore the political and legal implications of applying two constitutional texts in Cameroon between 1996 and 2019. As Enonchong explains, multi-textuality in Cameroon originated incidentally from transitional provisions in the 1996 Constitution, which sanctioned the partial and continued application of the prior 1972 Constitution. Although multi-textuality can offer continuity and stability during a purported transition from an authoritarian to a democratic regime, as Enonchong demonstrates, it can also open the door to efforts to undermine constitutionalism during that transition. Multi-textuality, therefore, can be Janus-faced, blending the promise for entrenching democracy with real risks of eroding it. This chapter assesses how to harness the potential of multi-textual constitutions, with specific reference to transitional contexts.

Chapter three, by Konrad Lachmayer, is titled 'The Beauty and the Beast: The Excessive Multi-Textualism of the Austrian Constitution'. Lachmayer explores the excessive multi-textualism in Austrian constitutional law, which is characterised by the co-existence of the founding constitutional document alongside hundreds of constitutional laws and even more constitutional provisions in statutory laws. Lachmayer probes the legal and political challenges arising from the complex multi-textual constitutional structure of the Austrian Constitution. These challenges include constitutional incoherence, legal uncertainty, and constitutional erosion.

Consideration is also given to how the Austrian Constitutional Court has performed its functions against the backdrop of such a highly fragmented constitutional framework. As Lachmayer shows, however, multi-textuality has come with advantages in Austria. Specifically, it has made possible pragmatic adaptation in the context of federal-state relations and European Union integration. He ultimately concludes that constitutional culture and practice are decisive to ensure constitutional integrity and to manage the complexity attendant to multi-textual constitutions.

We travel across the Atlantic Ocean for chapter four. In 'Canada's Multi-Textual Constitution', Mary Liston exposes what has been taken for granted or considered simply obvious in Canadian constitutional law: that Canada's constitution is multi-textual. The chapter explains the form and nature of the multi-textuality in Canada, and moreover draws from literary techniques to illustrate how to navigate and integrate different but fundamentally related texts in Canada, and by extension elsewhere. Drawing on literary theory to understand a text as any object that can be 'read,' the chapter builds on a broader socio-legal understanding of the phenomenon of a 'constitution.' Liston's analysis pays close attention to the growing importance of Indigenous constitutions in Canada. Liston also asks who has the authority to identify and name what counts as official or unofficial constitutional texts – a question that often arises in multi-textual jurisdictions.

In chapter five, Bruno Santos Cunha shines a light on 'Multi-Textuality by Amendment: The Brazilian Case'. The chapter explores the emergence of a multi-textual constitutional framework in Brazil following Constitutional Amendment No. 45/2004, which conferred upon certain international human rights treaties – the ones approved under a special legislative procedure – the same elevated status as constitutional amendments in the hierarchy of constitutional importance in the country. While these treaties are recognised under law as constitutional in nature and effect, they are not integrated into the founding text of the 1988 Constitution. The result is to create what Cunha describes as a parallel layer of constitutional norms. Cunha moreover details the historical, doctrinal, and political developments that prompted the choice to pluralise constitutional texts. He discusses how Brazilian courts have interpreted and applied these detached constitutional norms and considers the challenges of coherence and identification in Brazil's fragmented constitution.

Chapter six, 'Vertical and Horizontal Layers of the Lithuanian Constitution', is co-authored by Toma Birmontienė and Jolita Miliuvienė. They illuminate the 'composite codified' nature of the Constitution of the Republic of Lithuania and describe the constituent constitutional acts that form what is regarded in the country as 'the Constitution.' A multi-textual constitution by design, the Lithuanian Constitution, they explain, has been further amplified by its evolution through constitutional interpretation and state developments. In the course of detailing the evolution of the Lithuanian Constitution, they introduce the doctrine of supra-constitutional acts. Created by the Constitutional Court, this doctrine raises some doubt about the supremacy of the Constitution. Their chapter clarifies the design and operation of the Constitution, explains its growth and adaptability in a changing domestic and regional legal reality, and weighs the opportunities and challenges of multi-textuality in the Lithuanian constitutional order.

In chapter seven, titled 'There and Back Again: The Case of Mexico's Constitutional Forms Between Uni- and Multi-Textualism', Jaime Olaiz-González dives deeply into Mexico's constitutional history to uncover the country's cyclical shifts between uni-textual and multi-textual constitutionals forms. He explains that the country's first constitution in 1824 was multi-textual, consisting of the founding constitution and the Federalist Constitutive Act. The Constitutions of 1836, 1843, and 1857 were uni-textual, with a brief return to multi-textualism in 1847. He then shows that the current 1917 Constitution formally recognised its multi-textual form but operated as a uni-textual constitution until the 2011 Human Rights Reform. That year, a major constitutional reform elevated human rights treaties to constitutional rank, established the *pro persona* principle, and fostered doctrines like the block of constitutionality and block of conventionality in Mexico. These developments, Olaiz-González explains, marked a decade of dialogic, pluralist constitutionalism. But, as Olaiz-González shows, these dynamics gave way to reforms and resistance that ultimately reinstated a rigid uni-textual constitution. This chapter underscores the peculiarly Mexican phenomenon of alternation between uni-textuality and multi-textuality.

In chapter eight, Natalie Fox analyses 'The Tradition of Multi-Textuality in Poland' with a focus on the country's recurring reliance on multi-textuality. That tradition took the form of 'small constitutions' enacted in 1919, 1947, and 1992. Fox explains that these constitutional documents exhibit two defining features: temporality and incompleteness. They were designed to be provisional and incomplete, intended to bring stability to government, all while postponing an enduring and comprehensive constitutional settlement. Political actors turned to this technology in key transitional moments in the constitutional life of the country. These small constitutions had constitutional status but they regulated matters more commonly codified in ordinary law. As Fox observes, this 'duality' of small constitutions in Polish constitutional history simultaneously reflects their pragmatic utility and structural limitations.

Chapter nine brings us to Ukraine. In 'Exploring Macro-Constitutional Reality in Ukraine: Multi-Textual Insights from the Constitutional Court', Oleksandr Marusiak begins by observing that the 1996 Constitution of Ukraine is traditionally regarded as a single codified document, but he adds that at least three other documents exhibit characteristics of the country's supreme law: (1) the Act of Declaration of Independence of Ukraine, approved by referendum on 1 December 1991; (2) the Law of Ukraine 'On Adoption of the Constitution of Ukraine and Its Entry into Force', adopted immediately after the 1996 Constitution; and (3) the Rules of Procedure of the Verkhovna Rada of Ukraine, which, although formally an ordinary statute, has acquired special status from the Constitutional Court. His analysis seeks to understand the operation of the Constitution, and to demonstrate that multi-textuality has practical relevance in Ukraine beyond mere theory. Marusiak defines this state of affairs as Ukraine's 'macro-constitutional reality.'

In chapter ten, Leigha Crout examines 'Multi-Textuality in China: Revisions and Revolutions'. In practice, Crout explains, the Constitution is not the only source of constitutional norms in China. In addition to the Constitution, national 'Constitution-Related Laws' regulate state institutions, regional autonomy, constitutional rights, and state sovereignty. These special laws build upon or directly influence constitutionally codified rules and are often recognised as possessing semi-constitutional or wholly constitutional status. Other sources have also been regarded as indispensable and legally binding elements of China's Constitution. Crout analyses these various constitutional rules in China, evaluates the hierarchy and relationship among them, and delves into the benefits and complexities posed by multi-textuality in an authoritarian context.

In the penultimate chapter eleven, Dolunay Bulut demonstrates in 'Multi-Textuality and the Question of Constitutional Authorship' how a functional multiplicity can persist beneath the surface of the formal singularity of the constitutional text. Under the ruling AKP government, Bulut observes, the 1982 Turkish Constitution reveals two patterns of functional multiplicity: a secular multi-textuality employed by the republican regime to preserve its core characteristics, and a *de facto* Islamist legal pluralism under the AKP, which compartmentalises constitutionally entrenched social, political, and moral functions to consolidate its authoritarian rule. Bulut notes that while secular multi-textuality may have had questionable legitimacy, it nevertheless maintained internal normative coherence aligned with the core principles of the Constitution. In contrast, Bulut explains, the AKP's Islamist legal pluralism fragments constitutionally entrenched state authority by empowering religious sources and authorities, and by changing the fabric of the country.

Chapter twelve concludes the volume. In 'The Taliban's Multi-Textual Constitution: Cultivated Ambiguity as Authoritarian Technique', Amal Sethi argues that the Taliban regime governs through a multi-textual constitution composed of scripture, insurgency codes, doctrinal tracts, decrees, and relic texts. He illustrates how the regime sustains this system through what he terms 'cultivated ambiguity,' or the deliberate maintenance of uncertainty regarding source hierarchy and interpretation. According to Sethi, this technique provides the regime with policy flexibility, elite containment, tactical legitimacy, and foundational evasion. The chapter moreover compares Afghanistan with China, Iran, and Saudi Arabia to demonstrate that this strategy is characteristic of authoritarian regimes. In this way, Sethi shows that the Taliban's return to power in 2021 marked a rejection of codified constitutionalism but not an absence of constitutional order.

V. An Empirical Question

Constitutions are not always multi-textual. Many are uni-textual. But how common are uni-textual constitutions in the world? In this book, we suggest that there are fewer uni-textual constitutions than we might have thought. The US Constitution is not uni-textual in its legal form. Nor are the constitutions of Afghanistan, Austria, Brazil, Canada, Cameroon, China, Japan, Lithuania, Mexico, Poland, Turkey, and Ukraine. The conditions that led these constitutions to become multi-textual exist elsewhere in the world, and have similarly shaped those constitutions. Still, the question whether any constitutions are uni-textual can be answered only with the kind of detailed single-country jurisdictional studies featured in this book. Recognising that generalists without country-specific knowledge of the design and operation of a constitution could not give an authoritative answer to the question whether that constitution is multi-textual, this book engages specialists to relate the general theory of multi-textuality to the specific facts and socio-legal context of their country in order to assess whether their constitution is uni-textual or multi-textual. If we wish to classify any other constitution accurately as uni-textual or multi-textual, the same kind of in-depth study that each contributor has produced for this book must be performed. It is therefore an empirical question whether a constitution is uni-textual or multi-textual; theory alone cannot answer it, nor doctrine alone, nor certainly history alone. All insights are needed to answer the question.

The world's uni-textual constitutions include those that are legally a single canonical document. They need not be sociologically recognised as uni-textual in order to in fact count as uni-textual. The world's uni-textual constitutions also include those not yet amended, as well as those adhering to one or more of the appendative, integrative, and invisible models of amendment codification.[12] These three models of amendment codification eschew enacting new constitutional documents to the constitutional system to formalise a constitutional amendment. They instead alter the existing text of the original constitution, keeping it unchanged in its basic form. For example, in the appendative model, amendments are appended sequentially to the end of the constitutional document, with no alteration made to anything else anywhere in the text. Appendative amendments are simple additions to the existing constitution. In the integrative model, amendments are incorporated directly into the text of the original constitution. Integrative amendments are accompanied by notations or footnotes indicating what in the text has changed as a result of the amendment. And in the invisible model, amendments are likewise incorporated directly into the text of the original constitution, only without any notations or footnotes about what has changed, nor how. Invisible amendments alter the constitutional document without any indication that its text has been edited as a result of an amendment. None of these models of amendment codification pluralises the number of constitutional documents upon the enactment of an amendment. They all retain the documentary singularity of the constitution.

In theory, then, constitutions that adhere to these three models of amendment codification – appendative, integrative, and invisible – would qualify as uni-textual constitutions. One might assume that most constitutions reflect one of these three

[12] See R Albert, *Constitutional Amendments: Making, Breaking, and Changing Constitutions* (Oxford University Press, 2019) ch 6.

categories of amendment codification. Yet a recent study suggests fewer constitutions than we might imagine adhere strictly to a single model of amendment codification.[13] Instead, constitutions adopt a hybrid model blending two or more models of amendment codification, often including a fourth model that can be described as disaggregative. Under this disaggregative model, an amendment is memorialised in its own separate self-standing constitutional document that is disaggregated from the original constitution. In Brazil, Ethiopia, and the Republic of Georgia, for example, the standard practice of constitutional amendment reflects the strategic use of all four models of amendment codification.[14] The choice of which model of amendment codification to use for editing the constitution turns on the nature and scale of the amendment.

VI. An Agenda for Constitutional Research

This book endeavours to spark interest in the study and analysis of multi-textuality. The excellent chapters in this volume open our eyes to the unique form and operation of some multi-textual constitutions. Still, much remains for us to learn, and many questions remain to be asked about multi-textual constitutions. For instance, are there advantages to the multi-textual form in relation to constitutional development and regime transitions? On one view, multi-textuality creates flexibility in constitutional change. In a multi-textual regime, reformers can introduce changes to the constitutional system by adding a new document rather than overhauling or formally altering the founding charter. Separately, does multi-textuality relax amendment difficulty? Where a founding charter is too difficult to alter, legally enacted reforms may be impossible, leading to constitutional stagnation or extra-constitutional workarounds that undermine the rule of law. In these cases, does multi-textuality offer alternative avenues for reform beyond amending the founding text? Would reformers choose to enact a self-standing constitutional statute or alter an existing constitutional statute that exists apart from the founding constitution if they believe amending the founding document will be too legally or politically onerous? These questions probe whether a multi-textual constitutional system eases amendment difficulty by giving political actors multiple legal sites to codify constitutional reforms when it becomes clear that change is needed.

A second set of questions concerns the accommodation of difference and diversity in a polity. Multi-textuality may be well-suited to accommodating diversity within

[13] See R Albert, *The Architecture of Constitutional Amendments* (Hart Publishing, 2023).

[14] See B Cunha, 'The Codification of Constitutional Amendments in Brazil: Beyond the Appendative and Integrative Models' in R Albert, *The Architecture of Constitutional Amendments* (Hart Publishing, 2023) 75; M Nakashidze, 'Georgia's Model of Constitutional Amendment Codification' in R Albert, *The Architecture of Constitutional Amendments* (Hart Publishing, 2023) 245; Z Esehtu Degifie, 'The Amalgamation of Amendment Codification Models in Ethiopia: A Move Towards an Unwritten Constitution' in R Albert, *The Architecture of Constitutional Amendments* (Hart Publishing, 2023).

a state along legal, cultural, territorial, or other grounds. Does layering complex and even competing rules in multi-textual constitutions provide a sustainable base for composite legal systems to live fruitfully alongside one another, particularly in jurisdictions that are multi-juridical and multi-national? Does multi-textuality enhance constitutional stability by discouraging revolutionary breaks with the past and instead preserving continuity with prior legal orders or institutions? In a similar vein, to what extent does multi-textuality assist in bridging generations of constitutional norms? Adding new documents rather than altogether replacing the founding charter may make possible the selective conservation of an earlier generation of rights, rules, and structures in such a way that allows modern legal traditions to coexist with older ones, all within the same constitutional regime.

Other research questions present themselves. Does multi-textuality create a laboratory for innovation in constitutional design? Does multi-textuality make it easier for reformers to experiment with new institutions or rights without disturbing the founding charter? Do multi-textual constitutions guard against the problem of constitutional veneration, or are they just as susceptible to its risks as are uni-textual constitutions? One might hypothesise that spreading constitutional authority across separate documents could diffuse the excessive veneration that can attach to a uni-textual constitution. Reducing constitutional veneration, one might argue, could foster a healthier and more pragmatic approach to constitutional reform. An additional line of inquiry involves specification and specialisation: is it wise for a regime to focus separate constitutional texts on discrete subject matters? If yes, multi-textuality could be a profitable vehicle to that end. This focused approach to constitution-making could well create, in the end, a more comprehensive charter whose rules cover more ground than might be covered in a uni-textual constitution, if only because covering separate subjects in separate texts could avoid overburdening one single canonical constitutional document. Multi-textuality could also protect the form and content of the founding constitutional text.

For all its potential advantages, multi-textuality may likewise entail risks and challenges for constitutional governance and constitutionalism itself. Further research might inquire into the consequences of the formal fragmentation and complexity associated with the pluralisation of constitutional documents. Does multi-textuality make the constitution unwieldy, opaque, or inaccessible? Does the possibility of intra-constitutional constitutional conflict rise with the pluralisation of documents? Does the complexity of multi-textuality complicate the public's understanding of their constitution? Does it make the constitution comprehensible only to lawyers?

Multiple texts may also affect how the constitution is perceived. Does the pluralisation of texts diminish the educational or symbolic value of a constitution, insofar as a multiplicity of documents could make the document a less potent reflection of national unity and of the social contract that binds the governed to each other? Relatedly, if the multi-textual constitution is viewed as the exclusive domain of specialists, could that weaken the basis for civic education and public engagement? More concretely, does the intricacy of multi-textuality undercut the power of the people to hold government accountable given the deep information gap that might arise when the assemblage of constitutional documents is understandable only to legal and political elites?

A series of other questions presents itself in relation to judicial power in the face of multiple texts of constitutional status. Courts are the ones most routinely expected to harmonise conflicts between and among constitutional documents. Is there a risk of judicial aggrandizement in this context? Could a court improperly resolve a conflict between constitutional documents by prioritising the document it favours over the one that should more appropriately trump all others? Is there evidence that courts might step beyond their traditional role as interpreters of constitutional meaning into actively reshaping the architecture of the constitution? If this is a risk worth monitoring, what tools may political actors implement to aid them in that task, and how effective are those tools? And how to implement these tools consistently across time within the same jurisdiction? These are only a few of the many fascinating questions about multi-textuality that await future research.

VII. A Global Phenomenon

Multi-textuality is a global phenomenon in constitutional form. Constitutions often consist of layers of documents, including a combination of historical charters, constitutional amendments, annexes, super-statutes, international instruments, and other texts that together comprise the supreme law of the land. The prevalence of multi-textual constitutions calls for us to recast our study and understanding of how constitutions are made, how they are altered, how they are interpreted, and how they are ultimately replaced. The chapters in this book, all of them important and each authored by brilliant scholars attuned to how constitutions operate in both law and society, have launched us on an exciting journey to ascertain the facets, features, and failures of multi-textuality. Their chapters are essential because multi-textual constitutions are prevalent all around us today, and they will continue to be at the centre of our constitutional future. It is our responsibility not only to appreciate the theoretical foundations of this ubiquitous form of higher law, but also to build on its strengths and shore up its weaknesses in the service of the values of constitutionalism, democracy, and the rule of law.

1

Multi-Textual Constitutions in Japan: History, Functions, and Operations

MASAHIKO KINOSHITA

I. Introduction

In his comparative analysis of constitutional forms, Richard Albert distinguishes between *uni-textual* and *multi-textual* constitutions.[1] The former takes the form of a single, unified document serving as the supreme law of the land, whereas the latter comprises several separate texts that together possess constitutional supremacy. A typical example of a *multi-textual* constitution is the Canadian Constitution, which comprises a series of constitutional documents, including the Constitution Act 1867 and the Constitution Act 1982.[2]

Then, should Japan's Constitution be classified as a *uni-textual* or *multi-textual* constitutional model? The Japanese Constitution has appeared as a textbook example of a *uni-textual* constitution, both historically and in the present day. In fact, Japanese constitutional history features two successive codified constitutions: the Meiji Constitution[3] and the 1946 Constitution,[4] each existing as a single, unified document. Nevertheless, despite this appearance, Japan has never strictly conformed to the ideal of a *uni-textual* constitution. The Meiji Constitution shared constitutional supremacy with the Imperial House Law. During the transition from the Meiji Constitution to the 1946 Constitution under Allied occupation, the Potsdam Declaration and directives issued by the Supreme Commander for the Allied Powers (SCAP) operated as super-constitutional norms. Under the 1946 Constitution, the narrow scope of constitutional provisions and their relatively weak supremacy have elevated the status of constitutional statutes within Japan's constitutional order.

[1] R Albert, 'Multi-Textual Constitutions' (2023) 109 *Virginia Law Review* 1629.
[2] Constitution Act 1982, being Schedule B to the Canada Act 1982 (UK) c 11, s 52(2).
[3] Constitution of the Empire of Japan (promulgated 11 February 1889, entered into force 29 November 1890, repealed 3 May 1947).
[4] Constitution of Japan (promulgated 3 November 1946, entered into force 3 May 1947).

Unlike paradigmatic *multi-textual* jurisdictions such as Canada, the Japanese constitutional system has not neatly aligned with the three fundamental legal characteristics of multi-textual constitutions identified by Albert: (1) multiplicity, (2) asynchrony, and (3) shared supremacy.[5] However, it is also difficult to assert that the higher laws of Japan have been fully contained within a single integrated constitutional document, given the enduring presence of multiple constitutionally significant texts operating beyond the level of ordinary statutes. This chapter explores the history, functions, and operations of this distinctive Japanese version of constitutional *multi-textuality*.

This chapter divides the history of the Japanese Constitution into three periods – the Meiji Constitution period, the Occupation period, and the post-war period under the 1946 Constitution – and analyses the emergence and role of constitutional *multi-textuality* in each phase. First, it examines the Meiji Constitution period, focusing on the relationship between the Meiji Constitution and the Imperial House Law. Both documents were enacted simultaneously, each asserting supremacy within separate normative spheres, thereby giving rise to a dual constitutional order.[6] Second, it addresses the Occupation period, during which a super-constitutional authority, anchored in the Potsdam Declaration, operated above the ordinary Constitution. Finally, the chapter examines the current constitutional order established by the 1946 Constitution. Although the 1946 Constitution remains *uni-textual* in form, the substantial legal framework in Japan exhibits the functional characteristics of multiple constitutional statutes, akin to the systems found in the United Kingdom and New Zealand.

II. Dual Constitution Order

A. Meiji Constitution

In 1867, Yoshinobu Tokugawa, the last *Shogun*, returned government power to the Emperor (*Tennō*).[7] The era name (*gengō*) was changed to Meiji in the following year, marking the end of the feudal period and the beginning of Japan's modernisation. In its initial phase, the new Meiji government was led by those who had

[5] Albert (n 1) 1636.

[6] The Meiji era and the period during which the Meiji Constitution was in effect are not the same. The Meiji era, as an era name (*gengō*) denoting the reign of Emperor Meiji (Mutsuhito), spanned from 1868 to 1912. It was followed by the Taisho era (1912–1926), the Showa era (1926–1989), the Heisei era (1989–2019), and the current Reiwa era (2019–), each corresponding to the reign of a different Emperor. By contrast, the Meiji Constitution, which was promulgated during the Meiji era, remained in force from 1890 to 1947. In this chapter, the Meiji Constitution period refers to the period during which the Meiji Constitution was in effect.

[7] For a general overview of the Meiji Restoration, see S Matsui, *The Constitution of Japan: A Contextual Analysis* (Hart Publishing, 2011) 5–7; BL Walker, *A Concise History of Japan* (Cambridge University Press, 2015) ch 9; A Gordon, *A Modern History of Japan: From Tokugawa Times to the Present*, 4th edn (Oxford University Press, 2020) ch 5.

played key roles in the Emperor's restoration. Over time, however, public demand grew for the establishment of a parliament and the enactment of a constitution. The government, under the leadership of Hirobumi Itō – who would become Japan's first Prime Minister – began drafting a constitution modelled on those of German states such as Prussia, which featured a strong monarchy. On 11 February 1889, the Meiji Constitution was promulgated as a document granted by Emperor Meiji.

The Meiji Constitution represented a fusion of theocratic monarchy and constitutional democracy. Its legitimacy was grounded in ancient texts, such as the *Nihon Shoki* (*The Chronicles of Japan*), compiled in the eighth century under imperial directive.[8] The *Nihon Shoki* commences with mythological accounts, notably the narrative of the sun deity *Amaterasu*, who, as sovereign of the heavenly realm (*Takamagahara*), ordered her grandson *Ninigi* to govern the terrestrial realm of Japan. His descendants, forming the imperial lineage, eventually came to reign as emperors of Japan. Based on this divine lineage, the Meiji Constitution enshrined the core principle that supreme sovereignty – including the power to establish and amend the Constitution – resided in the Emperor.[9] This concept of imperial sovereignty is explicitly reflected in the Meiji Constitution, with Article 1 declaring that 'The Empire of Japan shall be reigned over and governed by a line of Emperors unbroken for ages eternal,'[10] Article 3 stating that 'the Emperor is sacred and inviolable,'[11] and Article 4 affirming that 'the Emperor is the head of the Empire, combining in Himself the rights of sovereignty, and exercises them.'[12]

Under the Meiji Constitution, constitutional scholars developed a distinction between *kokutai* (the essential nature of the state) and *seitai* (the form of government).[13] Both *kokutai* and *seitai* function as criteria for classifying a state's political system: *kokutai* changes depending on the location of sovereignty, whereas *seitai* changes depending on the method of exercising that sovereignty. While the Meiji Constitution was in effect, this distinction served as a criterion for determining the limits of constitutional amendments. The *kokutai* was understood as immutably determined by divine mandate, with sovereignty perpetually residing in the Emperor. Therefore, even constitutional amendments could not transfer sovereignty from the Emperor to any other entity, such as the people – not even the Emperor himself could alter the *kokutai*. Toshiyoshi Miyazawa's observation that the ultimate sovereign under the Meiji Constitution was, strictly speaking, not the Emperor but *Amaterasu* succinctly encapsulates the foundational logic of the Meiji constitutional order.[14]

Conversely, the question of whether sovereignty was exercised in a direct and despotic manner by the Emperor himself or through the involvement of various

[8] WG Aston (tr), *Nihongi: Chronicles of Japan from the Earliest Times to A.D. 697* (1896).
[9] Matsui (n 7) 9–10.
[10] Meiji Constitution (n 3) art 1.
[11] Meiji Constitution (n 3) art 3.
[12] Meiji Constitution (n 3) art 4.
[13] Y Hozumi, *Kenpō Teiyō Jō* [Outline of the Constitution, vol 1] 52–53 (Yūhikaku, 1910).
[14] T Miyazawa, *Kenpō* (5th rev edn) [Constitution] 28 (Yūhikaku, 1973).

state organs was regarded as a matter of *seitai* and a constitutional choice. This is equivalent to the acknowledgement that the choice between direct and indirect democracy remains valid even in a system where sovereignty resides with the people. While the Meiji Constitution embodied the *kokutai* that all governing authority should be derived from the Emperor's sovereignty, it did not adopt the *seitai*, which would have allowed the Emperor to exercise all that power directly and autocratically. Instead, it established a system in which the Emperor exercised his prerogatives in coordination with state organs.

Specifically, the Meiji Constitution stipulated that ministers of state were to advise the Emperor in exercising his prerogatives, and that the promulgation of laws and imperial ordinances required the countersignature of the responsible ministers.[15] Furthermore, it mandated that the enactment of legislation and the approval of state budgets were contingent upon the consent of the Imperial Diet.[16] The Imperial Diet consisted of the House of Peers and the popularly elected House of Representatives.[17] Voting eligibility was initially subject to various restrictions, but these were progressively eased, culminating in the extension of suffrage to all adult men in 1925. The Emperor retained the authority to veto the advice of ministers and decisions of the Imperial Diet; however, in practice, such veto powers were not exercised. Consequently, depending on how these constitutional mechanisms were implemented, the political system could, in effect, function as a constitutional monarchy broadly analogous to the British model.

B. Imperial House Law

The Meiji Constitution lacked certain fundamental components of governmental structure. Although it designated the Emperor as the sovereign, it did not specify who was to ascend to the throne. Article 2 merely stated, 'The Imperial Throne shall be succeeded to by Imperial male descendants, according to the provisions of the Imperial House Law,' thereby delegating the details of imperial succession – such as which male members of the imperial family would succeed, and in what order – to the Imperial House Law, a separate legal document.[18]

The Imperial House Law was enacted by Emperor Meiji on the same day that the Meiji Constitution was promulgated. It set forth provisions governing imperial succession, the regency, the status and scope of members of the imperial family, and the Imperial Household Council.[19] At the time, the idea that matters relating to the succession of the monarch and the monarch's family should be regulated not by the Constitution, but by house law (*Hausgesetz*), was widely accepted among

[15] Meiji Constitution (n 3) art 55.
[16] Meiji Constitution (n 3) arts 37, 64.
[17] Meiji Constitution (n 3) art 35.
[18] Meiji Constitution (n 3) art 2.
[19] Imperial House Law 1889.

European constitutional monarchies. The drafters of the Meiji Constitution and the Imperial House Law also shared this understanding: the latter was conceived as the law of the imperial family, fundamentally distinct from the former, which was the law of the state.[20] In other words, the Meiji Constitution was enacted through the Emperor's exercise of constituent power as head of state, whereas the Imperial House Law was enacted through the Emperor's exercise of patriarchal authority as head of the imperial family.

This distinction was also reflected in their respective modes of promulgation: the Meiji Constitution was publicly promulgated as a law of state, whereas the Imperial House Law, as an internal law of the imperial family, was not. In addition, state ministers countersigned the Meiji Constitution to indicate ministerial responsibility, but no such countersignatures appeared on the Imperial House Law.

Article 74 of the Meiji Constitution is central to understanding the relationship between the two:

> Article 74.
> (1) No modification of the Imperial House Law shall be required to be submitted to the deliberation of the Imperial Diet.
> (2) No provision of the present Constitution can be modified by the Imperial House Law.[21]

Constitutional amendment under the Meiji Constitution required the approval of two-thirds or more of both houses of the Imperial Diet. However, Article 74, Paragraph 1, states that the amendment to the Imperial House Law does not require the Imperial Diet's involvement. Instead, Article 62 of the Imperial House Law stipulated that such amendments required only that the Emperor consult with the Imperial Household Council and the Privy Council.[22]

The drafters' commentary on the Meiji Constitution explains the exclusion of the Imperial Diet from the amendment process of the Imperial House Law: 'Simply because the Imperial House Law is one that has been settled by the Imperial Family concerning their own affairs, and bears no relation to the reciprocal rights and duties of the Emperor or of His subjects towards each other.'[23] In other words, the Imperial House Law was conceived as governing internal affairs of the imperial family, unrelated to the rights and obligations of Japanese subjects, and therefore beyond the legal purview of the Imperial Diet. However, it is important to note that Article 74, Paragraph 2 explicitly prohibits any amendments to the Meiji Constitution from being effected through revisions to the Imperial House Law. This provision protects the more stringent constitutional amendment process from being circumvented by the comparatively simpler procedure for amending

[20] H Itō, *Teikoku Kenpō Kōshitsu Tenpan Gikai* [*Commentaries on the Constitution of the Empire and the Imperial House Law*] 143 (Kokka Gakkai, 1889).
[21] Meiji Constitution (n 3) art 74.
[22] Imperial House Law 1889 (n 19) art 62.
[23] H Itō, *Commentaries on the Constitution of the Empire of Japan*, 2nd edn (Miyoji Itō tr, 1906) 155–56.

the Imperial House Law. In his commentary, Hirobumi Itō referred to this provision as a 'special safeguard' for the Meiji Constitution.[24]

C. Development of the Imperial House Law

1907 was a pivotal year in the evolution of the Imperial House Law. One key development was the issuance of the Ordinance of the Formalities for Official Documents (*Kōshiki-rei*) as an Imperial Ordinance.[25] This ordinance defined the formalities for promulgating constitutional amendments, statutes, and other official documents. Notably, it extended these procedures to amendments to the Imperial House Law and to orders issued under its authority, requiring the countersignature of a Minister of State. This signified a reversal of the earlier practice of the drafters, who had withheld the public promulgation of the Imperial House Law on the grounds that it was an internal law of the imperial family. The Imperial House Law was now reclassified as a law of the state, accorded equal status with the Meiji Constitution and other statutes, and rendered subject to promulgation.

Second, the Imperial House Law was amended through the adoption of addenda to the original law. These Imperial House Law Addenda were issued twice: first in 1907 and again in 1918.[26] Interestingly, unlike typical Japanese legal reforms, which follow the 'invisible model' described by Albert – where amendments are incorporated into the original text – the Imperial House Law followed a model closer to the American 'appendative model,' in which changes are appended as separate documents.[27] The reason why such a special model was adopted for amending the Imperial House Law remains unclear. It is possible that the intention was to venerate the original law as an immutable, sacred text. A further interpretation holds that its amendment framework was modelled on the classical legal framework of ancient Japan.[28]

Third, beginning in 1907, a subsidiary legal framework began to emerge to give effect to the Imperial House Law, consisting primarily of imperial ordinances and Imperial Household Ministry regulations. Among the ordinances enacted under

[24] ibid 156.

[25] The Ordinance of the Formalities for Official Documents (*Koshiki-Rei*) (Imperial Ordinance No 6 of 1907, 1 February 1907).

[26] Imperial House Law Addendum (Meiji 40 Imperial House Law, 11 February 1907); Imperial House Law Addendum (Taisho 7 Imperial House Law, 28 November 1918).

[27] For models of constitutional amendment forms, see R Albert, *Constitutional Amendments: Making, Breaking, and Changing Constitutions* (Oxford University Press, 2019) ch 6. For the forms of amendment of Constitution and ordinary statutes in Japan, see M Kinoshita, 'The Form of Constitutional Amendments in Japan' in R Albert (ed), *The Architecture of Constitutional Amendments: History, Law, Politics* (Hart Publishing, 2023).

[28] K Harada, 'Meiji 40-nen Kōshitsu Tenpan "Zōho" Kō [A Study of the 1907 Imperial House Law Addenda]' (2003) 40(4) *Kokugakuin Hōgaku* 189, 207–13. The classical legal system (*ritsuryo*) codified in the early 8th century in Japan consisted of four types of law: *Ritsu*, *Ryo*, *Kyaku*, and *Shiki*. While the wording of the basic *Ritsu* and *Ryo* codes remained untouched, any necessary changes were made by issuing new regulations called *Kyaku*.

the authority of the Imperial House Law, many governed the legal relationships between members of the imperial family and ordinary citizens, reflecting the transformation of the Imperial House Law from a purely house law into an instrument of state law.

Miyazawa conceptualised the relationship between laws concerning the imperial household and ordinary state laws as a dual constitutional order.[29] According to him, both the Meiji Constitution and the Imperial House Law constituted the supreme law within their respective domains, with neither subordinate to the other. The legal system was thereby divided into two domains: laws concerning state affairs, governed by the Meiji Constitution, and laws concerning imperial household affairs, governed by the Imperial House Law. Miyazawa argued that this dual legal order was designed to circumscribe the legislative competence of the Imperial Diet.. Under the Meiji Constitution, all legislation, including constitutional amendments, required the consent of the Imperial Diet. However, matters relating to the imperial household were governed by a self-contained framework anchored in the Imperial House Law, which deliberately excluded the Imperial Diet from its purview.

A further important question left unresolved by the Meiji Constitution was whether it could be amended in a manner that would encroach upon the domain of the Imperial House Law. Miyazawa argued that, because the purpose of the Imperial House Law was to insulate imperial household affairs from parliamentary involvement, any constitutional amendment encroaching upon the domain of the Imperial House Law would be impermissible.

Under this dual constitutional order, conflicts between ordinary legislation and Imperial Household Ordinances were resolved based on their relevant scopes of application. Within the scope of the Meiji Constitution, ordinary legislation enacted with the involvement of the Imperial Diet took precedence over Imperial Household Ordinances. Conversely, within the scope of the Imperial House Law, Imperial Household Ordinances – issued without the participation of the Imperial Diet – prevailed over ordinary legislation.

This division of legal authority was given concrete expression in the 1907 amendment to the Imperial House Law, which clarified its scope relative to ordinary legislation. Under this amendment, ordinary statutes, such as the Civil Code, would not apply to legal relations between members of the imperial family and ordinary citizens when relevant special provisions existed in Imperial Household Ordinances.[30] Thus, regarding imperial household affairs, the Ordinances took precedence over ordinary statutes. In effect, the dual constitutional order enabled the imperial family to enjoy a distinct legal status, structured through imperial ordinances and insulated from parliamentary authority.

[29] T Miyazawa, *Kōshitsu-hō* [*Imperial House Law*] (Nihonhyōronsha, 1936) 1–15; T Miyazawa, *Kenpō Ryakusetu* [*Concise Treatise on Constitutional Law*] (Iwanami Shoten, 1942) 235–44.

[30] Imperial House Law Addendum 1907 (n 26) arts 7, 8.

D. The Functions and End of the Dual Constitutional System

The Meiji Constitution and the Imperial House Law satisfy two of the three defining features of a *multi-text* constitution as outlined by Richard Albert: multiplicity and shared supremacy. Both documents coexisted as supreme legal texts. However, unlike the Canadian and Israeli examples Albert examines, the Japanese case lacks asynchrony, as both texts were enacted simultaneously in 1889.

However, it is entirely conceivable that constitutional drafters intentionally adopt a *multi-textual* constitutional model from the outset. Indeed, in the Meiji era, the framers deliberately separated the Meiji Constitution and Imperial House Law into two coequal foundational documents to exclude the Imperial Diet from matters pertaining to the imperial family. Although it was theoretically possible to integrate both documents into a single constitution by employing a multitrack amendment mechanism, such an approach would have significantly increased the complexity of the constitutional text. A simpler dual-constitution structure likely offered greater benefits than a single complex constitution, such as enhancing the accessibility of each document to the general public.

Furthermore, the distinct codification of the Meiji Constitution and the Imperial House Law enabled the latter to be amended without requiring amendment of the former, which remained unaltered until 1946. Had the Imperial House Law been embedded within the Meiji Constitution, its amendment would have required constitutional revision. Although restricting amendments can enhance the symbolic authority of a legal code, excessive rigidity may hinder its responsiveness to evolving political and social conditions. Separating constitutional texts for domains subject to frequent change thus represents a strategic legal design that balances durability and adaptability.

However, the dual constitutional order was fundamentally incompatible with democracy, as it was deliberately designed to exclude the Imperial Diet from certain areas of state law-making.[31] Its validity depended entirely on the principle of imperial sovereignty and the Emperor's sacred inviolability. The 1946 Constitution dismantled this framework by stipulating that 'The Imperial Throne shall be dynastic and succeeded to in accordance with the Imperial House Law passed by the Diet.'[32] Before the 1946 Constitution came into effect, the 1889 Imperial House Law was abolished and replaced by a new Imperial House Law

[31] In contemporary comparative constitutional law, one also finds constitutional orders – exemplified by the role of the Chinese Communist Party Constitution in China or the constitutional status of Sharia law in Egypt – where a distinct normative framework, operating alongside or outside the ordinary constitution and legislative process, exercises a structurally significant function in governance. These arrangements may bear functional resemblance to the dual constitutional order of the Meiji Constitution period, albeit with significant differences in their respective constitutional foundations and historical contexts.

[32] 1946 Constitution (n 4) art 2.

enacted by the Imperial Diet, which holds only the status of ordinary legislation subordinate to the Constitution.[33]

III. Super Constitution

A. Potsdam Declaration

In July 1945, the Potsdam Conference was held in Potsdam, in the Soviet occupation zone of Germany, with Harry S. Truman, Winston Churchill, and Joseph Stalin in attendance. The conference resulted in the drafting of the Potsdam Declaration, issued on 26 July, which set out the terms for Japan's surrender across 13 articles. It demanded that Japan be placed under Allied occupation, while simultaneously clarifying the purpose of that occupation:

> 10. … The Japanese Government shall remove all obstacles to the revival and strengthening of democratic tendencies among the Japanese people. Freedom of speech, of religion, and of thought, as well as respect for the fundamental human rights shall be established.[34]
> 12. The occupying forces of the Allies shall be withdrawn from Japan as soon as these objectives have been accomplished and there has been established in accordance with the freely expressed will of the Japanese people a peacefully inclined and responsible government.[35]

The Potsdam Declaration is often described as a demand for Japan's 'unconditional surrender'; however, strictly speaking, this requirement applied only to the Japanese military. With respect to the Japanese government, the Declaration authorised Allied occupation only to the extent necessary to 'revive and strengthen democratic tendencies.'

The Potsdam Declaration warned that unless the Japanese government accepted its terms, Japan would face 'the utter destruction of the Japanese homeland.'[36] However, accepting these terms was not an easy decision for the Japanese government, as they were seen as potentially conflicting with the *kokutai*, the principle upholding the Emperor's sovereignty. A definitive move toward acceptance was not made until after the atomic bombings of Hiroshima and Nagasaki on 6 and 9 August. Even then, preserving the *kokutai* remained a primary concern. On 10 August, the Japanese government sought clarification from the Allied Powers,

[33] Imperial House Law, Act No 3 of 1947. Under the 1946 Constitution, the name of the Japanese legislative body was changed from the Imperial Diet (*Teikoku Gikai*) to the National Diet (*Kokkai*). Unlike its predecessor, the National Diet no longer includes an Emperor-appointed House of Peers; instead, it consists of the House of Representatives and the House of Councillors, both elected by popular vote.
[34] Proclamation Defining Terms for Japanese Surrender (Potsdam Declaration) (Potsdam, 26 July 1945) para 10.
[35] ibid para 12.
[36] ibid para 3.

asking whether the Declaration 'does not comprise any demand which prejudices the prerogatives of His Majesty as a Sovereign Ruler.'[37] In response, the US government, via Secretary of State James F Byrnes, issued a statement – later known as the Byrnes Note – without directly answering the question. Instead, Byrnes declared:

> From the moment of surrender, the authority of the Emperor and the Japanese Government to rule the state shall be subject to the Supreme Commander for the Allied Powers…[38]

He continued:

> The ultimate form of government of Japan shall … be established by the freely expressed will of the Japanese people.[39]

The Byrnes Note's assertion that the Emperor would 'be subject to' the Supreme Commander faced opposition, particularly from Japan's military leadership. Nonetheless, Emperor Hirohito eventually decided to accept the Potsdam Declaration on 14 August. The Allied occupation commenced on 28 August. On 2 September, the Japanese government officially signed the Instrument of Surrender to the Allied Powers, which reproduced the formulation of the Byrnes Note: 'The authority of the Emperor and the Japanese Government to rule the state shall be subject to the Supreme Commander for the Allied Powers.'[40]

This series of events surrounding Japan's surrender is understood to have significant implications not only on an international dimension but also for Japan's domestic legal order. According to Toshiyoshi Miyazawa's 'August Revolution' theory, Japan's acceptance of the Potsdam Declaration effected a transfer of constituent power from the emperor to the people without formal amendments to the Meiji Constitution.[41] Additionally, Jirō Tanaka argued that the signing of the Instrument of Surrender created supra-constitutional legal sources that stood superior to the existing constitution within Japan's domestic legal order. Tanaka explained that 'the Potsdam Declaration and the surrender documents constitute the constitutional basic law for the Allied occupation of Japan and form the most important legal source as the 'constitution of the constitution' of Japan under Allied occupation.'[42] In other words, these documents functioned as supra-constitutional

[37] Offer of Surrender from Japanese Government (10 August 1945) (1945) 13 *Department of State Bulletin* No 320, 205.

[38] The American Reply to the Japanese Offer of Surrender (The Byrnes Note) (11 August 1945) (1945) 13 *Department of State Bulletin* No 320, 206.

[39] ibid. Miyazawa interpreted this passage from the Byrnes Note as a demand that constituent power be vested in the people and, on this interpretation, regarded Japan's acceptance of the Potsdam Declaration as constituting the August Revolution. T Miyazawa, 'Nihonkoku Kempō seitan no Hōri [The Theory on the Foundation of the Constitution of Japan]' in *Kempō no Genri* [*Constitutional Principles*] (Iwanamishoten, 1967) 383.

[40] Instrument of Surrender (2 September 1945) (1945) 13 *Department of State Bulletin* No 321, 363, 364.

[41] Miyazawa (n 39) 38.

[42] J Tanaka, 'Rengōkoku no Kanri-ka ni okeru Nihon Gyōsei Hō [Japanese Administrative Law under Allied Occupation]' (1946) 64(5) *Hōgaku Kyōkai Zasshi* 265, 273.

texts, establishing a legal order that ultimately superseded the Meiji constitutional framework during the occupation period.

B. SCAP Directives

Following World War II, both Japan and Germany were occupied by the Allied Powers. In Germany, the existing government was entirely dissolved, and the Allies assumed direct control. In contrast, Japan retained its prewar government, which continued to function under the Meiji Constitution but operated under Allied supervision. A new command authority, the Supreme Commander for the Allied Powers (SCAP), was established to issue directives to the Japanese government, with General Douglas MacArthur of the United States appointed to this position.

SCAP's directives took various forms, including general orders, directives, and memoranda.[43] The directives encompassed a wide array of reforms, including constitutional amendments, the arrest and purge of wartime leaders, the dissolution of the *zaibatsu* (business conglomerates), land reforms, and the disestablishment of State *Shinto*.[44] They also introduced censorship and punitive measures to suppress criticism of and resistance to the occupation regime.

Although the Japanese government sought to implement SCAP directives in a manner consistent with the Meiji Constitution, the need for the Imperial Diet's approval of legislative changes posed a significant impediment. Legislative deliberations could be slow and unpredictable in outcome, paradoxically making democratic institutions obstacles to democratisation.

To address this issue, a special emergency Imperial Ordinance was issued by the Emperor on 20 September 1945, while the Imperial Diet was in recess.[45] This measure was grounded in Article 8 of the Meiji Constitution, which empowered the Emperor to issue emergency imperial ordinances with the force of law in cases of emergency when the Imperial Diet was not in session.[46] Commonly referred to as the Potsdam Emergency Imperial Ordinance, it enabled the Japanese government to execute SCAP directives directly through executive orders, bypassing the legislative process, and authorised the inclusion of penal provisions within such orders. Executive orders issued under this authority became known as the Potsdam Orders.

[43] ibid 273.

[44] For SCAP policies and their implementation, see AC Oppler, *Legal Reform in Occupied Japan: A Participant Looks Back* (Princeton University Press, 1976); Theodore Cohen, *Remaking Japan: The American Occupation as New Deal* (Herbert Passin ed, Free Press, 1987).

[45] Imperial Ordinance Concerning Orders to be Issued in Consequence of the Acceptance of the Potsdam Declaration (Potsdam Emergency Imperial Ordinance), Imperial Ordinance No 542 of 1945.

[46] Meiji Constitution (n 3) art 8.

C. The 1946 Constitution and the Super Constitution

During the occupation period, most legal provisions perceived as conflicting with the 1946 Constitution were repealed or amended. However, a more complex legal issue arose from the tension between the policies introduced under SCAP directives and the new constitutional framework. For example, the Potsdam Emergency Imperial Ordinance was criticised for infringing on the National Diet's democratic legislative authority. Additionally, land reform and the dissolution of the *zaibatsu*, both involving the compulsory expropriation of land and corporate shares at meager compensation, were deemed to violate the just-compensation requirement of Article 29(3).[47] Furthermore, following the conservative turn in occupation policy from 1948 onwards, various Potsdam Orders aimed at suppressing freedom of speech and labour movements were introduced, drawing criticism for their inconsistency with the 1946 Constitution's protections of free expression and labour rights.[48]

On this issue, Tanaka, positioning the Potsdam Declaration and the Instrument of Surrender as supra-constitutional legal sources, offered an explanation that can be broadly summarised into three points.[49] First, SCAP directives issued in pursuit of democratisation, as mandated by these supra-constitutional documents, constituted a form of supra-constitutional authority capable of amending or nullifying the ordinary Constitution. Second, even laws and orders formally enacted through the procedures established by the ordinary Constitution, when issued to implement SCAP directives, carried supra-constitutional force and thus superseded conflicting ordinary constitutional provisions. Third, the supra-constitutional status of SCAP directives remained unchanged despite the formal transition from the Meiji Constitution to the 1946 Constitution. The Supreme Court endorsed Tanaka's 'super constitution' theory, holding that legal institutions established under SCAP directives during the occupation possessed 'legal effect outside the Constitution,' independent of the 1946 Constitution.[50]

However, the validity of these supra-constitutional documents was confined to the occupation period. Upon the termination of the Allied occupation in 1952, the Potsdam Emergency Imperial Ordinance and the Potsdam Orders, considered inconsistent with the 1946 Constitution, were abolished. While these abolitions may appear to mark the final establishment of a legal system with the 1946 Constitution, unresolved issues remained. Certain policies introduced during the conservative turn of the occupation, such as restrictions on public servants' labour and political activities, were upheld as consistent with the new Constitution and

[47] 1946 Constitution (n 4) art 29(3).
[48] 1946 Constitution (n 4) arts 21, 28.
[49] J Tanaka, 'Potsudamu Kinkyū Chokurei o meguru Ikenron [On the Constitutionality of the Potsdam Emergency Imperial Ordinance]' (1949) 1 *Kōhō Kenkyū* 68, 82.
[50] Supreme Court, grand bench, 8 April 1953, 7 *Keishū* 775. See also Matsui (n 7) 27–28.

continued in effect. While conservative politicians criticised the 1946 Constitution as an 'imposed constitution,' liberal critics viewed these late-occupation regulations as 'imposed statutes.' Restrictions on public servants remain a contentious constitutional issue to this day.[51]

D. Functions and Challenges of the Super Constitution

Foreign military occupations are sometimes undertaken not solely to conduct military operations, but also to fundamentally transform the political and legal order of the occupied state. Such interventions are termed 'transformative occupations.'[52] The Allied occupation of Japan constitutes a paradigmatic case of a transformative occupation.

During the occupation, Japan's constitutional order assumed a two-tiered structure, which comprised a supra-constitutional layer and an ordinary constitutional layer. This bifurcated arrangement fulfilled important practical functions in facilitating the rapid and effective implementation of the occupation's democratisation programme. Democratisation may require the swift removal of the previous regime's leadership, the construction of democratic legal institutions, and far-reaching socio-economic transformations. However, these reforms often create substantive and procedural tensions within the ordinary constitutional order. Sweeping measures deemed necessary to lay the foundation for a constitutional democracy do not necessarily accord with the principles or procedures of a democratic constitution. In Japan, the establishment of a supra-constitutional authority, capable of superseding ordinary constitutional norms, provided a mechanism for navigating the legal and institutional dilemmas posed by rapid democratisation. While emergency provisions could have been incorporated into the new Constitution, doing so could jeopardise the long-term stability of democratic governance. For a newly democratised state, it may be safer to ground extraordinary powers, such as those exercised by SCAP, not in an ordinary constitution meant to endure beyond the transitional period, but in a supra-constitutional document intended to expire once the democratic transition is complete.

However, this is not to suggest that Japan's super-constitutional system was free of flaws. While supra-constitutional texts such as the Potsdam Declaration and the Instrument of Surrender conferred extraordinary powers upon SCAP, the mechanisms for controlling those powers were inadequate. Although broadly framed

[51] Supreme Court, grand bench, 25 April 1973, 27 *Keishū* 547 'the *Zennorin* case'; Supreme Court, grand bench, 6 November 1974, 28 *Keishū* 393 'the *Sarufutsu* case.'

[52] For discussions of transformative occupation, see N Bhuta, 'The Antinomies of Transformative Occupation' (2005) 16 *European Journal of International Law* 721; A Roberts, 'Transformative Military Occupation: Applying the Laws of War and Human Rights' (2006) 100 *American Journal of International Law* 580; GH Fox, 'Transformative Occupation and the Unilateralist Impulse' (2012) 94 *International Review of the Red Cross* 237.

obligations on SCAP, such as the need to implement democratic reforms, were imposed, such abstract mandates failed to provide effective constraints. In practice, the suppression of labour movements and socialist activity in the later phase of the occupation arguably exceeded what was necessary for democratisation.

An effective super-constitutional regime should include not only broad powers but also clearly defined limitations and oversight mechanisms. One possible safeguard might have been the creation of a dedicated super-constitutional tribunal, distinct from regular judicial bodies, to assess the conformity of occupation policies with the super-constitutional framework.

IV. Compact and Weak Constitution

In 1952, Japan regained its independence, marking the end of the era of super-constitutional governance. Since then, the 1946 Constitution has served as Japan's sole supreme law. Unlike the constitutional regime under the Meiji Constitution, in which the Imperial House Law existed as a parallel legal authority, no legal code today shares the same hierarchical status as the 1946 Constitution. On its face, the Japanese Constitution appears to exemplify a *uni-textual* constitution in its purest form. However, closer examination indicates that the Japanese constitutional system exhibits features of both *uni-textual* and *multi-textual* constitutional models.

A. Uni-Textual Large-C Constitution and Multi-Textual Constitutional Statutes

Although Albert does not expressly state this, his concept of *multi-textual* constitutions can be further classified into two distinct constitutional models. The first is the *multi-textual* 'large-C constitution' model, where a legally supreme and entrenched constitution is distributed across several documents, as exemplified by Canada.[53] The second is the *multi-textual* 'constitutional statutes' model, exemplified by the United Kingdom and New Zealand, where no codified large-C constitution exists, but multiple statutes are politically superior to ordinary statutes and are specially entrenched as so-called constitutional statutes.[54]

[53] The definition of large-C constitution here follows DS Law, 'Constitutions' in P Cane and HM Kritzer (eds), *The Oxford Handbook of Empirical Legal Research* (Oxford University Press, 2010) 376, 377 ('A large-c constitution is a legal document, or set of legal documents, that (1) proclaims its own status as supreme or fundamental law, (2) purports to dictate the structure, contours, and powers of the state, and (3) may also be formally entrenched, in the sense of being harder to amend or repeal than other laws').

[54] This chapter refers to statutes as constitutional statutes that are not legally entrenched in the same way as the large-C constitution but are politically difficult to amend through the ordinary legislative process.

Notably, even in jurisdictions with a large-C constitution – whether organised as *uni-textual* or *multi-textual* – it is still possible for multiple specially entrenched constitutional statutes to coexist alongside it.[55] While the centrality of the large-C constitution tends to overshadow these additional constitutional statutes, in substantive terms, these systems often operate within a tripartite structure composed of the large-C constitution, specially entrenched constitutional statutes, and ordinary statutes.

Japan's legal system established under the 1946 Constitution also includes statutes that, although formally classified as ordinary laws, function as small-c constitutions and are politically entrenched in a special manner.[56] Representative examples include Imperial House Law,[57] the Diet Act,[58] Cabinet Act,[59] Court Act,[60] Public Offices Election Act,[61] and the Local Autonomy Act.[62] Most of these were enacted by the Imperial Diet shortly after the promulgation of the 1946 Constitution and came into force concurrently with its implementation.[63] These statutes have largely remained unchanged since their enactment. Even when amendments have occurred, such changes have typically received support from both ruling and opposition parties – far exceeding the threshold required to initiate a constitutional amendment. In Japanese constitutional scholarship, such statutes are commonly referred to as 'subsidiary acts of the Constitution (*Kenpō fuzoku-hō*)';[64] in this chapter, they are referred to as 'constitutional statutes.'

Even in jurisdictions with a single large-C constitution, it is conceivable for multiple politically entrenched constitutional statutes to emerge. This observation calls into question whether any constitution can ever be truly *uni-textual* in practice. Of course, because the existence of a large-C constitution has a profound impact on a jurisdiction's constitutional order, there is merit in classifying constitutions as *uni-textual* or *multi-textual* by focusing solely on the structure of the large-C constitution – disregarding constitutional statutes – in jurisdictions where such a large-C constitution exists. For instance, although Japan's 1946 Constitution

[55] For constitutional statutes in jurisdictions with a large-C constitution, see S Stephenson, 'The Rise and Recognition of Constitutional Statutes' in R Albert and JI Colon-Rios (eds), *Quasi-Constitutionality and Constitutional Statutes: Forms, Functions, Applications* (Routledge, 2019) 27.

[56] The definition of small-c constitution adopted here follows Law (n 53) 377 ('A small-c constitution … consists of the body of rules, practices, and understandings, written or unwritten, that actually determines who holds what kind of power, under what conditions, and subject to what limits.').

[57] Imperial House Law (n 33).

[58] National Diet Act, Act No 79 of 1947.

[59] Cabinet Act, Act No 5 of 1947.

[60] Court Act, Act No 59 of 1947.

[61] Public Offices Election Act, Act No 100 of 1950.

[62] Local Autonomy Act, Act No 67 of 1947.

[63] The statute stipulating the procedure for amending the Constitution was not enacted until 2007 (Act on Procedures for Amendment of the Constitution of Japan, Act No 51 of 2007).

[64] M Ōishi, *Kenpō Chitsujo e no Tenbō* [*The Prospects of Constitutional Law and Order*] (Yuhikaku, 2008) 3–32. For a comprehensive study in Japanese comparing constitutional statutes in Japan and other jurisdictions, see Y Tomii, *Kenpō to Seitehō: Jun-Kenpō Ron* [Constitution and Statutes: The Theory of Quasi-Constitution] (Seibundō, 2024).

is also accompanied by several constitutional statutes, the legal order it established is markedly different from that of the Meiji Constitution period or the Allied occupation period, when multiple legally entrenched constitutional documents coexisted.

Nevertheless, this chapter emphasises that Japan's constitutional order – the small-c constitution – shares notable features with *multi-textual* constitutional systems observed in jurisdictions such as the United Kingdom and New Zealand. A distinction exists between Japan, on the one hand, and the United Kingdom and New Zealand, on the other, with respect to the presence of the large-C constitution. However, a more salient issue concerns the role of the large-C constitution within the broader small-c constitutional order.

The significance of a large-C constitution stems from its formal enactment through special procedures, its legal supremacy over statutes, and its entrenchment against ordinary legislative amendment.[65] These attributes distinguish it from constitutional and ordinary statutes and shape the nature of the small-c constitutional order in a distinctive manner. That said, the extent to which the large-C constitution governs the small-c constitution – its scope, supremacy, and degree of entrenchment – varies across jurisdictions. While such differences may appear to be a matter of degree, in extreme cases, they become differences in kind. Accordingly, in legal systems where the large-C constitution is narrowly scoped and weakly entrenched, the small-c constitution may come to resemble the constitutional arrangements found in the United Kingdom and New Zealand.

B. The 1946 Constitution as a Compact Constitution

Although Japan's 1946 Constitution is unquestionably the sole supreme law of the land, its substantive scope is relatively narrow and contains few detailed provisions. This can be quantitatively inferred from the 'Constitution Ranking' provided by the Comparative Constitutions Project (CCP).[66] According to this dataset, the Japanese Constitution contains only 4,998 words, ranking as the fifth shortest constitution globally. By contrast, the global median and mean lengths of national constitutions are 16,179 and 22,480 words.[67] For comparison, the United States Constitution contains 7,762 words, the South Korean Constitution 9,059

[65] See Stephenson (n 55) 29.

[66] Comparative Constitutions Project: Constitution Ranking (comparativeconstitutionsproject.org/ccp-rankings/, accessed 3 July 2025). For a study that uses the CCP dataset to compare the Japanese Constitution with those of other countries around the world, including the length of the text, see KM McElwain and CG Winkler, 'What's Unique About the Japanese Constitution?: A Comparative and Historical Analysis' (2015) 41 *Journal of Japanese Study* 249.

[67] KM McElwain, *Nihon-koku Kenpō no Fuhen to Tokui: Sono Kiseki to Teiryōteki Kōsatsu* [*The Universality and Originality of the Japanese Constitution in Quantitative Perspective*] (Chikura Shobō, 2022) 56.

words, the German Basic Law 27,379 words, and the Indian Constitution 146,385 words. This exceptional brevity suggests that many constitutional functions typically codified in formal constitutional texts elsewhere may instead be performed by statutes in Japan's legal system.

In fact, many provisions of the 1946 Constitution articulate general principles or policy directions, leaving specific content to subsequent legislation. Of its 103 articles, 33 contain sections that explicitly delegate detailed matters to legislation.[68] Key issues, such as nationality criteria, the number of legislative seats, and the electoral system, are not directly stipulated in the Constitution but are left to legislative enactment. Similarly, the relationship between the central and local governments is addressed only briefly in four articles.[69]

In Japan, the narrow scope of its large-C constitution and the critical role of constitutional statutes allow substantial reforms to government structure to be achieved without recourse to formal constitutional amendments. For example, the 1994 amendment to the Public Offices Election Act, which introduced proportional representation as one method for electing members of the House of Representatives,[70] and the 1999 amendment to the Local Autonomy Act, which significantly enhanced the autonomy of local governments,[71] would likely have required constitutional amendments in other jurisdictions. Makoto Ōishi, one of Japan's foremost contemporary constitutional scholars, has argued that the large-scale statutory reforms enacted from the 1990s through the 2000s have fundamentally transformed the constitutional order – rendering most earlier constitutional commentaries and textbooks obsolete – even though the 1946 Constitution remains formally unchanged.[72] This assertion aptly underscores the pivotal role that constitutional statutes play in shaping Japan's small-c constitutional order.

Although the presence of a large-C constitution formally distinguishes Japan from countries such as the United Kingdom or New Zealand, the functional structures of their constitutional orders reveal notable similarities. A large portion of Japan's constitutional norms is governed by constitutional statutes, much like those that constitute the *multi-textual* constitutional systems of the United Kingdom and New Zealand. Conversely, for example, although both the Japanese and the Mexican Constitutions are formally classified as *uni*-textual constitutions, the Mexican Constitution consists of a single large-C constitutional text with highly detailed provisions, extending even to specific guidelines for elementary school

[68] 1946 Constitution (n 4) art 2, art 4 para 2, art 5, art 7 items 5 & 8, art 10, art 17, art 24 para 2, art 26 paras 1 & 2, art 27 para. 2, art 29 para. 2, art 30, art 31, art 40, art 43 para. 2, art 44, art 47, art 49, art 50, art 59 para. 3, art 60 para 2, art 64, art 66 para 1, art 67 para 2, art 73 item 4, art 76 para 1, art 79 paras 1, 4 & 5, art 80 para 1, art 84, art 90, art 92, art 93 paras 1 & 2 art 95, art 102.

[69] 1946 Constitution (n 4) arts 92–95.

[70] Public Offices Election Act (n 61), as amended by Act No 4 of 1994.

[71] Local Autonomy Act (n 62), as amended by Act No 87 of 1999.

[72] Ōishi (n 64) 3–4, 34, 51–52.

education.[73] From a functional perspective, their substantive approaches to constitutional governance differ greatly.

C. The 1946 Constitution as a Weak Supreme Law

The influence of constitutional statutes within a jurisdiction is shaped not only by the scope of the large-C constitution but also by the degree to which its supremacy is institutionally secured. No matter how emphatically a constitution proclaims itself the supreme law of the land, such a declaration is merely aspirational unless backed by robust institutional mechanisms to ensure its enforcement. For instance, if the legislature retains ultimate interpretive authority over the large-C constitution, then, in practice, no meaningful hierarchical distinction exists between the large-C constitution and constitutional statutes.

In Japan, Constitutional practice under the 1946 Constitution has not secured strong supremacy of its large-C constitution. Although the Constitution explicitly vests the Supreme Court with the power of judicial review, nearly 80 years after its enactment, the Court has declared only 13 statutes unconstitutional. Notably, many of these rulings have relied on a narrow set of constitutional clauses: five concerning equality before the law and four relating to electoral matters. In most other constitutional contexts, the Court has adopted a deferential stance toward legislative judgments, thereby weakening the practical force of constitutional supremacy.

The most prominent example of this dynamic is Article 9 of the 1946 Constitution, commonly referred to as the 'pacifist clause.'[74] Its first paragraph declares that 'the Japanese people forever renounce war as a sovereign right of the nation,' and the second stipulates that 'land, sea, and air forces, as well as other war potential, will never be maintained.' Although there remains an ongoing debate about the original intent of Article 9, a literal reading appears to prohibit not only the use but also the possession of military force by the Japanese government.

In the immediate aftermath of World War II, Japan did not maintain its own military organisation. However, the outbreak of the Korean War in June 1950 prompted gradual rearmament. In 1954, the Self-Defense Forces Act was passed, formally creating the Self-Defense Forces (SDF) as a comprehensive military body encompassing land, maritime, and air divisions.[75] Despite long-standing academic claims that the SDF and its enabling statutes violate Article 9(2), the Supreme Court has declined to issue a ruling on their constitutionality. Presently, numerous statutes, including the Self-Defense Forces Act,

[73] Political Constitution of the United Mexican States (1917, as amended) art 3.
[74] 1946 Constitution (n 4) art 9.
[75] Self-Defense Forces Act, Act No 165 of 1954.

the Armed Attack Situations Act,[76] and the International Peace Cooperation Act (PKO Act),[77] operate on the presumption that the SDF is constitutional. This interpretation has been consistently upheld by the Cabinet Legislation Bureau, an agency operating under the Cabinet.[78] However, the resulting legal architecture departs considerably from the text of Article 9. In practical terms, Japan's military legal system is de facto governed by statutes rather than formal constitutional provisions that ostensibly regulate the use and possession of military force.

D. The Functions of Compact and Weak Constitution

The view that Japan's small-c constitutional framework consists of a compact and weak large-C Constitution supplemented by multiple constitutional statutes offers one explanation for an important paradox: despite having been enacted under foreign occupation in 1946, the Constitution has never been formally amended in its nearly 80-year history.[79]

Although debate persists over whether the 1946 Constitution was imposed by the occupying powers, it is widely acknowledged that much of its content was drafted by MacArthur's staff and reflects strong American influence. Conservative politicians, particularly within the Liberal Democratic Party (LDP), have framed these origins as evidence of foreign imposition, invoking this as a rationale for advocating revision in favour of a constitution rooted in traditional Japanese values. Such appeals resonate with segments of the population inclined toward patriotic sentiments. However, amending the Japanese Constitution requires a supermajority in both houses of the National Diet, followed by majority approval in a popular referendum. To meet these demanding thresholds, public opinion must reflect strong and widespread motivation for constitutional change. For such momentum to materialise, political leaders must do more than highlight psychological or ideological dissatisfaction; they must persuasively demonstrate that the 1946 Constitution poses tangible obstacles or inefficiencies in contemporary governance.

[76] Armed Attack Situations Act, Act No 79 of 2003.

[77] PKO Act, Act No 79 of 1992.

[78] For discussions on the constitutional review by the Cabinet Legislation Bureau, see K Fukuda, 'Towards an Institution-Independent Concept of Constitutional Review' (2023) 61 *Columbia Journal of Transnational Law* 387. Also, James C Fisher characterises the Cabinet Legislation Bureau's constitutional interpretations as 'non-statutory quasi-constitutional law,' clarifying their origins and functions (JC Fisher, 'The Quasi-Constitutionality of Non-Statutory Law' in Albert and Colon-Rios (eds) (n 55) 261.

[79] Occupation constitutions generally contain factors that cause instability. See Z Elkins, T Ginsburg, and J Melton, *The Endurance of National Constitutions* (Cambridge University Press, 2009) 118–19.

However, in practice, few issues have arisen that could not be resolved without amending the compact and weak 1946 Constitution.[80] The Constitution was groundbreaking in transferring sovereignty from the Emperor to the people, establishing democratic governance, and guaranteeing fundamental human rights. Although these core principles and norms were initially adopted under foreign pressure, as mandated by the Potsdam Declaration and SCAP directives, they have since gained broad domestic support and become deeply embedded in Japan's political culture. As a result, they have attracted relatively little sustained criticism. Moreover, the practical machinery of governance is primarily regulated by a body of constitutional statutes rather than the Constitution itself. Most operational or institutional challenges regarding the governmental system have therefore been effectively addressed through statutory amendments, rendering formal constitutional revisions unnecessary. An apparent exception is Article 9(2), which prohibits the maintenance of armed forces. As a matter of literal interpretation, this provision posed a significant legal obstacle to rearmament. However, the Supreme Court has consistently refrained from subjecting Article 9 to constitutional scrutiny, enabling rearmament to proceed through the legislative creation of the Self-Defense Forces and related statutes.

Had the 1946 Constitution been broader in scope and stronger in its supremacy, it might have produced institutional tensions requiring formal amendment. In such a scenario, criticisms could have extended beyond individual provisions to the entire constitutional framework, fueling conservative arguments about its coercive origins and prompting calls to revise even its democratic and human rights provisions.

In this respect, the limited scope of the large-C constitution – focused primarily on establishing a democratic system of governance while leaving many operational matters to ordinary statutes – can be seen as a stabilising factor. Thus, this structure has enabled the otherwise improbable coexistence of a coercively imposed constitution and a stable democratic order.

V. Conclusion

This chapter has traced the historical development of *multi-textual* constitutions in Japan and clarified their functions. In Japanese constitutional history, many constitutionally important matters have been placed outside documents formally entitled 'Constitution': during the Meiji Constitution period, matters concerning the imperial family were governed by the Imperial House Law; during the occupation period, extraordinary powers were vested in the SCAP under supra-constitutional documents; and under the 1946 Constitution, politically sensitive matters such

[80] For a discussion on the institutional factors contributing to the endurance of the 1946 Constitution, see S Yokodaido, 'Constitutional Stability in Japan not due to Popular Approval' (2019) 20 *German Law Journal* 263.

as military affairs have been effectively regulated by constitutional statutes. This practice of 'documentary outsourcing' has undoubtedly contributed to the stability of Japan's core constitutional documents, namely, the Meiji Constitution and the 1946 Constitution.

This characteristic of the Japanese constitutional order cannot be fully understood by focusing solely on the Meiji or 1946 Constitutions. The presence of a document formally labeled 'Constitution' naturally draws the attention of scholars in comparative constitutional law, often leading to an unwitting narrow focus on that single text. The concept of *multi-textual* constitutions offers a correction to this tunnel vision and encourages scholars to expand our analytical framework. Paradoxically, the insights afforded by this concept may prove even more valuable when applied to systems traditionally regarded as *uni-textual*, as in the case of Japan.

2

Multi-Textuality and Incrementalism in Cameroon's Democratic Transition

LAURA-STELLA ENONCHONG

I. Introduction

The Constitution of Cameroon is often considered a single exhaustive document (uni-textual), but one of the most intriguing phenomena in the country's constitutional evolution occurred between 1996 and 2019, when two constitutional texts were partially in force. This unfamiliar phenomenon may have raised some concerns, including concerns about locating Cameroon's constitution. Yet, unsettling as it may have appeared, the situation provided the continuity required during the country's transition from an authoritarian to a purportedly more democratic regime. This chapter employs the concept of multi-textual constitutions to explore the legal and political implications of that phenomenon in Cameroon. Multi-textual constitutions, as defined by Richard Albert, are constitutions consisting of 'multiple documents, each enacted separately with shared supremacy under law.'[1] While this alternative constitutional form affords great advantages and challenges uncommon in uni-textual jurisdictions, as this chapter demonstrates, in transitional contexts, its potential instrumentalism is of profound significance.

Following the promulgation of the 1996 Constitution, Cameroon was thrust into a state of multi-textuality through transitional provisions in that Constitution which allowed for the continued application of specific provisions of the previous 1972 Constitution. Driven by a prevailing pro-democratic vision, the 1996 Constitution introduced modern democratic features such as the Constitutional Council, the Senate, and decentralised regional authorities, which were to be established progressively. Until these institutions were created, the relevant institutions under the 1972 Constitution were to be maintained, effectively creating a state of multi-textuality in transition. That unique position afforded opportunities for the consolidation of a modern constitutional democracy by providing time and space

[1] R Albert, 'Multi-Textual Constitutions' (2023) 109(8) *Virginia Law Review* 1629, 1633.

for an incremental development of the prospective democratic institutions. This chapter argues that in practice, multi-textuality prolonged the transitional period, which in turn fostered political complacency and ultimately stalled democratic progress. It is further contended that in Cameroon, multi-textuality in transition functioned as a weapon of abusive constitutionalism, instrumental in entrenching competitive authoritarianism under the guise of gradual reform. The Cameroonian experience is instructive in expanding our understanding of multi-textuality and its potential impact on constitutional and political systems in transitional contexts. Moreover, it underscores the relevance of the social and political context in shaping democratic entrenchment beyond the formal existence of constitutional texts.

This chapter proceeds as follows. The next section discusses the critical juncture at which constitutional transformations led to the development of multi-textuality in Cameroon. That is followed by an analysis of some key features of multi-textuality as experienced in Cameroon. The penultimate section focuses on the controversial role of multi-textuality, highlighting how it simultaneously created opportunities for the incremental development of a modern democratic state while also fostering abusive constitutionalism. Drawing insights from the Cameroonian case, the chapter proceeds with some reflections on the theoretical and practical implications of multi-textuality in transitional contexts.

II. Historicising Constitutional Transformations and Multi-Textuality

Regarding multi-textual constitution-making, Albert suggests that such constitutional forms may arise either by design (reflecting a self-conscious choice of the constitutional drafters either at the time of constitution making or subsequently),[2] or through evolutionary processes such as formal amendments, political practice, or judicial interpretation.[3] Nevertheless, the foundational attributes of multi-textual constitutions suggest that their origins may incorporate elements of both design and evolution,[4] or may even be fortuitous.

Charting the origins of multi-textuality in Cameroon begins with the 1961 Constitution which created a Federal Republic. That Constitution made provision for some features of democracy, including the conditions for periodic elections into democratic institutions.[5] However, the pro-democratic institutions were progressively overshadowed by authoritarian tendencies. Despite its formal federal structure, the political system was in reality one that can be characterised as 'unitary federalism' because power was, instead, heavily concentrated in the central

[2] ibid 1640–41.
[3] ibid 1649–50.
[4] For instance, the origins of Lithuania's multi-textual constitutions, see ch 6 by T Birmontienė and J Miliuvienė, 'Vertical and Horizontal Layers of the Lithuanian Constitution'.
[5] See for instance, arts 2 and 3 of the Constitution of the Federal Republic of Cameroon 1961.

government. The ease with which Cameroon descended into authoritarianism can be attributed partly to the Federal Constitution itself, which created a strong executive president.[6] Having been modelled on the 1958 French Constitution, the establishment of a strong president in Cameroon was perhaps inevitable.[7] The Federal Constitution, however, vested in the President even far greater powers than envisaged under its French counterpart and ironically, the federal orientation of Cameroon did little to mitigate the overconcentration of powers in the president.

Cameroon's first President, Ahmadou Ahidjo, capitalised on these considerable presidential powers to construct an authoritarian state. Criticism of the government was silenced with repressive force and civil liberties were systematically undermined. Emulating the one-party states flourishing across Africa at the time, Ahidjo astutely engineered the dissolution of political parties to form a single political party called the Cameroon National Union (CNU), which he chaired.[8] In 1972, Ahidjo unexpectedly submitted proposals for a new constitution to a national referendum, with the primary aim to abolish the federal structure. In what has been described as the Glorious Revolution[9] in Cameroon, the 1972 Constitution was birthed through an overwhelming referendum vote in favour of establishing a unitary state.

Ahidjo's regime effectively eroded democracy and consolidated authoritarian rule under the highly centralised, presidential 1972 Constitution. It was this regime, with its flawed democratic framework and adversity to constitutionalism, that was inherited by President Paul Biya in 1982.[10] Upon assuming office, Biya maintained overarching authority over state institutions and used the military to further entrench his hold on power. The one-party system persisted, obliterating aspirations for the development of a vibrant political environment.

The 1990s, however, marked a critical juncture characterised by extensive constitutional, legislative and democratic reforms. A constellation of endogenous and exogenous factors triggered changes in the domestic political environment which prompted the reforms. Endogenous factors included the steep economic decline caused partly by corruption and mismanagement.[11] Exogenous factors included the democratisation conditions attached to economic assistance by

[6] M Etonga, 'An Imperial Presidency: A Study of Presidential Power in Cameroon' in N Kofele-Kale (ed), *An African Experiment in Nation Building: The Bilingual Cameroon Republic Since Reunification* (Westview Press, 1980) 151–55.

[7] The French Constitution grants extensive powers to the president, establishing unambiguously the supremacy of the executive. See R Elgie, *Political Leadership in Liberal Democracies* (Macmillan, 1996) 57–59.

[8] N Rubin, *Cameroon: An African Federation* (Pall Mall, 1971) 152–53; P Konings and F Nyamjoh, 'The Anglophone Problem in Cameroon' (1997) 35(2) *Journal of Modern African Studies* 207, 210.

[9] F Stark, 'Federalism in Cameroon: The Shadow and the Reality' (1976) 3(10) *Canadian Journal of African Studies* 423, 423.

[10] Konings and Nyamjoh (n 8) 2013.

[11] VJ Ngoh, 'Biya and the Transition to Democracy' in J Mbaku and J Takougang (eds), *The Leadership Challenge in Africa: Cameroon under Paul Biya* (Africa World Press, 2004) 434–37.

international financial institutions, such as the Bretton Woods Institutions, as well as growing global opposition to one-party states after the Cold War.[12] Together, these factors fuelled domestic demand for political liberalisation. After initial reluctance, Biya's government eventually conceded to reform pressures, notably through the enactment of the so-called Liberty Laws, which granted fundamental political freedoms such as freedom of assembly, speech, press and association. These reforms encouraged the proliferation of political parties, media outlets, civil society organisations and pressure groups.[13] The first multi-party presidential election was held in 1992. The opposition contested the election fiercely, but Biya's ruling party, now rebranded as the Cameroon People's Democratic Movement (CPDM),[14] retained power amid widespread allegations of gross electoral irregularities.[15]

The adoption of the 1996 Constitution culminated this series of political reforms aimed at transforming the political landscape from authoritarianism to democracy. The new Constitution was propagated as ushering in a new era for the separation of powers, democratic governance and human rights.[16] It introduced democratic features such as the Senate (the upper legislative chamber), the Constitutional Council and decentralised regional authorities. These developments were expected to consolidate the democratic reforms already underway.

It is important to note that the 1996 Constitution is not an entirely new document, but an extensively amended version of the 1972 Constitution, enacted pursuant to Law No. 96/06 of 18 January 1996 to amend the Constitution of 2 June 1972. It has since become accepted practice to refer to the amended version as the 1996 Constitution of Cameroon. The extent of the amendment has left somewhat unsettled the question of whether the changes to the constitution constitute an amendment or a replacement.[17] From a subjective perspective, the magnitude of changes suggests a replacement, in view of the substantial increase in the number of provisions (from 39 to 69 articles) and the substantive changes which distinguish the new constitution from its original form and orientation.

[12] ibid 432.

[13] ibid.

[14] CNU was transformed to the Cameroon People's Democratic Movement (CPDM) in 1985 with Biya as chair.

[15] Ngoh (n 11) 441–42; C Fombad and J Fonyam, 'The Social Democratic Front, the Opposition and Political Transition in Cameroon' in J Mukum Mbaku and J Takougang (eds), *The Leadership Challenge in Africa: Cameroon Under Paul Biya* (Africa World Press Inc., 2004) 470.

[16] SM Owona, 'Les Évolutions Constitutionelle en Afrique Noire Francophone: Recherches sur L'idéologie Dominante dans L'Élaboration des Constitutions au Cameroun (1990–2008)' (2019) 1 *Revue du Droit Public* 157, 167–68; L-S Enonchong, *The Constitution and Governance in Cameroon* (Routledge, 2021) 27.

[17] M Kamto, 'Dynamique Constitutionnelle du Cameroun Indépendant' (1995) 1, 2 & 3 *Revue Juridique Africaine* 7; MN Abada, 'Ruptures et Continuités Constitutionnelles en République du Cameroun: Réflexions à Propos de la Réforme Constitutionnelle du 18 Janvier 1996' (1998) 10(2) *Revue Africaine de Droit International et Compare* 308; M Ondoa, 'La Constitution Duale: Recherches sur les Dispositions Constitutionnelles Transitoires au Cameroun' (2000) 1(2) *Revue Africaine des Sciences Juridiques* 20; D Kamgaing, 'L'infra-Constitution Camerounaise: La Loi N° 96/06 du 18 Janvier 1996' (2021) 4 *Revue Internationale de Droit Comparé* 823.

This chapter is focused on the multi-textuality created by the transitional provisions of the 1996 amended version of the Constitution. Specifically, Article 67(1) provides that the new institutions created by the Constitution shall be set up progressively. In the meantime, Article 67(2) stipulates that the relevant existing institutions shall remain in place and continue to function until their successors are established. However, some provisions regulating the existing institutions were not replicated in the amended version. As a result, Articles 67(1) and 67(2) created a situation where two separate constitutional documents were in force – the 1972 Constitution as it stood prior to the January 1996 amendments and the amended version introduced by Law No.96/06. Thus, both the 1972 and 1996 Constitutions remained in force until the new institutions were put in place, the last of which, the decentralised regional authorities, was not established until 2019.

The above situation can be considered as multi-textuality in transition and the use of transitional provisions in constitutions is not uncommon. In fact, transitional provisions assume several roles, including the guarantee of stability and continuity of the state pending the establishment of a new regime or legal framework.[18] The transitional provisions in Cameroon's 1996 Constitution, however, were distinctive in that they facilitated the partial application of two constitutional documents for an indeterminate period.

III. Features of Multi-Textuality in Cameroon

Albert identifies three distinct legal features which set multi-textual constitutions apart from uni-textual constitutions. These are, multiplicity, asynchrony and shared supremacy.[19] These features are core to the idea of multi-textuality, but multi-textual constitutions may not necessarily reflect them all, in the same manner and forms or to the same degree.[20] In Cameroon, as noted in the preceding paragraph, the existence of two Constitutions (1972 and 1996) illustrates the feature of multiplicity. Asynchrony is evident in the fact that both constitutions were adopted at different times, by different constituent bodies and driven by specific prevailing political and social factors. The more intriguing feature is shared supremacy, which introduces important nuances to our understanding of this concept as a core feature of multi-textual constitutions. In the context of Cameroon, a closer look at the elements of hierarchy and entrenchment exposes the complexities that shared supremacy entails.

[18] L Pech, 'Les Dispositions Transitoire en Droit Constitutionnel' (1999) *Cahiers de Méthodologie Juridique* 1407, 1407–08; VR Manangou, 'Un État, Deux Constitutions: Analyse des Dispositions Transitoires de la Constitution Congolaise du 6 Novembre 2015' (2016) 19 *Recht in Afrika [Law in Africa]* 62, 64–66 ; D Landau, 'Transitional Norms in Constitutions' (2025) 1(50) *Yale Journal of International Law* 1.

[19] Albert (n 1) 1636.

[20] ibid.

On the first element of hierarchy, shared supremacy posits that 'the multiple documents of higher law are by default situated at the same elevated level of constitutional superiority … [n]one automatically trumps another.'[21] With regard to Cameroon, David Kamgaing argues that the 1996 Constitution is an infra-constitution, partly because it derives its validity from the 1972 Constitution and because there was no prevailing legal, political and social aspiration to replace the 1972 document.[22] Nevertheless, he places both Constitutions at the same level of normativity (shared supremacy), arguing that the 1996 Constitution is not hierarchically subordinate to the 1972 Constitution.[23] As both texts perform the same political and legal functions, they must be considered of equal normative significance.

Kamgaing's views rest on premises that are contentious for three principal reasons. First, the very notion of an infra-law presupposes a certain level of hierarchy and subordination, suggesting a more complex relationship between the two constitutions. Second, his argument regarding the source of the 1996 Constitution's validity neglects the significance of the transitional provisions within the 1996 text itself, which explicitly sanctioned the continued, albeit partial, operation of the 1972 document. Third, as discussed previously (and later in this chapter), the constitutional moment of the 1990s was driven by a prevailing aspiration to draft an entirely new constitution to break from the authoritarian legacy of the past. Nevertheless, Kamgaing's view of shared supremacy remains sound insofar as both Constitutions cover largely the same scope and assume the same normative and institutional functions.[24] Moreover, on a social and political level, both have been recognised as supreme normative instruments.

However, it is argued here that shared supremacy in Cameroon was of a partial nature. That situation arose, on the one hand, from the fact that the 1996 Constitution was superior in regard to the provisions it amended and certain new provisions it introduced. On the other hand, for new institutions provided for in the 1996 Constitution that had not been established in practice and thus remained non-existent, the corresponding provisions of the 1972 Constitution prevailed, to the extent that they had not been replicated in the 1996 text. For instance, Article 67(4) of the 1996 Constitution provides that, '[t]he Supreme Court shall perform the duties of the Constitutional Council until the latter is set up.' Among other responsibilities, the Constitutional Council is vested with jurisdiction in constitutional adjudication, which implied that the Supreme Court exercised that jurisdiction during the transition. The relevant provisions relating to that jurisdiction are shared between the 1972 and the 1996 Constitutions: while Articles 46 and 47 of the 1996 Constitution addressed constitutional review, in the absence of the Constitutional Council, the composition of the Supreme Court for such

[21] ibid 1639.
[22] Kamgaing (n 17) 837–41.
[23] ibid 837.
[24] ibid 841.

review was still governed by Article 33 of the 1972 Constitution. In fact, in 2002, in a petition relating to the constitutionality of the Standing Orders of the National Assembly, the Supreme Court referred to Article 67(4) of the 1996 Constitution to continue exercising its jurisdiction as defined in the 1972 Constitution.[25]

Turning to the second element of entrenchment, it is assumed that '[s]hared supremacy entails entrenchment, either legal or political.'[26] In the case of Cameroon, only the legal dimension was implicated. The transitional provisions relating to the new institutions in the 1996 Constitution demonstrate that only this text was specifically entrenched. Amendments under the 1996 Constitution require approval by an absolute majority of Parliament (meeting in congress). Where a second reading is requested by the President of the Republic, a two-third majority is required.[27] By contrast, the transitional provisions of the 1996 Constitution merely defined the extent to which the 1972 text remained applicable, viz, only until the new institutions were set up. When the Constitutional Council was finally established with the appointment of its members in 2018,[28] it went into operation. The first set of election petitions following the 2018 presidential elections were heard by the Constitutional Council, rather than the Supreme Court. No special procedure was required to repeal the remaining operative parts of the 1972 Constitution; repeal was automatic or implied as soon as the relevant conditions stated in the 1996 Constitution were fulfilled. That approach is not unusual, as the continued validity of the relevant provisions of the 1972 text was always intended as a provisional measure while the new institutions were being set up 'progressively.'[29]

It is also worth examining entrenchment within the 1972 Constitution itself. Under this Constitution, Cameroon had a unicameral Parliament. According to Article 36, '[a]n amendment presented to the Assembly on the initiative of the members or of the President of the Republic shall be passed by a majority of the membership of the National Assembly.' Presumably, that required a simple majority (50%+1), which did not appear to be particularly onerous. Interestingly, Article 36 prescribed a separate procedure for amendments initiated by a member of the National Assembly, which required the endorsement of at least a third of the Assembly before they could be introduced in Parliament. By contrast, the President faced no such preliminary requirement. Nevertheless, a one-third endorsement is an attainable threshold in most legislatures and amendments only required a majority to pass. On balance, the entrenchment of the 1972 Constitution seems rather weak. Etienne Temfack affirmed that the 1972 Constitution was not entrenched and the significant number of amendments (at least 10 amendments

[25] Cour Suprême Décision N° 001/CC/02-03 du 28 Novembre 2002, cited in Kamgaing (n 17) 840.

[26] Albert (n 1) 1639.

[27] Constitution of Cameroon 1996, art 63(3).

[28] Decree N°2018/105 of 07/02/2018 appointing members of the Constitutional Council.

[29] A similar argument has been made in relation to Congo's dual constitutions. See Manangou (n 18) 69–70.

between 1983 and 1992) reflected its flexibility.[30] In any case, it is unclear whether the 1972 amendment procedures remained valid during the transitory period. Even if they did, the low thresholds confirm that the 1972 Constitution was not entrenched.

Three important observations can be drawn from the above analysis. First, although multi-textuality in Cameroon occurred by amendment, it was neither the product of a self-conscious choice[31] nor the outcome of a deliberate developmental process. It seems more appropriate to describe it as a phenomenon incidental to the transitional measures aimed at consolidating a modern democratic state. That has further implications for our understanding of the features of multi-textuality, as will be shown in the following observations.

Second, multi-textual constitutions can reflect shared supremacy in a more complicated way. In Cameroon, the condition of partial shared supremacy appears to arise from the transitional context. Partial shared supremacy can raise some significant complexities, especially where constitutional documents overlap extensively or where constitutional adjudication is vigorous, allowing for multiple challenges of jurisdictional competence, conflict of laws and similar challenges.

Third, the question of entrenchment parallels that of partial shared supremacy. In transitional contexts in particular, it raises issues about the extent to which constitutional documents are truly entrenched.

IV. Incrementalism and Abusive Constitutionalism

The use of constitutional amendments to subvert democracy is not new; indeed, authoritarian regimes seem to prefer this 'covert' approach over more overt attacks on democratic institutions.[32] By deploying constitutional amendments, regimes can deflect criticism while enacting measures that effectively erode democracy under the guise of reinforcing it. This dynamic is exemplified by the situation in Cameroon, particularly during the period between 1996, when the current Constitution was promulgated, and 2019, when the last institutional arrangements introduced by the 1996 Constitution came into effect. This section aims to highlight the distinctive ways that multi-textuality was instrumental in sanctioning both incrementalism and abusive constitutionalism, which cumulatively facilitated political stagnation, the shrinking of the democratic space and the continuity of the authoritarian regime. The argument is developed in the two subsections below.

[30] EK Temfack, 'L'autorité de la Norme Constitutionnelle au Cameroun' (Université de Douala-Cameroun – D.E.A. de Droit Public 2005) www.memoireonline.com/12/08/1801/m_Lautorite-de-la-norme-constitutionnelle-au-Cameroun13.html.

[31] That can be contrasted with the Austrian position where multi-textuality occurred by design. See ch 3 by K Lachmayer, 'The Beauty and the Beast: The Excessive Multi-Textualism of the Austrian Constitution'.

[32] D Landau, 'Abusive Constitutionalism' (2013) 47(1) *University of California Davis Law Review* 189, 229–30.

A. The Janus Face of Incrementalism

The drafting of an entirely new constitution was the ultimate objective of opposition parties, nationalists and pro-democracy movements during the 1990s democratic awakening. However, the government wrestled control of the process from these groups and vested it instead in a presidentially appointed technical committee tasked with reviewing a presidential proposal for a revised constitution.[33]

In several respects, the failure to make comprehensive provisions for the new institutions in the 1996 Constitution may reflect a pragmatic response to the political momentum of the time, providing expedient solutions while leaving space for reflection and refinement of the institutions to be developed later. An alternative perspective, however, is that the government may have deliberately hijacked the constitution-making process to serve its own interests. By opting for an incremental approach to institutional reform, the government could covertly pursue its alternative political ambition under the guise of constructing a new democratic vision for the country. Incrementalism in constitution-making, especially in divided societies like Cameroon, can nonetheless be defensible, as it affords political actors the flexibility to construct stronger institutions over time, drawing on comparative good practices and adapting to evolving contextual realties. In such situations, applying different documents to regulate specific issues may be a strategic way to gradually construct a coherent and comprehensive constitutional system. Albert, for instance, notes that 'multi-textuality can be an effective tool to smooth the political terrain in a transition that proceeds incrementally rather than immediately.'[34] Similarly, Hanna Lerner recommends the use of tools such as ordinary legislation to defer the resolution of salient constitutional questions to a later date.[35]

Therefore, ostensibly, Cameroon's position was not entirely out of step. Multi-textuality in transition presented political actors, the government in particular, the tools to facilitate the incremental development of the modern democratic state envisioned at the time of the drafting of the 1996 Constitution. One such tool was the use of ordinary legislation to regulate the establishment and functioning of new institutions. For instance, regarding the Constitutional Council, Article 52 provides that '[a] law shall lay down the organization and functioning of the Constitutional Council, the conditions for referring matters to it as well as the procedure applicable before it.' The prospective law was intended as the mechanism through which the Constitutional Council, a hallmark of a modern democratic system, could foster the incremental development of constitutionalism

[33] J Takougang and M Krieger, *An African State and Society in the 1990s: Cameroon's Political Crossroads* (Westview Press, 1998) 183, 190; C Fombad, *Constitutional Law in Cameroon* (Wolters Kluwer, 2012) 29–30; Owona (n 16) 167.

[34] Albert (n 1) 1676.

[35] H Lerner, *Making Constitutions in Deeply Divided Societies* (Cambridge University Press, 2013) 44–46.

and the protection of human rights. It was incumbent upon the government and the legislature to ensure that the law eventually enacted brought to fruition an institution capable of delivering on that objective.

Article 14(6) makes similar pronouncements on the Senate, leaving the election of its members and related issues to be determined by law. A major advantage of introducing a bicameral parliament in Cameroon was the prospect of increased representation at the regional and local levels. Prior to 1996, each member of the National Assembly represented the entire nation,[36] whereas Senators were intended to represent both regional and local authorities[37] – an arrangement particularly relevant given the purported decentralisation of governance under the 1996 Constitution. Regional and local representation are not only essential features of diffusing democratic governance and participation across the country, but also, as Cosmas Cheka notes, serving as agents of good governance.[38] Moreover, as a second legislative chamber, the Senate offers the critical advantage of enhancing scrutiny in the legislative process. The National Assembly had historically been dominated by the ruling CPDM party, which at various points occupied over 80 per cent of the seats. That dominance produced inter alia, limited scrutiny of bills and executive actions. Due to the very disciplined majority of the ruling party, laws were often passed without critical deliberation or significant amendments, except for amendments on technicalities[39] which had no substantive implications on laws that were either inherently unconstitutional or infringed on fundamental rights. Thus, the creation of a second chamber was intended to enhance deliberative democracy and to increase oversight of both legislative processes and executive actions. Incrementalism, in this regard, provided remedial flexibility, allowing political actors the opportunity to refine and integrate new representative institutions throughout the transition.

Despite the potential benefits of incrementalism, it is not without dangers. One notable instance is the possibility of stagnation or derailment when no specific time limits are imposed on deferred transitional arrangements.[40] Donald Horowitz, for one, cautions against unguarded deferrals, warning of their tendency to cause delays that impede the timely resolution of important issues and may ultimately undermine the political transition.[41] That caution was borne out in Cameroon, where incrementalism was manifested in vague temporal commitments. While the Constitution stated that the new institutions shall be set up progressively (Article 67(1)), no timeframes were prescribed. Instead, the provision introduced an indeterminacy in its use of language along the lines of 'until such time that they

[36] Constitution of Cameroon 1996, art 15(2).

[37] Constitution of Cameroon 1996, art 20(1).

[38] C Cheka, 'The State of the Process of Decentralisation in Cameroon' (2007) 32(2) *Africa Development* 181, 181–82.

[39] Y Morse, 'The Legislature as Political Control: Change and Continuity in Cameroon's National Assembly (1973–2019)' (2021) 59(4) *Journal of Modern African Studies* 485, 491.

[40] Manangou (n 18) 72.

[41] D Horowitz, *Constitutional Processes and Democratic Commitments* (Yale University Press, 2021) 112.

are set up.' That ambiguity fostered democratic stagnation, as the establishment of the new institutions was deferred to the enactment of relevant legislative instruments, which in turn depended mainly on presidential initiatives. Over time, the political momentum for change dissipated, and with it, the political pressure to trigger the legislative initiatives. As a result, the relevant provisions of the 1972 Constitution continued to fill the void, rendering the legislative initiatives even less urgent. In the interval, pertinent questions remained unanswered, exacerbated by ambiguities and uncertainties about which constitutional arrangements were legally in force.[42] For example, Article 61 of the 1996 Constitution changed the territorial nomenclature from 'provinces' to 'regions,' yet the decentralised regional authorities envisioned in the Constitution did not become fully operational until 2019, following the promulgation of the Code on Regional and Local Authorities. Until then, decentralisation remained largely illusory.[43] Further uncertainties concerned the constitutional successor of the President of the Republic. The applicable provision of the 1996 text at the time, Article 6(4)(a), designated the Speaker of the Senate. Yet, in the absence of the Senate, it remained unclear whether the Speaker of the National Assembly maintained their position as the Constitutional successor pursuant to article 7 of the 1972 Constitution.

Thus, in the absence of the Senate, the Constitutional Council, or fully functioning decentralised regional authorities, the 1996 Constitution remained operative only partially. That partial application, along with the Constitution's inherent uncertainties, contributed to its diminished social legitimacy. It ultimately lost its symbolic standing as the fundamental law of the land, particularly due to its failure to enable the timely realisation of the democratic vison. A number of commentators have attributed the failed democratic process to delays in concluding the transition process, which allowed for the partial application of two constitutions with different ideological underpinnings. Magloire Ondoa notes that the 1996 Constitution is marked by its liberal democratic vision, in contrast to the 1972 Constitution.[44] However, as Serge Owona argues, the extensive delay in establishing liberal democratic institutions inhibited the transition to political pluralism and the rule of law.[45] Steve Bilounga reinforces that critique, arguing that the 'involuntary or deliberate omission' of a time limit for the establishment of new institutions created an undesirable indeterminacy and undermined the essence of the transition.[46]

[42] C Fombad, 'Some Perspectives on Durability and Change under Modern African Constitutions' (2013) 11(2) *International Journal of Constitutional Law* 382, 388.

[43] See generally, N Kofele-Kale, 'Local Governance under Cameroon's Decentralisation Regime: Is it all Sound and Fury Signifying Nothing?' (2011) 37(3) *Commonwealth Law Bulletin* 513.

[44] Ondoa (n 17) 26.

[45] Owona (n 16) 170–71, 176.

[46] ST Bilounga, 'La Crise de la Loi en Droit Public Camerounais' (2017) 11 *Les Annales de Droit* 21, 29–30, 55–56.

B. Abusive Constitutionalism

Abusive constitutionalism is evident not by dramatic attacks on the constitution, but by subtle constitutional amendments that gradually erode democratic institutions and practices.[47] In Cameroon, multi-textuality facilitated abusive constitutionalism by enabling the apparent changes introduced by the 1996 Constitution while simultaneously perpetuating the authoritarian dimensions of the 1972 text. The transitional provisions ensured a negative form of continuity, sustaining the authoritarian state through the partial application of both Constitutions and through the deliberate deferral of the pro-democracy features of the 1996 text. The concurrent application of the two constitutions shielded amendments to the 1996 Constitution from close scrutiny, allowing for the stealthy entrenchment of the authoritarian state. The Senate and the Constitutional Council in particular exemplify how ostensibly democratic constitutional amendments were abusively instrumentalised to consolidate presidential power and severely weaken political opposition.

When the Senate began functioning in 2013, the initial euphoria was short-lived. It soon became clear that cumulatively, the constitutional provisions and subsequent legislative instruments[48] governing the Senate largely replicated the flaws of the National Assembly, limiting its potential to enhance representation, deliberation and oversight. A key limitation derives from the mixed method of selecting senators. The Senate is composed of one hundred senators, with each of Cameroon's ten territorial regions represented by ten Senators. Of these, seven are indirectly elected at the regional level by an electoral college comprising regional and municipal councillors.[49] The other three are appointed directly by presidential decree.[50] All Senators serve a term of five years and are eligible for re-election or reappointment. A mixed selection method for a second legislative chamber is not inherently undemocratic, although it is important that the selection method is based on transparent rules and on principles that reasonably align with the rationale for creating a second chamber. In Cameroon, the Senate's democratic legitimacy is undermined in part by the presidential appointment of 30 per cent of its membership – a significant proportion, especially given the predominance of the ruling party in that institution. The electoral system, which remains significantly influenced by the government, in particular by the President, precludes free and fair elections. This systemic defect ensures that elections to representative bodies such as the National Assembly and Regional Councils have not broadened opposition representation. The election of Senators operates within that same defective system. In the 2018 senatorial elections, the opposition secured only seven of the

[47] Landau, 'Abusive Constitutionalism' (n 32) 229.
[48] Law N° 2016/011 of 27 October 2016 amending and supplementing certain provisions of Law N° 2013/006 of 10 June 2013 on the Standing Orders of the Senate; Electoral Code 2012, s 215(3).
[49] Constitution of Cameroon 1996, art 20(2).
[50] ibid.

70 elective seats.[51] Considering the restrictive electoral landscape, the President's appointment power further inhibits prospects for the opposition to gain any form of influence in the Senate. In fact, it perpetuates the predominance of the ruling party as the presidential appointment powers are not limited in any meaningful way. The only normative limitation relates to an age requirement[52] which has no relationship to the justification for establishing a senate nor does it add democratic features to the selection criteria or process. The President may therefore appoint at their pleasure. In practice, the appointees have been mainly members of the ruling CPDM party, with a tiny minority from members of opposition parties that have been co-opted into the government.

The composition of the third legislature, elected and appointed in 2023, is a staggering revelation of the extent of democratic erosion.[53] The CPDM swept all 70 elective seats in the Senate, while the President appointed an additional 24 CPDM Senators and six others, including three from opposition parties that have strategic political alliances with the government.[54] The bicameral experience has thus failed to produce the desired benefits of legislative oversight and deliberative democracy. In the absence of a credible electoral system and with a problematic appointment system to the Senate, the political majorities in both legislative houses coincide. The Senate has similarly been reduced to a compliant institution which fails to scrutinise legislative proposals or seriously challenge objectionable executive actions. The constitutional and legislative provisions have instead produced a Senate which functions primarily as a political instrument wielded unscrupulously by the political authorities.[55]

A parallel outcome can be observed with the Constitutional Council, further demonstrating that the 1996 Constitution effectively entrenches the ruling party and presidential domination of the political system, ultimately reinforcing the authoritarian character of the 1972 dispensation. Pursuant to Article 52 of the 1996 Constitution, legislative instruments were enacted in 2004 and 2012 to regulate the organisation and functioning of the Constitutional Council.[56] However, it did not become functional until 2018, following the appointment of its members by presidential decree[57] ahead of that year's presidential election. The Constitutional Council assumes key functions in consolidating constitutional democracy, particularly through its role in ensuring the regularity of presidential and parliamentary

[51] 'Cameroon: Landslide in Senate Poll' (2018) 55(4) *Africa Research Bulletin: Political, Social & Cultural Series* 21824, 21824B.

[52] Article 20(3) of the 1996 Constitution imposes a minimum age of 40 years for eligible candidates.

[53] P Zibi, 'Cameroon 2023 Senatorial Elections: The Heyday of the Dominant Party', ancl-radc.org.za/blog/cameroon-2023.

[54] Decree N°2023/188 of 31 March 2023 to appoint Senators.

[55] H Kouomegne Noubissi, *Décentralisation et Centralisation au Cameroun : Compétence entre l'Etat et les Collectivités Locales* (Harmattan, 2013) 85.

[56] Law N°2004/004 of 21/o4/2004 to lay down the organization and functioning of the Constitutional Council as amended by Law N°2012.015 of 21/12/2012.

[57] Decree N°2018/105 of 07/02/2018 appointing members of the Constitutional Council and Decree N°2018/106 of 07/02/2018 appointing the President of the Constitutional Council.

elections.[58] The Council's effectiveness in that regard is predicated on a number of factors, not least its accessibility and its independence.

Regarding accessibility, or standing, the ordinary citizen is generally excluded from the jurisdiction of the Council. In electoral matters, a petition can only be initiated by a candidate, a political party that participated in the election in the relevant constituency concerned, or a government representative.[59] Interest groups and civil society organisations, that often play influential roles in democracy promotion, are deprived of access to that avenue to help ensure the integrity of elections, a cornerstone of democracy.

These weaknesses are compounded by the Council's lack of independence, which emanates from an appointment system largely controlled by the President. The Council consists of eleven members appointed by the President for a renewable term of six years.[60] Of these, three are appointed directly by the President, two indirectly by the President,[61] and the other six nominated by the Speakers of the two Houses of Parliament – both of which, as discussed previously, are dominated by the ruling party. In effect, the President has control over the Council, bolstered by the incentive of term renewals for its members.[62] The lack of independence has been widely criticised as contributing to the Council's failure to decide electoral petitions impartially, with decisions routinely favouring the government, often through unreasoned or unauthoritative judgments.[63]

This analysis has unearthed some of the main obstacles to the effectiveness of the Senate and the Constitutional Council as vital institutions in the democratisation process. Neither institution has facilitated political party turnover, nor have they contributed to diminishing the ruling party's influence or the preponderance of the President in the political system. In line with David Landau's contention on the effects of abusive constitutionalism,[64] the amendments in Cameroon have instead reinforced a constitutional order in which the President and the ruling party face little constraints on their power and even fewer prospects for displacement.

V. Reflections on Multi-textuality in Transition

The preceding discussion of Cameroon's experience of multi-textuality prompts broader theoretical reflections on multi-textuality in transitional contexts, which this section aims to explore. These relate mainly to the issue of context and the origins of multi-textuality.

[58] Constitution of Cameroon 1996, art 48(1).
[59] Constitution of Cameroon 1996, art 48(2).
[60] Constitution of Cameroon 1996, art 51(1).
[61] Following nomination by the Higher Judicial Council chaired by the President.
[62] Constitution of Cameroon 1996, art 51(1).
[63] G Youmbi, 'Le Nouveau Conseil Constitutionnel Camerounais : La Grande Désillusion' (2019) 5 *Revue du Droit Public* 1377, 1407.
[64] Landau, 'Abusive Constitutionalism' (n 32) 213.

The background context in which multi-textuality arises during a transition has a bearing on the ultimate outcome of the process. The impetus for change may originate from the people expressing a commitment to a popular cause. Depending on the intensity of the movement for change, the government may be compelled to succumb to pressure, but without genuinely embracing the new vision. Under such circumstances, any purported actions aimed at advancing the transition are likely to be tainted by subtle impediments. As with many constitution-making processes, the principal engineers of change have decisive influence over the eventual content of the constitution. As such, if a reluctant government oversees a transition, especially unilaterally, multi-textuality can serve as the perfect tool to ensure that different constitutional texts are compatible with the government's overriding agenda, while also demonstrating putative features of change that nominally reflect the vision of the reform advocates. The veil of democracy may then suffice to suppress further demands for change, especially if the mere fact of transition is invoked repeatedly to justify piecemeal reforms.

Further, multi-textuality in transition can offer greater democratic value when it is developed by design. Where multi-textuality is the product of a self-conscious choice for a transitional period, constitutional actors are more likely to define the duration of the transition period and prescribe clear intervals for implementing measures that develop transitional institutions or processes incrementally. With such foresight, constitutional actors are also more inclined to prescribe clear expiration dates for transitional provisions or arrangements. As Albert demonstrates through an instructive example, the Italian experience of multi-textuality underscores the need to be prescriptive in relation to time, as a specific constitutional law adopted in 1947 defined when transitional arrangements ushering in a new regime would elapse.[65] Such provisions address the issue of indeterminacy and reduce uncertainty in identifying the applicable arrangements at any given time. Multi-textuality, as a constitutional feature, has an inherent limitation with regard to its capacity to complicate the determination of the scope of the constitutional text.[66] Introducing precise time limits offers the additional advantage of mitigating that problem by providing clarity on the scope of the constitutional text. Even where multi-textuality does not occur by design, measures need to be established to forestall potential abuse.

An additional problem with indeterminacy and delay is the gradual erosion of the momentum for change. In Cameroon, by the time the pro-democratic constitutional institutions were eventually established, the initial momentum for change had waned. In the absence of continued pressure, the government made

[65] Albert (n 1) 1642.

[66] Albert (n 1) 1660; D Michalsen, 'The Many Textual Identities of Constitutions' in K Gammelgaard and E Holmøyvik (eds), *Writing Democracy: The Norwegian Constitution 1814–2014* (Berghahn Books, 2014) 61.

no pretence to ensure that these institutions substantively reflected the spirit of the transition.

Whether multi-textuality occurs by design or otherwise, its benefits are more likely to materialise when mechanism have been put in place to ensure the transition is not derailed. An independent oversight mechanism can provide the scrutiny function, including the policing of time limits and the attainment of milestones.

VI. Conclusion

The foregoing discussion has drawn on Cameroon's experience of constitutional change to expand the discourse on multi-textual constitutions. It has shown how multi-textuality in Cameroon resulted incidentally from a purported constitutional amendment which included transitional provisions. These provisions paved the way for the partial and concurrent application of two constitutional texts with relatively differing ideological visions.

This chapter has also examined the features of multi-textuality in Cameroon, highlighting important nuances in relation to the elements of entrenchment and shared supremacy. Regarding the former, it has been argued that only the 1996 Constitution was legally entrenched. This may raise broader questions about whether entrenchment, as a feature of multi-textual constitutions, may be more fluid than originally conceived. However, the peculiar transitional nature of Cameroon's multi-textual constitutional context may indicate that different circumstances may produce different patterns in the behaviour of multi-textual constitutions. Further, as discussed previously, the shared supremacy of the 1996 and 1972 Constitutions is only partial. This again arises mainly from the transitional context, in particular from the transitional provisions which sanctioned the continued application of specific provisions in the 1972 Constitution, while deferring the application of parts of the 1996 Constitution indeterminately. The oscillation between texts ensured that neither constitution was fully supreme. This nuanced understanding of the hierarchy of multi-textual constitutional hierarchy may also suggest that there is some merit in looking into the more granular details of multi-textual constitutions to consider whether they can assume supremacy in the same way.

Multi-textual constitutions undoubtedly have invaluable advantages especially in transitional contexts. However, the experience in Cameroon has shown that the potentials can be easily obscured by prevailing circumstances and the absence of political will. Political actors in Cameroon adopted an incremental approach to democratic transition, opportunistically invoking whichever constitutional text that best advanced their immediate political objectives. The failure to prescribe specific timeframes for the complete break from the old order was a calculated attempt to ensure continuity of the authoritarian regime under the 1972 Constitution. Although the 1996 Constitution was presented as a new democratic vision, marked by the promise of democratic institutions, the prolonged delays in its implementation allowed the amendments to stealthily perpetuate the authoritarian state. These observations highlight the need to ensure that in transitional contexts, different constitutional documents purporting to oversee a transition integrate specific timeframes to clearly delineate the scope and extent of applicable provisions or documents. Moreover, they reveal how multi-textual constitutions, if unchecked, can serve as instruments for subverting democratic processes and institutions in transitional contexts.

3

The Beauty and the Beast: The Excessive Multi-Textualism of the Austrian Constitution

KONRAD LACHMAYER

I. Introduction

A. General Introduction

Multi-textual constitutions refer to national constitutional systems consisting of multiple documents that all enjoy equal constitutional supremacy, and are sometimes, but not always, entrenched through special procedures of constitutional change. These constitutions are characterised by multiplicity, asynchrony, and shared supremacy.[1] The Austrian Constitution is an example of this type of multi-textual constitution, as it consists of a multitude of documents and provisions of incredible variety. It incorporates historical documents, such as the Basic Law of 1867, a text that predates the *Bundes-Verfassungsgesetz* (B-VG), the Federal Constitutional Act of 1920, which is often regarded as the core of the Austrian Constitution. It includes constitutional amendment documents, such as the 1964 amendment, which raised international treaties, especially the European Convention of Human Rights (ECHR), to the constitutional level. Although the formal mechanism to constitutionalise international treaties was abolished in 2008, the ECHR and its additional protocols remain integral to Austrian constitutional law. More than 20 constitutional acts and several hundred constitutional provisions, including rights and their exceptions, comprise the Austrian Federal Constitution.

While Austrian constitutional law is characterised by supremacy, a further distinction must be made. On the one hand, there is a higher layer of constitutional law derived from the interpretation of the B-VG as the core document of

[1] R Albert, 'Multi-Textual Constitutions' (2023) 109 *Virginia Law Review* 1629, 1638.

the Constitution (without a separate or textually explicit constitutional basis). On the other hand, EU law supremacy also interacts with Austrian constitutional law. Thus, one might also think of multiple concepts of supremacy in the context of the Austrian Constitution. Finally, as Austria is a federal state, it must also be mentioned that the states (*Länder*) have enacted their own sub-federal state constitutional law, which again must comply with federal constitutional law.[2]

B. The Historical Dimension

In 2020, the Federal Constitutional Act of 1920 celebrated its 100th anniversary.[3] In recent years, the Austrian Federal President has praised the beauty of the Constitution,[4] crediting it with helping to resolve political conflicts in times of governmental crises. However, this laudatory view contrasts with the prevailing scholarly understanding of the Austrian Constitution as a ruin.[5] This perspective highlights the multi-textual structure of the Austrian Constitution.[6] In order to understand the development of constitutional multi-textualism in Austria, it is necessary to go back in time to the enactment of the first effective Austrian Constitution.

In 1867, more than 50 years before Hans Kelsen drafted the Constitution of the young Austrian Republic, Austria's first effective monarchical constitution was introduced. The decisive defeat of the Austrian Empire by Prussia in 1866 and the resulting weakening of imperial authority led to the Compromise (*Ausgleich*) with Hungary. This agreement restructured the empire into the Austro-Hungarian Empire and also included the enactment of a liberal constitution in the Austrian part of the monarchy.[7] This first effective constitution consisted of five Basic Laws (*Staatsgrundgesetze*), a structure that already illustrates an early emergence of multi-textual constitutionalism[8] in Austria, a feature that still has an impact today.[9]

[2] F Karlhofer, 'Sub-national Constitutionalism in Austria: a Historical Institutionalist Perspective' (2015) 7 *Perspectives on Federalism* 57, 67–71.

[3] K Lachmayer, 'The Austrian Constitutional Court' in A Jakab, A Dyevre and G Itzcovich (eds), *Comparative Constitutional Reasoning* (Cambridge University Press, 2017) 75, 76.

[4] Austrian Constitutional Court, '30th Constitution Day Celebrated with High-Level Guests' (1 October 2019) www.vfgh.gv.at/medien/30th_Constitution_Day.en.php.

[5] H Eberhard and K Lachmayer, 'Constitutional Reform 2008 in Austria: Analysis and Perspectives' (2008) 2 *ICL Journal* 112.

[6] ibid 119.

[7] G Stourzh, 'Die Entstehung des Staatsgesetzes über die allgemeinen Rechte der Staatsbürger vom 21. Dezember 1867 und seine unmittelbare Bedeutung [The Development of the State Law on the General Rights of Citizens of December 21, 1867 and Its Direct Significance]' (2018) 26(2) *Journal für Rechtspolitik [Austrian Journal for Law and Politics]* 95, 95–96.

[8] A closer examination reveals that even the enactment of the five State Basic Laws was accompanied by additional legislative acts. Moreover, some of the State Basic Laws delegates the task of establishing concrete legal rules to the parliament.

[9] Most prominently, the State Basic Law of the General rights of the Citizens of 1867 is still part of Austrian Constitutional Law (see Article 149 B-VG) and builds an important part of the Austrian fundamental rights.

After World War I, the Austrian monarchy collapsed, leading to the establishment of the First Austrian Republic. During the transitional period, various statutory acts were passed by the Provisional National Assembly (*Provisorische Nationalversammlung*), while the Constituent National Assembly (*Konstituierende Nationalversammlung*) adopted a multitude of transitional constitutional acts.[10] Several of these acts are still valid in Austrian constitutional law today.[11]

Against this backdrop of monarchical and transitional constitutional traditions of multi-textuality, the B-VG of 1920 can be understood, at least initially, as a codification or, in part, a consolidation of pre-existing constitutional documents, despite introducing significant innovative elements. However, the attempt to create a unified constitution ultimately failed. As in many other countries, transitional periods towards a democracy are marked by power struggles, often leading to 'imperfect' constitutional compromises. This was also the case in Austria. The conservative party and the socialist party failed to reach consensus on key 'ideological' questions, including the protection of fundamental rights (especially social rights),[12] the structure of the educational system, and the allocation of powers between the federation and the states (*Länder*).[13]

In this regard, the B-VG contains in its final provisions, most notably in Article 149 the statement that, besides the B-VG itself, other enumerated acts shall continue to apply as constitutional acts. These include, in particular, the Basic Law of 1867 on the General Rights of Citizens, along with further guarantees of fundamental rights, such as the 1862 Law on the Protection of Personal Freedom[14] and the 1862 Law regarding the protection against house searches.[15] The list also encompasses various transitional constitutional acts, including the Resolution of the Provisional National Assembly of 30 October 1918,[16] the 1919 Law on the Expulsion from the Country and the Takeover of the Assets of the House of Habsburg-Lorraine,[17] the

[10] E Wiederin, 'From the Federalist Papers to Hans Kelsen's "Dearest Child": The Genesis of the Austrian Constitutional Court' (2021) 76(2) *Zeitschrift für Öffentliches Recht [Austrian Journal for Public Law]* 313, 327.

[11] See eg the Resolution of the Provisional National Assembly of 30 October 1918 regarding the abolishment of censorship or certain provisions of the Treaty of St. Germain concerning eg borders (art 27-35), citizenship (art 70-82), or minority rights (art 62-9).

[12] M Stelzer, *The Constitution of the Republic of Austria: A Contextual Analysis*, 2nd edn (Bloomsbury Publishing, 2022) 10.

[13] ibid.

[14] Gesetz zum Schutze der persönlichen Freiheit, Imperial Law Gazette No. 87/1862.

[15] Gesetz zum Schutze des Hausrechtes, Imperial Law Gazette No. 88/1862.

[16] State Law Gazette No. 3/1918, which concerned the abolishment of censorship and the full establishment of freedom of association and assembly.

[17] Gesetz betreffend die Landesverweisung und die Übernahme des Vermögens des Hauses Habsburg-Lothringen (Act Concerning the Expulsion and the Seizure of the Assets of the House of Habsburg-Lorraine), State Law Gazette No. 209/1919.

1919 Law on the Abolition of the Nobility,[18] and Section V of Part III of the State Treaty of St. Germain of 1919.[19]

C. Further Structure of the Chapter

In that regard the Austrian Constitution does not deviate very much from other codified constitutions in incorporating the above-mentioned kind of transitional documents. However, the Austrian model of constitutional multi-textualism does not stop here, but goes far beyond this approach of formal and textual unification. To fully understand the complexities of constitutional multi-textualism in Austria, it is necessary to delve into the structural concepts embedded in the B-VG.

Accordingly, this chapter goes on to analyse the structure of the Austrian Constitution (Section II). Subsequently, a selection of challenges that multi-textualism entails will be discussed (Section III), as well as the more beneficial aspects and possibilities of the multi-textual structure (Section IV). Finally, a conclusion is drawn as to the meaning and implications of multi-textualism within the Austrian constitutional framework (Section V).

II. The Structure of the Austrian Constitution

A. Constitutional Laws and Constitutional Provisions

i. *The Multi-Textuality of Austrian Constitutional Law*

The multi-textuality of Austrian constitutional law was intentional from the beginning. The Constitution does not contain an incorporation clause. On the contrary, Article 44(1) B-VG already opens up the possibility of creating constitutional law in addition to the core document. This provision, which governs constitutional amendments, refers to 'constitutional laws or constitutional provisions contained in ordinary laws,' thereby enables the enactment of constitutional law outside the core document under two conditions. First, any such law has to meet the regular amendment requirements for constitutional law in Austria, which means that it has to 'be passed by the National Council … in the presence of at least half of the members and by a majority of two-thirds of the votes.'[20] Second, the law must be

[18] Gesetz über die Aufhebung des Adels, der weltlichen Ritter- und Damenorden und gewisser Titel und Würden (Act Abolishing the Nobility, Secular Orders of Knights and Dames, and Certain Titles and Dignities), State Law Gazette No. 211/1919.

[19] Staatsvertrag von Saint-Germain-en-Laye 1919 (State Treaty of St. Germain of 1919), State Law Gazette No. 303/1920.

[20] In contrast to the higher approval quorums of the first chamber of parliament, the Federal Chamber (second chamber) decides on constitutional matters with a simple majority. Article 44 para 2 B-VG

explicitly designated as a 'constitutional law' or 'constitutional provision.' If these two requirements are met, constitutional law may either be enacted as Federal Constitutional Acts (FCAs)[21] or incorporated into ordinary statutory legislation. The latter means that specific provisions (whole sections, individual paragraphs, or even single sentences) within an ordinary statutory law may be designated as constitutional provisions, if the Parliament votes separately on them with the required qualified two-thirds majority. The consequence of this framework is that Austrian constitutional law is rather fragmented. It thus consists of the core document (B-VG), additional acts recognised as constitutional law by the B-VG for historical (transitional) reasons,[22] approximately 20 FCAs, which are fully constitutional law, and roughly 550 constitutional provisions embedded within ordinary statutory law.[23]

Constitutional provisions serve many different purposes, each relating to the specific area of law being regulated. Usually, they create exceptions to the constitutional rules set out in the B-VG. In a constitutional system that includes an incorporation clause, most of these exceptions would not be permissible, as the legislature would be limited in its ability to enact statutory laws that depart from the existing constitutional framework. Austria's multi-textual approach offers a seemingly 'easier' alternative by allowing a new constitutional provision to be directly embedded within a specific statutory law, thereby creating targeted exemptions from the constitutional framework. This method opens up the possibility of deviating from constitutional norms by creating a constitutionally legitimised exception. A typical version of such a constitutional provision is the so-called 'competence coverage clause' (*Kompetenzdeckungsklausel*), which permits deviations from the constitutional allocation of powers between the federation and the *Länder*. In such cases, a constitutional provision inserted at the beginning of a statutory act declares that – irrespective of the constitutional allocation of powers (*Kompetenzverteilung*) – the entire competence for the subject matter of this particular statutory act belongs to the federation.[24] In this way, the constitutional provision formally authorises the deviation from the general allocation of powers by granting the competence to the federation. Additionally, the enactment of such a constitutional provision requires the consent of the second chamber of Parliament, the Federal Council (*Bundesrat*),

provides for an exception in the event that the constitutional jurisdiction of the federal states is to be restricted. In this case, a two-thirds majority quorum also applies.

[21] FCAs are distinguished from the core document, which is the B-VG (from 1920 as amended 1929 and re-enacted 1930).

[22] See Article 149 B-VG.

[23] Stelzer (n 12) 20.

[24] See eg with regard to recent examples K Lachmayer and E Wagenknecht, 'Country Report: Austria' in L Roberto Barroso and R Albert (eds), *The 2023 International Review of Constitutional Reform* (Constitutional Studies Program at the University of Texas at Austin in collaboration with the International Forum on the Future of Constitutionalism, 2024) 30, 33.

'to be given in the presence of at least half of the members and by a majority of two thirds of the votes.'[25]

In addition to their role in reallocating powers, constitutional provisions in Austria also serve various other functions. They may establish fundamental rights, such as Section 1 of the Data Protection Act (concerning a right to the protection of personal data). Conversely, they may introduce limitations on fundamental rights protections, such as in the area of administrative penalties (for example, Section 99 of the Road Traffic Act and Section 103 of the Motor Vehicle Act). They also address special institutional guarantees, such as the appointment of special legal protection officers under Section 57 of the Military Authorization Act and Section 91a of the Security Police Act. As most of the provisions concern particular rules in a specific area, they rarely establish general constitutional principles but must instead be considered within their specific legal context.[26]

The Austrian model of constitutional multi-textualism does not change the decision-making procedures for constitutional amendments. The only distinction lies in the labeling requirement: while amendments to the B-VG do not have to be explicitly labeled as constitutional law or constitutional provisions, any other constitutional act or provision must be labeled as such. Substantively, there is no legal differentiation between the different textual forms of constitutional law; all constitutional texts have the same normative relevance. Accordingly, any amendment or enactment of constitutional law is subject to the general rules of legal interpretation, especially the principles of lex posterior and lex specialis.

ii. Constitutional Amendments

When constitutional law and its amendments are considered in relation to each other, it becomes clear that the act of amendment itself constitutes a separate text that must be distinguished from the original constitutional law. Formally, constitutional law consists of the original version and all its subsequent amendments. The consolidated text is provided for convenience, but does not reflect the formal structure of constitutional law.[27] In this respect, multi-textualism operates in a temporal dimension, which is also relevant from the perspective of asynchrony.

An interesting example of this divergence is the 1964 amendment to the B-VG.[28] While Article I of the amendment (59/1964) changed the B-VG itself, Article II of the same amendment declared parts or entire texts of 13 international treaties to be constitutionally authorised. Notably, Article II No. 7 elevated the ECHR

[25] Stelzer (n 12) 31.
[26] Eberhard and Lachmayer (n 5) 114–15.
[27] By contrast, there is the concept of re-enactment, which creates a new consolidated version of the constitution including all amendments, see B-VG, Federal Law Gazette No. 1/1930.
[28] Federal Law Gazette 59/1964.

and its additional protocols to the constitutional level.[29] This form of normative integration of new texts into the constitutional sphere can only be found in the amendment text itself. Thus, certain constitutional amendments must be treated separately as they contain content that holds separate constitutional relevance.

Another temporal aspect concerns constitutional provisions governing the entry into force of constitutional provisions. Constitutional provisions do not exist solely in their substantive form, but are always accompanied by separate constitutional provisions specifying their effective date of entry into force. Thus, there are around 90 constitutional provisions in Austrian constitutional law that exclusively regulate the date of entry into force of other substantive constitutional provisions.

B. Constitutional Principles

The Austrian Constitution also contains a provision concerning a so-called total revision of the Constitution. Article 44(3) B-VG states that 'any total revision of the Federal Constitution … shall be submitted to a vote of the entire federal people.' This procedural requirement of an additional referendum, which complements the necessary two-thirds majority in the Parliament, has been interpreted by the Austrian Constitutional Court (ACC) to mean that the higher amendment requirements are to be understood as a higher layer of constitutional law.[30] This higher layer of constitutional law consists of those contents of the Austrian Constitution whose amendment would constitute a total revision. The ACC has identified these contents as the so-called 'constitutional principles' ('*Verfassungsprinzipien*') or core law of the Constitution ('*Baugesetze*').[31] These principles are not explicitly expressed within the constitutional text, but are recognised as an inherent concept of Austrian constitutional law, derived mainly through systematic interpretation of the provisions of the B-VG.[32] While the ACC initially identified democracy, federalism, and the republic form of government as core principles, in the 1950s, it added the rule of law, which also includes the separation of powers and fundamental rights.[33] Today, these six constitutional principles are understood as the core of the Austrian Constitution.[34]

[29] P Cede, 'Some aspects of the case law of the Austrian Constitutional Court on Art. 6 ECHR' (2009) 3 *ICL Journal* 27.

[30] Stelzer (n 12) 27.

[31] See Official Collection of the Judgments of the Austrian Constitutional Court (VfSlg) 2455/1952; A Jakab, 'Determining the Content of (Austrian) Constitutional Principles' in C Bezemek, M Potacs and A Somek (eds), *Vienna Lectures on Legal Philosophy, Volume 3: Legal Reasoning* (Hart Publishing, 2023) 1 (5).

[32] E Wiederin, 'The Evolution and Gestalt of the Austrian Constitution' in A von Bogdandy, PM Huber and S Ragone (eds), *The Max Planck Handbooks in European Public Law. Volume 2: Constitutional Foundations* (Oxford University Press, 2023) 23.

[33] Jakab (n 31) 1.

[34] See Lachmayer (n 3) 75 (102).

As a consequence, Austrian constitutional law is understood as consisting of two hierarchical layers: a higher layer of 'constitutional principles,' and a lower layer of 'ordinary constitutional law.'[35]

Only in one case, the legislature has deemed the higher layer of constitutional principles to be relevant: Austria's accession to the European Union. EU membership was considered to affect these principles, as the application of EU law would significantly change the Austrian models of democracy, federalism, and the rule of law. In recognition of this impact, a special FCA on Austria's Accession to the European Union[36] was enacted and consequently submitted to a referendum,[37] thereby fulfilling the constitutional requirements for a total revision of the Constitution. Most interestingly, this total revision is not visibly reflected in the constitutional text.[38] The transfer of legislative, administrative, and judicial competences to the EU is not expressed in any text, not even in the FCA on the accession itself.[39] One could argue that the EU treaties have also become – at least to a certain extent – part of Austrian constitutional law, which in turn creates an entirely new dimension of multi-textualism.[40]

The ACC has operationalised this constitutional hierarchy by asserting the authority to review 'ordinary constitutional law' against the standard of higher constitutional law. In effect, the ACC has granted itself the power to review constitutional law for compliance with the constitutional principles established by the ACC itself.[41] Interestingly, this multi-layered design of the Austrian Constitution has influenced the multi-textual structure of Austrian constitutional law, which has to be analysed in more detail.

C. International and European Law

i. *International Law*

As mentioned above, Austrian constitutional law also contains certain international treaties.[42] Previously, the Austrian Constitution permitted the authorisation of international treaties at the constitutional level, enabling the integration of

[35] Eberhard and Lachmayer (n 5) 116.

[36] Bundesverfassungsgesetz über den Beitritt Österreichs zur Europäischen Union (FCA on the Accession of Austria to the European Union), Federal Law Gazette No. 744/1994.

[37] C Herbst, 'Austria – Austrian Constitutional Law and Accession to the European Union' (1995) *European Public Law* 1 (2).

[38] Only certain provisions were included in the B-VG, which especially concern the effects on certain obligations of Austrian constitutional authorities (see below s II(C)(ii)).

[39] I Seidl-Hohenveldern, 'Constitutional Problems involved in Austria's accession to the EU' (1995) 33 Common Market Law Review 727–41.

[40] See below s II(C)(ii).

[41] M Stelzer, 'Limited Constitutional Amendment Powers in Austria' (2019) 21 *European Journal of Law Reform* 376, 377.

[42] E Handl-Petz, 'International Law in the Austrian Legal System' in B Verschraegen (ed), *Austrian Law – An International Perspective: Selected Issues* (Jan Sramek Publishing, 2010) 287, 331–32.

entire treaties, specific parts, or even individual provisions into the constitutional framework. The result was a multitude of new constitutional texts that must be considered when interpreting the Constitution. In the context of human rights protection, this approach opened up the possibility for significant developments in substance, but it also led to a deep formal fragmentation of human rights protection in Austria.[43]

This approach changed with the formal reform of Austrian constitutional law in 2008,[44] which abolished the possibility of directly authorising international treaties at the constitutional level.[45] Many of the treaties that had previously been granted constitutional status were either downgraded to the level of ordinary statutory law or have been repealed.[46] Since the reform, international law can only be integrated into Austrian constitutional law indirectly by enacting a new Federal Constitutional Act (FCA) that formally incorporates the relevant contents of a treaty. This was the case, for example, with the UN Convention on the Rights of the Child.[47] In 2011, the Austrian Parliament enacted an FCA on the Rights of the Child,[48] which selectively incorporated only a few rights from the UN Convention.

ii. European Union Law

Austria's accession to the EU, as described above, caused a total revision of the Austrian Constitution.[49] As a result, EU primary law – especially the Treaty on European Union (TEU), the Treaty on the Functioning of the European Union (TFEU), and the Charter of Fundamental Rights (CFR) – as well as secondary legislation such as regulations, and, to a certain extent, directives, not only has direct effect (at least to a certain extent) within Austria's legal system, but also enjoys primacy over domestic law, including constitutional law.[50] Thus, if there is a normative collision between Austrian and European law, it is EU law that must be applied. The importance of this European normative hierarchy cannot be overestimated. While Austrian constitutional law already offers a considerable textual complexity, the primacy of EU law adds an additional layer: potentially any act

[43] See Stelzer, *The Constitution of the Republic of Austria* (n 12) 190–94.

[44] See above s II(A).

[45] Handl-Petz (n 42) 299, 331–32.

[46] See Bundesverfassungsgesetz zur Bereinigung des Bundesverfassungsrechts [Federal Constitutional Act on the Consolidation of Federal Constitutional Law] (Erstes Bundesverfassungsrechtsbereinigungsgesetz – 1. BVRBG, [First Federal Constitutional Consolidation Act]), Federal Law Gazette I No. 2/2008.

[47] Convention on the Rights of the Child adopted 20 November 1989 by the General Assembly resolution 44/25, entry into force 2 September 1990.

[48] Bundesverfassungsgesetz über die Rechte von Kindern, Federal Law Gazette I No. 4/2011.

[49] See above s II(B).

[50] A Posch, 'Community law and Austrian constitutional law' (2008) 2 *ICL Journal* 272, 279; K Lachmayer, 'The Constitution of Austria in International Constitutional Networks: Pluralism, Dialogues and Diversity' in A Albi and S Bardutzky (eds), *National Constitutions in European and Global Governance: Democracy, Rights, the Rule of Law* (TMC Asser Press, 2019) 1271, 1274.

of European legislation may supersede a concrete provision of Austrian constitutional law. [51] In addition, Austrian law must be interpreted in conformity with Union law.

To reflect this fundamental integration, Austrian constitutional law also contains a dedicated, albeit limited, chapter on the European Union (Articles 23a–k B-VG).[52] These provisions serve as domestic constitutional links that connect Austrian constitutional law with EU constitutional law, presupposing the EU Treaties as their foundations. Thus, the Austrian constitutional texts cannot be fully understood without reference to Union law. For instance, the Constitution refers to EU institutions such as the European Parliament, the Council, or the European Court of Justice, whose competences and functions derive exclusively from the EU Treaties and not from domestic rules.[53] Moreover, Article 50 B-VG governs the domestic process for approving amendments to the EU Treaties, which constitutionally requires approval of both chambers of the Austrian Parliament by a two-thirds majority and would also require a referendum if the amendment significantly interferes with Austria's constitutional principles.

In a famous decision, the ACC declared that certain rights enshrined in the CFR, insofar as they correspond to provisions of the ECHR, are to be recognised as fundamental rights under the Austrian Constitution.[54] The Court's rationale was to ensure that individuals could seek constitutional protection for violations of rights enshrined in the CFR to the ACC. This decision perfectly illustrates the interrelation between Austrian constitutional law and European constitutional law.[55]

III. Challenges

A. Introduction

The founding father[56] of the Austrian Constitution, Hans Kelsen, could not have foreseen the far-reaching effects of the formal design of Austrian constitutional law, which has been shaped by the political culture of the Second Republic and has led to various constitutional problems. These problems include the lack of clarity across more than 1,000 constitutional provisions and the lack of a robust

[51] Lachmayer (n 50) 1277.
[52] ibid 1278.
[53] See R Schütze, *European Constitutional Law*, 3rd edn (Oxford University Press, 2021) 73–150.
[54] See Austrian Constitutional Court, 14.3.2012, U 466/11 et al, English version: www.vfgh.gv.at/downloads/VfGH_U_466-11__U_1836-11_Grundrechtecharta_english.pdf; see also G Kristoferitsch, 'The Charter of Fundamental Rights of the European Union to be treated like Constitutional Law (2013) 7 *ICL Journal* 88–92.
[55] For a structurally distinct approach to incorporating EU law into the constitutional order, see also ch 6 by T Birmontienė and J Miliuvienė, 'Vertical and Horizontal Layers of the Lithuanian Constitution'.
[56] Wiederin, 'From the Federalist Papers to Hans Kelsen's "Dearest Child"' (n 10).

constitutional culture within the Austrian government, which tends to overrule judgments of the Constitutional Court (even in cases of human rights violations).[57] As a result, constitutional patriotism has not taken root, and fundamental rights remain largely unknown to the Austrian population, being scattered across more than 20 different documents.[58]

A political attempt in the early 2000s to reform Austrian constitutional law both formally and substantively – by reframing the Constitution into a newly structured, coherent text – led to the establishment of an Austrian Convention (2003–2005).[59] However, it ultimately proved unsuccessful in achieving its reform objective.[60] The Austrian Convention attempted to address the overall situation of what could be described as a confusing constitution.[61] However, once excessive multi-textualism has taken hold, it is not so easy to put the genie back into the bottle. The long-standing challenges of unification and incorporation remained unsolved in Austria. Nevertheless, at least the proliferation of multi-textualism was curbed to some extent by efforts to streamline the Constitution in 2008.[62]

B. Unconstitutional Constitutional Law

In the context of the multi-layered understanding of Austrian constitutional law, the case law of the ACC has been crucial in defining the boundaries of constitutional principles. A particularly significant example dates from 2001, in an ACC case concerning the legal protection of public procurement.[63] The Federal Procurement Act contained a constitutional provision (section 126a), which declared that all 'provisions of provincial law in force … regarding the organization and jurisdiction of bodies responsible for legal protection in the area of public procurement shall be deemed not to be contrary to federal constitutional law.' According to the legislative documents, this temporary provision was intended to safeguard the status quo of the public procurement control bodies in the states under federal constitutional law. However, in a previous case, the ACC had already declared the concept of legal protection in question to be unconstitutional.[64] In order to circumvent the Constitutional Court's control

[57] Eberhard and Lachmayer (n 5) 115.

[58] See K Lachmayer and R Rothmann, 'Zur Kenntnis der Grundrechte: Einblicke einer explorativen Studie in Österreich' (2023) *Zeitschrift für Rechtssoziologie* [*Journal of Sociology of Law*] 300, 314–25.

[59] P Gerlich, 'The Constitutional Convention in Austria: A Parallel Campaign with Ambivalent' (2005) 3 *Journal for Comparative Government and European Policy* 52.

[60] Eberhard and Lachmayer (n 5) 112–13; M Stelzer, 'Constitutional Change in Austria' in X Contiades (ed), *Engineering Constitutional Change: A Comparative Perspective on Europe, Canada and the USA* (Routledge, 2012) 7, 12.

[61] Stelzer, 'Constitutional Change in Austria' (n 60) 28.

[62] See the constitutional amendment Federal Law Gazette I No. 2/2008; see also Eberhard and Lachmayer (n 5) 118–22.

[63] Official Collection of the Judgments of the Austrian Constitutional Court (VfSlg) 16.327/2001.

[64] Official Collection of the Judgments of the Austrian Constitutional Court (VfSlg) 15.578/1999.

over the question concerned, the Parliament enacted a constitutional provision designed to exclude the contested provisions from constitutional review. The federal legislature did not, however, explicitly declare the specific provision on legal protection to be a constitutional provision, but instead included the above-mentioned provision, which in turn declares the provisions identified as unconstitutional by the ACC 'not to be contrary to federal constitutional law.' From both a lex posterior and a lex specialis perspective, this legislative manoeuvre derogated the general provisions of constitutional legality in this specific context. From a constitutional perspective, the legislature politically reclassified an unconstitutional norm as constitutional, which exceeded the proper function of constitutional law. This action reflects a political misuse of constitutional authority, revealing an unwillingness to accept judicial findings of unconstitutionality. An imminent effect was the removal of any further control by the Constitutional Court in that regard.

In reaction to these developments, the ACC concluded that the constitutional provision itself was unconstitutional as a violation of the constitutional principles. Furthermore, the ACC identified a violation of the rule of law principle, where the ordinary constitutional legislature suspended the Constitution, even if this only concerned a specific part of the legal order. 'It is indeed a core element of constitutional law to ensure that the ordinary constitutional legislature should not be able to remove the authoritativeness of the Constitution for a certain area of the legal system.'[65] Such a provision would not only violate the 'principle of the authoritativeness of the Constitution but also the competence of the Constitutional Court to review norms.'[66] Both must be regarded as core elements of the rule of law principle of the Federal Constitution of Austria.

The ACC thus made it clear that the use of the constitutional provision must be limited if it is to serve the purpose of suspending the Constitution in a certain area of law.

C. Constitutional Identification

The large number of constitutional acts and provisions makes it difficult to have a proper overview of Austrian constitutional law. Although the labeling obligation facilitates the identification of constitutional provisions, it remains challenging to maintain a comprehensive overview in the absence of an enumerative list. On the one hand, it is typically possible to identify relevant provisions within specific areas of law, as they are embedded in the corresponding statutory law. On the other hand, it is difficult to follow the dynamics of newly enacted constitutional provisions, although recent enhancements to the Austrian Legal Information System

[65] Official Collection of the Judgments of the Austrian Constitutional Court (VfSlg) 16.327/2001.
[66] ibid.

have improved access to legal texts.[67] Given this complexity, it is evident that the sheer volume of constitutional law has become a significant obstacle. Introducing limits on the overall length of the Constitution would definitely improve the coherence and accessibility of Austrian constitutional law.

D. Constitutional Elevation

The concept of constitutional provisions in the Austrian context can be understood as a mechanism of constitutional elevation. In most cases, such provisions are not used to establish new substantive constitutional rules, but to create exceptions to existing constitutional rules.[68] Through this process, statutory law that would otherwise contradict constitutional law is elevated to the constitutional level as an exception, but only with regard to a specific, concrete case. This practice poses a structural problem: it fosters the perception that constitutional compliance is not necessary, but that deviations from constitutional norms can be easily legitimised through formal elevation. This undermines the coherence and the significance of constitutional rules and principles.

In an act of judicial self-entrenchment, the ACC has even elevated certain parts of the CFR to the constitutional level in 2012.[69] While the provisions of the CFR have been generally treated as statutory rights domestically, the case law of the Court has allowed constitutional review of Austrian statutory law against CFR rights.[70] Given the enormous effects of this constitutional re-evaluation of the CFR on Austria's legal system, it is possible to speak of a constitutional super-elevation.

E. Constitutional Conflicts

In addressing constitutional conflicts as a challenge inherent to multi-textualism, Richard Albert argues as follows:

> The disaggregated nature of multi-textual constitutions moreover creates the possibility of conflict between two or more constitutional documents. When one latter-adopted constitutional document comes into interpretive conflict with an earlier-adopted constitutional document, the conflict must be resolved to bring clarity to the meaning of the Constitution. In cases like these, the authoritative arbiter of the meaning of the Constitution must resolve the conflict.[71]

[67] See the Federal Legal Information System (Rechtsinformationssystem des Bundes) www.ris.bka.gv.at/.

[68] Eberhard and Lachmayer (n 5) 114.

[69] See s II(C)(ii).

[70] Kristoferitsch (n 54); H Verdino, 'The Charter of Fundamental Rights of the European Union as Review Standard in Proceedings before the Constitutional Court' (2013) 7 *ICL Journal* 93–94.

[71] Albert, 'Multi-Textual Constitutions' (n 1) 1672.

The above-mentioned case law of the ACC concerning unconstitutional constitutional amendments exemplifies this dynamic. The ACC effectively asserted the existence of superior constitutional limits by declaring a constitutional provision unconstitutional.[72] This constitutional conflict was a direct result of the multi-textual approach of Austrian constitutional law. The conflict between the legislature and the ACC culminated in the Court's exercise of its role as the final arbiter of constitutional meaning.

Regular conflicts between different amendments are resolved through legal derogation. The problem of creating a multitude of exceptions to constitutional rules, as well as the sporadic constitutional elevation of statutory provisions that would otherwise violate fundamental rights, show further challenges for the ACC to find proper interpretative answers.

F. Constitutional Erosion and Inflexibility

The overall arbitrary practice of enacting constitutional provisions to shield statutory legislation that would otherwise infringe constitutional law illustrates a general deficit within Austrian constitutional culture. The principle of constitutional supremacy – that statutory law must conform to the Constitution – has been structurally undermined. The limits established by the ACC are very wide and still leave significant leeway for the legislature to create constitutional exceptions.[73]

Besides its negative effect on respect for constitutional supremacy, the proliferation of constitutional texts also limits the legislature's flexibility in enacting new statutory law, as existing constitutional provisions must be considered and often cannot be easily amended due to higher majority requirements in the Parliament. While constitutional amendments have typically been politically possible for decades, growing political polarisation and the lack of a two-thirds parliamentary majority for the governing parties have made it increasingly difficult. The adjustment of the right to the protection of personal data (section 1 of the Data Protection Act[74]) in the context of the enactment of the European General Data Protection Regulation (GDPR)[75] can serve as an example. While this amendment of Austrian constitutional law could have been a technical issue, the government did not have the necessary majority and was politically unable to find a consensus

[72] See above s III(B).

[73] In the context of Hungary, this well-established Austrian bad habit was criticised as an expression of authoritarianism by not respecting the constitutional court. See eg K Lane Scheppele, 'Constitutional Revenge' (*VerfBlog*, 4 March 2013) verfassungsblog.de/constitutional-revenge/.

[74] Bundesgesetz zum Schutz natürlicher Personen bei der Verarbeitung personenbezogener Daten [Federal Act on the Protection of Individuals with regard to the Processing of Personal Data, Datenschutzgesetz, Data Protetion Act – DSG], Federal Law Gazette I No. 165/1999.

[75] Regulation (EU) 2016/679 on the protection of natural persons with regard to the processing of personal data and on the free movement of such data, OJ [2016] L 119/1.

with the opposition parties.[76] Ultimately, the amendment was not agreed upon and remained unadopted to this day, with no indication that it will be implemented in the future. Although the amendment may not be seen as a politically or legally important, it does highlight the lack of flexibility inherent in Austria's system of excessive multi-textualism.

IV. Possibilities

From a comparative perspective, Austrian constitutional law can serve as an illustration of the complex interplay between different constitutional documents and the strategies developed (especially by the ACC) to navigate this formal constitutional design. Austria presents a clear example of excessive multi-textualism, offering scholars a rich case study of the many different versions of challenges such a fragmented and layered constitutional structure can generate.

As far as the possibilities of multi-textualism are concerned, the Austrian experience shows how textual flexibility relativises the constitutional text, viewing it not as a sacred charter but as a technical instrument.[77] Austria's instrumental approach to constitutional law – despite the existence of a prominent founding father of the Austrian Constitution[78] – has never fostered constitutional veneration or constitutional patriotism in Austria.[79] Instead, it has facilitated political compromises in a democracy and has enabled a more flexible integration of European Union law. The constitutional elevation of the ECHR allowed the further development of fundamental rights in Austria without sparking internal political conflicts. Interestingly, the 2008 limitation on the constitutional adoption of international treaties has since limited the adoption of new fundamental rights or the integration of other new international treaties at the constitutional level.[80]

Multi-textualism has also had a positive impact on the allocation of powers between the federation and the *Länder*. By using competence coverage clauses, it was easier to find political solutions for the necessary harmonisation of certain areas of law across federal and state levels. Although one could claim the opposite, arguing that this technique has eroded federalism in Austria, it nonetheless shows how long-standing conflicts can be overcome. In this regard, constitutional multi-textualism has also become a tool for suppressing deeper political conflicts, particularly concerning federalism or fundamental rights, opting for the easier option of adding up new constitutional documents without trying to directly resolve these underlying discrepancies.

[76] A Anderl and D Schelling, 'Datenschutzregime mit österreichischen Eigenheiten' *Der Standard* (16 May 2018) www.derstandard.at/story/2000079662346/datenschutzregime-mit-oesterreichischen-eigenheiten.

[77] Stelzer, *The Constitution of the Republic of Austria* (n 12) 20.

[78] Wiederin, 'From the Federalist Papers to Hans Kelsen's "Dearest Child"' (n 10) 325–27.

[79] Albert, 'Multi-Textual Constitutions' (n 1) 1685–93.

[80] Handl-Petz (n 42) 299; Eberhard and Lachmayer (n 5) 119.

However, this instrumental approach also carries risks, particularly in times of populism, when constitutional values may be easily ignored and undermined.[81] Interestingly, through the introduction of constitutional principles, the ACC has created a very broad but still strong mechanism for constitutional resilience against authoritarianism, establishing this higher layer of constitutional law. The protective function of this framework would be exhausted if a majority of the population were to vote in favour of abolishing these values in a referendum. The overall ease of creating exceptions did not, remarkably, lead to a state of emergency or constitutional exemptions during the COVID-19 pandemic. Austria's approach to the pandemic remained within the constitutional framework and did not attempt to establish any form of constitutional exceptionalism.[82]

Finally, another layer of multi-textualism in the context of Austrian constitutional law concerns multilingual constitutionalism. Austria's official state language is German,[83] but there are also ethnic minorities, particularly Croatian and Slovenian communities in the south and southeast of the country,[84] who are guaranteed certain language rights under the Constitution.[85] However, the opportunity to adopt a multilingual constitutional text was never taken up in Austria. This absence has epistemic implications, as it limits the possibilities of linguistic minorities in the constitutional framework and may be seen as a missed chance for inclusive nation-building.

V. Conclusions

The beauty of the Austrian Constitution lies not in its multi-textualism, but in its core document, which established clear principles and rules for situations of governmental crisis. The B-VG, as Kelsen's legacy, has been enriched over the past century and today includes many elements characteristic of modern constitutions.[86]

[81] K Lachmayer and K Fredy Hinterberger, 'Challenges of liberal democracy in Austria: Lessons Learned from Current Government Crises' in B Mathieu and G Katrougalos (eds), *The Crisis of Liberal Democracy: Diagnostics and Therapies* (Intersentia, 2023) 127–38.

[82] K Lachmayer, 'Constitutional Compliance or Governmental Mismanagement? Rights Limitations in Austria from Lockdowns to Compulsory Vaccination' in A Vedaschi (ed), *Governmental Policies to Fight Pandemic: The Boundaries of Legitimate Limitations on Fundamental Freedoms* (Brill, 2024) 115, 117–18).

[83] See Article 8 B-VG.

[84] K Lachmayer and N Sonntag, 'An Introduction to Austrian Legal Culture' in S Koch and M Mikkel Kjølstad (eds), *Handbook on Legal Cultures. A Selection of the World's Legal Cultures* (Springer International, 2023) 75 (77).

[85] N Sonntag, 'Minderheiten und Recht: Eine Einführung am Beispiel Österreichs [Minorities and the Law: An Introduction to the Case of Austria]' (2010) 1 E*uropäisches Journal für Minderheitenfragen [European Journal for Migration Issues]* 4–32; R Vouk, *70 Years Article 7. Relevant, obsolete, met, superseded* (Mohorjeva druzba, 2025) 129–52.

[86] Nevertheless, many aspects of the Austrian Constitution remain open to improvement. For a detailed analysis, see K Lachmayer, 'Southern Lessons for Constitutional Law: A View from Austria' in U Kischel (ed), *Southern Lessons for Constitutional Law* (Mohr Siebeck, 2026) 11–34.

But it is also part of Kelsen's legacy to have designed a constitution with built-in flexibility for multi-textualism. By conceiving the constitution as a set of rules for the political arena (*Spielregelverfassung*),[87] Kelsen refrained from embedding preambles or other substantive objectives in constitutional law. In his view, in a democracy, these decisions are a matter for the parliament to decide on a statutory level.[88]

The Austrian constitutional culture of the Second Republic of Austria (since 1945), however, has made excessive use of the possibilities of multi-textualism enshrined in the Constitution. Constitutional provisions were enacted for a variety of reasons and created a multitude of constitutional exceptions, a practice the ACC has sought to constrain by setting quantitative and qualitative limits on the enactment of constitutional provisions. Regarding fundamental rights, multi-textualism has allowed for the creation of a multitude of new rights, which, however, remain largely unknown to the people as they are fragmented and dispersed across numerous constitutional texts. This fragmentation poses an ongoing challenge for the effective communication and understanding of constitutional rights, both within legal discourse and among the broader population.

Looking beyond the domestic dimension and including the sphere of European Union law, a whole new and even more complex world of multi-textualism (as well as multilingualism) opens up, which also has a significant impact on the Austrian Constitution. Although this impact may not be immediately apparent when looking at the text of Austrian constitutional law itself, it becomes evident through the relevant jurisprudence of the ACC and the CJEU, which reveals the quantitative and qualitative dimensions of this interaction.

Multi-textualism might simplify the process of constitutional amendments as well as complicate the constitutional system as a whole. The challenge posed by the resulting complexity must ultimately be resolved by the constitutional actors responsible for interpreting and applying the Constitution. Much more important than the formal design, however, is the constitutional culture of a country, meaning how constitutional actors deal with constitutional texts and values, especially in times of crisis. While democratic decline can be observed in many countries around the world, Austrian constitutionalism has continued to develop over the last 30 years, grounded in the principles of democracy, the rule of law, and human rights.[89]

[87] H Eberhard and K Lachmayer, 'Rule of Law in Austria' in *Understandings of the Rule of Law in various Legal Orders of the World* (*Rule of Law Wiki* 2011).

[88] Stelzer, *The Constitution of the Republic of Austria* (n 12) 20.

[89] See regarding recent developments in Austria the annual contributions in LR Barroso and R Albert (eds), *The International Review of Constitutional Reform (2022–2026).*

4

Canada's Multi-Textual Constitution

MARY LISTON

Uniformity is not in the spirit of our constitution. We have not a single community in this country. … This is the fact embodied in the law. It may be wise or unwise, according to the preferences and predilection of every one, but this is the basis of our constitution. Diversity is the basis of our constitution.[1]

I. Introduction

This chapter aims to do two things: (1) to bring to the surface what has been taken for granted or considered simply too obvious to dwell on in Canadian constitutional law; and (2) to encourage legal scholars to embrace techniques derived from other disciplines for handling and interpreting multi-textual constitutions. The first objective challenges the view that constitutions are unitary and uniform sources of legal norms. Canada, for example, has a constitution that is located in more than one place, one text, and one time. Even further, Canada's Constitution is not only multi-textual, but could also be considered a *multi-textual corpus*.[2]

The second objective makes use of insights from other disciplines that offer sophisticated techniques for understanding and managing groups of interconnected texts that must be interpreted *together*. The main disciplines that share this skill set are history, literary theory, philology, and theology. These techniques and

[1] References re The Weekly Rest In Industrial Undertakings Act, The Minimum Wages Act, And The Limitation of Hours of Work Act [1936] SCR 461 521 (Rinfret J).

[2] A paradigmatic example of a *textual corpus* in literature (and familiar in popular culture) is JRR Tolkien's oeuvre. Medievalist and Tolkien scholar Gergely Nagy sets out how Tolkien's *The Silmarillion* refers to two different things: (1) the book of this title; and (2) 'the products of Tolkien's practically lifelong creative process' which includes *The Hobbit*, *The Lord of the Rings* trilogy, and a large number of other documents. I make use of this distinction to further redescribe the 'Constitution of Canada' (ie, a constitution comprised a plurality of texts under that title) as a multi-textual corpus which includes a number of texts that are part of (though not always acknowledged) Canada's lifelong creative process of constitution-making. See G Nagy, '*The Silmarillion*: Tolkien's Theory of Myth, Text and Culture' in SD Lee (ed), *A Companion to J.R.R. Tolkien The Legendarium* (Wiley Blackwell, 2014) 107.

devices are not 'foreign' to law, and I endeavour to demonstrate their relevance through my redescription of the Canadian Constitution as multi-textual. My hope is that this game-changing book will open a fruitful and exciting path for legal scholars in their approach to interpreting, researching, teaching, and writing about multi-textual constitutions.

I begin by setting out, following Richard Albert's lead in his important article, 'Multi-Textual Constitutions,'[3] the concept of a multi-textual constitution. I then turn to consider the Canadian Constitution first as a 'simple' multi-textual constitution in Section III. Section IV presents a deeper and more complex understanding of Canada's multi-textual Constitution, using different literary techniques to illustrate how we can navigate and integrate different but fundamentally related texts. In this section, I also interrogate the conventional notion of 'text' by suggesting that – drawing on literary theory and semiotics – a text is any object that can be 'read.' This line of argument necessarily builds on a broader socio-legal understanding of 'constitution.' The implications of this broader understanding of 'text' will be explored through a few examples. Prominent in this analysis is the growing import of Indigenous constitutions in a decolonising Canada. I then consider the question of who has the authority to identify and name what counts as official or unofficial, constitutional texts in Section V. I conclude with some thoughts on future questions and directions for research.

II. Uni- vs Multi-Textual Constitutions

In his article 'Multi-Textual Constitutions,' Albert begins by challenging the traditional distinction between written and unwritten constitutions as both 'incorrect and misleading.'[4] This is because all constitutions are written down in some way and most contain unwritten norms such as principles, conventions, or rules. The written constitution is usually a positive document, while the unwritten constitution takes on a different shape due to its particular jurisdictional context and often forms what is now increasingly called an 'invisible' constitution that complements the 'visible' written constitution.[5]

The traditional way of describing constitutions obscures another interesting and salient reality: some jurisdictions work with one supreme document, while others rely on multiple documents. From this starting point, Albert defines uni-textual constitutions as those whose written elements appear in a single document, which,

[3] R Albert, 'Multi-Textual Constitutions' (2023) 109 *Virginia Law Review* 1629.

[4] ibid 1631.

[5] See, eg, the pieces in this collection: R Dixon and A Stone (eds), *The Invisible Constitution in Comparative Perspective* (Cambridge University Press, 2018). Dixon and Stone set out various understandings of constitutional invisibility as comprising a 'sphere' that is textual, extra-textual and sociological. This chapter complements their understanding of the invisible constitution. 'The Invisible Constitution in Comparative Perspective' in ibid 1, 3–4. In the American context, see LH Tribe, *The Invisible Constitution* (Oxford University Press, 2008).

in turn, is treated as the *only* positive source of higher law.[6] In other words, a single, authoritative text contains the main constitutional norms for that jurisdiction.[7] In his analysis, the American Constitution is the 'world's paradigmatic example.'[8] But, as he turns to other jurisdictions, this idea of a unitary, unified constitutional text increasingly appears as an example of American exceptionalism – at least in popular culture.[9]

By way of contrast, Albert's conception of multi-textual constitutions is that these constitutional orders consist of multiple constitutional documents, each potentially enjoying shared constitutional authority or status, and each potentially (sometimes, but not always) entrenched under special procedures of constitutional change.[10] Multi-textual constitutions may exist at national, subnational, and supranational levels.[11] They may take the form of founding texts, basic organic laws possessing constitutional status, or standalone constitutional amendments.

Multi-textual constitutions, Albert writes, share three features: (1) a multiplicity of texts; (2) asynchrony, meaning the documents are not adopted concurrently; and (3) shared supremacy.[12] Canada exhibits these first three features. Canada has two main written constitutions – the Constitution Act 1867[13] (originally the British North America Act 1867) and the Constitution Act 1982[14] – that were created over time and have shared constitutional supremacy.

Multi-textual constitutions can be created intentionally by design or through ad hoc or evolutionary processes over time. These modes are not mutually exclusive. Finally, multi-textual constitutions may also be later consolidated into a uni-textual form.[15] When created by design, Albert suggests three models: (1) a founding document that references other documents of higher law; (2) a founding document that anticipates the later creation of such documents; and (3) a founding document that enumerates other documents which are understood to comprise the constitution.[16] As will be explained below in Section IV, Canada clearly reflects the first and third models, while its alignment with the second is unclear.

[6] Albert, 'Multi-Textual Constitutions' (n 3) 1633.

[7] Dag Michalsen suggests that pre-modern constitutions were often unwritten in contrast to the mono-textual modern constitutions of the late eighteenth century. D Michalsen, 'The Many Textual Identities of Constitutions' in K Gammelgaard and E Holmøyvi (eds), *Writing Democracy: The Norwegian Constitution 1814–2014* (Berghahn Books, 2014) 62. On the model of a modern constitution, see Z Elkins and T Ginsburg, 'What Can We Learn from Written Constitutions?' (2021) *Annual Review of Political Science* 321.

[8] Albert, 'Multi-Textual Constitutions' (n 3).

[9] This is because the US also has other essential documents related to the Constitution such as the Emancipation Proclamation of January 1, 1863 and the Northwest Ordinance (An Ordinance for the Government of the Territory of the United States, North-West of the River Ohio, 1787). One could also add A Hamilton, J Madison and J Jay, *The Federalist Papers* (Bantam, 1982) and The Gettysburg Address. For a fuller list, see Albert, 'Multi-Textual Constitutions' (n 3) 1635, n 14.

[10] ibid 1633.

[11] ibid; see also n 11 therein.

[12] ibid 1636–40.

[13] Constitution Act 1867 (UK), 30 & 31 Vict, c 3, reprinted in RSC 1985, App II, No 5.

[14] Constitution Act 1982, being Schedule B to the Canada Act 1982 (UK) 1982, c 11.

[15] Albert, 'Multi-Textual Constitutions' (n 3) 1647.

[16] ibid 1641.

For multi-textual constitutions created through evolutionary processes, Albert proposes these three models: (1) formal amendments entailing the pluralisation of constitutional texts; (2) political practice in the lawmaking process and the 'dialogic interactions of political actors' in constitutional politics;[17] and (3) judicial interpretation that confers constitutional status on particular documents.[18] Again, Canada clearly fits within the third model and, at times, the second. Due to the difficulty of amending the Constitution under its current procedural rules, recent formal amendment activity has been limited.[19] Canada's mode of constitutional interpretation and the existence of an unwritten constitution each enable the constitution to grow in an evolutionary manner over time.

Both uni-textual and multi-textual constitutions can be recognised in the popular imagination as 'the constitution.' Although it is easier for lay persons to comprehend uni-textual models, Albert demonstrates that multi-textualism in and of itself does not hinder either popular understanding or endorsement. He then works through the concept through a survey of multi-textual features and constitutional arrangements across a range of jurisdictions.

III. Canada's Multi-Textual Constitution: the Simple Version

We can understand Canada's multi-textual Constitution as a simple construct or in a more complex sense. Section III presents Canada's 'simple' multi-textualism, while Section IV presents the more complex version.

It is unsurprising that Canada's Constitution would align with Albert's concept of multi-textuality. This is because Canada understands itself to be multi-juridical – a jurisdiction with many coexisting legal systems: (1) the original Indigenous legal orders; (2) Quebec's civil law tradition, with common law governing its public law; and (3) the broader common law system encompassing both private and public law. Canada has gone beyond legal pluralism (ie, a mere descriptor of a polity with more than one legal order) to explicitly recognise three different and valid sources of law. A metaphor used by some Indigenous scholars to illustrate this multi-juridical reality is that of a complex braid of hair. Because of the multiplicity of Indigenous legal orders in Canada, the braid contains more than three single strands.[20] Instead, it is comprised of many strands woven together, with two larger, distinctly coloured

[17] ibid 1649.

[18] ibid 1656.

[19] For a list of contemporary amendments, see www.canada.ca/en/intergovernmental-affairs/services/about-canada.html. For an in-depth analysis of amendments see R Albert, *Constitutional Amendments: Making, Breaking, and Changing Constitutions* (Oxford University Press, 2019).

[20] See Oleksandr Marusiak in ch 9 'Exploring Macro-Constitutional Reality in Ukraine: Multi-Textual Insights from the Constitutional Court' in this volume, who talks about Ukraine's Constitution as a 'complex interplay of multiple layers' 173.

strands standing out from the rest: the common law and the civil law.[21] Canada's multi-juridical nature therefore inevitably entails a multi-textual constitutional order, one that includes numerous Indigenous constitutions.[22]

Canada is clearly multi-textual in a 'simple' sense, with its two authoritative positive constitutional documents mentioned earlier: the Constitution Act 1867[23] (originally the British North America Act 1867[24]) and the Constitution Act 1982. Among other matters, the 1867 text sets out core aspects of Canada's unwritten constitution, primarily the three branches of government and the division of powers. The 1982 text sets out the bill of rights,[25] interpretive provisions, Aboriginal rights, and the amending formulae, which provide a mechanism for ongoing formal constitutional evolution.

These two documents share constitutional supremacy and are considered co-equal. The Foreword to the official *Consolidation of the Constitution Acts, 1867 to 1982* makes this co-equality clear:

> This consolidation contains the text of the *Constitution Act, 1867* (formerly the *British North America Act, 1867*), together with amendments made to it since its enactment. The *Constitution Act, 1982* contains the *Canadian Charter of Rights and Freedoms* and other provisions, including the procedure for amending the Constitution of Canada.[26]

If we were to stop here at the existence of two constitutional documents, we would arrive at the conventional account of the Canadian legal order as a 'simple' multi-textual Constitution.

Since Canada is a federal state, we could also complexify this simplicity a little without doing much harm. We might, for example, include the provincial

[21] For an illustration of such a braid, see 'Weaving Legal Traditions: An Animated Insight into Canada's Multi-Juridical Identity (*Reconciliactionyeg*, 19 October 2023) www.reconciliactionyeg.ca/post/weaving-legal-traditions-an-animated-insight-into-canada-s-multi-juridical-identity. See also D Lindberg, '(Re)bundling nêhiyaw âskiy: Nêhiyaw Constitutionalism Through Land Stories' in S Xavier and others (eds), *Decolonizing Law: Indigenous, Third World and Settler Perspectives* (Routledge, 2021); J Borrows and others (eds), *Braiding Legal Orders: Implementing the United Nations Declaration on the Rights of Indigenous Peoples* (McGill-Queen's University Press, 2019).

[22] J Borrows, *Canada's Indigenous Constitution* (University of Toronto Press, 2010).

[23] David Schneiderman, following Peter Russell (both Canadian constitutional scholars), notes that it is a mistake to treat the Constitution Act 1867 as Canada's first Constitution. He and Russell argue that it is, in fact, Canada's fifth and is preceded by: (1) Royal Proclamation of 1763; (2) Quebec Act of 1774, 14 Geo III c 83 (UK); (3) Constitutional Act of 1791, 31 Geo III c 31 (UK); the Act of Union in 1840; and then finally (4) the Constitution Act 1867. See D Schneiderman, 'Unwritten Constitutional Principles in Canada: Genuine or Strategic?' in Dixon and Stone (eds) (n 5) 517. As a teaching subject, constitutional law, however, usually does not spend much time on these earlier documents. See also P Russell, 'Chapter 3 Confederation' in *Constitutional Odyssey: Can Canadians Become a Sovereign People?*, 2nd edn (University of Toronto Press, 1993) and J Webber, *The Constitution of Canada: A Contextual Analysis*, 2nd edn (Hart Publishing, 2021).

[24] Eric Adams underscores how Canada's first constitution was 'strategically renamed to cut ties with its past.' 'Canadian Constitutional Identities' (2015) 38(2) *Dalhousie Law Journal* 311, 339.

[25] Canada's bill of rights is the Canadian Charter of Rights and Freedoms, s 7, Part 1 of the Constitution Act 1982, being Schedule B to the Canada Act 1982 (UK), c 11.

[26] Department of Justice Canada, *A Consolidation of The Constitution Acts 1867 to 1982* (Her Majesty the Queen in Right of Canada, represented by the Minister of Public Works and Government Services, 2012) iii.

constitutions[27] as part of Canada's formal multi-textual constitutional order. Because of Canada's multijuridical nature, we might designate a foundational text like Quebec's Civil Code[28] as a constitutional text. This provincial Civil Code governs interpersonal and property relations in the province (ie, equivalent to the body of private law in a common law legal system). Its preamble states that the Civil Code

> comprises a body of rules which, in all matters within the letter, spirit or object of its provisions, lays down the *jus commune*, expressly or by implication. In these matters, the Code is the foundation of all other laws, although other laws may complement the Code or make exceptions to it.

For Quebec, the Civil Code also expresses the province's identity as the home of the Quebec nation and its distinct society.

We could again stop here. But constitutional multi-textualism runs much deeper in Canada, and it is to this more complex multi-textual constitutionalism that I now turn.

IV Canada's Deep Multi-Textualism[29]

When we step back, look through a long historical lens, and pay close attention, it becomes clear that Canada's Constitution is actually a 'complex' of texts. Canadians do refer to the Constitution in this manner, at least when invoking a small set of foundational documents. But, if legal and political actors were to reflect more deeply on Canada's constitutional context, they might recognise that this multi-textualism entails more than a mere plurality of documents. Instead, it can be understood, in the literary sense, as a *textual corpus*: 'a collection of sometimes inconsistent texts, tracing a relatively stable narrative over a very long period of time, involving a huge cast of characters.'[30] To grasp how such a corpus might be read together and interpreted, one might turn to analogous bodies of work, such as collections of medieval manuscripts, complex religious canons,[31] or the oeuvres of authors whose ideas unfold across multiplicitous texts.

[27] See eg An Act to amend and continue the Act 32-33 Victoria chapter 3; and to establish and provide for the Government of the Province of Manitoba, 1870, 33 Vict, c 3 (Can).

[28] Civil Code of Québec, CQLR c CCQ-1991 ('Civil Code'). Recollect that the public law aspects of Quebec's provincial legal order are governed by the common law principles and, where statutes are concerned, a hybrid of civilian and common law approaches.

[29] I borrow the term 'deep' from Canadian philosopher Charles Taylor, who uses this adjective to describe the model of complex, asymmetrical federalism that characterises Canada. He also uses it in a broader sense to recommend that Canada should acknowledge and accept 'a plurality of ways of belonging' to Canada and being Canadian. C Taylor, 'Shared and Divergent Values' in G LaForest (ed), *Reconciling the Solitudes: Essays on Canadian Federalism and Nationalism* (McGill-Queen's University Press, 1993) 183. See also J Tully, *Strange Multiplicity: Constitutionalism in an Age of Diversity* (Cambridge University Press, 1995).

[30] Nagy, '*The Silmarillion*' (n 2) 108.

[31] On the Christian Bible, see JJB Combrink, 'Multiple Meaning and/or Multiple Interpretation of a Text' (1984) 18 *Neotestamentica* 26.

As noted in the Introduction, one of this chapter's aims is to bring this insight to the forefront of Canadian constitutional discourse.[32] Doing so, I argue, adds interpretive 'depth' to both our understanding and our scholarship. Toward the end of this chapter, I will revisit the idea of a 'relatively stable narrative over a very long period of time' to propose several avenues and directions for future research.

To begin developing this deeper account of Canada's constitutional multi-textualism, the present section turns to literary theory for methodological guidance and analytical perspective. Canada's positive constitutional texts provide many 'clues' pointing to the existence of a larger textual corpus, one that gives the Constitution its depth and complexity. The literary or metafictional techniques that I reference to are: intertextualism, transtextualism, extratextualism, hypertextualism,[33] and (weak) closure.[34]

A. Intertextualism

Intertextualism refers to 'the effective presence of one text in another which takes place by means of plagiarism, quotation or allusion.'[35] For those of us working in cognate disciplines – history, literature, philology, philosophy, theology – this form of multi-textualism is familiar terrain. It appears in legal texts as well, primarily through quotation and allusion.

In Canada's constitutional law, three illustrative examples of intertextualism can be found in sections 52(2), 25, and 35(1) of the Constitution Act 1982. Section 52(2), for instance, conveys the following:

[32] As discussed earlier, multi-textualism is also necessarily related to Canada's 'invisible' constitution. For a larger discussion of Canada's invisible constitution, see VA MacDonnell, 'Rethinking the Invisible Constitution: How Unwritten Constitutional Principles Shape Political Decision-Making' (2019) 65(2) *McGill Law Journal* 175.

[33] For a discussion of the first four terms, see M Jesús Martínez Alfaro, 'Intertextuality: Origins and Development of the Concept'(1996) 18(1/2) *Atlantis* 268, 280–81. Alfaro looks to post-structuralist thinking about narrative – such as the work of Gérard Genette – as well as the influence of Russian theorist of the novel, Mikhail Bakhtin and his work on dialogism, for her conception of intertextuality. This chapter will not touch on paratextuality understood as 'the relations between the body of a text and its title, subtitle, epigraphs, illustrations, notes, first drafts, and other kinds of accessory signals which surround the text and sometimes comment on it.' ibid 281. Nor will it explore architextuality – 'the generic category a text belongs to' – though this chapter clearly assumes that we are dealing with the legal genre of a constitutional text and the subgenre of a multi-textual constitution. ibid. On the 'genre' of the constitution text, see G Frankenberg, 'Comparing Constitutions: Ideas, Ideals, and Ideology – Toward a Layered Narrative' (2006) 4(3) *International Journal of Constitutional Law* 439; RA Ferguson, '"We Do Ordain and Establish": The Constitution as Literary Text' (1987) 29 *William & Mary Law Review* 29.

[34] GS Morson, 'Narrativeness' (2003) 34 *New Literary History* 59, 71.

[35] Alfaro (n 33) 280 (citing both Julia Kristeva and Gérard Genette for the notion of intertextuality). In some respects, I use intertextualism similarly to how Akhil Reed Amar uses *intra*textualism as a label for the method for structural analysis of text: 'Intratextualists read a word or phrase in a given clause by self-consciously comparing and contrasting it to identical or similar words or phrases elsewhere in the Constitution.' My use is broader – hence intertextualism – since the comparative exercise involves other documents. See A Reed Amar, 'Intratextualism' (1999) 112(4) *Harvard Law Review* 747.

Constitution of Canada

52 (2) The Constitution of Canada includes

(a) the Canada Act 1982, including this Act;
(b) the Acts and orders referred to in the schedule; and
(c) any amendment to any Act or order referred to in paragraph (a) or (b).

(emphasis added)

The word 'includes' signifies that the Constitution is open-ended: it is neither confined to the consolidated text nor to the 30 documents enumerated in the schedule. This inclusion clause reaffirms the constitutional status of any amendments to this collection of documents.[36] It also implicitly acknowledges elements of the unwritten constitution, such as constitutional conventions rooted in Westminster parliamentary practice.

Section 25 provides another example:

Aboriginal rights and freedoms not affected by Charter

25 The guarantee in this Charter of certain rights and freedoms shall not be construed so as to abrogate or derogate from any aboriginal, treaty or other rights or freedoms that pertain to the aboriginal peoples of Canada including

(a) any rights or freedoms that have been recognized by the Royal Proclamation of October 7, 1763; and
(b) any rights or freedoms that now exist by way of land claims agreements or may be so acquired.

(emphasis added)

Section 35(1) echoes and reinforces this recognition:

Recognition of existing aboriginal and treaty rights

35 (1) The existing aboriginal and treaty rights of the aboriginal peoples of Canada are hereby recognized and affirmed.

(emphasis added)

These two provisions provide further textual evidence of Canada's multi-textualism and its textual corpus. For Indigenous Peoples, the Royal Proclamation of 1763[37] stands as a foundational document, often characterised as the *Magna Carta* of Crown-Indigenous relations, because it established the treaty-making process between Indigenous Peoples and the Crown. The Proclamation certainly holds constitutional significance and arguably possesses – though as yet to be determined by the Supreme Court of Canada – domestic constitutional status. I emphasise *domestic* here because the Proclamation is formally a British legal instrument.

[36] For a more detailed discussion of the inclusion clause, see Albert, 'Multi-textual Constitutions' (n 3) 1661–66.

[37] George R, Proclamation, 7 October 1763, reprinted in RSC 1985, App II, No 1.

Moreover, the body of treaties signed between Canada and Indigenous Peoples, while not always treated as such by the Canadian state, must be understood as both constitutive and constitutional texts.[38] A third category of foundational text consists of land claims agreements which affirm Aboriginal title and, for Indigenous communities, acknowledge their special constitutive relationship with the land itself. Taken together, sections 25 and 35(1) convey a strong sense of Canada's multi-textual constitutionalism and its nature as a *corpus*, one that referentially incorporates other foundational documents as well as numerous signed treaties.

A second kind of intertextualism exists in Canada's Constitution. The Preamble to the Constitutional Act 1867 sets out the desire to unite what were then Upper Canada (now Ontario), Lower Canada (now Quebec), and the Maritime provinces into a federal state and, importantly for our purposes, states:

> Whereas the Provinces of Canada, Nova Scotia, and New Brunswick have expressed their Desire to be federally united into One Dominion under the Crown of the United Kingdom of Great Britain and Ireland, with a Constitution similar in Principle to that of the United Kingdom. …
>
> (emphasis added)

We can understand the underlined text as a form of allusion that indirectly incorporates multiple features of the British constitutional tradition. Here I would note that, in literary studies, the term 'allusion' does not necessarily carry the same power of incorporation that it does in law. This seemingly innocuous wording in the Preamble, then, functions to incorporate both the unwritten and written elements of the Constitution of the United Kingdom into the Canadian constitutional order.[39] Written law was incorporated at the founding of the colony, so long as it had not been rejected, overridden, or otherwise modified by the Canadian legal system.[40] This includes statutes such as the Act of Settlement 1701, a foundational UK statute that predates Canada's Constitution and has been affirmed in case law as part of Canada's multi-textual constitutional order.[41] Finally, the

[38] Canada recognises 70 historic treaties signed between 1701 and 1923 by the Crown and 364 First Nations communities. Canada also recognises 27 modern treaties, the first of which was signed in 1975 (the James Bay and Northern Quebec Agreement). For an analysis of how treaties comprise an 'integral part' of the Constitution of Canada, see S Grammond, 'Treaties as Constitutional Agreements' in P Oliver, P Macklem and N Des Rosiers (eds), *The Oxford Handbook of the Canadian Constitution* (Oxford University Press, 2017) 305, 306.

[39] Several chapters in this volume consider the function of preambles. Leigha Crout discusses the different interpretations of the Preamble in China's Constitution and suggests that the New Left's interpretive approach that is 'realistic, contextual, and organic' can produce illiberal results. See ch 10 by L Crout, 'Multi-textuality in China: Revisions and Revolutions' 191, 193.

[40] See eg the rules laid down with respect the incorporation of laws in the former British colonies in *Cooper v Stuart* (1889), 14 App. Cas. 286 (JCPC).

[41] An Act for the further Limitation of the Crown and better securing the Rights and Liberties of the Subject, 12 & 13 Will 3 c 2. For judicial recognition of this document, see *Reference re Remuneration of Judges of the Provincial Court (PEI)* [1997] 3 SCR 3 [83]: 'I am of the view that judicial independence is at root an unwritten constitutional principle, in the sense that it is exterior to the particular sections

Preamble adverts to the institutional structure of the constitutional order, not all of which is specified in the text. For example, Canada's first-past-the-post electoral system is not directly codified but only implied in the text of the Preamble and in certain provisions in the Constitution Act 1867 that refer to electoral districts, and no more.

Unwritten constitutional law (or, as discussed earlier, Canada's 'invisible Constitution') includes constitutional conventions, the Crown's prerogative power, and the entire body of constitutional principles.[42] The Supreme Court of Canada affirmed this multi-textual constitutional vision in *Reference re Secession of Quebec*, where it held:

> The 'Constitution of Canada' certainly includes the constitutional texts enumerated in s. 52(2) of the *Constitution Act, 1982.* Although these texts have a primary place in determining constitutional rules, they are not exhaustive. The Constitution also 'embraces unwritten, as well as written rules', as we recently observed in the *Provincial Judges Reference, supra*, at para. 92. Finally, as was said in the *Patriation Reference, supra*, at p. 874, the Constitution of Canada includes
>
> 'the global system of rules and principles which govern the exercise of constitutional authority in the whole and in every part of the Canadian state.'
>
> These supporting principles and rules, which include constitutional conventions and the workings of Parliament, are a necessary part of our Constitution because problems or situations may arise which are not expressly dealt with by the text of the Constitution. In order to endure over time, a constitution must contain a comprehensive set of rules and principles which are capable of providing an exhaustive legal framework for our system of government. Such principles and rules emerge from an understanding of the constitutional text itself, the historical context, and previous judicial interpretations of constitutional meaning. …[43]

This passage illustrates the depth of Canada's multi-textualism. Grounded in the Preamble but augmented through judicial interpretation, Canadian constitutionalism has come to rely on two guiding metaphors: the *living tree* and the *architecture* metaphors. These metaphors function not only as interpretive tools but also as indicia of intertextualism and transtextualism (the focus of the next subsection), signaling the very existence of Canada's deep multi-textualism. Shaped and surrounded by these unwritten constitutional norms and metaphors, the written text, according to constitutional scholars Zachery Elkins and Tom Ginsburg, comes to act as a 'kind of semiotic for the actual, unwritten constitution.'[44]

of the *Constitution Acts*. The existence of that principle, whose origins can be traced to the Act of Settlement of 1701, is recognised and affirmed by the preamble to the Constitution Act 1867. The specific provisions of *the Constitution Acts, 1867 to 1982*, merely "elaborate that principle in the institutional apparatus which they create or contemplate": *Switzman v. Elbling*, 1957 CanLII 2 (SCC), [1957] S.C.R. 285, at p. 306, *per* Rand J.'

[42] See the Hon. Justice Malcom Rowe and Manish Oza, 'Structural Analysis and the Canadian Constitution' (2023) 101 *Canada Bar Review* 206, 207.

[43] *Reference re Secession of Quebec*, [1998] 2 SCR 217 at [32].

[44] Elkins and Ginsburg, 'What Can We Learn' (n 7) 328.

The *living tree* metaphor is the older of the two[45] and authorises a dynamic and progressive approach to constitutional interpretation, especially in relation to unwritten constitutional principles which can be used to 'fill gaps' in the written text.[46] In contrast, the *architecture* metaphor is literally structural: it invites readers to engage in multi-levelled interpretation in order to understand how the text's components or parts relate to one another.[47] Functionally, the 'interpretive use of structural analysis typically aims at coherence in our constitutional arrangements, while the gap-filling role aims at comprehensiveness.'[48]

These kinds of intertextual connections may be explicit or implicit in the constitutional text, but can be brought to the surface through the use of these two metaphors and their associated interpretive methodologies. To take one example, the principle of the separation of powers does not explicitly appear anywhere in either the 1867 or 1982 Acts.[49] Yet this unwritten principle is widely understood to illuminate the structure set out in the Constitution Act 1867, which delineates the three branches of government: executive, legislative, and judicial. Judicial decisions invoking the separation of powers make explicit what is only implicit in the text: that power in Canada's constitutional order is distributed across distinct institutions, each exercising different functions.

These two metaphors help guide courts in determining when and how to fill such interpretive gaps in the constitutional text. Part III of the Constitution Act 1867, for example, sets out Executive Power in Section 9: 'The Executive Government and Authority of and over Canada is hereby declared to continue and be vested in the Queen.' On its face, this synecdochical language suggests the Monarch exercises complete governmental authority in Canada. But in practice, this is completely false. Moreover, the Constitution Act 1867 makes no mention of the Prime Minister or Cabinet. To reconcile these textual omissions with the actual practice of the Westminster system, constitutional interpreters rely on unwritten

[45] See *Edwards v Canada (Attorney General)*, 1929 CanLII 438 (JCPC) [106-07]: 'The B.N.A. Act planted in Canada a living tree capable of growth and expansion within its natural limits. The object of the Act was to grant a Constitution to Canada.' In this case, the UK's Judicial Committee of the Privy Council interpreted the word 'person' to include both male and female persons so that women would be eligible to be appointed to the Senate.

[46] Canada has generally embraced a dynamic approach to interpretation in public law and has eschewed originalist approaches to legal texts, both statutory and constitutional. The middle ground – textualism – is also approved. On Canada's rejection of originalist approaches to interpretation, see the Hon. Justice Ian Binnie, 'Interpreting the Constitution: The Living Tree vs Original Meaning' (1 October 2007) Policy Options 104.

[47] Rowe and Oza argue that these two metaphors mandate a *methodology* called structural analysis that legal interpreters can use to identify valid unwritten norms and then to give them effect through interpretation and textual gap-filling. Rowe and Oza (n 42) 208.

[48] ibid 217.

[49] As Lord Diplock adverts, speaking of the Jamaican constitution, the separations of powers is often taken for granted in constitutional texts: 'Because of this a great deal can be, and in drafting practice often is, left to necessary implication from the adoption in the new constitution of a governmental structure which makes provision for a legislature, an executive and a judicature. It is taken for granted that the basic principle of separation of powers will apply to the exercise of their respective functions by these three organs of government.' *Hinds v the Queen* [1976] 1 All ER 353 (JCPC) 359.

principles and architectural or structural reasoning. As Canadian legal scholar Mark Walters puts it, 'judges are constructing bridges over the waters that separate islands of constitutional text, creating a unified and useable surface.'[50]

The *architecture* metaphor is thus essential to the idea that the constitutional text itself aspires to internal integrity and coherence, with its various parts harmoniously relating to each other.[51] The Supreme Court captures the essence of this metaphor in the *Senate Reform Reference*:

> [26] These rules and principles of interpretation have led this Court to conclude that the Constitution should be viewed as having an 'internal architecture', or 'basic constitutional structure': *Secession Reference*, at para. 50; *OPSEU v. Ontario (Attorney General)*, 1987 CanLII 71 (SCC), [1987] 2 S.C.R. 2, at p. 57; see also *Supreme Court Act Reference*, at para. 82. The notion of architecture expresses the principle that '[t]he individual elements of the Constitution are linked to the others, and must be interpreted by reference to the structure of the Constitution as a whole': *Secession Reference*, at para. 50 … . In other words, the Constitution must be interpreted with a view to discerning the structure of government that it seeks to implement. The assumptions that underlie the text and the manner in which the constitutional provisions are intended to interact with one another must inform our interpretation, understanding, and application of the text.[52]

The Court's reasoning in the *Trial Lawyers*[53] case illustrates how both of these metaphors can work in tandem, but places particular emphasis on how the *architecture* metaphor invites and structures the interpretation of multiple texts to achieve constitutional 'fitness':

> [24] On its face, s. 92(14) does not limit the powers of the provinces to impose hearing fees. However, that does not mean that the province can impose hearing fees in any fashion it chooses. Its power to impose hearing fees must be consistent with s. 96 of the *Constitution Act, 1867* and the requirements that flow by necessary implication from s. 96. This follows from two related tenets of constitutional interpretation.
>
> [25] First, particular constitutional grants of power must be read together with other grants of power so that the Constitution operates as an internally consistent harmonious whole. Thus s. 92(14) does not operate in isolation. Its ambit must be determined, not

[50] MD Walters, 'Written Constitutions and Unwritten Constitutionalism' in G Huscroft (ed), *Expounding the Constitution: Essays in Constitutional Theory* (Cambridge University Press, 2009) 264.

[51] This is what legal philosopher Ronald Dworkin famously called 'fit' in his theory of interpretation. See R Dworkin, 'Law as Interpretation' (1982) 9(1) *Critical Inquiry* 179, 194; R Dworkin, *Law's Empire* (Belknap, 1986).

[52] *Reference re Senate Reform*, 2014 SCC 32. See also K Glover, 'Structure, Substance and Spirit: Lessons in Constitutional Architecture from the *Senate Reform Reference*' (2014) 67 *SCLR* 221.

[53] *Trial Lawyers Association of British Columbia v British Columbia (Attorney General)*, 2014 SCC 59, [2014] 3 SCR 31 ('*Trial Lawyers*'). Along with the two written provisions from the Constitution Act 1867, the Majority read into the text the unwritten principles of the rule of law and access to justice in order to determine that British Columbia's provincial hearing fee scheme should be struck down as unconstitutional. This enabled the Majority to broaden the scope of s 96 at the expense of s 92(14) and add content to the unwritten constitutional principle of access to justice. The Dissent found the scheme to be a valid exercise of provincial power and suggested judicial activism on the part of the Majority. For a similar case involving the visible and invisible constitution, the architecture metaphor, and structural analysis, see *Toronto (City) v Ontario (Attorney General)*, 2021 SCC 34, [2021] 2 SCR 845.

> only by reference to its bare wording, but with respect to other powers conferred by the Constitution. In this case, this requires us to consider s. 96 of the *Constitution Act, 1867*.
>
> [26] Second, the interpretation of s. 92(14) must be consistent not only with other express terms of the Constitution, but with requirements that 'flow by necessary implication from those terms': *British Columbia v. Imperial Tobacco Canada Ltd.*, 2005 SCC 49, [2005] 2 S.C.R. 473, at para. 66, per Major J. As this Court has recently stated, 'the Constitution must be interpreted with a view to discerning the structure of government that it seeks to implement. The assumptions that underlie the text and the manner in which the constitutional provisions are intended to interact with one another must inform our interpretation, understanding, and application of the text': *Reference re Senate Reform*, 2014 SCC 32, [2014] 1 S.C.R. 704, at para. 26 (emphasis added).
>
> [27] It follows that in determining the power conferred on the province over the administration of justice, including the imposition of hearing fees, by s. 92(14), the Court must consider not only the written words of that provision, but how a particular interpretation fits with other constitutional powers and the assumptions that underlie the text.

Structural arguments nevertheless have the potential to informally amend the Constitution. The power of the Supreme Court to make explicit or to introduce new structural features through constitutional interpretation therefore creates concerns about the potential misuse of judicial power through interpretation, as it does in other jurisdictions.[54]

B. Transtextualism

Transtextualism is broader than intertextualism and can refer to everything explicit or latent that relates one text to another,[55] as well as the 'textual transcendence of the text' itself.[56] It could, for example, relate to the so-called small 'c' unwritten constitution, which includes political constitutionalism and extra-constitutional sources such as judicial interpretations, institutional practices, foundational documents outside the formal constitution, discretionary decisions made by constitutional actors, and moral or political philosophical values.[57] This subsection focuses on extra-constitutional documents and other foundational documents located outside both the constitutional text and the territorial boundaries of Canada. Nevertheless, they may be read *together* since they are interrelated. The constitutional texts considered in this section also engage in metatextuality, that is, 'the relation, usually called 'commentary,' which links one text with another that

[54] On this point, see T Birmontienė and J Miliuvienė's discussion of the Lithuanian Constitutional Court in this volume, see ch 6 'Vertical and Horizontal Layers of the Lithuanian Constitution' 129–30. Judicial activism is the term that captures this kind of misuse of judicial power. See eg the discussion in R Hirschl, *Towards Juristocracy: The Origins and Consequences of the New Constitutionalism* (Harvard University Press, 2004). See also the judicial disagreement in *Trial Lawyers* (n 53).

[55] Alfaro (n 33) 280.

[56] G Genette, *Palimpsests: Literature in the Second Degree* (University of Nebraska Press, 1997) 1.

[57] See LB Solum, 'Originalism and the Invisible Constitution' in Dixon and Stone (eds) (n 5) 61.

comments on it without quoting it or, even without mentioning it at all.'[58] Texts often influence each other in subtle ways not immediately visible on the surface. This subsection will consider two examples: the first involves provincial constitutional texts; the second involves the Canadian Charter of Rights and Freedoms.

The first example is Quebec's Civil Code. The preamble to the Civil Code suggests that this text is 'in harmony' with both the Charter of the French Language[59] (a legal document that designates French as the common and official language of Quebec) and the Charter of Human Rights and Freedoms[60] (a human rights document that is a precursor to the Canadian Charter of Rights and Freedoms). Viewed through the lens of transtextualism, one might conclude that these three interrelated texts together form a multi-textual provincial constitution. If that goes too far in the eyes of some constitutional scholars, it is at the very least arguable that each is a text of great constitutional significance – perhaps quasi-constitutional status – at the provincial level, and is viewed by the political community of Quebec as constitutionally constitutive.

The second example is the Canadian Charter of Rights and Freedoms. Here, I suggest that constitutional relations not only cut across the Canadian jurisdiction but also extend beyond its borders. This is the most dynamic aspect of *trans*textualism. The example also brings us closer to the idea of a textual corpus and textual genealogies. Looking at the historical development of the Charter, we can see an interconnected web of constitutional texts that have directly contributed to and informed its creation.[61] The genealogy might be traced as follows: Magna Carta, 1215; the 1689 Bill of Rights;[62] the 1787 Constitution of the United States and its Bill of Rights; the 1789 Declaration of the Rights of Man and of the Citizen in France; the 1948 Universal Declaration of Human Rights;[63] the 1953 European Convention for the Protection of Human Rights and Freedoms; the 1960 Canadian Bill of Rights;[64] the 1962 Ontario Human Rights Code; the 1966 International Covenant on Civil and Political Rights and the International Covenant of Social, Economic and Cultural Rights;[65] the 1975 Quebec Charter of Human Rights and Freedoms; the 1977 Canadian Human Rights Act; and then, finally, the Charter itself in 1982. Like members of an extended constitutional family, each of these

[58] Alfaro (n 33) 281.

[59] Charter of the French Language CQLR c C-11.

[60] Charter of Human Rights and Freedoms CQLR c C-12.

[61] Note that Canada still requires incorporation of international documents at both the federal and provincial levels. International norms, however, are persuasive and given great weight in Canadian jurisprudence. In this respect, Canada parallels the material openness to international norms and texts as Brazil does, but differs from the Brazilian case as described by Bruno Santos Cunha in this volume where international human rights treaties can attain constitutional status while remaining separate from the Brazilian Constitution. See ch 5 by B Santos Cunha, 'Multi-textuality by Amendment: The Brazilian Case'.

[62] An Act Declaring the Rights and Liberties of the Subject and Settling the Succession of the Crown, 1 William & Mary Sess 2 c 2).

[63] GA Res 217(111), UN GAOR, 3d Sess, Supp No. 13, UN Doc. A/810 (1948) 71.

[64] SC 1960, c 44.

[65] Both were adopted by the UN in 1966 but did not come into force until 1976.

texts forms part of the Canadian Charter's lineage, and the Charter could not have come to existence in its current form without these antecedents. This form of transtextualism involves more than simply reading documents alongside one another; rather, it reflects a structural webbing of related texts.[66]

C. Extratextualism

Extratextualism encompasses constitutional 'texts' located outside the conventional notion of a written text. Here, one must extend the concept of 'text' to include artifacts, actions, practices, events, and other forms of communication that convey meaning and can be 'read' – much like the broader interpretive framework employed in disciplines such as literary studies, cultural studies, anthropology, and semiotics. Not only are these materials located outside the conventional constitutional text, they also challenge conventional legal conceptions of what constitutes a text.

In a decolonising jurisdiction like Canada, this broader form of multi-textualism is becoming increasingly salient. The most important and illustrative set of such extratextual texts comes from Indigenous legal orders. This is because the status of many texts will change when an Indigenous perspective is taken into account. Texts that were formerly viewed as non-constitutional in significance will be given a new status as Canada re-reads its constitutional history. These include both oral histories of a constitutional nature[67] and extratextual physical objects that serve as constitutional expressions.

In eastern Canada, diplomatic treaty negotiations between Indigenous Peoples and European powers often involved the exchange of gifts and other artefacts, such as wampum belts.[68] A very early example, dating to 1613, is the Two Row Wampum belt, called *Gaswéñdah* in the Mohawk language.[69] Made from glass beads woven onto fabric, the belt represents a mutual treaty agreement between the Five Nations of the Haudenosaunee (or Iroquois) and representatives of the Dutch government in what is now upstate New York. It depicts two boats, rendered in purple beadwork, each navigating in parallel a shared river of life, with neither steering the other's course. Each boat carries the life, laws, and

[66] Note that we could also move forward in time to see how the Charter, in turn, has influenced the development of constitutional texts in other jurisdictions. A prominent example is its direct influence on the drafting of Chapter 2 Bill of Rights in the Constitution of the Republic of South Africa. See Constitution of the Republic of South Africa Act No 108 of 1996.

[67] *Delgamuukw v British Columbia*, [1997] 3 SCR 1010 which first recognised oral history as a source of evidence in Aboriginal title cases. This oral history can include origin stories and other forms of traditional knowledge.

[68] See J Borrows, 'Wampum at Niagara: The Royal Proclamation, Canadian Legal History, and Self Government' in M Asch (ed), *Aboriginal and Treaty Rights in Canada: Essays on Law, Equity, and Respect for Difference* (University of British Columbia Press, 1997) 155.

[69] For an illustration, see www.onondaganation.org/culture/wampum/two-row-wampum-belt-guswenta/.

peoples of its respective culture, while the white rows between the boats represent peace, friendship, and perpetuity. This constitutional text communicates an ideal relationship based on mutual respect, reciprocity, self-determination, and interconnection. Because the Five Nations span what is now southern Canada and the northern United States, the Two Row Wampum 'crosses' borders and possesses constitutional significance for Haudenosaunee in both countries. In Canada, wampum belts were once considered a symbol of treaty agreement, but were later relegated to the status of historical artefacts, seen primarily as culturally significant only to local Indigenous communities. Today, however, as Canada re-evaluates its constitutional history in light of its relationship with Indigenous Peoples, such a 'text' are increasingly recognised as having legal and constitutional significance.[70]

The full extent of this extratextual multi-textualism remains to be uncovered in Canadian constitutionalism. Its contours will continue to emerge alongside the evolving relationship between Indigenous and non-Indigenous communities in Canada.[71] Political resistance to formally acknowledging this form of extratextual constitutionalism is inevitable.[72] Nevertheless, no doubt exists that these texts carry constitutional 'weight' within the Canadian legal and political order.[73]

D. Hypertextualism[74]

Hypertextualism locates constitutional meaning beyond the conventional written text, in pre-texts (such as drafts, interim, or transitional constitutions prior to the finalised document), texts derived in any manner from earlier sources through imitation or transformation, and post-texts (including texts not

[70] Another example would be a 'covenant chain' which could be depicted with beads in a wampum belt or through an actual metal chain of linked silver medallions. These 'texts' are simultaneously artefacts, symbols of relationships, and legal documents. The covenant chain represented the actual 'chain' which was a series of agreements (alliances, peace and friendship treaties, economic relations, and so on) between the British and the Haudenosaunee beginning in the 17th century. Periodically, the metal covenant chain would be taken out to be 'polished' and renewed to symbolise the same for the relationship. See MD Walters, 'Brightening the Covenant Chain: Aboriginal Treaty Meanings in Law and History After *Marshall*' (2001) 24(2) *Dalhousie Law Journal* 75.

[71] A third example would be the legal significance of an eagle feather in many Indigenous cultures. See A Mills, *Eagle Down Is Our Law: Witsuwit'en Law, Feasts, and Land Claims* (University of British Columbia Press, 1994).

[72] See also Boast and Blumhardt who both touch on the fears that this kind of multi-textualism would generate in New Zealand, including the anxiety that it could, as Boast suggests from the perspective of the settler legal order, 'unnecessarily complicate things.' RP Boast, 'Recognising Multi-textualism: Rethinking New Zealand's Legal History' (2006) 37 *Victoria University of Wellington Law Review* 547, 582; H Blumhardt, 'Multi-textualism, "Treaty Hegemony" and the Waitangi Tribunal: Making Sense of 19th Century Crown-Māori Negotiations in Te Urewera' (2012) 43 *Victoria University of Wellington Law Review* 263, 284–86.

[73] Blumhardt (n 72) 272.

[74] Though not considered in this chapter, the more literal meaning of hypertextualism has salience and will have increasing import for what we mean by multi-textualism as constitutional orders become better connected, textually and though interpretation, in cyberspace.

originally considered part of the constitution but that have come to be, or are coming to be, recognised as having constitutional significance).[75] These sorts of texts possess the most uncertain positive legal status and may overlap significantly with sociological understandings of a constitution.[76] Dag Michalsen describes this form of intertextuality as the 'constitution as derivative texts,' and examines how these derivative texts have become interwoven with Norway's constitution through social practice and popular culture. He illustrates how nationalist ideology enables constitutional integration of derivative texts such as the national language, anthem, flag, and selected works of music, art, architecture, and literature.[77] In a similar vein, Eric Adams writes: 'Today, Canada's constitution serves as an object of law for lawyers, a set of rules for governments, and as a repository of politics for political scientists and journalists. A constitution is, of course, all of those things, but a constitution also consists of the stories a nation tells about itself.'[78]

Some of these 'texts' may possess constitutional status in local communities, but not in the eyes of the larger national or legal community. There is therefore a fair bit of overlap between extra- and hypertextualism in the Canadian context. Métis scrip records provide one example.[79] In 1870, the Canadian federal government created the scrip system specifically for Métis people, issuing scrip (a document like a certificate or voucher used in place of legal tender) either in the form of money or land, in lieu of negotiating treaties.[80] This allowed the federal government to acquire land from the Métis with relative ease to facilitate western development, with the ultimate aim of extinguishing Métis land rights.

A conventional view of scrip would treat these documents as ephemera, of local or historical interest only. A broader legal view may recognise their relevance to contract or property law. But what about constitutional law? For the Métis community, scrip is close tied to questions of Aboriginal land, title, and self-government, and is thus recognised as having constitutional significance. As it now stands, scrip does not possess formal constitutional textual status and is not part of Canada's multi-textual Constitution. It may, however, come to acquire such status as the complex relations between Canada's multi-textual Indigenous

[75] Genette (n 56) 7.

[76] Here I follow Mark Tushnet in distinguishing between the constitutional text and the nation's constitution, the constitution encompassing the text itself, institutions, historical understandings, and other phenomena. *Why The Constitution Matters* (Yale University Press, 2010).

[77] Michalsen (n 7) 67–73.

[78] Adams (n 24) 313. See also M Rosenfeld, *The Identity of the Constitutional Subject: Selfhood, Citizenship, Culture and Community* (Routledge, 2010).

[79] The Métis are one of the three Indigenous groups that are recognised in the Constitution Act 1982. Section 35(2) defines Aboriginal Peoples of Canada: '(2) In this Act, aboriginal peoples of Canada includes the Indian, Inuit and Métis peoples of Canada.' The Métis Nation originated in Western Canada and describes communities of mixed European and Indigenous ancestry, though designation and issues around membership are complex and subject to disagreement.

[80] See *Daniels v Canada (Indian Affairs and Northern Development)*, 2013 FC 6 (CanLII), [2013] 2 FCR 268 and *Daniels v Canada (Indian Affairs and Northern Development)*, 2016 SCC 12, [2016] 1 SCR 99 for a fuller treatment of the scrip system.

constitutional orders and the multi-textual non-Indigenous constitution continues to evolve – and as we continue to benefit from the work of Indigenous scholars and legal historians. A similar process is underway in other jurisdictions, such as New Zealand.[81]

V. Who Recognises the Texts That Comprise a Multi-Textual Constitution?

Both extratextualism and hypertextualism remind us that the act of identifying and formally recognising what counts as a constitutional text is inherently political. It is also deeply tied to questions of power and justice. If we remain too conventional and complacent in our understanding of multi-textual constitutions, we risk engaging in acts of textual hegemony, that is, displacing, alienating, and rejecting texts that another community regards as constitutional (and may be seen as such even from within the rejecting legal order). This chapter, along with others in this volume, reminds us to attend to such forms of hegemony in the designation of constitutional significance.

Textual hegemony is a particularly pressing issue in the treatment of texts from Indigenous legal orders. Another, more overlooked, example stems from the dominance of the English language and culture in Canada: the absence of a legally authoritative French version of the Constitution Act 1867.[82] Though a French translation exists, it does not have the force of law, since this Act was enacted by the Parliament of the United Kingdom in English only. Although Canada has managed to get by with this historical anomaly, in principle, it should be corrected, but in practice, it likely will not be, for fear of reopening the Constitution for negotiation.

VI. Dialogue, Evolution, Transition, and Transformation – Future Directions

The turn to multi-textualism has perhaps raised more questions than it has answered. For example, what should the constitutional status of various fundamental texts located within and outside a particular jurisdiction be? Can there ever truly be a uni-textual constitution under modern conditions of legal and cultural diversity? And, what analytical tools are necessary for law students to engage with the nuances and complexities that multi-textualism generates?

[81] Boast discusses similar issues with deeds of cession, confiscation agreements, and regional pre-emptive agreements between the Māori and the colonial state in New Zealand. Boast (n 72) 554–60.

[82] F Larocque and L Cardinal, 'Canada's Bilingual Constitution: An Unfulfilled Obligation' (2022) 31(3) Constitutional Forum 7, 2022 CanLIIDocs 4242, canlii.ca/t/7n0sm.

As the epigraph to this chapter indicates, I follow the Canadian tradition in valorising the many forms of diversity, including textual diversity. At the same time, this chapter remains mindful of the disadvantages and risks that attend multi-textualism, many of which are highlighted in other contributions to this volume.[83] Multi-textualism can be used instrumentally or abusively by any branch of government. It can also create further disharmony and irreconcilability.[84] In comparison, uni-textualism seems to promise certainty, simplicity, and closure.

But multi-textualism may also function as a generative 'platform'[85] where these issues can (hopefully) be worked out while constitutional transitions unfold. Multi-textualism, marked by its open-endedness, inherently provides 'feedback loops' where texts and communities can, over time, dialogue about narrative and meaning.[86] The weak closure that its offers to the constitutional narrative may, in fact, be its strength, and the techniques and tools drawn from other disciplines may produce a rich and textured legal analysis of constitutional paths – whether they are evolving, transitioning, transforming, stagnating, or regressing.[87] Rather than anchoring constitutional meaning in a singular moment, multi-textualism enables us to perceive multiple constitutional moments across time. It may even help us anticipate new moments by disclosing the conflicts and tensions embedded in the existing constitutional narratives. For Canada, multi-textualism will be a necessary platform for understanding the constitutional futures continually shaped by multijuridicalism and its attendant textual complexity.

[83] In this volume, see ch 2 by L-S Enonchong, 'Multi-textuality and Incrementalism in Cameroon's Democratic Tradition', ch 3 by K Lachmayer, 'The Beauty and the Beast: The Excessive Multi-Textualism of the Austrian Constitution' and ch 12 by A Sethi, 'The Taliban's Multi-Textual Constitution: Cultivated Ambiguity as Authoritarian Technique'.

[84] See ch 11 by D Bulut, 'Multi-textuality and the Question of Constitutional Authorship'.

[85] Crout (n 39) 199 (considering how multi-textuality may provide a platform for discussing and negotiating the divergent constitutional values and projects in a divided political community).

[86] As used in ch 8 by N Fox, 'The Tradition of Multi-Textuality in Poland' in this volume.

[87] Morson (n 34) 69–72.

5

Multi-Textuality by Amendment: The Brazilian Case

BRUNO SANTOS CUNHA

I. Introduction

Until 2004, Brazilian constitutional and international law scholars actively debated the hierarchy and status of international treaties within the national legal system, particularly whether such treaties should be considered at the same level as domestic laws or hold a distinct, superior position. This debate largely centered around the interpretation of the 1988 Constitution, which left open questions about the hierarchical placement and binding force of international agreements in the domestic legal order. Some scholars argued that any international treaty approved by the National Congress acquired a status equivalent to ordinary federal law and, therefore, could be repealed by a simple majority in each House, the same quorum required for ordinary federal laws.

The debate was settled with the enactment of Constitutional Amendment No. 45 in 2004, which introduced Article 5, §3° to the Constitution. This provision establishes that international human rights treaties and conventions approved by both houses of the National Congress, in two rounds of voting with a three-fifths majority, shall be equivalent to constitutional amendments. Following this reform, international treaties may now be ratified and incorporated into Brazilian law through three distinct procedures: (i) human rights treaties approved by a simple majority in each House of Congress acquire the status of ordinary federal law; (ii) human rights treaties approved under the new procedure set out in Article 5, §3° acquire constitutional status equivalent to constitutional amendments; and (iii) treaties that do not concern human rights are incorporated with the status of ordinary federal law, regardless of the quorum by which they are approved.[1]

Notably, international human rights treaties and conventions approved under Article 5, §3° create separately codified constitutional laws that may change the

[1] See discussion in Section IV below.

meaning of the Constitution but leave the master text unchanged. These treaties and conventions are not integrated into the original text of the Constitution nor listed in the appendix of amendments. The outcome of this arrangement is a constitution composed of multiple texts (or a multi-textual constitution), each enjoying the same level of constitutional supremacy. This chapter aims to discuss how the Brazilian constitutional practice regarding international treaties and conventions on human rights falls within Richard Albert's proposed framework of multi-textual constitutions.[2] The main idea is to identify the challenges that this new notion of multi-textuality may pose to the regular operation of the Brazilian constitutional system.

This chapter first explores the historical development of constitutional pluralisation in Brazil, focusing on fundamental rights and the recognition of rights outside the main text of the Constitution. Section II examines how the 1988 Constitution's open-ended catalogue of fundamental rights has supported the recognition of materially constitutional rights beyond the master text, including through interpretive constructions such as penumbras. Section III examines the role of constitutional amendments in pluralising constitutional texts, discussing Albert's theory on multi-textuality[3] and the shift introduced in the Brazilian scenario by Constitutional Amendment No. 45 in 2004. Section IV analyses the hierarchical status of international treaties within the Brazilian legal system, with particular attention to the Federal Supreme Court's (STF) relevant jurisprudence and its implications for multi-textuality. Section V addresses judicial perceptions of multi-textuality, examining how courts treat constitutional norms outside the main text and evaluating whether Brazil's Constitution can be considered truly multi-textual. Section VI concludes by reflecting on what Brazil's experience reveals about the promises and tensions of multi-textual constitutionalism, including the relationship between the master text, supra-legality, and separately codified constitutional norms.

II. Fundamental Rights and the Idea of Pluralisation of Constitutional Texts in Brazil

The Brazilian Constitution of 1988 explicitly articulates that the rights enumerated within its text do not constitute an exhaustive list of all rights enjoyed by Brazilians. According to the Constitution, fundamental rights are not confined to a formal enumeration but embrace a material dimension as well. This is exemplified by the material openness of the catalogue of fundamental rights, explicitly enshrined in Article 5, §2º, which states that 'the rights and guarantees expressed in this Constitution do not exclude others deriving from the regime and principles

[2] R Albert, 'Multi-Textual Constitutions' (2023) 109 *Virginia Law Review* 1629.
[3] ibid.

adopted by it, or from international treaties to which the Federative Republic of Brazil is a party.' This inclusive clause, rejecting a closed list of constitutional rights, continues to challenge both legal scholars and courts, particularly regarding its true scope and meaning.

Legal scholars of fundamental rights have long recognised that the express constitutional openness enshrined in Article 5, §2º reflects the understanding that fundamental rights exist in both formal and material terms. In this regard, Samuel Fonteles argues that formal fundamentalisation means that anything sovereignly designated as fundamental by the Constitution must be considered as such. At the same time, Fonteles continues, nothing prevents the Constitution from affirming the existence of fundamental rights outside the formal text, which may derive from other legal sources.[4] These rights, though not formally codified in the Constitution, would be considered materially fundamental because they impact the basic structure of the State and society. Fonteles concludes that, within the current Brazilian constitutional framework, especially in light of Article 5, §2º, 'there will be fundamental rights not written in the Constitution, but possessing the same weight as those expressly enshrined within it.'[5] This perspective highlights the constitutional openness to recognising fundamental rights beyond the formal text, acknowledging their material significance in shaping the nation's constitutional order.

These fundamental rights, considered implicit in the Brazilian legal system, often become the subject of intense debate regarding their exact scope and reach. Their effective recognition largely depends on inferences drawn from what are known as penumbral areas (*zonas de penumbra*). As such, these rights are not always immediately clear, but their recognition evolves through judicial and scholarly reasoning that fills the gaps left by the constitutional text. Consequently, the identification and application of these rights require a dynamic and interpretive approach, which allows courts to adapt the Constitution to emerging social, political, and cultural realities, even when those rights are not expressly outlined within its provisions. Building on Fonteles' parallel between the Brazilian experience and the American example from *Griswold v Connecticut*,[6] penumbral areas refer to legal spaces in which the Constitution, while not explicitly addressing certain rights, allows for their identification through interpretation, often grounded in broader constitutional rights, principles, or judicial decisions.[7]

Although Justice Douglas did not originate the concept of penumbras, it was in his opinion in *Griswold*[8] where the metaphor gained traction as a means to designate implicit constitutional rights in the American context.[9] Douglas reasoned

[4] S Fonteles, *Direitos fundamentais* (Juspodivm, 2024) 27–28.

[5] ibid 28.

[6] *Griswold v Connecticut*, 381 US 479 (1965).

[7] Fonteles (n 4) 90.

[8] For a complete history of the penumbra metaphor, see B Henly, '"Penumbra": The Roots of a Legal Metaphor' (1987) 15 *Hastings Constitutional Law Quarterly* 83–92.

[9] See RG Dixon Jr, 'The *Griswold* Penumbra: Constitutional Charter for an Expanded Law of Privacy?' (1965) 64 *Michigan Law Review* 197; MDS Prickett, 'The Right of Privacy: a Black View of *Griswold v. Connecticut*' (1980) *Hastings Constitutional Law Quarterly* 177.

that certain rights, such as the right to marital privacy, though not explicitly stated in the US Constitution, could be inferred from the fundamental guarantees expressly protected in the Bill of Rights. As he wrote, 'specific guarantees in the Bill of Rights have penumbras, formed by emanations from those guarantees that help give them life and substance.'[10] On this basis, the US Supreme Court struck down a Connecticut statute forbidding the use of contraceptives, holding that it unconstitutionally violated the right to marital privacy located within the penumbra of the specific guarantees of the Bill of Rights.

Beyond the idea of penumbras, Justice Goldberg's concurring opinion in *Griswold* brought forward another important reflection on enumerated rights. According to him, '[t]he language and history of the Ninth Amendment reveal that the Framers of the Constitution believed that there are additional fundamental rights, protected from governmental infringement, which exist alongside those fundamental rights specifically mentioned in the first eight constitutional amendments.'[11] Goldberg emphasised that the Ninth Amendment – which states that the enumeration of certain rights in the Constitution does not imply the absence of others – provided sufficient authority to support the Court's recognition of a fundamental constitutional right to marital privacy.

This framework for identifying implicit fundamental rights informs both Brazilian and American constitutional interpretation, reinforcing the conviction that constitutional meaning transcends the formal text and supporting the pluralisation of constitutional texts. From this perspective, constitutional rights may not only emerge from the explicit provisions of the Constitution but can also be inferred from other legal sources, reflecting the evolving nature of the constitutional order.

Although the recognition of implicit fundamental rights with constitutional status outside the formal text is well-established in Brazil, the prevailing understanding has focused on the existence of materially constitutional norms that enshrine fundamental rights outside the text of the Constitution. However, the idea of the pluralisation of constitutional texts goes beyond the material aspect to encompass the formal dimension. In other words, pluralisation recognises that there may be norms that are both formally and materially constitutional, even when located in texts other than the main text of the Constitution. At least to date, this phenomenon has not been systematically analysed in Brazil through the lens of the pluralisation of constitutional texts or multi-textuality. These concepts suggest that a constitution, in a broader sense, may consist of multiple documents, each with equal constitutional supremacy. In this sense, pluralisation and multi-textuality indicate that the constitutional legal order can extend beyond the written text of the Constitution, incorporating other legal instruments and documents that hold

[10] *Griswold* (n 6) 484.

[11] ibid 488. The Ninth Amendment to the US Constitution reads as follows: The enumeration in the Constitution, of certain rights, shall not be construed to deny or disparage others retained by the people.

constitutional status both formally and materially, and, in an interconnected way, shape the nation's legal order.

The next step in this analysis is to examine how Brazilian constitutional practice regarding international treaties and conventions on human rights, especially following Constitutional Amendment No. 45 in 2004, aligns with Albert's framework of multi-textual constitutions. Before delving into this, however, it is essential to establish a clear understanding of Albert's theoretical foundations of multi-textuality.[12] This theoretical grounding will provide the necessary lens through which to assess the evolving role of international human rights instruments within the Brazilian constitutional order.

III. Multi-textuality and the Pluralisation of Constitutional Texts Through Constitutional Amendments

Classifying constitutions based on their attributes, forms, rights, structure, and parameters has long occupied a central place in constitutional law. This is particularly true in comparative constitutional studies, where the distinctive task of contrasting the constitutions of different nations – based on their similar or unique characteristics – has often made such classifications a prominent focus of legal scholarly inquiry.

In the social sciences, classification serves a purpose beyond the mere, immediate exposition of the world. It is not undertaken for its own sake, but is employed with a specific goal in mind: to provide a structured framework to guide analysis within a particular study.[13] From a functionalist perspective, the value of a classification lies not in its inherent truth or falsity, but in how effectively it serves the purpose for which it was created. Genaro Carrió emphasises that the instrumental criterion of utility defines the merit of classifications. As he points out,[14]

> Classifications are neither true nor false, they are useful or useless [or, they may be misleading]; their advantages or disadvantages are contingent upon the interest that guides those who formulate them, and on their fertility in presenting a field of knowledge in a way that is more easily understandable or richer in desirable practical consequences.

In this spirit, Richard Albert observes that classifying constitutions as either written or unwritten has historically been 'the basic building block in constitutional studies.'[15] This traditional binary, however, is challenged by Albert, who argues that it overlooks more complex forms of constitutions, such as multi-textual ones. He contends that the written–unwritten distinction is not only misleading but also

[12] Albert (n 2).
[13] K Jaspers, *Introdução ao pensamento filosófico* (Cultrix, 2011) 89.
[14] G Carrió, *Notas sobre derecho y lenguaje*, 3rd edn (Abeledo-Perrot, 2006) 99.
[15] Albert (n 2) 1631.

insufficient to capture the full range of constitutional forms across different legal systems, prompting a rethinking of how constitutions should be categorised.

For Albert, the written–unwritten distinction 'overlooks and obscures the most important formal distinction among the constitutions of the world: some constitutions consist of a single, supreme document of higher law while others consist of multiple documents, each enacted separately with shared supremacy under law.'[16] By contrast, the study of multi-textuality in constitutions offers key advantages (or potential promises, in Albert's words), such as increased flexibility in adapting to new realities, the capacity for incremental constitutional reform, and a check on excessive constitutional veneration.[17] By having multiple texts of equal constitutional status, these constitutions can evolve more gradually and pragmatically, facilitating necessary reforms while preventing rigid adherence to a single document.

Albert identifies two pathways to multi-textuality. The first is express design, where multiple texts are deliberately crafted as sources of constitutional law and may or may not be consolidated into a single document over time.[18] The second is unplanned evolution, primarily driven by 'the dialogic interactions of political actors and by the impulse of constitutional politics,'[19] where the constitution organically develops through the addition of new texts, each gaining constitutional status without a central design.

Within unplanned evolution, Albert describes three distinct categories of multi-textuality: (1) the pluralisation of constitutional texts when new rules cannot be incorporated into an existing uni-textual constitution; (2) the evolution of a uni-textual constitution into a multi-textual one through political practice, where political actors treat certain ordinary laws as having constitutional status; and (3) the pluralisation of constitutional texts through judicial interpretation, whereby courts elevate external texts to constitutional standing.[20]

The Brazilian case of multi-textuality fits the first category identified by Albert. It first emerged from a practical situation where the constitutional incorporation of an international norm could not be accommodated, in formal terms, within the existing uni-textual Constitution. To address this, the necessary instrument was introduced through a constitutional amendment. Moreover, the very process of establishing this multi-textuality involved another constitutional amendment. To study and analyse this process – marked by two constitutional amendments that led to multi-textuality in Brazil – it is necessary to address, even if briefly, the evolution and history of constitutional amendment codification in Brazil, which helps to explain this phenomenon.

[16] ibid 1633.
[17] ibid 1634.
[18] ibid 1640.
[19] ibid 1649–50.
[20] ibid 1649–59.

Throughout Brazil's 200-year constitutional history, the codification of constitutional amendments changed little from the first Constitution of 1824 to the eighth and current Constitution of 1988. This period was characterised by a recurring shift between two main models of amendment codification.[21] The appendative model adds amendments sequentially at the end of the constitutional text, altering norms without changing the original structure. In contrast, the integrative model incorporates amendments directly into the original text as interwoven clauses, preserving the external form of the Constitution despite substantive alterations.

From 1824 until 2004 (including the first 16 years under the 1988 Constitution), Brazil employed a mix of these two models, without mandating a specific model for any specific amendment. Although the recognition of materially constitutional norms outside the constitutional text was possible – in line with the recognition of implicit fundamental rights discussed in the previous section – the formal pluralisation of the constitutional text had not yet taken shape. Therefore, there was no recognition of a norm with both material and formal constitutional status outside the explicit text of the Constitution. This system persisted throughout various constitutional phases in Brazil, shaping the evolution of the country's constitutional order until the significant shift introduced by Constitutional Amendment No. 45 in 2004, which redefined the scope and nature of constitutional changes, particularly in relation to international human rights treaties.

With the approval of Constitutional Amendment No. 45 in 2004, the Constitution of 1988 established a distinct model for the codification of specific amendments. This constitutional change marked the emergence of a mandatory multi-textual Constitution in Brazil, recognising the possibility of formal and material constitutional norms (and not just fundamental rights) existing outside the main text of the Constitution. The amendment added a new provision to Article 5, §3º, which states that 'The international human rights treaties and conventions which are approved in each House of the National Congress, in two rounds of voting, by three-fifths of the votes of their respective members, shall be equivalent to constitutional amendments.' Once approved for incorporation according to the specific procedure now established in the Constitution, an international human rights treaty is considered an integral part of Brazil's Constitution, both materially and formally. Multi-textuality, therefore, is explicitly expressed and automatically follows from this specific process of constitutional change.

This new provision from 2004 established a distinct process for the approval of international human rights treaties, positioning them at the same level as constitutional amendments (or 'equivalent to constitutional amendments') without altering the original text of the Constitution. Following Albert's classification of the basic

[21] For a more detailed overview of the history of constitutional amendments and their codification in Brazil, see B Cunha, 'The Codification of Constitutional Amendments in Brazil: Beyond the Appendative and Integrative Models' in R Albert (ed), *The Architecture of Constitutional Amendments* (Hart Publishing, 2023).

models for codifying constitutional amendments,[22] this arrangement fits within the disaggregative and invisible models. In the invisible model, amendments are incorporated into the constitution without any visible indication of where or how the changes have occurred. The original text remains unmarked, and readers cannot easily discern what has been altered, added, or removed. By contrast, the disaggregative model involves constitutional changes that are codified in separate documents or even in unwritten norms, rather than being integrated into the main constitutional text. This model combines features of the appendative, integrative, and invisible models, allowing for changes to be codified in distinct sites, which may include separately codified constitutional laws that alter the meaning of the constitution without changing the original text itself.

In essence, Article 5, §3° creates a mandatory model for codifying international human rights treaties that may modify the meaning of the Constitution without integrating them into the main text. As such, these treaties remain invisible within the constitutional structure, neither integrated into the original document nor indicated in the amendment appendix, and are instead considered 'separately codified constitutional laws.'[23]

Given this innovation, analysing the status of international treaties within the Brazilian legal system, both before and after Constitutional Amendment No. 45, becomes crucial. Particular attention must be given to how the STF clarified their hierarchical status and the broader implications for the theory and practice of multi-textuality, as this shift has reshaped the constitutional landscape and the relationship between domestic and international law in Brazil.

IV. The Status of International Treaties Within the Brazilian Legal System and the Recognition of a Multi-textual Constitution

Between 2004 and 2025, following the new constitutional provision of Article 5, §3°, which introduced and supported the idea of multi-textuality in Brazil, the Brazilian National Congress approved three constitutional amendments (or instruments with equivalent constitutional force) incorporating international human rights treaties and conventions into the Brazilian legal and constitutional system. These include: (i) the Convention on the Rights of Persons with Disabilities and its Optional Protocol (New York, 2007), adopted in 2009; (ii) the Marrakesh Treaty to Facilitate Access to Published Works for Persons Who are Blind, Visually Impaired or Otherwise Print Disabled (Marrakesh, 2013), adopted in 2018; and

[22] For an in-depth discussion on the distinct models of codification of constitutional amendments, see especially R Albert, *Constitutional Amendments: Making, Breaking, and Changing Constitutions* (Oxford University Press, 2019) ch 6.

[23] ibid 235.

(iii) the Inter-American Convention against Racism, Racial Discrimination and Related Forms of Intolerance (Guatemala, 2013), adopted in 2022.

Regarding these international human rights instruments, there is no dispute among legal scholars or within the courts that, once approved under the procedures of Article 5, §3°, they possess both formal and material constitutional status, with an equivalent standing to constitutional amendments. However, questions remain in relation to other groups of international norms potentially incorporated into the Brazilian legal system: (i) human rights treaties incorporated after 2004 without following the Article 5, §3° procedure; (ii) human rights treaties incorporated prior to 2004; and (iii) treaties on subjects unrelated to human rights. The main question, then, is to define the actual status of these distinct international treaties within the Brazilian legal system, particularly in light of STF interpretations, and to assess the implications of such recognition within the broader context of Brazil's plurality of constitutional texts (multi-textuality).

The status of international human rights treaties in Brazil has been a subject of discussion since the original drafting of the 1988 Constitution. First and foremost, it is impossible to engage in this debate without recognising that the Article 5, §2°[24] expressly provides that the rights enumerated within the constitutional text are not exhaustive of all rights enjoyed by Brazilians. In this regard, the 1988 Constitution explicitly rejects the notion of an exhaustive catalogue of constitutional rights and, moreover, affirms that such rights may derive from 'international treaties to which the Federative Republic of Brazil is a party,' thus opening the door for the incorporation of international treaties into the broader framework of constitutional rights in Brazil.

Since 1988, the wording of Article 5, §2° has been interpreted by some Brazilian legal scholars as authorising the constitutional incorporation of rights and guarantees from international human rights treaties ratified and integrated, under the then-prevailing procedure, into Brazil's domestic legal system. According to this interpretation, these rights and guarantees are regarded as if they were written directly in the Constitution, effectively becoming part of the Brazilian constitutional framework. Citing various important legal scholars in international and constitutional law who support the constitutional hierarchy and immediate applicability of these treaties within Brazil's legal system, Valerio Mazzuoli suggests that the rights and guarantees expressly enumerated in the constitutional text do not preclude those arising from international treaties to which Brazil is a party. This, he argues, is because the Constitution itself integrates these treaty-based rights into its catalogue of protected rights, thus expanding its *bloc de constitutionnalité* (constitutional block).[25] Reaffirming his position in favour of the direct

[24] The clause reads as follows: *The rights and guarantees expressed in this Constitution do not exclude others deriving from the regime and principles adopted by it, or from international treaties to which the Federative Republic of Brazil is a party.*

[25] V Mazzuoli, 'O novo §3° do art. 5° da Constituição e sua eficácia' (2005) 167 *Revista de Informação Legislativa* 95.

applicability and constitutional status of all human rights treaties, irrespective of the procedural rules established by Constitutional Amendment No. 45 in 2004, Mazuolli explains that

> the most plausible conclusion that can be reached regarding the interpretation of the new §3° of Article 5 of the Constitution is that this new constitutional provision does not annul the interpretation according to which international human rights treaties ratified by Brazil already have the status of (materially) constitutional norms as a result of the express provision in §2° of the same Article 5 of the 1988 Constitution. In other words, all international human rights treaties to which the Federative Republic of Brazil is a party have a materially constitutional nature and status under the interpretation of §2° of Article 5 of the 1988 Constitution, but they will only have the effects of equivalence to constitutional amendments (ie, they will only formally integrate the Constitution, with all the consequences inherent to such integration) if approved, in each House of the National Congress, in two rounds, by three-fifths of the votes of their respective members, in accordance with the new §3° of Article 5 of the Brazilian constitutional text.[26]

For Mazzuoli, then, the distinguishing feature regarding the status of international human rights treaties incorporated into the Brazilian legal system lies precisely in their formal integration into the Constitution. He argues that all such treaties, once incorporated, are materially constitutional by virtue of the constitutional openness enshrined in Article 5, §2°, regardless of the incorporation procedure.[27] In other words, once incorporated through the opening clause provided for in Article 5, §2°, human rights treaties would have only a material constitutional status; on the other hand, once incorporated through the new procedure outlined in Article 5, §3°, they would be both formally and materially constitutional. However, this interpretation has not been the one historically endorsed by the STF.

Before the 1988 Constitution, the question regarding the hierarchy of international treaties and their relationship with domestic law had already been debated within the STF.[28] At least until 1977, the STF maintained through several precedents that international treaties held primacy over domestic legislation. As an example, it recognised the primacy of international treaties over subsequent domestic legislation in two landmark cases decided, respectively, in 1943 and 1951.[29]

However, this jurisprudential stance shifted in 1977, when the Court ruled in RE 80.004/SE that international treaties, once incorporated, held the same status as ordinary laws within the domestic legal system. This meant they could be revoked by subsequent legislation or set aside in favour of specific national laws. The case involved a conflict between the Geneva Convention Providing for a

[26] ibid 111.

[27] ibid.

[28] A Moreira Maués, 'Supralegalidade dos tratados internacionais de direitos humanos e interpretação constitucional' (2013) 18 *SUR – Revista Internacional de Direitos Humanos* 217.

[29] See Federal Supreme Court, ACi 7872, Judgment of 11 October 1943 jurisprudencia.stf.jus.br/pages/search/colac10036/false; Federal Supreme Court, ACi 9587/DF, Judgment of 12 August 1951, jurisprudencia.stf.jus.br/pages/search/sjur24893/false.

Uniform Law for Bills of Exchange and Promissory Notes (1930), which had been incorporated into Brazil's legal system, and a later domestic law. The Court upheld the validity of the subsequent law, which altered provisions previously addressed by the Convention, holding that 'the Convention and the law would exist at the same hierarchical level, meaning the former could not prevail over future law'[30] (*lex posterior derogat priori*).

This restrictive judicial interpretation persisted without significant changes even after the promulgation of the current Constitution in 1988. Despite the constitutional innovation introduced by Article 5, §2º, the Court continued to treat international treaties primarily as having the status of ordinary laws within the domestic hierarchy. This position was reaffirmed in two STF decisions in 1995 and 1997, which confirmed that international treaties, regardless of subject matter, hold the status of ordinary laws. In both cases, the Court maintained that, once incorporated into the Brazilian legal system (by a simple legislative majority, under the standard procedure for internalising international norms at that time), treaties are treated as equivalent to national legislation, subject to the same rules and authority.

In judgment HC 72.131/RJ, decided in 1995, the issue at hand was a conflict between provisions of the American Convention on Human Rights (ACHR), adopted and incorporated by Brazil in 1992, and Decreto-Lei No. 911 of 1969. The first point of contention concerned the scope of civil imprisonment. The 1988 Constitution prohibits civil imprisonment, except for debtors of alimony obligations and for unfaithful bailees who unjustifiably refuse to return property to its rightful owner. By contrast, Article 7, §7 of the ACHR stipulates that 'no one shall be detained for debt,' except for those subject to 'the orders of a competent judicial authority issued for nonfulfillment of duties of support.' Meanwhile, the 1969 domestic law specifically regulated the possibility of civil imprisonment for unfaithful bailees, in accordance with the exceptions provided in the Brazilian Constitution.

Maintaining its position that incorporated international norms have the status of ordinary law, the STF held that the provision of the ACHR, despite being subsequent, contained general principles that did not override the application of the specific rules governing the figure of the unfaithful bailee in Brazil. As explained by Frederico Augusto Leopoldino Koehler,

> Not every new treaty revokes a previous law that conflicts with it. It is required that, in addition to being new, the treaty must be capable of revoking the previous law, and this only happens when both normative types are either general or both are special. This is the primacy of *lex posterior generalis non derogat legi priori speciali*, meaning that the special rule, even if older, prevails over the general rule.[31]

[30] G Ferreira Santos, 'Treaties X Human Rights Treaties: A Critical Analysis of the Dual Stance on Treaties in the Brazilian Legal System' (2013) 15 *European Journal of Law Reform* 22.

[31] F Augusto Leopoldino Koehler, 'Hierarquia dos tratados internacionais em face do ordenamento interno: um estudo sobre a jurisprudência do STF' (2007) 14 *Revista ESMAFE* 152–53.

Two years later, in 1997, the hierarchy of international norms in relation to domestic law returned to the spotlight before the Federal Supreme Court. In ADI 1480/DF, an extensive discussion took place regarding the 1982 Termination of Employment Convention (an International Labor Organization Convention to which Brazil had adhered in 1995). The debate centred on the compatibility of this Convention with the 1988 Federal Constitution. Regarding the topic of the status of international treaties within Brazilian law, the STF summarised its position as follows:

> In the Brazilian legal system, international treaties or conventions are hierarchically subordinated to the normative authority of the Constitution of the Republic. As a result, international treaties that, once incorporated into the domestic legal system, formally or materially violate the text of the Constitution will have no legal value.
>
> Once regularly incorporated into domestic law, international treaties or conventions occupy the same planes of validity, effectiveness, and authority as ordinary laws within the Brazilian legal system, creating, therefore, a mere normative parity between them and acts of public international law. Precedents.
>
> In the Brazilian legal system, international acts do not have hierarchical primacy over domestic legal norms. The potential precedence of international treaties or conventions over infraconstitutional domestic rules will only be justified when the situation of antinomy with the domestic legal system requires, for resolving the conflict, the alternative application of the chronological criterion (*lex posterior derogat priori*) or, when applicable, the criterion of specialty. Precedents.[32]

Based on the cases discussed above, it can be observed that the STF adopted a relationship of normative parity between ordinary laws and treaties. In the event of a conflict between laws and treaties, the chronological criterion (*lex posterior derogat priori*) should be applied or, when applicable, the criterion of specialty (*lex specialis derogat generalis*).[33]

Despite some scholarly disagreement,[34] the Court had by then consolidated the idea of normative parity between international norms and domestic law. However, ongoing academic criticism, coupled with new cases reaching the Court's docket, eventually led to the emergence of a new chapter in the long-standing discussion regarding the hierarchy of international norms incorporated into Brazilian law.

The growing global recognition of human rights, particularly through regional systems such as the ACHR and the Inter-American Court of Human Rights in Costa Rica (IACHR), began to exert a tangible influence on the STF by 2000. In judgment RHC 79.785/RJ, the STF acknowledged that international human rights treaties, although still subordinate to the Constitution in the legal hierarchy, should be endowed with a 'supra-legal force.' This recognition allowed for

[32] See Federal Supreme Court, ADI 1480/DF, judgment of 4 September 1997 portal.stf.jus.br/processos/detalhe.asp?incidente=1646696.

[33] Koehler (n 31) 152.

[34] For a synthesis of these legal scholars' arguments, see Mazzuoli (n 25).

the direct application of such treaties against ordinary laws, though not against the Constitution itself. A particularly notable contribution comes from Justice Sepúlveda Pertence, who, in his opinion, introduced the idea of the 'supra-legal' status of international human rights treaties within the STF, albeit with some uncertainty. As he stated:

> Still with uncertainties not sufficiently matured, I tend to accept the granting of supra-legal force to human rights conventions in order to give direct application to their norms – even, if necessary, against ordinary law – whenever, without violating the Constitution, they complement it, specifying or expanding the rights and guarantees contained therein.[35]

The debate over the status of international norms in Brazil took a decisive turn with the enactment of Constitutional Amendment No. 45 in 2004, which, as previously discussed, solidified the concept of multi-textuality in both formal and material terms. It also established at the constitutional level a dual distinction: first, between international human rights norms and other international norms; and second, between those incorporated through the procedure granting them constitutional amendment status and those that retain the status of ordinary legislation.

Nevertheless, the idea of the supra-legal status of international human rights norms, which had already been gaining traction,[36] was firmly established by the STF in 2008 with the ruling in RE 466.343/SP.[37] The case concerned civil imprisonment for a defaulting fiduciary debtor, specifically whether failure to return an asset could justify incarceration. Interpreting the Brazilian Constitution in conjunction with Article 7, §7 of the ACHR,[38] the STF held that the only constitutional exception to the prohibition on civil imprisonment applies to alimony debtors, as explicitly recognised in the ACHR. As a result, the Court invalidated all infraconstitutional provisions permitting the imprisonment of defaulting fiduciary debtors. Two excerpts from the ruling are worth mentioning, respectively from Justice Gilmar Mendes and Justice Celso de Mello:

> The supra-legal normative status of international human rights treaties ratified by Brazil, therefore, renders inapplicable any conflicting infraconstitutional legislation, whether enacted before or after the act of accession. [Justice Gilmar Mendes]
>
> When it comes to international human rights treaties, they must be regarded as normative instruments occupying an intermediate position, granting them a status superior to that of ordinary domestic laws, yet still subordinate to the authority of the Federal Constitution. [Justice Celso de Mello]

[35] See Federal Supreme Court, RHC 79.785/RJ, judgment of 29 March 2000 jurisprudencia.stf.jus.br/pages/search/sjur15842/false.

[36] ibid.

[37] See Federal Supreme Court, RE 466.343/SP, judgment of 3 December 2008 jurisprudencia.stf.jus.br/pages/search/sjur323/false.

[38] ACHR – Article 7, §7. No one shall be detained for debt. This principle shall not limit the orders of a competent judicial authority issued for nonfulfillment of duties of support.

The STF reaffirmed the principle that international human rights norms, regardless of the incorporation procedure, hold an inherently superior status to ordinary domestic law, enabling them to override conflicting national legislation. The Court then clarified that there are two procedures for ratifying international treaties in Brazil: the original procedure requiring a simple majority vote in each house of Congress, and the newer procedure introduced by the 2004 constitutional amendment, which requires two separate supermajority votes in each house. The Court further distinguished the hierarchical status of treaties based on their subject matter and the ratification procedure. Treaties on subjects unrelated to human rights ratified through the original procedure are equivalent to federal law and can be repealed by subsequent federal law. In contrast, human rights treaties ratified through the same procedure hold a status above ordinary federal law,[39] while those ratified through the 2004 procedure are equivalent to constitutional amendments and can only be repealed by another constitutional amendment. This doctrinal differentiation established by the STF has significantly contributed to the broader understanding and acceptance of multi-textuality within the Brazilian constitutional framework.

V. Judicial Perceptions of Multi-textuality

This section analyses the judiciary's perceptions of potential constitutional norms codified outside the main text of the Constitution, exploring the practical application of multi-textuality. The aim is to assess how courts value these norms and whether they distinguish between norms within the constitutional text compared to those outside it. Ultimately, this analysis seeks to determine if a truly multi-textual Constitution exists in Brazil. This will be conducted by examining cases in which the STF has invoked one of the three multi-textual constitutional amendments enacted in Brazil, using their formally and materially constitutional provisions as interpretative or decision-making parameters. These three amendments, approved by the Brazilian National Congress in 2009, 2018, and 2022,[40] stem from interna-

[39] Here are some international human rights treaties that were incorporated into the Brazilian legal system through the simplified procedure and, as a result, hold supra-legal status: (1) Inter-American Convention to Prevent and Punish Torture, adopted by Brazil on 20 July 1989; (2) United Nations Convention on the Rights of the Child, adopted on 24 September 1990; (3) International Covenant on Civil and Political Rights, adopted on 24 January 1992; (4) International Covenant on Economic, Social and Cultural Rights, adopted on 24 January 1992; (5) American Convention on Human Rights, adopted on 25 September 1992; (6) Inter-American Convention on the Prevention, Punishment, and Eradication of Violence against Women, adopted on 27 November 1995.

[40] The Convention on the Rights of Persons with Disabilities and its Optional Protocol (New York, 2007), adopted in 2009; The Marrakesh Treaty to Facilitate Access to Published Works for Persons Who are Blind, Visually Impaired or Otherwise Print Disabled (Marrakesh, 2013), adopted in 2018; The Inter-American Convention against Racism, Racial Discrimination and Related Forms of Intolerance (Guatemala, 2013), adopted in 2022.

tional human rights treaties and conventions incorporated into the Brazilian legal system through the procedure established in Article 5, §3º of the Constitution.

A key benchmark for the existence of an effectively multi-textual Constitution in Brazil is the STF's consistent application of the Convention on the Rights of Persons with Disabilities, incorporated into the Brazilian legal system in 2009 with the status of a constitutional amendment. In two distinct cases, ADI 5.357 MC-Ref/DF[41] and RE 1.096.905 AgR/MG,[42] the STF assessed the legality of private educational institutions charging additional fees for providing specialised services and accommodations for students with disabilities. The Court ruled such charges unconstitutional, as private institutions are required to ensure inclusive education without imposing additional financial burdens on students with disabilities. Applying the constitutional norm derived from the Convention regarding equal access to education, the Court invalidated conflicting infraconstitutional interpretations and established that private schools are obligated to adapt their services to accommodate students with disabilities without discrimination or additional costs. This jurisprudence reaffirmed the Convention's binding constitutional authority and reinforced the principle that norms with formal and material constitutional status, though external to the main constitutional text, can serve as direct parameters for judicial review and constitutional interpretation.

The STF extended this reasoning in judgment HC 151.523/SP,[43] reaffirming the Convention's constitutional status and direct applicability. The Court ruled that the continued confinement of an individual in a psychiatric custody hospital after the extinction of their criminal liability was unconstitutional. Based on the Convention's guarantee of the 'full and effective participation and inclusion in society' (Article 3, 'c'), the Court emphasised that persons with physical, mental, intellectual, or sensory disabilities should not be subject to institutionalisation as the default measure. Instead, social reintegration – not indefinite confinement – must guide judicial and political decisions in such cases. This case exemplifies the active operation of multi-textuality with full constitutional authority.

The STF further reinforced this constitutional framework in ADI 7.028/AP,[44] ruling that the broad definition of disability established by the Convention, which holds constitutional status, could not be restricted by subnational legislation. In this case, the State of Amapá enacted a law limiting eligibility for public school admissions by defining disability narrowly as physical, mental,

[41] See Federal Supreme Court, ADI 5.357 MC-Ref/DF, judgment of 9 June 2016 jurisprudencia.stf.jus.br/pages/search/sjur359744/false.

[42] See Federal Supreme Court, RE 1.096.905 AgT/MG, judgment of 29 March 2021 jurisprudencia.stf.jus.br/pages/search/sjur444107/false.

[43] See Federal Supreme Court, HC 151.523/SP, judgment of 27 November 2018 jurisprudencia.stf.jus.br/pages/search/sjur396251/false.

[44] See Federal Supreme Court, ADI 7.028/AP, judgment of 19 June 2023 jurisprudencia.stf.jus.br/pages/search/sjur482605/false.

or sensory impairments, and by requiring medical documentation to certify disability status, thereby diverging from the broader definition adopted at the national level and set by the Convention. The STF declared the state law unconstitutional, reaffirming that subnational entities cannot narrow the concept of disability or impose additional burdens that undermine rights guaranteed by international treaties with constitutional status. More broadly, the ruling offers a practical application of multi-textuality, confirming that subnational legislative action is impermissible when it contradicts or restricts the scope of provisions contained in international human rights treaties incorporated as constitutional amendments.

Since the Convention on the Rights of Persons with Disabilities was incorporated with constitutional amendment status in 2009, it has been the most frequently invoked multi-textual constitutional norm in the jurisprudence of the STF. The Court has consistently reaffirmed the Convention's constitutional authority, using it to invalidate state and federal legislation, as well as conflicting legal interpretations. In contrast, the other two multi-textual amendments, incorporating international human rights norms in 2018 and 2022, have yet to generate a comparable body of case law. Although initial claims invoking these newer amendments as constitutional parameters have already reached the STF, the Court has yet to issue a landmark ruling that fully tests the application of multi-textuality in relation to these norms.

VI. Conclusion

The consolidation of multi-textuality in Brazil, driven by Constitutional Amendment No. 45/2004, represents a distinctive phenomenon in comparative constitutional law. By introducing a specific mechanism for incorporating international human rights treaties, the Brazilian legal system has developed a model of multi-textuality in which these treaties attain constitutional status while remaining separate from the main text of the Constitution. This model aligns with Albert's theoretical framework, which contemplates that formally and materially valid constitutional norms may coexist outside the primary constitutional text without necessarily being fully integrated into it. The STF's practical application of this model reinforces its effectiveness: international human rights treaties incorporated under Article 5, §3° of the Brazilian Constitution have served as autonomous parameters for judicial review, exerting a direct influence on constitutional interpretation and supporting the establishment of binding precedents.

However, the consolidation of constitutional multi-textuality in Brazil is not without interpretative and institutional challenges. The distinction established by the STF between international treaties with supra-legal status and those equated with constitutional amendments has generated uncertainties regarding the applicability and limits of these norms within the national legal system. In particular, it remains unclear how extensively the Court will operationalise the concept of supra-legality.

Nevertheless, while the legislature and judiciary have taken steps toward solidifying the normative authority of these new constitutional texts, ongoing scholarly inquiry remains essential for evaluating the long-term impact of multi-textuality on Brazil's constitutional stability. This is especially crucial for understanding the interaction between the original constitutional text, formally constitutional norms outside it, and the judicial mechanisms that ensure coherence and applicability within the constitutional system – subjects that merit deeper exploration in future analysis.

6

Vertical and Horizontal Layers of the Lithuanian Constitution

TOMA BIRMONTIENĖ AND JOLITA MILIUVIENĖ

I. Introduction

The concept of constitutional multi-textuality challenges the traditional perceptions of constitutions as single cohesive legal documents. Multi-textual constitutions consist of multiple documents with shared legal supremacy, thereby challenging conventional understandings of constitutional unity[1] and rejecting the dichotomy between written and unwritten constitutions. The theoretical foundations for analysing multi-textual constitutions can be traced to broader inquiries into constitutional pluralism and modularity, which examine how constitutions incorporate diverse sources of legal authority shaped by historical contingencies, political compromises, and external influences.[2] These interactions underscore the dynamic and multi-layered composition of constitutional authority, where historical texts coexist with modern amendments.

The Lithuanian Constitution of 1992 exemplifies this phenomenon through a unique constitutional design that integrates multiple constituent acts, creating a layered and dynamic framework of constitutional governance. This multi-textual nature is not only reflected in the Constitution's foundational design, where constituent acts adopted both prior to and following the its promulgation are endowed with supreme constitutional authority, but also in its ongoing evolution through judicial interpretation. Such a composite structure situates the Lithuanian Constitution at the intersection of codified integrity and fluid adaptability, raising questions about its coherence, hierarchy, and practical application. This chapter explores the theoretical and practical dimensions of the Lithuanian Constitution's multi-textuality, revealing how it fulfils all three features common to

[1] R Albert, 'Multi-Textual Constitutions' (2023) *Virginia Law Review* 1632, 1633.

[2] DJ Galligan and M Versteeg, *The Social and Political Foundations of Constitutions* (Cambridge University Press, 2013) 36.

the multi-textual constitutions: multiplicity, asynchrony, and shared supremacy.[3] Also, the Lithuanian experience reflects the dynamic interplay between historical legacies and contemporary developments that shaped the emergence of the new Constitution adopted following Lithuania's re-establishment of the independent state.

The authors aim to analyse the Lithuanian Constitution by drawing on constitutional jurisprudence, historical documents, and contemporary legal commentary to unpack the multifaceted interactions between the main body of the Constitution and its constituent acts. By examining the Lithuanian case, this chapter contributes to the broader discourse on multi-textual constitutionalism, offering insights into how such frameworks reconcile their composite nature with demands for coherence, stability, and responsiveness, while navigating historical continuity, legal innovation, and practical governance within an interconnected legal landscape.

II. Lithuanian Constitutional Traditions

The traditions of constitutional law can be understood very broadly – as the body of constitutional law developed over different historical periods, as a set of recurring fundamental principles underpinning constitutional provisions, or as particular methods of interpreting the constitutional text.[4] In interpreting the current Constitution of the Republic of Lithuania, it is imperative to consider both its historical foundations and contemporary context. Traditions and continuity allow us to situate the constitutional system within a temporal continuum, linking past, present, and future.[5]

Lithuanian historical constitutional heritage begins with the Lithuanian Statutes of 1529, 1566, and 1588 (see Section II(A)). Constitutional heritage also includes the Constitution of the Polish-Lithuanian Commonwealth of 3 May 1791 (see Section II(B)) and the Lithuanian interwar constitutions (see Section II(C)), each of which contributed to the development of Lithuania's constitutional identity.

A. The Lithuanian Statutes as a Legal Foundation of the State of Lithuania

The most significant historical sources of Lithuanian constitutional law include the Lithuanian Statutes of 1529, 1566, and 1588, which had an impact not only on the

[3] Albert (n 1) 1638.

[4] T Birmontienė, 'Traditions of Lithuanian Constitutional Law' in D Jočienė (ed), *Thirty Years of Constitutional Justice: Tempore et Loco* (Constitutional Court of the Republic of Lithuania 2024) 693.

[5] E Jarašiūnas, 'Constitutional traditions and constitutional continuity' in G Goda (ed.) *Nuo nacionalinės konstitucijos iki transnacionalinio konstitucionalizmo* (Constitutional Court of the Republic of Lithuania 2024) 68.

development of law in Lithuania, but also on the legal traditions of other states. The enduring importance of Statutes is reflected in the preamble to the current Constitution of the Republic of Lithuania of 1992, which explicitly references them.[6] They are also invoked in the jurisprudence of the Constitutional Court of the Republic of Lithuania to highlight the historical foundations of certain legal institutions.[7]

Lithuania is distinguished by its rich constitutional tradition, which dates back to the early sixteenth century. The Lithuanian Statutes, beginning with the first enacted in 1529, stood out in Europe for their systematic codification and broad scope. They encompassed not only civil and criminal law but also constitutional provisions on state governance and incorporated democratic principles of individual rights within an estate-based society. For instance, the Lithuanian Statute of 1529 proclaimed the principle of the *equal and uniform* application of written laws to all individuals. Section Four, concerning 'inheritance by women and the giving of girls in marriage,'[8] was particularly advanced for its time in addressing the legal status of women. Notably, it placed a strong emphasis on protecting widows' rights to guardianship over their children, safeguarding women's property and inheritance rights, and establishing these rights as an independent area of legal regulation. The Statutes likewise recognised the importance of the protection of other personal freedoms, further underscoring the progressive character of Lithuanian's early constitutional heritage.[9]

B. The Constitution of the Polish-Lithuanian Commonwealth of 3 May 1791 as the First Codified Constitution in Europe and the First Historical Composite Constitution

One of the most prominent historical constitutional documents is the Constitution of the Polish-Lithuanian Commonwealth of 3 May 1791 (hereinafter the Constitution of 3 May 1791). It marked the culmination of political, social, and

[6] The preamble to the 1992 Constitution of the Republic of Lithuania proclaims that: 'The Lithuanian Nation … having based its legal foundations on *the Lithuanian Statutes* and *the Constitutions of the Republic of Lithuania*, … striving for an open, just, and harmonious civil society and a State under the rule of law, by the will of the citizens … adopts and proclaims this Constitution.'

[7] Ruling of 13 May 2005 Žin 2005 No 63-2235; ruling of 8 July 2005 Žin 2005 No 87-3274.

[8] *The Statute of Lithuania. Statuta Lituaniae 1529* (Artlora, 2002) 86–90.

[9] For example, Section IV of the Lithuanian Statute of 1529, in its Article 15 titled 'Princesses, Lords' Widows and Girls May Not Be Married against Their Wills, but Only with Their Consent,' prescribed that 'We also promise by our sovereign grace and generosity that we ourselves and our descendants shall protect princesses (kniaginy), lords' widows, princesses (kniazheny), maidens and girls in their freedoms, [and] will not force them to marry anyone without their consent. But each of them [may] freely marry anyone [she] pleases with the counsel of her friends.' *The Statute of Lithuania. Statuta Lituaniae 1529* (Artlora, 2002) 89.

economic reforms carried out by the Commonwealth in the second half of the eighteenth century[10] and created a constitutional monarchy.

The Constitution of 3 May 1791 is recognised as the first codified, composed (sometimes called textual) constitution in Europe, predating the French Constitution of 3 September 1791. It embodied several modern legal and political ideas of the time, drawing inspiration from United States Constitution of 1787, the ideals of the French Revolution, and the shared statehood experience of the Polish and Lithuanian nations.[11] Its core principles – constitutional supremacy, separation of powers, respect for law, judicial independence, and the aspiration for a state governed by the rule of law – continue to be fundamental tenets of democratic constitutions today.

Despite these progressive features, the Constitution of 3 May 1791 remained bound to the estate-based social order and did not embrace the egalitarian principles of the French Declaration of the Rights of Man and of the Citizen of 1789, particularly the notion of equality of all. Even so, the Constitution outlived its brief formal lifespan of about 14 months, enduring as a symbol of statehood and constitutionalism, especially in the historical memory of both Lithuania and Poland as they strove to restore sovereignty after the loss of independence.[12]

The Constitution of 3 May 1791 can be regarded as an early instance of multi-textual constitution. A complementing act – the Reciprocal Guarantee of Two Nations (also called the Mutual Pledge of Two Nations) – was adopted on 22 October 1791 and became a constituent part of the Constitution of 3 May 1791. This act formally established the equal status of Lithuania and Poland within the framework of their common state.

C. The Revival of Lithuanian Constitutional Traditions during the Twentieth-century Interwar Period

The constitutional traditions of the State of Lithuania were revived only after its proclamation of independence at the beginning of the twentieth century. On 16 February 1918, the Council of Lithuania adopted the Act of Independence, establishing the modern State of Lithuania. Several provisional constitutions were adopted in 1918 and 1920,[13] each elaborating important human rights provisions. For instance, Article 27 of the provisional Constitution of 1918 declared universal suffrage and voting rights of women, while Article 16 of the provisional Constitution of 1920 introduced the prohibition of the capital punishment.

[10] E Raila, *1791 m. gegužės 3 d. Konstitucija* [*Constitution of 3 May 1791*] (Vilnius Academy of Arts Press, 2001) 66.

[11] Birmontienė (n 4) 696.

[12] ibid 613.

[13] V Andriulis, R Mockevičius and V Valeckaitė, *Lietuvos valstybės teisės aktai: 1918 II.16–1940.VI.15* (Teisės institutas, 1996) 2–7.

In the history of Lithuanian constitution-making, the Constituent Assembly (*Seimas*) played a special role. On 1 August 1922, it adopted the Constitution of the State of Lithuania, which reflected European constitutional trends influenced by the so-called Weimar Constitution of 1919 and instituted a liberal parliamentary republic. Before the Russian occupation of Lithuania in 1940, two additional permanent Constitutions were adopted in 1928 and 1938, although these are generally not regarded as democratic.

After the restoration of Lithuania's independence at the end of the twentieth century, as the country sought to rejoin the international community of democratic states, Lithuania's rich constitutional traditions served as a significant reference point for drafting the Constitution of the Republic of Lithuania of 1992. Although its early twentieth-century constitutions were unified legal acts, Lithuania's historical unique experience also included a multi-textual, composite codified constitutional framework. This was exemplified by the afore-mentioned multi-layered structure of the first European constitution – the Constitution of 3 May 1791 – which was complemented by an act ensuring equality between the Grand Duchy of Lithuania and the Kingdom of Poland within the Polish-Lithuanian Commonwealth.

Thus, constitutional multilayeredness may also be considered as an enduring and integral element of Lithuania's constitutional tradition, reflected in the development of the 1992 Constitution. The Constitutional Court of Lithuania has recognised the importance of these traditions, which not only aligned with broader European constitutional traditions, but also, at certain historical junctures, surpassed them in the depth of constitutional ideas, the strength of legal entrenchment, and the commitment to human rights protections.

III. The Structure of the Lithuanian Constitution of 1992 and its Modification

The Constitution, adopted on 25 October 1992 by referendum, is a combination of constitutional innovations and traditions.[14] It is classified as a composite codified constitution. Today, it comprises the main text and four constituent constitutional acts explicitly listed in Article 150, forming a multi-document constitutional framework. Under the principle of the integrity of the Constitution enshrined in Article 6, these constituent constitutional acts are integral to the Constitution and hold the same legal force of the Constitution, sharing its exclusive authority within the legal system. Notably, these acts differ in their dates of adoption, purposes, and legal character.

Thus, the Lithuanian Constitution, characterised by multiplicity, asynchrony, and shared supremacy, clearly reflects the three core features of multi-textuality

[14] Jarašiūnas (n 5) 62–84.

described by Richard Albert[15] and offers a valuable model for analysing multi-textual constitutions. This section examines in further detail the form and structure of the current Lithuanian Constitution. Sections III(A) and III(B) explore the acts added to the Constitution at the time of the Constitution's adoption, revealing that its multi-textuality was embedded in its original design, while Sections III(C) and III(D) introduce two other constituent acts incorporated into the Constitution through subsequent constitutional evolution.

A. From Restoration to Constitution: Lithuania's Pre-Constitutional Framework after Regaining Independence in 1990

Before delving into the details of the structure of the Constitution of 1992, it is worth examining briefly the historical context leading to its adoption, particularly the key events and documents that significantly influenced the constitutional text, some of which later became the constituent parts of the Constitution itself.

After half a century of Russian occupation, Lithuania regained its independence on 11 March 1990. On the second day of its sitting, the newly elected Supreme Council of the Republic of Lithuania, where the political reform movement held an absolute majority, renamed itself the Constituent Assembly and adopted the Act on the Re-establishment of the Independent State of Lithuania. The Act of 11 March 1990 made clear that the restoration of independence of the State of Lithuania was grounded in the legal continuity of the Lithuanian state established in 1918. Therefore, first of all, to underscore that the Lithuania's statehood had de jure never ceased to exist,[16] the Constitution of 1938 was briefly restored – though only for a few minutes. As that Constitution was not at all suited to contemporary realities,[17] its validity was immediately suspended. On the same day, the Provisional Basic Law (1990) was enacted as a single, easily amendable document to serve as a transitional constitution until the adoption of a permanent one.

Drafting of the new Constitution began soon after. However, Soviet Russia did not react well to Lithuania's independence and sought to undermine it internationally by spreading speculations about the legitimacy of the Act of Independence of 1990 and the transitional Constitution. In response, the Supreme Council-Constituent Assembly decided to hold a general poll (plebiscite) on the provision that 'The State of Lithuania shall be an independent democratic republic'. This provision was supported by 90.40 per cent of participating voters in the plebiscite

[15] Albert (n 1) 1629.

[16] D Žalimas, 'Main legal and political issues on the continuity of the Republic of Lithuania' (2000) 1(17) *Politologija* 3–18.

[17] The Constitution of 1938 extremely strengthened presidential powers and left the country subject to an authoritarian regime.

of 9 February 1991.[18] The outcome was formalised through the adoption of the Constitutional Law of 11 February 1991 on the State of Lithuania, which subsequently became a constituent part of the new Constitution of 1992. Furthermore, this affirmation of Lithuania's status as an independent democratic republic was consolidated in Article 1 of the new Constitution's main text.

On 8 June 1992, in response to external attempts to incorporate Lithuania into the Commonwealth of Independent States (a political union of former Soviet republics dominated by Russia), the Supreme Council adopted the Constitutional Act on the Non-Alignment of the Republic of Lithuania to Post-Soviet Eastern Alliances (hereinafter the Constitutional Act of Non-Alignment). Drawing on the Acts of 16 February 1918 and 11 March 1990 on the restoration of the independent state of Lithuania, as well as the will of the entire nation expressed in the plebiscite of 9 February 1991, the Supreme Council declared that Lithuania would never, in any form, join any new political, military, economic, or other state unions and commonwealths created on the basis of the former so-called Soviet Union. It further affirmed that any such efforts would be regarded hostile to the independence of Lithuania.

B. The Multiplicity of the Constitution of 1992 since its Adoption: the Main Body of the Text and Two Constituent Parts adopted Prior to the Constitution

The Lithuanian Constitution, adopted on 25 October 1992, consists of a main body of 154 articles. As mentioned before, Article 150 listed the constituent parts of the Constitution. At the moment of its adoption, two constituent constitutional acts, both adopted prior to the Constitution itself, were recognised: the aforementioned Constitutional Law of 11 February 1991 on the State of Lithuania (hereinafter the Constitutional law on the State of Lithuania) and the Constitutional Act of 8 June 1992 on the Non-Alignment of the Republic of Lithuania to Post-Soviet Eastern Unions. The principle of the integrity of the Constitution, enshrined in Article 6, affirms the harmonious nature of the Constitution as an integral act and establishes that all constituent parts possess equal legal force. Accordingly, the two constitutional acts have the same supreme legal power as the main body of the Constitution.[19]

The Constitutional Law on the State of Lithuania gave legal effect to the most successful referendum in Lithuanian history (even the adoption of the Constitution itself garnered slightly fewer votes cast in favour). It established the provision that

[18] J Žilys, 'Lietuvos valstybės konstitucingumo raida 1990 m. atkūrus nepriklausomybę [Development of Lithuanian Constitutionalism in 1990 After Re-instauration of Independence]' in J Miliuviene and others (eds), *Lietuvos konstitucinė teisė* (Mykolas Romeris University, 2022) 148.

[19] The Constitutional Court, only in 2020, *expressis verbis* stated that those constituent parts have the legal force of the Constitution.

'The State of Lithuania shall be an independent democratic republic,' which consequently became the content of Article 1 of the 1992 Constitution. The Constitutional Law on the State of Lithuania also sets strict rules for the amendment of this provision, making any alteration next to impossible: it requires votes of not less than three-quarters of all Lithuanian citizens of Lithuania cast in favour in a general poll. Later, the Constitutional Court clarified that even this rigorous procedure cannot amend all elements of that provision.[20] The Constitutional Court held that two of the three eternal constitutional values – independence and democracy – are enshrined therein and are therefore unamendable. Recognising the constitutional act's paramount importance in shaping the constitutional order, the drafters of the 1992 Constitution deemed it necessary not only to incorporate its core statement into Article 1, but also reinforce it by preserving the entire act as an integral constituent part of the Constitution.

The Constitutional Act on the Non-Alignment reflects Lithuania's historical experience and was intended to prevent the recurrence of developments like the 1940 occupation by Soviet Russia. The act provides that: (i) Lithuania intends to maintain good mutual relations with all countries that were part of the Soviet Union, (ii) any efforts to incorporate Lithuania into new alliances formed on the basis of the former Soviet Union are illegal, and (iii) the presence of Russian military forces on Lithuanian territory is unlawful. This third provision was particularly important from a constitutional perspective, since it elevated to constitutional status the prohibition of Russian military presence in the territory of Lithuania.[21] The systematic interpretation of this act played a crucial role in developing Lithuania's constitutional doctrine of national security and state defence; it also gave birth to one of the most important constitutional principles – the principle of the geopolitical orientation of the state (discussed in Section IV(B)).

C. Multiplicity by the Evolution: the Third Constituent Part of the Constitution, Emerged from the Interpretation of the Constitution

Alongside the Constitution, the Law on the Procedure for the Entry into Force of the Constitution (hereinafter the Law on Entry into Force), containing transitional provisions and certain constitutional additions, was adopted in the same referendum of 25 October 1992. Article 152 of the Constitution refers to this law, stating that it shall regulate the procedure for the entry into force of the Constitution and its separate provisions. However, when the Constitution was adopted, the Law on Entry into Force was not considered part of the Constitution nor attributed the

[20] Ruling of 24 January 2014 TAR 478; ruling of 11 July 2014 TAR 10117.
[21] The last Russian troops did not withdraw from Lithuanian territory until 31 August 1993.

same legal force; instead, it was regarded as an ordinary law supplementing the Constitution.

This understanding persisted until the Constitutional Court, in its ruling of 29 October 2003, held that the Law on Entry into Force – having been adopted together with the Constitution by the Nation in the referendum, and containing provisions inseparably related to certain provisions and principles of the Constitution, supplementing others, or establishing the particularities of their implementation – could not be considered a non-constituent part of the Constitution. Consequently, it could not possess lower legal force than the Constitution itself.

Thus, the Lithuanian Constitution acquired its third constituent part by way of judicial interpretation. The legislature subsequently followed the Constitutional Court's reasoning and formally amended Article 150 to list the Law on Entry into Force as an equal constituent part of the Constitution. Although the amendment was enacted only on 13 July 2004, it is generally considered that the Lithuanian Constitution has comprised its third constituent part since the Constitutional Court's 2003 ruling. Even though this law was originally designed to regulate the transitional period until the Constitution was fully implemented, it also contains provisions that remain in effect as long as the Constitution itself is in force (for instance, the text of the oath of parliamentarians). These enduring provisions continue to pay a role in the formation of official constitutional doctrines.

D. The Occurrence of Asynchrony: Constitutional Act on Membership of Lithuania in the European Union as the Fourth Constituent Part of the Lithuanian Constitution since 2004

Given the specific *sui generis* nature of the European Union (EU) – marked by shared competences in designated areas and the autonomous power to adopt binding legislation – Lithuania's accession to the EU required constitutional amendments. Despite that several constitutional provisions had to be amended to align with the *acquis communautaire*, the Lithuanian Parliament chose not to alter the main text extensively. Instead, it supplemented the Constitution with the Constitutional Act on Membership of the Republic of Lithuania in the European Union (hereinafter referred to as the Act on EU Membership) and amended the list of the constituent parts of the Constitution in Article 150. By this evolutive amendment, Lithuania's membership in the EU, already approved by the Lithuanian nation in a referendum, was constitutionally confirmed.[22] This new addition expanded the list of constitutional values by introducing new elements tied to European integration. Soon afterwards, the Constitutional Court emphasised that fully-fledged

[22] Ruling of 13 December 2004 Žin No 181-6708.

participation of Lithuania in the EU is a constitutional imperative, derived from the sovereign will of the People and recognised as a constitutional value in itself.[23]

The Act on EU Membership allowed the transfer of some competences to the European institutions; it also enshrined the rule of collision, consolidating the priority of the application of EU legal acts, with the sole exception of the Constitution itself.[24] This supplementation of the Constitution helped preserve the integrity of the main text by preventing multiple amendments, as EU membership obligations involve the competences of all state institutions.

Consequently, this Act had an important impact on the content of the overall content of the Constitution and introduced considerable implications for the interpretation of its provisions. Some constitutional provisions acquired new substantive content and required reinterpretation (see Section IV(A)), while others were interpreted from the outset with this new constitutional layer in mind. This dynamic was further exemplified when the Constitutional Court invalidated a constitutional amendment concerning currency issuance due to procedural violations. The Court declined to reinstate the prior version of the provision, which had granted exclusive currency issuance rights to the Bank of Lithuania, reasoning that the constitutional reality in Lithuania had fundamentally changed. In light of the Act on EU Membership and Lithuania's accession to the Eurozone in accordance with its EU commitments, reinstating the prior text would have created internal contradictions and inconsistencies within the constitutional framework. This development demonstrates that the incorporation of new constituent parts has the potential to alter constitutional definitions and their interpretation, even in areas that may not initially appear to be directly linked to European regulations.

IV. Visible and Invisible Constitutional Developments Determined by Constitutional Multi-Textualism

The multi-textuality of the Lithuanian Constitution certainly affects the development of constitutional doctrine. In accordance with the principle of integrity of the Constitution, the various components of the Lithuanian Constitution should not be regarded as a mere collection of separate documents, but rather as a single, codified, and composite legal act of supreme legal force. There are no differences in legal hierarchy or legal force among these constituent parts. Collectively, they perform the classical function of a constitution: reflecting constitutional identity and preserving historical continuity in shaping the constitutional design.[25]

The jurisprudence of the Constitutional Court shows both the opportunities and challenges presented by the multi-textuality of the Lithuanian Constitution.

[23] Rulings of 24 January 2014 TAR 478; ruling of 11 January 2019 TAR 439; ruling of 6 February 2020 TAR 14609.

[24] Ruling of 14 March 2006 Žin No 30-1050.

[25] A Jakab, 'Constitutional Identity' (2016) *Oxford Studies in European Law* 12–15.

For instance, the principle of integrity of the Constitution means that the content of one constituent part may influence the interpretation of a 'primary' constitutional norm. In some cases, the previously established meaning of a constitutional norm has changed and required reinterpretation following the adoption of a new constituent part (see Section IV(A)). It is also argued that any future amendments must be made with due regard to the existing components of the constitutional framework, and that in some cases, specific alterations of the Constitution may be impermissible if they contradict those components (see Section IV(B)). Finally, in the course of developing official constitutional doctrine, potential new layers have emerged that supplement the explicitly enumerated parts of the Constitution (see Section IV(C)).

A. The Reinterpretation of the Official Constitutional Doctrine due to the Adoption of New Constituent Part of the Constitution

In the jurisprudence of the Constitutional Court, the interpretation of the Constitution is understood as the clarification of its explicit and implicit provisions and principles, which contributes to the ongoing development of the constitutional doctrine, including its modification. The addition of new provisions to Article 150 of the Constitution has inevitably incorporated content that was previously absent. Given the principle of textual integrity enshrined in Article 6, all constitutional provisions must now be coherently interpreted in light of this expanded content. In effect, three consequences can be distinguished: (1) the need to modify or reinterpret certain aspects of the existing constitutional doctrine to avoid contradictions; (2) the necessity to reinterpret 'classic' constitutional concepts more liberally than was envisaged at the moment of adoption; and (3) a new understanding of the sources that inform constitutional interpretation.

The first consequence of adding new constitutional components to the Constitution is that, in some cases, the existing constitutional doctrine must be reinterpreted. One example concerns the typology of governmental acts. The constitutional doctrine developed by the Constitutional Court in its rulings of 23 November 1999[26] and 29 November 2001[27] stated that absolutely 'all matters of state governance assigned by the Constitution and laws to the competence of the Government are decided by means of adopting resolutions,' as explicitly provided in Article 95 of the Constitution. This understanding treated resolutions as the only constitutionally permissible type of governmental acts. However, the adoption of the Act on EU Membership in 2004 rendered this interpretation tenable. The Constitution, as supplemented by this constitutional act, expanded the types of legal acts that the Government is empowered

[26] Ruling of 23 November 1999 Žin No 101-2916.
[27] Ruling of 29 November 2001 Žin No 102-3636.

to adopt, by expressly providing that 'the Government may adopt decisions or resolutions.' In its ruling of 27 June 2007,[28] the Constitutional Court confirmed this shift, emphasising that the Government has the right to adopt different types of acts, each with different features. For instance, the requirement to immediately publish all acts issued by the Government does not apply to decisions concerning EU matters. This evolution raises the broader question of how durable existing interpretations of constitutional provisions remain in the face of new constituent components.

Second, certain constitutional provisions have acquired different content when reinterpreted in light of the Act on EU membership. For instance, the principle of geopolitical orientation emerged in constitutional doctrine in 2011.[29] This principle, reflecting Lithuania's commitment to European and transatlantic integration, is systematically manifested in both negative and positive forms in the 1992 Constitution's composite parts. In its negative dimension, which was recognised from the beginning, the principle of geopolitical orientation defines the limits that Lithuania must not overstep when it participates in global or regional integration, a constraint derived from the Constitutional Act on the Non-Alignment. Conversely, in its positive dimension, the principle of geopolitical orientation establishes the state's constitutional direction toward state's geopolitical integration and promotes dynamic, active engagement in that path, as expressed in the Act on EU Membership.

An example of how the new components to the Constitution has led to a more liberal content of an 'old' constitutional provision can be seen in evolving interpretation of the constitutional conception of the family. In its ruling of 28 September 2011, the Constitutional Court recognised that while marriage remains the most common basis for family formation and undoubtedly holds exceptional value to society, the Constitution also protects families formed outside marriage.[30] The Court emphasised that the constitutional concept of the family is defined by the substance of relationships (such as mutual responsibility between family members, understanding, the voluntary assumption of rights and duties, etc.), rather than by the formal expression of those relationships. In 2019, the Court went further by stating that the constitutional concept of the family is gender neutral.[31] Finally, in 2025, the Court stated that same-sex persons also might form a family under the Constitution.[32]

All these rulings made extensive reference to the jurisprudence of European supranational courts and reflect the evolving realities of contemporary society. However, as one drafter of the Constitution recalled, 'in 1992, the drafters of the Constitution considered the family based on marriage to be such a self-evident category that there

[28] Ruling of 27 June 2007 Žin No 72-2865.
[29] Ruling of 15 March 2011 Žin No 3-1503.
[30] Ruling of 28 September 2011 Žin No 118-5564
[31] Ruling of 11 January 2019 TAR No 439
[32] Ruling of 17 April 2025 TAR No 6803

was no major discussion; there was no need to convince each other of what marriage and family meant or to clarify what legal reality we would create.'[33]

It can be assumed that a more liberal concept of the family – compared to the self-evident concept held by the drafters of the Constitution – would have evolved in the constitutional doctrine in any event, particularly given the strong influence of the living Constitution doctrine in Lithuanian constitutional law. Nevertheless, there is no doubt that Lithuania's accession to the EU and its desire to speed up integration into the community of Western legal systems accelerated this doctrinal development.

Third, the expansion of the Constitution through new components – particularly when they introduce entirely new content that must be taken into consideration in the interpretation of constitutional provisions – has broadened the sources used in constitutional interpretation. The classic constitutional doctrine maintains that the Constitutional Court, in interpreting the Constitution, is bound only by the Constitution itself and the official constitutional doctrine established by the final acts of the constitutional review institution. Other external legal sources, such as the jurisprudence of supranational courts or foreign constitutional courts, may serve as sources of inspiration but hold no binding authority. Even then, their use is contingent on whether the constitutional judge accepts the theory of the 'borrowing' or 'migration' of constitutional ideas.[34]

However, following Lithuania's accession to the EU, the Constitutional Court articulated a new commitment, binding on itself, to take EU law into account when interpreting constitutional provisions in areas of shared competence. In its decision of 20 December 2017, the Court underlined that EU law is a source for constitutional interpretation in the areas wherever Lithuania shares or confers competences on EU institutions. In such areas, there are no grounds for interpreting the Constitution in a manner that differs from how these matters are regulated under EU law.[35]

The relationship between constitutional law and EU law has become one of the most salient issues in many European states. At first glance, the new constitutional development might appear to provide an answer to the fundamental question of how to reconcile the supremacy of the national Constitution with the direct application and primacy of EU law, as well as how to ensure the harmonious functioning of these distinct legal systems, each rooted in diverse national legal systems. However, the reality is far more complex. The Constitutional Court's 2017 decision effectively placed EU law in the areas of shared competence (which are numerous!) on a constitutional footing. The absence of clear limits on this new approach raises more questions than it answers. EU law is a complex legal system,

[33] E Jarašiūnas, 'Šeimos koncepcijos pagrindai 1992 m. Lietuvos Respublikos Konstitucijoje [Fundamentals of family conception in the 1992 Lithuanian Constitution]' (International Conference 'Family in Changing Society', 2007) www.lrs.lt/docs3/kad5/w5_istorija.show5-p_r=5979&p_k=2.html.

[34] S Choudhry, *The Migration of Constitutional Ideas* (Cambridge University Press, 2007).

[35] Decision of 20 December 2017, lrkt.lt/en/court-acts/search/170/ta1843/content.

composed not only of the founding treaties and the jurisprudence of the Court of Justice of the European Union (CJEU), but also of secondary EU law, including directives and regulations. Hence, these secondary legal sources should not serve as guidelines for interpreting the Constitution. Otherwise, it can be expected that constitutional provisions might be interpreted in the light of secondary legislation or even lower-ranking EU legal sources – risks subordinating constitutional interpretation to legal instruments that may later be invalidated by the CJEU for inconsistency with primary EU law.[36] Such an outcome would directly undermine the fundamental principle of the supremacy of the Constitution over all other legal acts.

Consequently, constitutional interpretations that engage newly added content must be approached prudentially and remain anchored in constitutional fundamentals. Even considering the Act on EU Membership, the Constitutional Court's newly established interpretive rule should, at the very least, be subject to clear limits that may possibly be elaborated in future rulings, clarifying when and to what extent EU law should be taken into account in constitutional interpretation. Such limits are essential to ensure that fundamental constitutional values are not undermined (in line with the Solange doctrine)[37] and that the identity and traditions of the Lithuanian Constitution are preserved, despite the expansion of its constituent parts.

B. The Multiplicity Constraint on Constitutional Amendments

The constituent parts of the Constitution also impose certain limits on future constitutional amendments. The principle of internal coherence (or the imperative to avoid internal contradictions) precludes constitutional amendments that would introduce contradictions within the constitutional framework. The Lithuanian Constitutional Court has formulated a doctrine of limitations on constitutional amendments, holding that three of the four current constituent parts of the Constitution constitute substantive limitations on constitutional amendments.[38]

The Constitutional Court identified three types of substantive limitations on constitutional amendments: absolute, quasi-absolute, and relative (or conditional). The scope and applicability of each limitation depend on the specific constituent parts involved, as the circumstances of their adoption and their legal nature shape their impact on the Constitution's amenability.

At the core of this doctrine lies the theory of eternal clauses – an absolute prohibition against amending, denying, or undermining certain constitutional

[36] For more, see T Birmontienė, 'Konstitucinė teisė ir tarptautinė bei Europos Sąjungos teisė: kas diktuoja teisės sistemų sąveikos ribas?' in *XXI amžiaus iššūkiai tarptautinei teisei: Liber amicorum Sauliui Katuokai* (collection of scientific articles) (Mykolas Romeris University, 2020) 71–101.

[37] J Miliuviene, 'Influence of "Soft Law" on the Development of Constitutional Jurisprudence' (Doctoral Dissertation, Mykolas Romeris University, 2020).

[38] Rulings of 24 January 2014 and 14 July 2014.

elements under any circumstances, by any entity with amendment powers, including the Nation itself. The foundational values of the State of Lithuania and the Constitution as a social contract – namely, state independence and democracy – derive from the Constitutional Law on the State of Lithuania and are enshrined in Article 1 of the Constitution. The innate nature of human rights is inseparable from these two principles, as democracy cannot exist without respect for human rights. Any denial or amendment of these constitutional values would abolish the restored 'independent State of Lithuania, founded on democratic principles,' as proclaimed in Lithuania's Act of Independence of 16 February 1918, and would defy the will of citizens expressed in the general plebiscite of 1991, the results of which are reflected in the Constitutional Law on the State of Lithuania. Thus, the Constitutional Law on the State of Lithuania effectively safeguards the Constitution and the State against 'committing democratic suicide.'[39]

The Constitutional Court has further linked the principles of independence and democracy to the constitutional principle of geopolitical orientation. Drawing on historical lessons learned from the Russian occupation and Lithuania's forced incorporation into the so-called Soviet Union, the Constitutional Court held that the Constitutional Act on the Non-Alignment warrant the same level of protection as Article 1 of the Constitution and the Constitutional Law on the State of Lithuania. As such, the Constitutional Act on the Non-Alignment may only be altered by a general plebiscite, requiring the approval of no less than three-fourths of all citizens with the active electoral right to vote. Given the near-impossibility of reaching such results, this limitation amounts to a de facto absolute restriction, designed to preserve the state's independence and democratic orientation.

Finally, relative limitations on constitutional amendments ensure that no provision of the Constitution may be amended in a manner that contravenes Lithuania's obligations arising from its EU membership, unless the Nation first decides to withdraw from the EU through the same process by which it joined, ie a national referendum. Until such a referendum takes place, any constitutional amendment that contradicts Lithuania's EU obligations is deemed unconstitutional. In this way, the Constitutional Court has effectively precluded attempts, often driven by populist rhetoric, to 'save' the national identity of Lithuania or even curtail human rights under the guise of protecting 'traditional' values from the perceived influence of the 'rotten West.'

In conclusion, these substantive limitations on the alteration of the Constitution, along with the principles stemming from the integrity and internal coherence of the Constitution, including its constituent parts, provide a solid framework for guiding and constraining constitutional alterations in the future.

[39] D Žalimas, 'The Principle of the Geopolitical Orientation of the State in the Constitution of the Republic of Lithuania' (24 October 2014) www.lrkt.lt/data/public/uploads/2015/04/zalimas_en2014-10-24.pdf.

C. The Role of the Constitutional Court in Interpreting the Form of the Constitution: New Constituent Parts?

As discussed earlier, the constituent parts of the Lithuanian Constitution came into being through different processes – some were adopted together with the Constitution, or even prior to it, while others were introduced through formal constitutional amendments or developed over time through official constitutional doctrine.

Judicial interpretation of constitutional provisions is essential if we believe in the longevity of a living constitution. The interpretation of constitutional provisions and principles must be based on objective and well-founded arguments in order to achieve the integrity and coherence of the Constitution, maintain the balance of constitutional values, and sustain the vitality of the legal foundation of society and the state. Undoubtedly, such judicial powers can be justified only if the Constitutional Court and its judges are independent, and if their decisions are founded on convincing constitutional reasoning. Without these safeguards, judicial interpretation risks becoming unjustified constitutional activism, potentially driven by the aim of developing new doctrines that lack sufficient basis in the Constitution itself.

From this perspective, one could argue that the Constitutional Court's doctrine concerning the interpretation of constitutional provisions – when it expands the scope of constituent parts by reassessing their constitutional status and amendment procedures – risks exceeding the permissible limits of doctrinal development. This concern is especially pertinent in relation to the so-called doctrine of 'supra-constitutional acts,' formulated in the Court's ruling of 30 July 2020, which introduced a new conceptual structure and hierarchy of constitutional acts.

Consequently, not all constitutional acts referred to in the constitutional jurisprudence as inseparable from the text of the Constitution should necessarily be treated as formal constituent parts, as is the case with the Law on Entry into Force. It is, therefore, reasonable to consider whether this precedent to add more constituent parts in the course of interpreting the Constitution implies the possibility of more constituent parts that might emerge in the future in the same way, ie through the interpretation of the Constitution, and what impact they could have on the further development of constitutional doctrine.

In this context, the ruling of the Constitutional Court of 30 July 2020 was somewhat revolutionary in identifying (or inventing) a new hierarchy of constitutional acts. The Court highlighted the importance of the historical *fundamental constitutional acts* of the State of Lithuania, which include the Resolution of the Council of Lithuania of 16 February 1918 (Act of Independence) and the Act of the Supreme Council of the Republic of Lithuania of 11 March 1990 on the Re-establishment of the Independent State of Lithuania (referred to in Section III(A)), as well as the Declaration of the Council of the Lithuanian Freedom Fight Movement of 16 February 1949.

The Constitutional Court underscored that the current Constitution emerged from the historical fundamental constitutional acts of Lithuania, drawing parallels between specific provisions in the present Constitution and those contained in the historical acts. The Constitutional Court ultimately concluded that these historical fundamental constitutional acts 'have supra-constitutional force, as they may not be denied by any constitution of the State of Lithuania.'[40] However, as regards the hypothetical future constitutions of Lithuania referenced in the ruling, which are said to have no force to override those fundamental acts, it would have been necessary to clarify in what constitutional manner such future constitutions might be adopted and how they would relate to the current Constitution.

Moreover, the ruling of 30 July 2020 and the doctrine it developed regarding the fundamental constitutional acts of the State of Lithuania are not fully in line with certain provisions of the Constitution of 1992 itself.[41] It is worth noting that the statehood of Lithuania spans centuries and cannot be reduced only to the restoration of independence in the early twentieth century. The preamble to the Constitution situates the foundations of the State of Lithuania in a broader historical context, referring to acts beyond those enumerated in the Court's ruling (for instance, the Lithuanian Statutes). The constitutional traditions of Lithuania are thus more substantive and extensive than the set of fundamental constitutional acts emphasised by the Court,[42] although some of them are particularly important.

While it is clear that at least two of the above-mentioned historical acts (excluding the Declaration of 1949) are inseparable from the Constitution, and that the Constitutional Court had referred to them on many occasions in its jurisprudence[43] even prior to this listing, the question still remains whether this makes them a constituent part of the Constitution. Even if this is so, it is obvious that those acts differ from the constituent constitutional acts that have been analysed before, at least in terms of their legal force, which, as described by the Constitutional Court, is different in that they have 'supra-constitutional force.' For the moment, Article 150 has not been further amended to incorporate these fundamental acts, and there are no initiatives to expand the established list of constituent parts of the Constitution. Thus, it is an open issue whether they will remain a significant part of Lithuania's constitutional developments solely within the Court's jurisprudence.

Some authors have argued that the so-called doctrine of supra-constitutional acts is better understood as an academic construct,[44] and therefore, it should not be regarded as having the same legal consequences as formally recognised

[40] Ruling of 30 July 2020 TAR No 14847.

[41] Birmontienė (n 4) 636.

[42] ibid.

[43] For instance, the Constitutional Court ruling of 18 March 2014 TAR No 3226.

[44] T Birmontienė, 'Konstitucinė doktrina ir Konstitucijos interpretavimo (ne)laisvė [Constitutional doctrine and (il)liberty of constitutional interpretation]' in D Pūraitė-Andrikienė and A Juškevičiūtė-Vilienė (eds), *Konstitucinė justicija Lietuvoje: trys veiklos dešimtmečiai* (Vilnius University Press, 2024) 38–39.

constitutional texts. Even if the Court's attempt to reshape the constitutional law paradigm in 2020 calls for substantial fine-tuning to ensure consistency in the perception of constitutional law, it is unlikely to have any practical impact on the legal system of Lithuania in operation.[45]

Therefore, the doctrine of acts that have supra-constitutional force, as formulated in the Constitutional Court's ruling of 30 July 2020, should be regarded as an unsuccessful attempt to establish a new constitutional structure. This raises concerns regarding the Constitutional Court's power to interpret the Constitution so broadly as to introduce new structural features without formal amendment. The historical aspects in the developed constitutional doctrine warrant closer scrutiny, which also applies to the so-called doctrine of supra-constitutional acts, as historical constitutional provisions from the past cannot be altered or denied.

V. Conclusions

The historical traditions of Lithuanian constitutionalism date back to the sixteenth-century Statutes of Lithuania. The first European constitution, adopted in 1791, was already composite and multi-textual. Although its structure was shaped by the historical circumstances of the time, it is evident that the multi-layered nature of the constitution can be justified by its very essence – its aim to reflect the actual situation in the development of the state and, at times, to clarify what was not sufficiently explicit or utterly omitted in the main text. It can be argued that static constitutions, unaccompanied by supplementary texts or judicial interpretation by independent courts, risk becoming façades, serving as mere decorations of non-democratic states.

The Lithuanian experience testifies that different layers or constituent parts of the Constitution may be adopted alongside the Constitution itself, whether by original design or through developments that emerge at a later stage. These additions arise primarily through two processes: the formal procedure of constitutional amendments or the interpretative practices of the Constitutional Court. Consequently, their impact on the development of national constitutional law is also multifaceted. On the one hand, a multi-textual constitutional structure helps preserve the core body of the constitutional text from radical or frequent amendments, thereby safeguarding the stability and integrity of the constitutional framework. Adding constituent parts to the Constitution also provides an opportunity to broaden and enrich the understanding of unamended constitutional provisions, ensuring that they remain responsive to evolving societal needs and challenges. On the other hand, the activism of the Constitutional Court demonstrates that additional layers can be integrated through judicial interpretation, effectively bypassing the formal

[45] E Kūris, 'Doctrinal Experimenting with the Constitution in Lithuania: On the Structure of the Constitution, the Non-Amendability of Constitutional Provisions, and the Legal Force of "Pre-Constitutional" Acts' (2023) *Review of Central and East European Law* 95–133.

amendment process. This approach excludes the direct or representative participation of the Nation, which is the primary source of constitutional authority.

Therefore, when constitutional courts interpret constitutional provisions and reveal their multi-layered nature, it is crucial to assess all relevant circumstances and the potential implications. This is a particularly sensitive undertaking, especially when the objective is to reintroduce important acts of constitutional significance from the past into the presence – and future – constitutional framework. The Lithuanian case reflects both the promise and the risks of this process. A successful example is the amendment of Article 150 of the Constitution, which formalised the list of constituent constitutional parts following the Constitutional Court's interpretation that the Law on the Procedure for the Entry into Force of the Constitution must be regarded as a constituent part of the Constitution. By contrast, a questionable development is the so-called doctrine of supra-constitutional acts, introduced in the Constitutional Court's ruling of 30 July 2020, which seeks to replace the traditional hierarchical structure of constitutional provisions with a new framework. The emergence of this doctrine illustrates the disputable expansion of the Constitutional Court's powers and its insufficient insights into the essence of the Constitution. This can be assessed as an attempt to impose an artificial structure on the Constitution – one that is not based on fundamental constitutional provisions, including the long-standing Lithuanian traditions of constitutionalism, referred to in the preamble of the Constitution.

7

There and Back Again: The Case of Mexico's Constitutional Forms Between Uni- and Multi-Textualism

JAIME OLAIZ-GONZÁLEZ

I. Introduction

In a groundbreaking article in 2023, Richard Albert not only rejected the canonical relevance of the binary classification of constitutions as written or unwritten as a false distinction, but also introduced a more contemporary and functional framework based on the actual formal configuration of constitutions around the world: the distinction between uni-textual and multi-textual constitutions.[1] As Albert contends:

> The false distinction between written and unwritten constitutions comes at a great cost. It overlooks and obscures *the most important formal distinction* among the constitutions of the world: some constitutions consist of a single, supreme document of higher law *while others consist of multiple documents, each enacted separately with shared supremacy under the law.* [These] constitutions are therefore unlike *uni-textual* constitutions whose written elements appear in a single document that is treated as the only supreme law of the land. I call them *multi-textual* constitutions. Multi-textual constitutions differ from single-text constitutions on the major markers of constitutional life: their initial design, their ongoing evolution, their authoritative interpretation, and their formal amendment.[2]

This excerpt summarises in a nutshell the basic differences between uni-textual – the world's dominant model of constitutional codification – and multi-textual constitutions, which are fundamentally characterised by three features: (1) *multiplicity*, as multi-textual constitutions are comprised of a plurality of

[1] R Albert, 'Multi-Textual Constitutions' (2023) 109 *Virginia Law Review* 1631–32.
[2] ibid 1633 (emphasis added).

documents endowed with the same authoritative signal as higher law;[3] (2) *asynchrony*, since these documents are not adopted nor enacted at the same time, but rather emerge through an incremental process of constitutional construction;[4] and (3) *shared supremacy*, in light of their common placement at the top of the constitutional hierarchy – all functioning, without distinction, as higher law, and therefore constituting the supreme law of the land.[5]

Though multi-textual constitutions have been part of constitutional reality for decades, the identification of their features, challenges, and possibilities – as formulated by Albert[6] – remains largely uncharted territory in the field of comparative constitutionalism.

This chapter aims to adapt Albert's distinctive theory of multi-textual constitutions to the case of Mexico. As we will explore, the Mexican case may appear fall outside some of the proposed categories and offers an interesting case study for broadening the scope of inquiry into multi-textual constitutions, their formulation, and their complex operational codes.

As we will see, Albert's categorisation of constitutional forms proves particularly useful in settings deeply influenced by legal formalism and constitutional symbolism,[7] where the constitution is treated more as an object of reverence than as the sum of fundamental societal arrangements drawn from diverse sources but carrying equal authoritative force. For instance, if experts on the Mexican Constitution were asked whether Mexico reflects a uni-textual or a multi-textual model, it is very likely that, due to the enduring formalist tradition, most would categorise it as uni-textual. As we will demonstrate, however, this categorisation would be far from accurate.

II. Mexico's Early and Middle Constitutions: Between Uni- and Multi-Textualism

In Mexico's extensive nineteenth-century constitutional tradition – reflected in five different constitutional texts: 1824, 1836, 1843, 1847, and 1857 – the country alternated between uni-textual and multi-textual constitutions. Except for the Constitutions of 1824 and 1847, each of these texts enjoyed exclusive supremacy as the single authoritative document of higher law. This trend is evident in the case of the Constitutions of 1836 and 1843, whose languages unequivocally affirm their exclusive constitutional supremacy, leaving no doubt as to their status at the apex of the constitutional pyramid.

[3] ibid 1636–37.
[4] ibid 1637–38.
[5] ibid 1639–40.
[6] ibid 1660–93.
[7] J Olaiz-González, *Transformaciones políticas y cambio constitucional en México: Reflexiones en torno a su evolución histórica y sus problemas contemporáneos* (Tirant Lo Blanch, 2023) 55–62.

The Constitutions of 1836 and 1847, respectively known as the Seven Laws and the Constitutive Act and Reforms, may suggest a degree of multi-textuality due to their titles, which appear to denote a plurality of separate and independent documents, but this is misleading, as each of these constitutions was in fact written as a single, unified text. Nonetheless, as we are about to discover, one of these constitutions fits the uni-textual model, while the other, notwithstanding its apparent exclusive supremacy, functioned as part of a multi-textual constitutional form.

This section analyses how each Constitution articulated its distinctive model of textualism.

A. The Early Constitutions

The identification of uni-textual constitutions is, most of the time, self-explanatory: the constitutional text typically contains an explicit provision designating that single document as the exclusive supreme law of the land. By contrast, such explicit assertions are rarer in the case of multi-textual constitutions. Nonetheless, there are instances in which multiple constitutional texts that share the status of higher law also recognise their shared constitutional authority. This was the case with Mexico's first Constitution, adopted in 1824.

Even though the dominant official narrative of Mexico's Founding emphasises that it was predicated on a single constitutional text – the Constitution of 1824 – in fact, Mexico's constitutional tradition was born multi-textual. Prior to the adoption of the Constitution in October of 1824,[8] the Constituent Assembly had issued in January the *Acta Constitutiva de la Federación* (The Federalist Constitutive Act),[9] which outlined the form of government, the separation of powers, and the federalist character of the nascent republic. It is interesting to see the language that these two foundational documents employ in acknowledging their respective shared constitutional authority, particularly in their provisions establishing the federal form of government, the amendment mechanism, and the explicit unamendability of specific constitutional norms. The following language from Articles 6, 24, and 35 of the Federalist Constitutive Act underscores the shared supremacy of both documents:[10]

> **Article 6.** Its constituent parts are independent, free, and sovereign states, insofar as it pertains exclusively to their internal administration and government, as detailed *in this Act and in the General Constitution.*[11]

[8] Constitución Federal de los Estados Unidos Mexicanos, 4 de Octubre de 1824 [Mexican Constitution of 1824]. See www.diputados.gob.mx/biblioteca/bibdig/const_mex/const_1824.pdf.

[9] Acta Constitutiva de la Federación, 31 de Enero de 1824 [The Federalist Constitutive Act of 1824]. See www.diputados.gob.mx/biblioteca/bibdig/const_mex/acta.pdf.

[10] ibid.

[11] ibid art 6 (emphasis added).

> **Article 24.** The constitutions of the states may not contradict *this Act nor the provisions of the General Constitution;* therefore, they may not be enacted until the latter is published.[12]
>
> **Article 34.** *The General Constitution and this Act* guarantee to the states of the federation the form of government adopted in the present law; and each state is likewise bound to uphold the federal union at all costs.[13]
>
> **Article 35.** This Act may only be amended at the time and under the terms prescribed by the General Constitution.[14]

The Constitution of 1824 followed suit with the Federalist Constitutive Act pertaining in affirming the multi-textual character of the Founding in the following terms:

> **Article 170.** To reform or add *to this constitution or the constitutive act,* all the rules shall also be observed, which are required for the formation of laws except that the president shall not have the right to make the observations of article 106.[15]
>
> **Article 171.** Those articles *of this constitution and of the constitutive act* which establish the liberty and independence of the Mexican nation, its religion, form of government, liberty of the press and the division of the supreme powers of the Union and of the states can be never be changed.[16]

A close analysis of both documents, particularly in light of the dates of their adoption, evinces that the Federalist Constitutive Act was enhanced – and in some respects completed – by the Constitution of 1824. Together, they comprised the supreme law of the land until 1836, when Mexico's founding multi-textual constitution was replaced for the first time by a uni-textual document claiming exclusive supremacy. The so-called Seven Laws of 1836[17] and the Organic Bases of 1843[18] replaced the federalist model with a centralised form of government organised into departments, following the influence of the French tradition. In the case of the 1836 Constitution, although it appears to comprise seven separate laws, each predicated on an independent document, the reality is that all seven were contained within a single constitutional text that enjoyed exclusive supremacy as higher law. Notwithstanding, the language of the 1836 Constitution introduced a degree of confusion: when outlining the amendment mechanism – the so-called *Constitutional Variations*[19] – the text spoke of the *constitutional laws* (ie, the Seven Laws comprising the Constitution), creating the impression that each was a standing-alone document, when in fact it was the opposite – as we have explained:

[12] ibid art 24 (emphasis added).
[13] ibid art 34 (emphasis added).
[14] ibid art 35.
[15] Mexican Constitution of 1824 (n 8) art 170 (emphasis added).
[16] ibid art 171 (emphasis added).
[17] Leyes Constitucionales, 29 December 1836 (Seven Constitutional Laws of 1836). See www.diputados.gob.mx/biblioteca/bibdig/const_mex/const_1836.pdf.
[18] Bases de organización política de la República mexicana, 13 June 1843 (Organic Bases of 1843). See www.diputados.gob.mx/biblioteca/bibdig/const_mex/bases-1843.pdf.
[19] These *Variations* were regulated in the Seventh Constitutional Law of 1836.

> **Article 2.** Any modifications attempted after that period shall necessarily observe the requirements set forth in Article 12, paragraph 10, of *the Second Constitutional Law*; in Article 26, paragraphs 1 and 3; in Articles 28, 29, and 38 of *the Third Constitutional Law*; and in Article 17, paragraph 2, of *the Fourth.*[20]

Despite this confusing language, it was clear that all the constitutional laws were entrenched as higher law, requiring a vote of two-thirds of Congress and a majority of the departments to enact any *variation* to a constitutional law or provision.

The Organic Bases of 1843 more explicitly established a supermajoritarian amendment mechanism, likewise requiring a two-thirds vote in Congress to approve any constitutional amendment. Its language clearly highlights the distinction between this supreme constitutional document and ordinary laws, particularly in its provisions governing amendment powers,

> **Article 202.** Alterations or reforms to these bases may be made at any time. In the laws issued on this matter, all provisions applicable to ordinary laws shall be observed, with the sole distinction that for any vote, regardless of its nature, exactly two-thirds of the votes in both Chambers shall be required – no more, no less. In these cases, the Executive shall exercise the authority granted under section 20 of Article 87.[21]

However, the uni-textual trend was interrupted by the Constitutive Act and Reforms of 1847,[22] which reinstated the constitutional regime of 1824, including its multi-textual character. Paragraph III of the Preamble to the Constitution of 1847 makes this particularly clear:

> **III.** That the Constitutive Act and the Federal Constitution, enacted on January 31 and October 24 of 1824, *together form the sole Political Constitution of the Republic.*[23]

B. The Middle Constitution

The Middle Constitution of 1857[24] was characterised by embracing a uni-textual constitutional form, but it also reveals some interesting features regarding entrenchment and the dynamics involved in shifting from multi-textual to uni-textual systems.

It is important to recall that the Middle Constitution of 1857 was preceded by the restoration of the 1847 Constitution, which itself reinstated the multi-textual constitutional regime of 1824. In addition, between 1855 and 1873, Mexico experienced a distinctive period of evolutive multi-textualism, in which the

[20] Article 2 of the Seventh Constitutional Law of 1836 (emphasis added).

[21] Article 202 of the Organic Bases of 1843.

[22] Acta Constitutiva y de Reformas Constitucionales, 18 May 1847 [Constitutive Act and Reforms of 1847]. See www.diputados.gob.mx/biblioteca/bibdig/const_mex/reformas-1847.pdf.

[23] Preamble of the Constitutive Act and Reforms of 1847, emphasis added.

[24] Constitución Federal de los Estados Unidos Mexicanos, 5 February 1857 [Mexican Constitution of 1857]. See www.diputados.gob.mx/biblioteca/bibdig/const_mex/const_1857.pdf.

Constitutions of 1847 and 1857 co-existed with the so-called Reform Laws.[25] These laws were championed by President Benito Juárez and liberal reformists who aimed at reducing the influence of the Catholic Church in political, social, and economic life. They nationalised Church property, regulated marriage as a civil contract, and established religious freedom – an act that effectively dismembered the existing constitutional order by abrogating the eternity clause that had recognised Catholicism as the sole official religion in Mexico as provided in the Constitutions of 1824 and 1847. These laws also eliminated the political and social privileges of clergy members, including their right to vote and run for public office.

The Reform Laws were deeply consequential in Mexico's constitutional development and enjoyed a quasi-constitutional status. In recognition of their growing influence on constitutional politics, President Sebastián Lerdo de Tejada – Juárez's successor – proposed to Congress a project of amendments to incorporate the Reform Laws into the text of the Constitution of 1857, thereby affirming their unequivocal constitutional authority.[26] These amendments were passed in 1873 and from then on, the Constitution of 1857 assumed a fully uni-textual form.[27]

The case of the Reform Laws and their incorporation, through the 1873 amendments, into the text of Middle Constitution of 1857 resembles what Albert describes as 'multi-textualism by consolidation,'[28] since the Reform Laws co-existed and shared constitutional supremacy – between 1855 and 1873 – with the existing Constitutions of 1847 and 1857, respectively.[29]

Additionally, the Middle Constitution of 1857 introduced a provision pertaining to the supremacy clause which, in light of Albert's distinction between uni-textual and multi-textual constitutions, may appear both confusing and problematic:

> **Article 126.** This Constitution, the laws of the Congress of the Union enacted pursuant thereto, and all treaties made or to be made by the President of the Republic with the approval of Congress, shall be the Supreme Law of the entire Union. The judges in every State shall be bound by said Constitution, laws, and treaties, notwithstanding any provisions to the contrary that may exist in the Constitutions or laws of the States.[30]

As we will see, the ramifications of this textual ambiguity proved particularly challenging in clarifying the constitutional form of Mexico, not only in the case of the Middle Constitution, but even more importantly, in the Modern Constitution of

[25] I Flores, 'La Constitución de 1857 y sus reformas: A 150 años de su promulgación' in D Valadés and M Carbonell (eds), *El proceso constituyente mexicano. A 150 años de la Constitución de 1857 y 90 de la Constitución de 1917* (Universidad Nacional Autónoma de México, Instituto de Investigaciones Jurídicas, 2007) 292–316, 320–24 archivos.juridicas.unam.mx/www/bjv/libros/5/2389/12.pdf.

[26] ibid 296–98.

[27] J Olaiz-González, 'Caught between. On the Distinctive Character of Mexico's Model of Amendment Codification' in R Albert (ed), *The Architecture of Constitutional Amendments: History, Law, and Politics* (Hart Publishing, 2023). This article explores in more depth the integrative mode of codification of the Reform Laws when they were incorporated to the text of the Constitution of 1857.

[28] Albert (n 1) 1647–48.

[29] F Serrano Migallón, *La Constitución Política de la República Mexicana de 1857 y las Leyes de Reforma* (Secretaría de Gobernación, 2015) 108–14.

[30] Mexican Constitution of 1857 (n 24) art 126 (emphasis added).

1917. The language of Article 126 of the Constitution of 1857 was carried over verbatim into Article 133 of the Constitution of 1917.[31] On its face, this provision appears to support a multi-textual reading of the Mexican constitutional order, since it grants constitutional supremacy to a combination of sources: the constitutional text of 1917, the laws enacted by Congress under its authority, and the treaties made by the President with Congress' approval. Altogether, these are to be regarded as 'the Supreme Law of the Union.' However, this language is ultimately misleading for several reasons.

First, notwithstanding that this provision explicitly requires that the enactment of federal laws be pursuant to the Constitution, it was not clear that the laws of Congress enacted in accordance to the Constitution were not at the same hierarchical level of it, that they were not subordinated to it, since the very language of Article 133 treating them 'as the supreme law of the Union,' provided the opposite: that altogether with the treaties approved by the Senate, they should be regarded as the supreme law of the land with shared constitutional supremacy.

Second, and unlike the clause governing laws enacted by Congress, the provision is silent on whether the treaties made by the President and approved by the Senate should be pursuant to the Constitution. This omission creates further ambiguity, and as we will see, these confusions eventually necessitated clarification by the Supreme Court, which affirmed the exclusive supremacy of the Constitution and the subordination of both congressional laws and international treaties to it. As we will explore in the next section, both constitutional practice and judicial interpretation played an important role in resolving this conundrum.

III. The Modern Constitution of 1917: Embracing Uni-Textualism

The regime inaugurated by the Constitution of 1917 was characterised by the coexistence of two seemingly contradictory elements: the formal preservation of the multi-textual system articulated in Article 133, and the effective consolidation of a uni-textual model as the dominant operational code of Mexico's constitutional politics. In a nutshell, while the Constitution formally established multi-textualism, as we are about to explain in this section, uni-textualism became, in practice the de facto exclusive constitutional form.

[31] Constitución Federal de los Estados Unidos Mexicanos, 5 February 1917 (Mexican Constitution of 1917). *See* www.diputados.gob.mx/LeyesBiblio/ref/cpeum/CPEUM_orig_05feb1917_ima.pdf. Article 133 provided: 'This Constitution, the laws derived from the and enacted by the Congress of the Union, and all the treaties made and execute by the President of the Republic, with the approval of Congress, *shall be the supreme law of the country*. The judges of each state shall observe the Constitution, the laws derived from it and the treaties, despite any contradictory provision that may appear in the constitutions or laws of the states' (emphasis added).

Mexico's enduring formalist legal tradition, combined with single-party rule between the 1920s and the mid-to-late 1990s, produced a political climate in which separation of powers was merely nominal and the Constitution functioned mainly as a symbolic instrument.[32] The Supreme Court played a limited role, focusing mainly on private adjudication, and, along with a deferential legislative branch, routinely rubber-stamped the policies and legislation promoted by the Executive, which concentrated nearly all political authority.[33] The other branches were expected to serve merely as passive transmission belts for presidential directives.

Against this backdrop, the confusion created by the wording of Article 133 regarding the supremacy clause and its multi-textual implications – particularly the alleged shared authority of federal legislation and treaties with the Constitution – was addressed in two ways.

In the case of federal legislation, it was the legislative process itself and the application and enforcement of these laws that gave rise to a kind of rule of recognition.[34] Through this consistent and widely accepted practice, all political actors and officials came to acknowledge that these laws – notwithstanding the language of Article 133 – were hierarchically subordinated to the Constitution and did not in any sense shared constitutional supremacy with it.

With respect to the status of treaties in the constitutional order, it became necessary for the Supreme Court to ascertain whether those made by the President and approved by the Senate were at the same level as the Constitution and federal legislation, as Article 133 suggests. Assuming a hierarchical, formalist, and centralist view of constitutional supremacy, the Court's early interpretations placed treaties not only below the Constitution but also subordinate to federal laws.

Hence, the formal but misleading appearance of multi-textualism in Article 133 was eventually clarified and rejected. The constitutional hierarchy was established as follows: the Constitution stands as the exclusive supreme law of the land, followed by federal legislation enacted in accordance with it, and then international treaties – subject first to congressional approval, and, after a 1934 amendment to Article 133, to Senate approval.

Eventually, this hierarchy would change during the transformative 1990s, when the Court first recognised that treaties shared the same hierarchy as federal laws,[35] and finally concluded that, because treaties are made on behalf of the Mexican State, approved by the Senate as a representative of the federal pact and negotiated at the federal level, they should be considered superior to federal laws.[36]

[32] J Ramón Cossío Díaz, *Sistemas y modelos de control constitucional en México* (Universidad Nacional Autónoma de México, Instituto de Investigaciones Jurídicas, 2017) 33–90.

[33] ibid 84–90.

[34] Albert (n 1) 1653–55. The rule of recognition is what Albert describes in this article as 'political practice.'

[35] G del Semanario Judicial de la Federación, Pleno de la Suprema Corte de Justicia de la Nación, *Tesis Aislada P. C/92,* December 1992, at sjf2.scjn.gob.mx/detalle/tesis/205596. This precedent established that treaties and federal laws shared equal normative status.

[36] Semanario Judicial de la Federación y su Gaceta, Pleno de la Suprema Corte de Justicia de la Nación, *Tesis Aislada P. LXXVII/99,* November 1999, at sjf2.scjn.gob.mx/detalle/tesis/192867.

IV. The Constitutional Transformations of 1994 until 2011: Shifting to Multi-Textual Gear

This hierarchical framework, which had long reinforced the de facto dominance of uni-textualism despite the formal multi-textual language of Article 133, persisted until 1992, when the Mexican judiciary began experiencing a radical overhaul, which some scholars have described as a constitutional revolution.[37] That year, the Reformative Power of the Constitution enacted a consequential amendment that elevated the status of the Supreme Court to a full-fledged constitutional court with plenary powers of judicial review, establishing it as the ultimate custodian and interpreter of the Constitution and the final arbiter of constitutional disputes between branches of government and the states.

This institutional transformation coincided with the consolidation of a long process of political liberalisation that paved the way for the end of single-party rule and the deconcentration of political power formerly concentrated in the Executive branch.[38] Over time, political power was gradually redistributed among the legislative and judicial branches, the states, and various constitutional agencies. This redistribution established a more decentralised system, grounded in political plurality and judicial independence and aimed at the effective protection of rights. The Supreme Court became instrumental in preserving this new democratic configuration. This broader process was also characterised by growing societal demands for the effective protection of rights against government abuse, further shaping the Court's evolving function.

Empowered with an unprecedented mandate for judicial scrutiny, the Court embarked on a gradual revision of the hierarchical relationship between federal laws and treaties within the constitutional framework. Departing from the dominant approach that had governed for decades interpretation of the supremacy clause, the Court set an influential precedent in *Tesis Aislada 9/1999*, holding that 'international treaties occupy a position above federal statutes and below the Constitution.'[39] This marked a turning point, initiating a drastic constitutional change that disrupted the entrenched practice of constitutional uni-textualism. This process was reinforced by a landmark decision from the Inter-American Court of Human Rights (the Inter-American Court).

A. The Radilla Pacheco Case

The wave of constitutional change in Mexico was triggered from abroad by a momentous decision of the Inter-American Court in the *Radilla Pacheco* case. Involving the forced disappearance of a Mexican social activist in the 1970s, the

[37] Cossío Díaz (n 32) 91–162.

[38] Olaiz-González (n 7).

[39] Semanario Judicial de la Federación y su Gaceta, Pleno de la Suprema Corte de Justicia de la Nación, *Tesis Aislada P. LXXVII/99,* November 1999, at sjf2.scjn.gob.mx/detalle/tesis/192867.

case marked a watershed in the interaction between the American human rights system and Mexico's constitutional framework. The decision established, among other things, that the crime of forced disappearance is continuous in nature, imposing an ongoing obligation on the State to investigate the victim's whereabouts and prosecute those responsible. Failure to do so would incur international responsibility, as it did in this case.

This decision triggered a normative earthquake in Mexico's constitutional system. In response to this and subsequent decisions,[40] the Supreme Court expanded the constitutionally progressive interpretative approach it had initiated in 1999. It marked a decisive shift in Mexico's constitutional jurisprudence, compelling courts, particularly the Supreme Court, to reconceptualise the constitutional status of international human rights obligations and the State's responsibilities under them. This critical jurisprudential shift laid the groundwork for one of the most significant constitutional transformations in Mexico: the Human Rights Reform of 2011, which, in Richard Albert's terms, constituted a genuine constitutional dismemberment.[41]

As the following section will show, the Inter-American Court's decisions became an integral building block of constitutional change in Mexico, with major implications for its constitutional form.

V. The Constitutional Amendment on Human Rights of 2011: The Case of Evolutive Multi-Textualism by Formal Amendment and Judicial Interpretation

The great leap towards multi-textualism came in the form of a constitutional amendment that, due to its sweeping departure from traditional formalism, amounted to a progressive and evolutive constitutional dismemberment.[42]

This momentous amendment, passed in 2011, inaugurated a new constitutional regime within the original text of the Constitution of 1917 by introducing two radical changes in its language and, consequently, in its operational code: a revised first paragraph of Article 1 and the addition of two new ones. These changes established a new constitutional canon based on shared supremacy between the Constitution and the international human rights treaties ratified by Mexico.

The amendment elevated to constitutional status all human rights treaties ratified by the Mexican Senate and incorporated a very innovative formula grounded

[40] To comply with this momentous decision from the Inter-American Court of Human Rights, Mexico's Supreme Court integrated the so-called *Expediente Varios 912/2010,* that established an illustrative precedent on a good practice of judicial performance to comply with international rulings on human rights.

[41] R Albert, *Constitutional Amendments: Making, Breaking, and Changing Constitutions* (Oxford University Press, 2019) 61–86.

[42] J Olaiz-González and J Mario de la Garza, 'Through the Looking Glass: Towards a Classification of Constitutional Dismemberments in Mexico' in R Albert (ed), *Comparative Constitutional Reform in Latin America* (Routledge) (forthcoming).

in the *pro persona* principle, which mandates that the norm most favourable and protective of the individual must prevail in the event of a contradiction or conflict between such treaties and the Constitution. This elevation was predicated on the revised language of Article 1, which encapsulated the core transformative contents of the amendment.[43] To appreciate the magnitude of this change, we may contrast the previous and revised versions of Article 1:

> **[Prior to the Amendment of 2011]**
>
> **Article 1.** In the United Mexican States, every individual shall enjoy the guarantees granted by this Constitution, which may not be restricted or suspended except in the cases and under the conditions established herein.
>
> **[Language of the Amendment of 2011]**
>
> **Article 1.** In the United Mexican States, all persons shall enjoy the human rights **recognized in this Constitution and in the international treaties to which the Mexican State is a party,** as well as the guarantees for their protection, whose exercise may not be restricted or suspended except in the cases and under the conditions established in this Constitution.
>
> **[Additions]**
>
> The norms relating to human rights shall be interpreted in accordance with this Constitution and with the relevant international treaties, **favoring the broadest protection of individuals at all times.**
>
> All authorities, within their competence, have the obligation to promote, respect, protect, and guarantee human rights in accordance with the principles of universality, interdependence, indivisibility, and progressiveness. Consequently, the State must prevent, investigate, sanction, and repair human rights violations in the terms established by law.[44]

Surprisingly, Article 133 remained intact despite the hierarchical revolution introduced by the amendment to Article 1, retaining the original language of the 1917 Constitution:

> **Article 133.** This Constitution, the laws derived from the and enacted by the Congress of the Union, and all the treaties made and execute by the President of the Republic, with the approval of the Senate, shall be the supreme law of the country. The judges of each state shall observe the Constitution, the laws derived from it and the treaties, despite any contradictory provision that may appear in the constitutions or laws of the states.[45]

[43] J Olaiz-González, 'La Reforma al Artículo 1ro. en materia de derechos humanos como desmembramiento constitucional: una alternativa para la mutabilidad constitucional incremental' in H Ramírez García and J María Soberanes Díez (eds), *El artículo 1° constitucional: la teoría constitucional de los derechos humanos* (Universidad Nacional Autónoma de México, Instituto de Investigaciones Jurídicas, 2021) 349–82.

[44] Article 1 of the Mexican Constitution of 1917, as amended by decree on 10 June 2011 (emphasis added).

[45] Article 133 of the Mexican Constitution of 1917. It is worth noting that this provision has been amended only once, in 1934, reflecting the allocation in the Senate of the approval powers of international treaties. In the original text of the Constitution, Article 133 referred in broader terms to Congress, and not to the Senate.

Notwithstanding the fact that Article 133 was not amended – as we are about to see – it was recontextualised within a broader human rights framework and came to function more as a gateway to constitutional pluralism than as a narrow clause of legal supremacy. In this case, it appears that the Reformative Power of the Constitution chose to rely on the Supreme Court's clarifying role to reinterpret the provision, instead of amending its text through the 2011 reform.

The amendment to Article 1 marked the culmination of an extended process not only of political liberalisation and institutional consolidation, but also the deep and gradual incorporation of new normative and jurisprudential trends aimed at a more effective and comprehensive protection of rights within a liberal democracy framework. It signaled a paradigm shift in both the judicial role and the legal profession.[46] Both judges and attorneys had to prepare themselves to navigate this new regime characterised by the shared supremacy of the Constitution and international human rights treaties, with the protection of human dignity at its core.[47] As we are about to see, the amendment created a two-pronged system in which domestic constitutional norms and international human rights obligations were expected to function in coordination to broaden the scope and effectiveness of human rights protection in Mexico, consistent with the great compact of international human rights law.

Very soon, the Supreme Court assumed a leading role in implementing this new constitutional regime. Through its jurisprudence, it developed a new grammar of constitutional harmonisation and established a revised operational code centered on what came to be known as the *block of constitutionality*.[48] Judicial interpretation thus became the vehicle for giving full effect to the amendment, leading to the articulation of three basic concepts now underpinning the Court's human rights jurisprudence. The differentiation of these concepts – each with distinct normative scope, function, and interpretive implications – was crucial and illustrated the Court's views on the evolving multilevel constitutionalism framework.

A. The Block of Constitutionality

The block of constitutionality refers to a body of constitutional norms that, while not all located within the original constitutional text, are considered to have constitutional rank, thus serving as authoritative parameters for interpreting constitutional provisions. This doctrine, inspired by similar constructions in other

[46] H Fix-Fierro and J Martínez-Uriarte, *Derechos humanos. Cien años de evolución de los derechos en la Constitución mexicana* (México, Fondo de Cultura Económica, 2018).

[47] P Salazar (coord.), *La reforma constitucional sobre derechos humanos. Una guía conceptual* (Instituto Belisario Domínguez, Senado de la República, 2014) 19–20.

[48] A Pozas-Loyo, C Saavedra-Herrera and F Pou-Giménez, 'When Lore Leads to More: Constitutional Amendments and Interpretation in Mexico 1917–2020,' (2023) 48(2) *Law & Social Inquiry* 1–32.

Latin American countries such as Colombia, Brazil, and Argentina,[49] was judicially recognised and consolidated in *Contradicción de tesis 293/2011*.[50]

The block of constitutionality comprises the original constitutional text – particularly its substantive provisions on rights protection and the preservation of constitutional democracy, international human rights treaties ratified by the Senate, federal statutes deriving directly from constitutional mandates, and relevant Supreme Court precedents. Together, these components serve both as an interpretive framework and a normative extension of the Constitution, enabling courts to scrutinise the compatibility of laws not only with the Constitution itself but also with this broader set of constitutionally ranked norms, all claiming constitutional supremacy.

B. The Standard of Constitutional Regularity

This standard of constitutional regularity serves as the methodological benchmark against which the validity and constitutionality of legal norms and state actions are assessed. It includes both the constitutional text and norms of equivalent hierarchy, including those within the block of constitutionality. The Supreme Court has established that any law, regulation, administrative act, or even judicial decision may be measured against this standard to determine its conformity to constitutional mandates.

Unlike the block of constitutionality or the block of conventionality, which denote substantive sets of norms, the standard of constitutional regularity is a procedural or analytical framework that guides constitutional control or scrutiny. Under this standard, a federal law may be challenged before the Supreme Court on grounds of incompatibility, using both the Constitution and applicable treaty norms as points of reference.

C. The Block of Conventionality

The block of conventionality is the most distinctive feature of Mexico's multi-textual constitutional mix, referring to the body of international human rights law – particularly the American Convention on Human Rights and the interpretative decisions of the Inter-American Court – that domestic judges are obliged to observe and apply.

[49] These Latin American countries incorporated human rights treaties into their constitutional framework in the last decade of the past century. Colombia did it by design in the Constitution of 1991, whereas Argentina and Brazil did it by evolution via formal amendments in 1994 and 1998, respectively.

[50] Semanario Judicial de la Federación y su Gaceta, Pleno de la Suprema Corte de Justicia de la Nación, *Contradicción de tesis 293/2011*, 3 September 2013, at www2.scjn.gob.mx/ConsultaTematica/PaginasPub/DetallePub.aspx?AsuntoID=129659.

The Supreme Court explicitly recognised this doctrine following the *Radilla Pacheco* decision[51] and strengthened it in key rulings such as *Contradicción de tesis 293/2011* and *Contradicción de tesis 21/2011*,[52] which established the obligation of conventionality control. Its function is to ensure that domestic law conforms to international human rights obligations, particularly when domestic norms are ambiguous, silent, or in conflict with treaty-based standards. Judges at all levels are obligated to perform ex officio conventionality control, assessing whether the norms or acts they apply align with human rights treaties and the jurisprudence of the Inter-American Court. While its scope overlaps with the block of constitutionality, it is particularly relevant when treaty norms offer broader protections than the Constitution.

Therefore, the clearest expression of the new multi-textual regime is the recognition of both blocks – of constitutionality and conventionality – as equally authoritative standards for ascertaining constitutional regularity. The interplay among these three frameworks reflects the Supreme Court's move toward a multi-normative and pluralist constitutional model that, in the spirit of the 2011 amendment, blurred rigid hierarchies and promoted interoperability between constitutional and international human rights law.

In sum, the momentous shift from uni-textualism to multi-textualism triggered by the 2011 amendment exemplifies Albert's evolutive multi-textualism,[53] but with an interesting twist: it began at Time One via formal amendment,[54] became fully entrenched at Time Two via judicial interpretation,[55] and, as the next section will show, was later put to test by foreign courts.

VI. The Risks of Multi-Textualism: The Problem of Internalisation of International Human Rights Law

It is no exaggeration that the 2011 amendment inaugurated the richest period of constitutional interpretation and adjudication in the modern history of the Supreme Court and federal judiciary.[56] It ushered in a new paradigm that required judges to develop analytical tools to reconcile the language of the Constitution and the contents of the panoply of applicable treaties, generating an outstanding progeny of precedents aimed at maximising human rights protection. In light of the depth and enduring impact of its jurisprudence, it is fair to describe the period between 2011 and 2024 – when the constitutional separation of powers began

[51] *Radilla Pacheco v Mexico*, Judgment, Inter-Am Ct H R (ser C) Num 209 (23 November 2009).

[52] Semanario Judicial de la Federación y su Gaceta, Pleno de la Suprema Corte de Justicia de la Nación, *Contradicción de tesis 21/2011*, 9 September 2013, at www2.scjn.gob.mx/ConsultaTematica/PaginasPub/DetallePub.aspx?AsuntoID=124100.

[53] Albert (n 1) 1649–59.

[54] ibid 1650–52.

[55] ibid 1656–59.

[56] Fix-Fierro and Martínez-Uriarte (n 46).

to unravel under a populist governing coalition – as the Gilded Age of Mexico's Supreme Court.

This process of domestic jurisprudential refinement and consolidation was accompanied by the growing influence from the Inter-American System for the Protection of Human Rights, especially through several salient decisions of the Inter-American Court against Mexico. These cases addressed the practices of the so-called *arraigo* and preventive or pre-trial detention, both of which were authorised by domestic criminal statutes and, at the time, embedded in the constitutional text – though the *arraigo* was eventually removed. Specifically, Article 19 of the Mexican Constitution mandated judges to impose automatic pre-trial imprisonment for a list of specific crimes. As we are about to see, this mandate conflicted with the block of conventionality.

Both practices – *arraigo* and automatic pre-trial detention – constituted unjustified deprivations of personal liberty and violations of due process. Their indeterminate duration and lack of legal substantiation contravened the rights provided in the American Convention on Human Rights. The Inter-American Court confirmed these violations in two momentous decisions with major ramifications in Mexico's constitutional system.

The first case, *Tzompaxtle Tecpile et al. v Mexico*,[57] involved the unlawful and arbitrary detention of Jorge Marcial Tzompaxtle Tecpile, Gerardo Tzompaxtle Tecpile, and Gustavo Robles López by Federal Police agents when the victims were stopped on the road between Veracruz and Mexico City. The Inter-American Court found that the State had violated multiple rights, including personal liberty, the presumption of innocence, the right not to self-incriminate, the right to a fair trial, and the right to judicial protection. It also declared that Mexico had failed to adapt the domestic legal provisions required by Article 2 of the Convention. The Court ordered Mexico to annul its domestic provisions authorising pre-procedural *arraigo* and to align its legal framework on pre-trial detention with the rights and obligations provided in the American Convention.[58] Notably, the Court referred broadly to 'domestic legislation' without further specifications pertaining to the hierarchy of the provisions – either at a constitutional or statutory level – to be adapted. As we are about to see, that changed with the *García Rodríguez* case.

The second case, *García Rodríguez et al. v Mexico*,[59] involved Daniel García Rodríguez and Reyes Alpízar Ortiz, who were held in pre-trial detention for more than 17 years. The Court declared that both *arraigo* and pre-trial detention violated numerous rights, including personal liberty, the right to be heard, the presumption of innocence, equality before the law, and judicial guarantees. It again concluded that Mexico had failed to fulfil its obligations under Article 2 of the Convention and ordered the repeal of domestic legal provisions relating to pre-procedural *arraigo* and pre-trial detention. But the Court initiated an unprecedented dynamic

[57] *Tzompaxtle Tecpile et al. v Mexico*, Judgment, Inter-Am Ct H R (ser C) Num 470 (7 November 2022).
[58] ibid 56–57 at [253].
[59] *García Rodríguez et al. v Mexico*, Judgment, Inter-Am Ct H R (ser C) Num 482 (25 January 2023).

by ordering, for the first time in explicit terms, that Mexico adapt its legal system, *including its constitutional provisions* via formal amendment, to bring it to conformity with the Convention:

> **301.** With regard to the concept of mandatory pre-trial detention, this Court orders the State, as it has done in other cases, 279 to adapt its legal system, **including its constitutional provisions,** so that it is compatible with the American Convention. For such purposes, the State must take into consideration the provisions of paragraphs 154-163 and 184 of this judgment, which establish the requirements that such measures must satisfy in order to be compatible with said treaty.[60]

Incorporating these two decisions into Mexico's legal system – an illustrative example of what Harold Koh describes as the internalisation of international law[61] – entailed a series of difficulties that required the compliance of Congress. For the first time, the Inter-American Court ordered Mexico to implement all levels of legislative changes, including amending the Constitution, to harmonise its constitutional framework – Article 19 in particular – with the American Convention of Human Rights. After months of deliberate delay, however, the governing coalition in Congress openly defied the Court's mandate. Instead of narrowing or repealing Article 19, it adopted an amendment expanding the list of offenses subject to automatic pre-trail detention, and therefore broadening the application of a measure that was unequivocally rejected by the Inter-American Court as inconsistent with the rights and principles of the American Convention of Human Rights. This intransigent stance by Mexico's political elite was unprecedented, setting the country on a regressive path toward reinstating a uni-textual constitutional form that, in practice, seeks to abrogate the multi-textual system created by the 2011 human rights amendment.

This section demonstrates the dynamics set in motion by contemporary practices of multi-textualism, which involve not only dialogue between the legislature and the judiciary, but also at times a contentious exchange with foreign courts. These dynamics show that multi-textualism is not only an academic concept, but also a practical issue of the utmost relevance when assessing the performative dimension of constitutional forms.

VII. Back to Uni-Textualism: The 2024 Amendment on Constitutional Supremacy

The 2024 constitutional supremacy amendment to Article 105 materialised Mexico's regression to a uni-textual constitutional model. By barring judicial review of constitutional amendments and restricting the *erga omnes* effects of *amparo* judgments,

[60] ibid 76 at [301].
[61] H Hongju Koh, 'The 1994 Roscoe Pound Lecture: Transnational Legal Process' (1996) 75 *Nebraska Law Review* 181.

the reform stripped away the plural normative foundations that had briefly launched Mexico into contemporary multi-textualism. In particular, it explicitly renders all constitutional amendments unchallengeable before the Supreme Court: constitutional controversies (*controversias constitucionales*), actions of unconstitutionality (*acciones de inconstitucionalidad*), and *amparo* trial (*juicio de amparo*) 'that aim to contest additions or reforms to the Constitution' are now procedurally inadmissible.[62] By the same token, the amended Amparo Law mandates that when a court strikes down a statute as unconstitutional, the ruling 'only benefits the involved parties, without general effects.' These changes dismantle the core mechanisms of the prior multi-textual regime: substantive judicial review of constitutional changes and the *erga omnes* reach of rights-protective judgments.[63]

This reform represents a strategic consolidation of constitutional power in the hands of the governing majority, with decidedly authoritarian overtones. By insulating the constitutional text, as amended by the majority, from judicial scrutiny, the reform entrenches the majority's will as the *only* source of higher law. Proponents explicitly invoke a majoritarian mandate to justify this overhaul, effectively placing the political majority's will above the Constitution itself. Such reasoning is emblematic of contemporary democratic backsliding: under the guise of 'supremacy,' a dominant coalition uses legal change to weaken checks and balances and concentrate power.[64] By foreclosing external or counter-majoritarian inputs in constitutional governance, the reform moves Mexico's system away from the dialogic dynamics of multi-textualism and toward majoritarian unilateralism.

The result is a constitutional order where pluralism and normative dialogism are severely eroded. Under the previous multi-textual model, multiple authoritative texts and actors could interact in defining supreme law – for example, domestic judges applying international human rights treaties or jurisprudence as supreme constitutional norms. This created a space for normative dialogue between the Constitution and international human rights law, between courts and the legislature, and even between national and supranational judicial bodies. That interplay is now systematically curtailed. The political majority's absolute control over the constitutional text reigns supreme and uncontested, shutting down the reciprocal influences that once animated multi-textual constitutionalism's vision of higher law pluralism.

Between 2011 and 2024, Mexico's constitutional system exhibited quintessential features of multi-textualism: a plurality of texts (the Constitution and human rights

[62] Decreto por el que se reforma el primer párrafo de la fracción II del articulo 107, y se adiciona un quinto párrafo al artículo 105, de la Constitución Política de los Estados Unidos Mexicanos, en materia de inimpugnabilidad de las adiciones o reformas a la Constitución Federal. See dof.gob.mx/nota_detalle.php?codigo=5742105&fecha=31/10/2024#gsc.tab=0.

[63] Decreto por el que se reforman y derogan diversas disposiciones de la Ley de Amparo, Reglamentaria de los artículos 103 y 107 de la Constitución Política de los Estados Unidos Mexicanos. See dof.gob.mx/nota_detalle.php?codigo=5751769&fecha=13/03/2025#gsc.tab=0.

[64] A Aguiar Aguilar, R Castro Cornejo and A Monsiváis-Carrillo, 'Is Mexico at the Gates of Authoritarianism?' (2025) 36(1) *Journal of Democracy* 50–64, dx.doi.org/10.1353/jod.2025.a947883.

treaties) sharing the apex of the legal hierarchy, and multiple interpreters (domestic and international courts) engaged in shaping constitutional identity. However, recent political developments have steadily eroded this spirit. The past decade, especially under the current administration, has been marked by concerted efforts to re-centralise constitutional authority and curtail judicial autonomy. Even before the 2024 amendment, the Supreme Court had largely deferred to the Constituent Power doctrine, treating constitutional amendment power as inherently sovereign and beyond substantive judicial scrutiny. Sporadic progressive voices on the Court urged recognition of implicit limits on the reform power by invoking basic structural principles, but these remained a minority view.[65]

In consequence, the Mexican Constitution now embodies a rigid and centralist uni-textual model. The constitutional text, as amended by the political majority, is treated as the exclusive source of supreme law, insulated from any external normative challenge or override. In Albert's framework, Mexico has journeyed 'there and back again' between constitutional forms, shifting from a traditionally uni-textual regime, to a brief decade-long experiment of multi-textualism after 201,1 and now returning decisively to uni-textual orthodoxy. Under the current model, all constitutional authority converges on a single constitutional text that admits no peer. International human rights treaties and jurisprudence, once approaching equal footing with the Constitution, have been relegated to a subordinate status, effectively stripped of any constraining force on legislators or the reformative power. Judicial rulings, no matter how principled, cannot alter or annul what the constitutional text, as amended, prescribes beyond the individual case at hand. The normative ecosystem of Mexican constitutionalism has thus contracted dramatically – it is monological rather than dialogical, with the constitutional text, as defined by those in political power, monopolising the conversation.

This system is 'rigid' in that it fortifies the formal amendment process as the sole avenue for legal change: once an amendment is approved by the required majority, neither courts nor international norms may scrutinise it. It is 'centralist' in that it concentrates ultimate interpretative and lawmaking authority in the federal center – specifically in the dominant coalition – sidelining the dialogic processes that once gave voice to minority perspectives and transnational standards.

In sum, the 2024 supremacy reform marked a definitive break from the plural, multi-textual constitutionalism that Mexico briefly embraced over the past decade. What remains is a unitary constitutional order governed by a majoritarian logic of supremacy. The Constitution, amendable at will by a supermajority, has become supreme, exclusive, and beyond normative challenge. This shift carries profound implications: it consolidates an authoritarian tilt in Mexico's constitutional trajectory and extinguishes the pluralist promise of the 2011 reforms. The reversion to uni-textualism may insulate the incumbent majority's

[65] M Velasco-Rivera and J Colón-Ríos, 'On the Legal Implications of a 'Permanent' Constituent Power' (2023) 12(2) *Global Constitutionalism* 269–97, doi.org/10.1017/S2045381722000223.

constitutional agenda from external interference, but it does so at the expense of core democratic safeguards: pluralism, institutional balance, and external checks that had begun to take root as counterweights to absolute textual supremacy. Mexico's constitutional framework, once cautiously open to multiple sources of higher law, has swung back to a single-text focus, leaving the constitutional text 'supreme' in theory, and the majority's power supreme in practice. The long-term consequences of this rigid uni-textual turn will unfold in the years to come, but its immediate effect is clear: a more closed and hierarchical constitutional order, dominated by political fiat and stripped of the normative space that once allowed for the plural dialogues essential to a healthy multi-textual constitutional democracy.

VIII. Conclusion: There and Back Again – The Case of Performative Uni-Textualism

Mexico's constitutional evolution – beginning as a multi-textual system in 1824, interrupted by a shift to uni-textualism from 1836 to 1846, reinstated, at least formally, as multi-textual from 1847 to 1917, followed by the consolidation of a symbolic uni-textual tradition from 1917 to 1994, transformed by the momentous constitutional reforms of 1994 and 2011, and ultimately reversed by the reinstallation of uni-textualism in 2024 – reveals the dynamic character of constitutional forms and their inherent challenges and possibilities.

'There and Back Again,' the subtitle of J.R.R. Tolkien's *The Hobbit*,[66] aptly captures Mexico's latest shift from the multi-textual constitutional regime established by the 2011 human rights amendment to a de facto uni-textual system in which relevant political actors and institutions overtly defy decisions from the Inter-American Court – decisions that, under the rule of recognition and the jurisprudence of the 2011 regime, enjoyed constitutional authority.

The constitutional transformations of the past quarter-century in Mexico were of epic scale, instrumental in shaping the country into a full-fledged constitutional democracy. A shift of this magnitude required an evolution from its simplistic constitutional form of uni-textualism to a much more sophisticated and challenging one such as multi-textualism, achieved through consequential formal amendments and key judicial interpretations – both domestic and international. This new multi-textualism consolidated two blocks of shared supremacy: the block of constitutionality and the block of conventionality. Altogether, this mix enhanced the protection of human rights in Mexico – until a dark period of constitutional regression steered the system back to a uni-textual track, with gradual obliteration of the legacy of the 2011 human rights amendment.

[66] JRR Tolkien, *The Hobbit: Or There and Back Again* (Allen and Unwin, 1937).

If this process teaches us anything, it is that constitutional transformations – like social change – unfold along a continuum,[67] an inherently dialectic process marked by both progress and retrogression.[68] Therefore, the most pressing challenge for present and future generations of lawyers and judges is to persevere in finding creative ways to preserve the multi-textual constitutional form, broaden the scope for rights protection in Mexico, and ultimately, strengthen its constitutional system.

[67] W Michael Reisman, S Wiessner and AR Willard, 'The New Haven School: A Brief Introduction' (2007) 32 *Yale Journal of International Law* 575.

[68] W Michael Reisman, 'Development and Nation Building: A Framework for a Policy-Oriented Inquiry' (2008) 60 *Maine Law Review* 311. In this article, Michael Reisman contends that '[From] a policy-oriented perspective, not all change is considered development; changes incompatible with human dignity can be characterized as retrogressions or as "disdevelopmental."'

8

The Tradition of Multi-Textuality in Poland

NATALIE FOX[†]

I. Introduction

In the history of Polish constitutional law, the term 'Small Constitutions' has been commonly used to refer to temporary constitutional acts that played a crucial role in transitional periods. Notably, this term was not introduced by the legislator but emerged in common usage, becoming an integral part of Polish political and constitutional doctrine. This phenomenon is closely linked to three key periods of constitutional transformation in which Poland has resorted strategically to multi-textuality. First, in 1919, before World War II, the newly independent Republic of Poland required an interim legal framework before establishing a stable constitutional order. Second, in 1947, just after World War II, the political landscape was dominated by the growing influence of communist forces, necessitating legal adjustments that paved the way for a socialist system. Third, in 1992, the transition from communism to democracy required a temporary constitutional arrangement to facilitate systemic change while ensuring stability after the collapse of the Soviet Union. Throughout all three distinguishable periods of constitutional transformation, the constitution-making process experienced delays. The primary objective was the adoption of a new full constitution where all constitutional matters were included into a single, one binding document of the highest position within the domestic legal order. Consequently, legislative measures adopted in the mentioned transitional periods were of a provisional nature and inherently incomplete in their content. Thus, the constitutional framework comprised of several

[†] The theses of this chapter were presented during the Ninth Annual Conference of the International Society of Public Law ICON·S (titled 'Island and Ocean: Public Law in a Plural World') held in New Zealand at the Te Herenga Waka – Victoria University of Wellington (3–5 July 2023). The publication has also been supported by funds from the Faculty of Law and Administration, Jagiellonian University, granted within the Priority Research Area Society of the Future under the Excellence Initiative – Research University programme at the university.

constitutional acts and political documents, each regulating a different aspect of constitutional matters, together forming a composed constitution.

This chapter provides a topical and contextual outline of the multi-textuality of Poland's Small Constitutions, which is associated with the transition periods and the dispersion of various written acts of the constitution. Enacted during periods of political transformation, the Small Constitutions of 1919, 1947, and 1992 served as temporary constitutional provisions regulating the foundations of the political system. Naming the designation of each act of constitutional significance as a Small Constitution applies exactly in practice to one resolution and two statutes. Instead, the constitutional order was derived from multiple coexisting acts that collectively shaped the framework of the state's functioning. This phenomenon resulted from both political and legal circumstances, as well as the desire for an evolutionary change of the state system, which required a gradual adjustment of existing regulations. First, it should be emphasised that Small Constitutions created at different historical moments reflecting diverse content and varying levels of detail, but also they had some common features. They regulated only a part of the matter under scrutiny usually being the subject of constitutional regulation, and were intended to be temporary, resulting primarily from the period and circumstances in which they were created. Moreover, they undoubtedly fell within the scope of constitutional acts, resulting from their positions in the legal system in force at a given time, from their contents, and sometimes from their names. Second, Small Constitutions did not replace existing constitutions, but many acts or political documents of constitutional rank were in force at that same time. The drafters of this interim constitutional acts consistently regarded them as provisional and contingent legal instruments, intended to regulate the fundamental principles of the state system only until the adoption of a permanent formal constitutional act. The period of their applicability provided an opportunity to test new state system, including governmental structures and assess the adequacy of the adopted legal provisions. Naturally, the Small Constitutions established the legal framework for the functioning of the state during transitional periods. However, constitutional practice did not always align with the normative assumptions of these acts, as political conditions ultimately played a decisive role.

II. Drivers of Multi-Textuality

Upon the restoration of Poland's Independence Day on 11 November 1918, after 123 years of partitions, the statehood was reborn in entirely new constitutional realities. There was a necessity to build a new state system with virtually no possibility of returning to specific pre-partition solutions. The constitutional foundations were created from scratch because it was impossible to simply reconstruct previously existing solutions. The adoption of an interim constitutional document was preceded by the issuance of the 22 November 1918 Decree on the highest representative authority of the Republic of Poland[1] clearly granted in the title to the Provisional Chief of State Józef Pilsudski. On the one hand, so-called November Decree constituted a clear censorship in shaping the system of the reborn state, and on the other hand opened a new stage in which the state authorities' activities acquired a legal basis. Thus, this act was to a certain extent constitutional in nature,[2] defining some of the most important elements of the state system, such as the political system of central authorities or the principles of lawmaking. The actual power exercised by the Chief of State received legal sanction and became a temporary and provisional basis for the state's functioning. Thus, it stipulated a time perspective for its functioning, which would end with the constitution of the Legislative Sejm.[3] In addition to the clearly defined period of office, the Chief of State's authority was limited to a certain extent by the obligation to submit all his issued legislative acts (decrees) to the Legislative Sejm for approval at its first session.[4] Failure to meet this condition would result in losing their binding force. With the existing political consent, based on the November Decree's provisions, subsequent legal acts constituting the basis for the state's functioning were issued in a short time. At that time, there was a generally accepted view that the state system must be based on a strong parliament until a new constitutional document of a higher law would be adopted.[5]

The genesis of the Small Constitution of 1919,[6] as well as the political conditions surrounding its adoption – such as the lack of a clear majority in the Sejm, the difficult situation in which the state found itself, and the existing system of government – resulted from being an act (resolution) that could only function in a transitional period. From the standpoint of its content, the resolution stipulated fundamental rules concerning the state system, which determined its constitutionality. In practice, the primary systemic and political feature was dualism of the activities of major state authorities, which did not exclude the necessary cooperation, but which appeared to be more significant and prominent than could be implied merely by the content of the Small Constitution itself.[7] The term 'constitution' was neither used nor given the rank of a statute as an act of primary legislation. This resolution took on a highly peculiar form that did not correspond to its meaning. It was due to the strong fear of the legislator at the time that the title of the act, and especially the introduction of the term 'constitutional act,' could give rise

[1] Journal of Laws of the Polish State, No. 17, item 41; hereafter, November Decree.

[2] In this context see especially S Rogowski, 'Małe konstytucje (1919 – 1947 – 1992)' (1999) 2 *Przegląd Sejmowy* 14.

[3] November Decree, art 1.

[4] November Decree, art 3.

[5] S Krukowski, 'Mała Konstytucja z 1919 r.' in M Kallas (ed), *Konstytucje Polski. Studia monograficzne z dziejów polskiego konstytucjonalizmu* (Państwowe Wydawnictwo Naukowe, 1990).

[6] The resolution of 20 February 1919, entrusting Józef Piłsudski with the further exercise of the office of the Chief of State (Journal of the Laws of the Polish State, No. 19, item 226).

[7] In the Small Constitution of 1919, the state authorities included: the Legislative Sejm with the Marshal at its head, the Government consisting of the President of the Council of Ministers and ministers, as well as the Chief of State. *See* Part II of the Small Constitution of 1919.

to significant controversies, resulting in the near impossibility for the Sejm to take power, and consequently, the continuation of its exercise by the Chief of State on the previous principles.[8]

Comprising two parts, the Small Constitution of 1919 was exceptionally laconic and synthetic. Part I contained the Sejm's acceptance of Piłsudski's statement on resigning from the office of the Chief of State and gratitude 'for the hard work of holding the office in the service of the Fatherland.' Therefore, it lacked any normative content and had a declaratory nature. In its short introduction, Part II contained the statement entrusting Piłsudski with the further exercise of the Chief of State's power on the indicated 'principles' and specifying the period of holding the office 'until the statutory adoption of the content of the Constitution, which will specify in principle the provisions on the organization of the supreme authorities in the Polish State.'[9] The adopted conditions for the exercise of power by the Chief of State were regulated in five short points and in fact constituted the foundations of the system. His competences fell within the scope appropriate for the Chief of State while placing him in the branch of executive power. In turn, the Sejm was granted sovereign and legislative power. The Small Constitution of 1919 did not provide for legislative competences of other bodies and did not specify the scope of the legislative matter or entities with legislative initiatives (in practice, the state of legislative exclusivity was granted to the Sejm, interrupted by the three-month activity of both the State Defense Council and the government). As a result, constitutional practice did not match the hypothetical patterns. In practice, the domination of the Chief of State was limited by the Sejm, and it was necessary to make the most important decisions by consensus.[10]

Assuming a dualist structure of the executive branch in the Small Constitution of 1919, the Legislative Sejm, as the sovereign, subordinated both the Chief of State and the government. The Chief of State was directly subordinated, while the government was placed under the Sejm's influence through its participation in the appointment of its members by the Chief of State and through the institution of ministerial responsibility. An additional mechanism reinforcing the subordination of the executive bodies – and serving as a safeguard for the Sejm – was the requirement of countersignature for every act (decree) issued by the Chief of State, which had to be endorsed by the relevant minister. In this manner, responsibility for every act of the Chief of State extended to both executive bodies, thereby introducing the principle of dual responsibility, as an exceptionally rare construction. This arrangement weakened the position of the government in relation to the Sejm, as in the event of a conflict, the government (or a minister) could not rely on

[8] See Rogowski (n 2) 17.

[9] This very name replaced the functioning of the concept of the Republic of Poland in the November Decree.

[10] See A Ajnenkiel, *Od rządów ludowych do przewrotu majowego: zarys dziejów politycznych Polski 1918–1926* (Państwowe Wydawnictwo Wiedza Powszechna, 1977) 79.

the support of the Chief of State in implementing its policies, given that the Chief of State stood in the same position in relation to the Sejm.[11]

Certainly, it should be stated that the Small Constitution of 1919 fulfilled its role in the so-called provisional constitutional period of 1918–1922, characterised by dynamic events that made up the activities aimed at rebuilding the state system. Consequently, this state of affairs favoured the creation of a short, synthetic, and temporary act (resolution). Although it built flexible foundations for the functioning of the state system, due to its brevity and the limitation of its content, it did not comprehensively shape the fundamental constitutional foundations.[12] The Small Constitution of 1919 was replaced by the March Constitution adopted in 1921,[13] but the state authorities that were created under the Small Constitution continued to function until November 1922, pending the parliamentary elections. A month later, the Chief of State Józef Piłsudski resigned from his office. The challenge was to find a way to define the constitutional framework of the state's system, as the content of the Small Constitution was undoubtedly insufficient to achieve this objective. Its deficiencies were supplemented through interpretation based on general principles of law and constitutional practices of other countries. The form of the state system established by it was unachievable from the very beginning. The supremacy of the Sejm, combined with the underdeveloped provisions regarding executive bodies, was intended to provide the political and legal basis for weakening the institutional position of the executive.[14]

III. Challenges of Multi-Textuality

The path leading to enact Small Constitution of 1947[15] as a temporary legal and systemic solution was much longer and more complicated than during the period of 1918–1919. The content of the Constitutional Statute was shaped in the context of radical systemic changes following the end of World War II, whose outcome significantly influenced the existing balance of political forces. International conditions led to solutions that brought about the dominance of the political new camp, which resulted in the creation of the Provisional Government of the

[11] M Pietrzak, *Rządy parlamentarne w Polsce w latach 1919-1926* (Spółdzielnia Wydawniczo-Handlowa 'Książka i Wiedza', 1969) 50.

[12] On this view see R Kraczkowski, 'Mała konstytucja z dnia 20 lutego 1919 r.' in RJastrząbski and M Zubik (eds), *Małe Konstytucje. Ustawy zasadnicze okresów przejściowych 1919-1947-1992* (Wydawnictwo Sejmowe, 2014) 23–26.

[13] Act of 17 March 1921 Constitution of the Republic of Poland (Journal of Laws of the Republic of Poland, No. 44, item 267, amended and supplemented by the Act of 2 August 1926, Journal of Laws of the Republic of Poland, No. 78, item 442); hereafter March Constitution of 1921.

[14] W Komarnicki, *Polskie prawo polityczne (geneza i system)* (Wydawnictwo Uniwersytetu w Białymstoku, 2008) 86–87.

[15] Constitutional Statute on the system and scope of operation of the highest organs of the Republic of Poland, adopted by the Legislative Sejm on 19 February 1947 (Journal of Laws of the Republic of Poland, No. 18, item 71).

Republic of Poland, a formally uniform and internationally recognised, albeit politically diverse centre of power. By virtue of the violation of the rule of law, the priority was the preparation for and holding of free elections, which would result in the formation of a parliament fully capable of determining the basic constitutional framework of the state system. However, the official results of the popular elections on 19 January 1947 brought about a change in the political and legal circumstances. In the state of affairs at that time, the opposition held no real influence on the manner of creation and the form of the constitutional provisions adopted by the Legislative Sejm. The latter, fulfilling its main role as a constituent assembly, quickly began to adopt provisions that would remain in force until the new constitution was established, creating a multi-textual temporary basis for the functioning of the state.[16] The Sejm commenced its activity on 4 February 1947 and on the same day, at its opening ceremony, adopted – before the Small Constitution of 1947 – the Constitutional Act on the election of the President of the Republic of Poland.[17] The legislative rush and numerous procedural simplifications diminished the likelihood of a substantive discussion on both the principles of electing the president and the constitutional sources of the position of the Sejm and its powers. Moreover, the scope of the head of state's power or other branches of government was not defined. Thus, a state system based on such generally outlined principles could not function for a long period while maintaining the principle of legalism.[18] Apart from the provisions relating directly to the detailed specifications of the procedure for electing the president, Article 1 of the mentioned above Constitutional Act of 4 February 1947 regulated the important issue of constitutional authorisation for the Legislative Sejm and its powers, as well as for the other acts it issued, in the form of a reference to previously applicable regulations. The Sejm's right to elect head of the state[19] resulted from a legal constitutional statute (the March Constitution of 1921) and a political document (Manifesto of the Polish Committee of National Liberation of 22 July 1944[20]), as well as being a result of the nationwide referendum of 1946.

The Small Constitution of 1947 was accompanied from the beginning by the clear intention to give it the character of a constitutional act, as indicated by its relative formalities – a long title and a special procedure for amending it[21] – and despite all reservations concerning the regulation's scope, due to its

[16] See especially M Kallas, 'Ukierunkowania polityczno-prawne małej konstytucji z 19 lutego 1947 r.' in R Jastrząbski and M Zubik (eds), *Małe Konstytucje. Ustawy zasadnicze okresów przejściowych 1919-1947-1992* (Wydawnictwo Sejmowe, 2014) 63–64.

[17] Journal of Laws of the Republic of Poland, No. 9, item 43; hereafter Constitutional Act of 4 February 1947.

[18] In this context see Rogowski (n 2) 24 and Kallas (n 16) 59.

[19] The President of the Republic of Poland was elected for a seven-year term at a special coinvented session of the Sejm by an absolute majority of votes. Articles 3 and 7 of the Constitutional Act of 4 February 1947.

[20] Journal of Laws of the Republic of Poland, No. 1; hereafter Manifesto of 1944.

[21] By a qualified majority of two-thirds of the statutory number of Members of the Sejm. Article 30 of the Small Constitution of 1947.

content. This Constitutional Statute was also characterised by its departure from the principle of the separation of powers (present previously in the March Constitution of 1921) and its replacement with the doctrine of the unity of state power,[22] which strengthened the Sejm's position only in theory, considering the existing legal status. Additionally, the tradition of the parliament's bicameralism was broken by theoretically granting a prominent role to the Legislative Sejm, concurrently introducing a certain balance of power by reinforcing the constitutional positions of the government and the head of the state. Both the powers granted to the executive branch (government) to issue decrees with the force of law and the indicated position of the head of the state did not fit into the classical framework of the parliamentary system.[23] Departing from the principle of separation of powers was significant for the ruling party in the context of formulating new constitutional principles of the socialist state. However, the most significant limitation of the Sejm's position, making the parliamentary system an illusory construction, resulted from political conditions, which included the actual single-party system due to the legal opposition's disappearance from the political arena.

By comparing the scope of the acts on which the Legislative Sejm relied in the Constitutional Act of 4 February 1947 and the Small Constitution of 1947, fundamental similarities can be found. It should be emphasised that Article 1 of the Small Constitution of 1947 defined the powers of the Legislative Sejm, as the body of the 'supreme authority of the Polish Nation,' to decide 'on the system and scope of activity of the highest bodies of the Republic of Poland,' regulations and other bases for its operation – the basic assumptions of the March Constitution of 1921, the principles of the Manifesto of 1944, the principles of the legislation on national councils and the social and systemic reforms confirmed in a nationwide referendum of 30 June 1946. The construction of this provision did not result in the principle of the applicability of the March Constitution of 1921, replaced by the Small Constitution of 1947, and, as it seems, the legal provisions of the Manifesto of 1944 of that were amended by this constitution. The binding force of the remaining provisions of the Manifesto of 1944, which had the nature of a political declaration, as well as other 'principles' and 'reforms' listed in the Small Constitution of 1947, contained in ordinary acts or decrees, continued to exist, because they were not provisions of a constitutional nature. They only formed the basis for shaping the legislator's will to formulate the content of the Small Constitution in one way or another. Multi-textuality reflects a strategic approach to constitutional evolution, particularly in times of transition and reform. In Poland, the practice of employing multiple constitutional texts, as exemplified by

[22] A complete rejection of the separation of powers in the structure of state organs, in favour of the unity of state authority see S Rozmaryn, 'W jakim zakresie obowiązuje dziś Konstytucja z 17 marca 1921 r.' (1948) 1 *Państwo i Prawo* 20.

[23] In this context see especially Z Rykowski, 'Pozycja Sejmu Ustawodawczego w systemie najwyższych organów Rzeczypospolitej Polskiej' in M Rybicki and J Ciemniewski (eds), *Sejm Ustawodawczy Rzeczypospolitej Polskiej 1947–1952* (Zakład Narodowy im. Ossolińskich, 1977) 181.

the Small Constitution of 1947, illustrates a nuanced method of governance that allows for flexibility and gradual adaptation to changing political landscapes. The concept involves maintaining several foundational legal documents simultaneously, providing a framework that can accommodate incremental changes without necessitating abrupt or total overhauls.

The adoption of the temporary constitutional act made it possible to legitimise the legal acts previously issued by the State National Council and the Polish Committee of National Liberation. The latter acted as the legal, temporary executive authority and served to introduce new solutions into the existing legal order. At the same time, allowed defining and thus limiting the role played by the March Constitution of 1921 in the political system, while denying the validity of the April Constitution of 1935,[24] which was the basis for the actions of the Polish state authorities exiled in London by emphasising its illegality due to the method of its adoption and undemocratic content. As a result of referring to the validity of the March Constitution of 1921, the 'property' of which was theoretically recognised in the Manifesto of 1944 as 'the only binding legal constitution, legally adopted,' the state's continuity was maintained, unquestioned on both international and domestic grounds.[25] These actions constituted an attempt to legitimise the government based on the assumptions of the March Constitution of 1921.

In this context, it is necessary to note two different concepts emerging from the approach to the constitutional principles regulating this period of applying the Small Constitution of 1947. On one hand, a simple continuation of the system according to the provisions of the March Constitution of 1921 was assumed, with only minimal changes and without references to acts issued within the period of 1944–1946. The project of the Polish People's Party was significant, based on the view that the March Constitution of 1921 was binding 'in its entirety' – until the adoption of the full constitution – and 'in particular,' the provisions contained in Chapters I–V, only 'with changes introduced later by the Constitutional Act of February 4, 1947.'[26] On the other hand, the concept of the new principles of the transitional system was presented only with a general and enigmatic reference to the March Constitution of 1921. Such a project was presented by the Polish Workers' Party and the Polish Socialist Party, proposing a new structure of the system of power, based generally on the basic assumptions of the March Constitution of 1921 and on the principles contained in other acts. Therefore, it did not follow from the literal wording of the Manifesto of 1944 that the March

[24] Constitutional Act of 23 April 1935 (Journal of Laws of the Republic of Poland, No. 30, item 227); hereafter April Constitution of 1935.

[25] The Manifesto of 1944 stated, 'the State National Council and the Polish Committee of National Liberation operate on the basis of the March Constitution of 1921, the only legally binding constitution, adopted.'

[26] These changes consisted of the Legislative Sejm's adoption of the competences of the Senate, resulting from the March Constitution of 1921 and thus the concentration of all legislative competences and the definition of the bodies appointed to execute the laws (the prime minister and the ministers).

Constitution of 1921 would remain in force until the adoption of a new (full) constitution. Its 'basic assumptions' were to remain in force until 'the convening of the Legislative Sejm elected in a universal, direct, equal, secret and proportional vote, which will adopt a new constitution as an expression of the will of the nation'.[27] The authorities' position on this matter was not clearly specified, which was the basis for divergent assessments both in the doctrine of constitutional law and among politicians regarding the scope of the validity of the assumptions of the March Constitution of 1921.[28]

In principle, there was general respect for the March Constitution of 1921, but as a whole, it was considered a closed chapter in the history of Polish constitutional law.[29] Therefore, the basic political and programmatic documents and legal acts constituting the foundations of the new system were issued relatively quickly, and a new system of state authorities was created. Notwithstanding formal references to the existing legal and constitutional system, the adopted acts fundamentally changed the previous system, which resulted from different axiological assumptions. The pace of these actions was influenced by the ruling political party's desire to continue its previous strategy of formally observing democratic rules. This continuity signaled that for some time, there would still be at least a formal coexistence of acts originating from the Second Polish Republic and those issued at the end or after the end of the war by the State National Council and its appointed bodies. It should be stressed that, except for the validity of the basic assumptions of the March Constitution of 1921, in practice, entire groups of provisions of the said constitution were also incorporated into the content of legal acts, in particular, the Small Constitution of 1947. This procedure was also followed in legal acts of lower rank, repeating individual articles contained in legal acts from the period of the Second Polish Republic 'in accordance with the needs of the new system'.[30] However, all of this integration functioned in a situation defined by the political composition of the Sejm and the exercise of actual power by one ruling political party.

The Small Constitution of 1947 highlights two features characterising this normative act. The first refers to the scope of its regulations, which was markedly narrower than that commonly applied in constitutions in formal sense. The incompleteness of the Small Constitution of 1947 was expressed primarily in the lack of

[27] See the Manifesto of 1944.

[28] On one hand, it is emphasised in the literature that the influence of the March Constitution of 1921 on the political system of the state during the Legislative Sejm was more apparent than real. See A Burda, *Polskie prawo państwowe* (Państwowe Wydawnictwo Naukowe, 1977) 134. On the other hand, it is suggested that it was not significant but a one-off since it was clearly revealed only in legal acts of constitutional rank in the beginning of 1947 and was no longer visible later. See K Działocha, 'Wstęp' in K Działocha and J Trzciński (eds), *Zagadnienie obowiązywania Konstytucji marcowej w Polsce Ludowej 1944–1952* (Zakład Narodowy im. Ossolińskich, 1977) 5.

[29] In this view see P Sarnecki, 'Konstytucja marcowa a rozwój konstytucjonalizmu polskiego' (2001) 2 *Przegląd Sejmowy* 34–36.

[30] W Skrzydło and W Zakrzewski, 'Mała Konstytucja z dnia 19 lutego 1947 r. – geneza i znaczenie' (2012) 3 *Przegląd Prawa Konstytucyjnego* [Const. L. Rev.] 17.

regulations concerning issues usually present in twentieth-century constitutional acts. It should be pointed out that there is no regulation of the basic principles of the political and socioeconomic system, the structure of local authorities and self-government, the armed forces, and, in particular, civil rights and obligations.[31] In Article 1 of the Small Constitution of 1947, referring to the principles formulated in other acts was an attempt to give them a constitutional importance. The remaining gaps would be filled by future legislation, gradually replacing the acts in force to date. A specific supplement to the Small Constitution of 1947 was the Legislative Sejm's unpublished and adopted (in the form of a resolution) declaration on the implementation of civil rights and freedoms, dated 22 February 1947.[32] It was a response to the opposition's criticism and society's negative impression of the lack of codification of civil rights and freedoms, which resulted from the maximum limitation of the possibilities of giving them universally binding legal force. The legal rank of the issued declaration was significantly reduced by the non-statutory form, and its content was far from those of democratic models. In particular, it should be emphasised that the declaration contained a definition of civil rights and freedoms that differed from that in the March Constitution of 1921 stated that 'their exploitation in the fight against the democratic system of the Republic of Poland should be prevented by statutes'.[33] This formulation at most indicated the self-commitments of the Sejm, declaring that in its constitutional and legislative work and in exercising control over the activities of the Government and determining the basic direction of the State's policy – it will continue to implement basic civil rights and freedoms.[34] The limited treatment of the issue of rights and freedoms and the complete omission of civic duties meant, especially in the political context of the time, that the incompleteness of the Small Constitution in this respect constituted its significant deficiency.[35] The second feature of the Small Constitution of 1947 – subsequent to its incompleteness – was its temporality. Its period of validity was unspecified, but according to the position adopted in Article 1, it would be in force 'until the entry into force of the new Constitution,' which would be adopted by the Legislative Sejm during

[31] Rogowski (n 2) 23–24.

[32] Hereafter Declaration of 22 February 1947.

[33] Declaration of 22 February 1947.

[34] K Działocha, 'Źródła prawa dotyczące Sejmu Ustawodawczego' in M Rybicki and J Ciemniewski (eds), *Sejm Ustawodawczy Rzeczypospolitej Polskiej 1947–1952* (Zakład Narodowy im. Ossolińskich, 1977) 70–72; see also Skrzydło and Zakrzewski (n 30) 23–24.

[35] The Declaration of 22 February 1947 created such rights and freedoms as equality before the law regardless of nationality, race, religion, gender, origin, position or education; personal inviolability, protection of citizens' life and property; freedom of conscience and challenge, freedom of scientific research and publishing its results and freedom of artistic creation; freedom of the press, speech, associations, meetings, public gatherings, and demonstrations; the right to vote and be elected to state authorities; inviolability of the home; secrecy of correspondence and other means of communication; the right to file complaints, petitions, and applications to the appropriate state authorities; the right to work and rest; the right to security in cases of inability to earn money; the right to education; care for the family and for the mother and child; and protection of health and the ability to work. See Declaration of 22 February 1947.

its five-year term.[36] Understood in this sense, temporality allowed a significant extension of the validity of the rules of the transitional period, which could nonetheless be shortened at will if political circumstances justified it. It transpired that there were no obstacles to its extension, which occurred with the adoption of the Act of 15 December 1951 on changing the deadline for the development of the draft constitution and extending the Legislative Sejm's term of office.[37] The formal reason for this state of affairs was the assessment that the Sejm would not manage to present the final version of the draft constitution by the original deadline of 4 February 1952. Ultimately, it was extended by four months due to the extension of the Sejm's term of office by another six months. From this perspective, the reasons for the delay were both political and ideological since they concerned determining the essence of the prevailing constitutional system of the state.

The Small Constitution of 1947 became the binding fundamental law until the adoption of the Constitution of the Polish People's Republic of 22 July 1952.[38] Importantly, new provisions adopted until then were not granted constitutional status because the communist authorities aimed to gradually take full control over the state and lay the foundations for a new socialist constitution. In this way, they avoided the need to subsequently adapt existing provisions to new constitutional regulations.[39] Thus, the changing political conditions reduced the legal acts in force during the constitutional provisional period of 1947–1952 to superficial and facade-like provisions that served as negative constitutional patterns.[40] To some extent, its content referred to the March Constitution of 1921, but in reality, it was only an illusion concealing the real system of exercising power, subordinated in principle to the leading role of the ruling party. This situation, together with the adopted principle of 'a common path to socialism' based on the growing dependence on Soviet models, meant that when constructing the next new constitution, almost no solutions contained in the Small Constitution of 1947 were applied due to its weak legal significance and political role. The content of the fundamental constitutional principles remained an open issue. The ruling camp in the legal and constitutional sphere at that time was characterised by its desire to use the adoption of the constitution in the politics and propaganda of the ruling groups by politicising the content of constitutional concepts, which was achieved mainly by their interpretation.[41]

[36] Article 6 of the Small Constitution of 1947.

[37] Journal of Laws of the Republic of Poland, No. 1, item 1.

[38] Journal of Laws of the Polish People's Republic, No. 33, item 232.

[39] J Wawrzyniak, 'Treść małej konstytucji z 1947 r.' in R Jastrząbski and M Zubik (eds), *Małe Konstytucje. Ustawy zasadnicze okresów przejściowych 1919-1947-1992* (Wydawnictwo Sejmowe, 2014) 84 Skrzydło 86.

[40] See K Kersten, *Narodziny systemu władzy. Polska 1943–1948* (Wydawnictwo Libella, 1986).

[41] In this vein, see Rogowski (n 2) 29.

IV. Lessons of Multi-Textuality for Poland and the World

Multi-textuality opens new possibilities for the constitutional-making process. The Small Constitutions were enacted during exceptional historical times, at turning points in the state's and the political system's history.[42] Their adoption held both political and symbolic significance, influencing international and domestic perceptions. Rather than providing exhaustive regulations, they sketched the broad outlines of systemic changes while maintaining a provisional nature. These acts were typically the result of political compromise during times of crisis, when divergent political visions complicated the adoption of a constitution in a formal sense – one, binding act (document) of higher law. The two main characteristics of the Small Constitutions – on the one hand, their temporary (provisional) nature and on the other hand, incompleteness (limited scope) – reinforced each other in a feedback loop. Because these constitutional acts (one resolution and two statutes) were intended to function only until the adoption of a new constitution in a formal sense, they were necessarily narrow in scope, focusing on essential matters to maintain constitutional order.

A characteristic feature of a basic laws is that they refer, directly or indirectly, to the previously operative constitutional order. New single, supreme formal constitutions are established on foundations constructed from the previous accumulated constitutional and political experience of the state system. On one hand, solutions or institutions that have proven effective in practice and have been positively evaluated are maintained (albeit sometimes with modifications). On the other hand, certain measures are deliberately abandoned in order to avoid the problems or ambiguities that accompanied their implementation. Often, the framers of constitutions act with the aim of filling gaps or remedying the errors and uncertainties that emerged in prior constitutional practice. Undoubtedly, the political and constitutional system in Poland during 1919-1989 and in the period 1989-1997 – as the nation moved toward the enactment of a new constitution – were marked by numerous flaws and erroneous solutions, resulting primarily from misguided ideological principles. Particularly striking was the gap between theory and practice, characteristic of the 'realities of socialism,' as well as between formal solutions and their content. The 'constitutional moments', leading to systemic changes, such as the Polish Round Table Talks, showed the existence of a strong and active political centre, with huge social support, focused on the traditions and slogans of the Independent and Self-Governing Trade Union called Solidarity. A general vision of political and constitutional changes emerged, based on democratic patterns. The complicated legal situation that arose after the popular elections on 4 June 1989 also did not favour the calm construction of constitutional solutions. It should be also emphasised that the Constitution of the Polish People's Republic of 1952 was still in force, along with numerous amendments that broke its coherence, including the

[42] R Albert, 'Multi-Textual Constitutions' (2023) 109 *Virginia Law Review* 1676.

changes introduced by the Act of 7 April 1989 amending the Constitution of the People's Republic.[43] Nevertheless, in constitutional practice, general principles and normative rules had to be transformed into solutions with a much greater degree of specificity. The adoption of a formal constitution became the fundamental goal, shadowed by a general conviction that it was impossible to improve the existing solutions without a deep new constitutional design.[44]

During the 1989–1992 changes to the state's political system occurred in an evolutionary manner. In the changing political situation, characterised by increasingly noticeable divisions in the political camp of Solidarity and the growing criticism of the Polish Round Table decisions, ultimately led to significant changes in the matter of work on the new constitution, pushing back the prospect of its adoption. Work on the new constitutional statute, initiated in the beginning of 1990 by creating two separate Constitutional Committees in the Sejm and the Senate (both chambers independently and separately worked on the new constitution), was interrupted due to the Sejm dissolving itself on 10 March 1990 before the end of its term. The disintegration of the Solidarity camp, which had been ongoing since the spring of 1990, was crowned only by the presidential elections of 25 November 1990, won by Lech Wałęsa, who then assumed this office. In the years 1989–1991, a veritable 'constitutional chaos' resulted from the growing conflict between the Sejm and the president and, to some extent, the government. During this period, there were two separate constitutional projects, providing for the institution of government regulations with the force of law, which were not finalised in the form of a constitutional act (statute) despite the initiation of the legislative procedure. Moreover, the Sejm proposing in a new constitution a parliamentary system and the upper chamber (Senat) preferring a presidential system.[45] Constitutional scholars consider 1991 the most difficult year of the transformation period and emphasise that even the strongest proponents of finalising the constitutional design had to capitulate to the prevailing political situation.[46] Nonetheless, in mid-1991, the concept of adopting an temporal constitutional document emerged, bearing the features of a provisional and incomplete constitutional act. This was caused by concerns about the state's stability in the face of the constitutional system's inconsistency and the significant fragmentation of political forces.

Ultimately, with the first full-democratic general elections on 27 October 1991, Sejm began working, focused on preparing an interim constitutional act.

[43] Journal of Laws of the Polish People's Republic, No. 19, item 101; hereafter April Amendment of 1989.

[44] M Granat and K Granat, *The Constitution of Poland. A Contextual Analysis* (Hart Publishing, 2019).

[45] See H Suchocka, 'Check and Balances Under the New Constitution of Poland' (1998) 45 *St. Louis-Warsaw Transatlantic L.J.* 69, 74; R Mojak, 'Geneza, prawnoustrojowe zasady i prawne procedury tworzenia i uchwalenia Konstytucji Rzeczypospolitej Polskiej z 2 kwietnia 1997 r.' (2018) 4 *Gdańskie Studia Prawnicze* 108.

[46] J Ciemniewski, 'Podział władz w „małej konstytucji' (kilka uwag o stosunkach między parlamentem a rządem)' in Maria Kruk (ed), *„Mała konstytucja' w procesie przemian ustrojowych w Polsce*, (Wydawnictwo Sejmowe, 1993) 24.

In practice, the form and content of the Small Constitution of 1992[47] were created by many factors. It emerged from several years of systemic transformation, gradually redefining statehood and leading to a complete change of the system as new political and social conditions took shape. In fact, it was created differently from the previous Small Constitutions, albeit with certain similarities in circumstances and conditions. It should be emphasised that in this constitutional transformation process there was no need to reconstruct the basic elements of the state system from scratch. Nonetheless, it was necessary to properly modify and adapt them to the new systemic realities.

The Small Constitution of 1992 shared the defining characteristics of transitional constitutional acts. First, there was no doubt about its constitutional nature, as evidenced by both the title of the statute – Constitutional Statute – and its content, consisting of regulations that were unquestionably included in the constitutional matter.[48] In this context, it should be highlighted that the Small Constitution of 1992 did not comprise all sources of law in force during that constitutional period. By repealing the Constitution of the Polish People's Republic of 1952 and its subsequent amendments, some of the provisions of that act were left in force, which, regardless of the location and time of adoption, had the same legal force. In this respect, Article 77 of the Small Constitution of 1992 was important as it precisely specified which provisions of the previous fundamental act remained in force, meaning that no important areas of state and social life were beyond the reach of constitutional norms.[49] Such state of affairs was characteristic of the transitional period in 1992–1997, constitutional scholars dealing with a composed constitution, where apart from the Small Constitution of 1992 the older constitutional provisions and those of the Constitutional Act of 23 April 1992 on the Procedure for Preparing and Adopting the Constitution of the Republic of Poland[50] were in force.[51] A common feature of the Polish transitional constitutional order was the coexistence of multiple constitutional acts and political documents, each regulating a certain section of the constitutional matter. However, it was intended as a provisional measure and led to numerous difficulties in practice. In the Small Constitution of 1992, first the sticking point was the legitimacy of leaving certain provisions in their current form, or the lack of new regulations (in the field of civil rights or the system of sources of law and the omission of the issue of courts,

[47] Constitutional Statute of 17 October 1992, on mutual relations between the legislative and the executive powers of the Republic of Poland and the local self-government Journal of Laws of the Republic of Poland, No. 84, item 426.

[48] M Kruk, 'Praktyka konstytucyjna pod rządami małej konstytucji z 1992 r.' in R Jastrząbski and M Zubik (eds.) *Małe Konstytucje. Ustawy zasadnicze okresów przejściowych 1919-1947-1992* (Wydawnictwo Sejmowe, 2014) 119.

[49] On its basis, the provisions of Chapters 1, 4, and 7, with the exception of Article 60, paragraph 1, Article 61, paragraph 3, Chapters 8 and 9, with the exception of Article 94, and Chapters 10 and 11 remained in force.

[50] Journal of Laws of the Republic of Poland, No. 67, item 336.

[51] The Small Constitution of 1992 operated alongside the Constitution of the Polish People's Republic of 1952, some of whose provisions were abrogated while others remained in force. See Kruk (n 48) 119–21.

particularly the regulation of the Constitutional Tribunal). Second, its temporality of the Small Constitution of 1992 was clearly defined in the introduction to streamline the activities of the highest state authorities and was intended to apply until the adoption of a new Constitution. Third, the Small Constitution of 1992 also met the criterion of the incompleteness of the scope of its regulations.[52] The basic principles on which this interim constitutional statute was based included the principle of the separation of powers, the predominance of elements of the parliamentary system, with the presence of numerous regulations typical of the presidential system, the bicameral parliament, the strong position of deputies and senators with a free mandate and extensive parliamentary immunity, elements of referendum as a form of direct democracy, the balance between the position of the president and the government, on the one hand, and the maintenance of the previous positions of the local government officials, on the other hand. The Small Constitution of 1992 did not introduce any fundamental novelties, but at most, it contained solutions that had long been absent from Polish constitutional law or partially adopted regulations that were previously in force.

The period of systemic transformation under the Small Constitution of 1992 was not merely a transitional phase or a time of awaiting a new constitution, during which provisional institutions were established. Rather, it was primarily a further stage in the construction of a new state system, regarded as a period of testing new constitutional principles and institutions – essentially a constitutional trial period. The adoption of the Small Constitution of 1992 resulted in the petrification of certain institutions and procedures previously introduced into the constitutional order, as indicated by the restoration of the second chamber of parliament (Senat) or the institution of presidential general elections.[53] The accepted constitutional practice was to rely on previously binding or draft regulations, adapting some of them directly into the act while leaving others in force within the framework of previously issued legal acts. The Small Constitution of 1992 was a transitional legal regulation – an incomplete constitution. By its nature, it was a temporary act in force until the adoption of the new constitution. Consequently, the Small Constitution of 1992 would be a fragmentary and framework act, meaning that in some areas, there would be a reference to ordinary laws (statutes). The characteristics of the content of the Small Constitution of 1992 justified the statement that a number of issues requiring constitutionalising remained outside its text. At the same time, this act regulated many issues belonging to ordinary legislation. While drafting worked – mainly for political reasons – the legislator decided not to choose a specific political system. As a result, institutions and solutions characteristic of both the parliamentary-cabinet and semi-presidential systems were introduced into the Small Constitution of 1992. The guiding idea of the creators of

[52] Despite the fact that the Small Constitution of 1992 was a broad statute consisted of 78 articles divided into 6 chapters, whereas the Small Constitution of 1947 had 32 articles divided into 9 chapters.

[53] M Kruk, 'Wstęp' in M Kruk (ed), *'Mała konstytucja' w procesie przemian ustrojowych w Polsce* (Wydawnictwo Sejmowe, 1993) 8.

this act was to ensure a stable government given the condition of the parliament's political fragmentation.[54] From 1992 to 1997, no fundamental changes occurred in either external or internal conditions, except for the change of power resulting from the parliamentary elections, which is normal feature of a democratic system.

Constitution-making process on the preparation of a one, single document of a higher position in a legal system (constitution in formal sense) was carried out, albeit at a varying pace. In total, seven drafts of the fundamental (basic) law were submitted, with the first reading beginning in September 1994. These drafts were then sent to the Constitutional Committee of the National Assembly to prepare a unified draft (bill), which was adopted in January 1997. The relatively slow pace of the Committee's work resulted from various disputes and controversies that hindered the development of a common position. Finally, the currently being in force Constitution of the Republic of Poland was ratified on 2 April 1997 [55] by the National Assembly – the joint chambers of Parliament (Sejm and Senat). Polish Constitution of 1997 is a supreme, single document (act) of highest position in the sources of domestic law, enacted as a constitutional statute (basic law) subsequently approved in a nationwide referendum held on 25 May 1997. This fundamental constitutional statute has an independent value and is an expression of the stability of the democratic tradition of the state. It has three special characteristics. First, its special form consists of a specific name – only this act is referred to as the 'Constitution' or 'Basic Law'. The most important aspect is the specificity of the procedures for creating and amending the constitution, which significantly differ from the procedure for passing ordinary laws.[56] It is a rigid constitution – it has a higher legal authority than ordinary statutes, which consequently means that these statutes cannot amend the constitution and must be consistent with it (around this principle, so-called constitutional judiciary has emerged).[57] However, the Polish Constitution of 1997 does not contain relatively immutable or unchangeable constitutional provisions.[58] Second, the constitution's special content encompasses the scope of the matters that it regulates and the manner of regulating them. The scope of the matters regulated by the constitution is universal in the sense that the modern constitution regulates all systemic issues. The so-called 'thematic triad', which means building the content of the

[54] Rogowski (n 2) 44.

[55] Journal of Laws of the Republic of Poland, No. 78, item 483; hereafter the Polish Constitution of 1997.

[56] A bill to amend the Constitution shall be adopted by the Sejm by a majority of at least two-thirds of votes in the presence of at least half of the statutory number of deputies and by the Senate by an absolute majority of votes in the presence of at least half of the statutory number of senators. Article 235(3) of the Polish Constitution of 1997.

[57] L Garlicki, *Polskie prawo konstytucyjne. Zarys wykładu* (Wolters Kluwer, 2024) 45.

[58] L Garlicki, 'Aksjologiczne podstawy interpretacji konstytucji' in M Zubik (ed), *Dwadzieścia lat transformacji ustrojowej w Polsce. 51. Ogólnopolski Zjazd Katedr i Zakładów Prawa Konstytucyjnego, Warszawa 19-21 czerwca 2009 r.* (Wydawnictwo Sejmowe, 2010) 99 and also see L Garlicki, 'Normy konstytucyjne relatywnie niezmienialne' in J Trzciński (ed), *Charakter i struktura norm konstytucyjnych* (Wydawnictwo Sejmowe, 1997) 140–48.

constitution around three basic issues, defining the general principles of the state system,[59] fundamental rights, freedoms, and obligations[60] and the system of the supreme authorities of the state, the scope of their competences, and mutual relations between the executive, legislative and judicial branch. Third, the special legal force involves giving the constitution its highest place in the system of statutory law. It is currently a formal (uniform) constitution – all constitutional matters are included in one binding document (act) with the highest position in the legal sources – which is a statute of constitutional importance. In this context, every act must be compatible with it, and no act may be contrary to it (positive and negative aspects). Therefore, when considering the Polish Constitution of 1997, it is essential to bear in mind that there exists a single supreme constitutional act – and, of utmost importance, all three of its characteristics – special form, content and legal force – must coexist simultaneously.[61]

Transformations in the Polish political system after the fall of communism required significant legal and constitutional changes. The transition from a socialist state to a democratic republic necessitated the adoption of temporary solutions before a comprehensive and permanent constitution could be established. The creation of the Small Constitution of 1992 was a crucial step in this process, regulating the fundamental principles of governance and defining the relationships among state authorities. Although initially, there was no intention to enact another temporary and incomplete legal act, it is justified to regard the Small Constitution of 1992 as a constitutional act 'on the way' to the adoption of the Constitution of the Republic of Poland of 1997. In the Polish experience, multi-textuality has played a pivotal role during crucial periods such as the post-Communist transition and earlier historical shifts. It acted as a mechanism to bridge legal and political divides, often serving as an intermediate step towards a more comprehensive and permanent constitutional settlement. This strategy not only facilitated political negotiation and compromise during periods of uncertainty but also enabled the legal system to adapt creatively to the realities of governance. Therefore, multi-textuality should not be seen merely as a legislative complexity, but as a powerful tool that inspires innovative pathways to constitutional development, accommodating the need for both stability and progress in national law.

V. Conclusion

Small Constitutions of 1919, 1947 and 1992 reflect the turbulent history of Poland in their efforts to establish an independent state and its political system. Undoubtedly, these temporary and incomplete acts (one resolution and two

[59] Chapter I of the Polish Constitution of 1997.
[60] Chapter II of the Polish Constitution of 1997.
[61] This is a widely accepted and commonly presented constitutional perspective put forward by Garlicki (n 57) 48–56.

constitutional statutes) comprise a hallmark of constitutional law and political practice, playing a crucial role in the interim transitional periods. A distinctive feature of Poland's Small Constitutions was their multi-textual tradition, which allowed for flexible adoption of existing constitutional solutions to dynamic political changes. While their fragmented structure sometimes led to interpretational challenges, it also provided the advantage of enabling incremental reforms. In the transition periods new legal solutions could be tested before committing to a new constitution, ensuring a smoother adoption of constitutional regulations.

Despite similarities in their purposes, the conditions and intentions that led to the adoption of temporary constitutional acts varied significantly in timing, form, and content.

1. The Small Constitution of 1919 was enacted shortly after Poland regained its independence following World War I. It was not a constitutional statute but a parliamentary resolution containing only a few essential provisions. The intention was to adopt a supreme, single constitution rapidly; however, due to the complexities of defining the state's system, this process took longer than expected. The November Decree significantly influenced the solutions introduced in this act.
2. The Small Constitution of 1947 was established after World War II as a result of the policies of the ruling political camp. It introduced gradual constitutional changes by incorporating provisions from the previous system while adapting them to new political realities. However, these rules were often fragmented and lacked coherence, leaving certain legal and institutional gaps that required further clarification and adjustment over time. This constitutional statute was more extensive than its 1919 predecessor, but it deliberately omitted provisions on civil rights freedoms, and obligations.
3. The Small Constitution of 1992 was the most recently adopted among the three, following the political transformations of 1989–1991. The initial goal was to quickly implement a formal (uniform) constitution and completely abandon the previous system. However, due to the complexity of Poland's evolving legal status, the legislator decided to introduce a temporary and provisional constitutional regulation in the form of an extensive and detailed constitutional statute. This act aimed to serve as a foundation for the future formal constitution, a process complicated by numerous constitutional amendments made between 1989 and 1991. The 1997 Constitution of Poland builds upon the foundational principles established in earlier constitutional frameworks that guided the country's systemic transition, with particular reference to the Small Constitution of 1992.

Small Constitutions served as milestones, marking significant moments of change and embodying expectations related to democratic constitutional mechanisms in the absence of well-defined constitutional concepts. In this context, political and propaganda effects on national relations of branches of government were also of paramount importance. The Small Constitutions roughly regulated systemic issues, sketching rather than exhaustively detailing them, while assuming their almost programmatic provisionality, which incidentally determined the narrow scope of regulation of temporary constitutional acts. The more ideological the foundation for a Small Constitution's adoption, the more easily its provisions became detached from social reality. While the legislature or the framers intended these constitutions to remain in force for a short period, in practice, they often lasted several years. This extended duration allowed for the development of certain constitutional practices that influenced subsequent constitutional arrangements. Small Constitutions regulated the foundations of the political and constitutional state system remaining in force until the adoption of a new, full formal constitution. The experience of Poland's Small Constitutions demonstrates that during transition periods, legal flexibility and multi-textuality can be as important as formal constitutional coherence. Their value lay not only in their content but also in their adaptability to shifting political realities. Analysing these constitutional moments offers valuable insights into the mechanisms of systemic evolution and the role performed by constitutional law in state transformations. Ultimately, the Small Constitutions of 1919, 1947 and 1992 fulfilled their role as temporary constitutional acts, laying the groundwork for subsequent comprehensive constitutional regulations, such as the Polish Constitution of 1997.

9

Exploring Macro-Constitutional Reality in Ukraine: Multi-Textual Insights from the Constitutional Court

OLEKSANDR MARUSIAK

I. Introduction: Implied Multi-Textuality of the Constitution of Ukraine

Richard Albert's theory of multi-textual constitutions, as both a term and category in the field of public law,[1] invites scholars to re-examine the traditional binary framework of 'written/unwritten' constitutions that has long dominated academic discourse. This attempt to reframe constitutional texture as a complex interplay of multiple layers not only offers a new approach to understanding the 'large-C' paradigm but also raises important questions, particularly for jurisdictions with a codified constitution.

The 1996 Constitution of Ukraine[2] provides an interesting case. At first sight, it does not exhibit any of the foundational characteristics of multi-textual constitutionalism – (1) *multiplicity*, (2) *asynchrony*, and (3) *shared supremacy*.[3] Few would dispute that Ukraine's Constitution is a single codified document of supreme authority, especially when compared to constitutional systems that distribute foundational authority across multiple equally binding instruments, such as those of Israel or Sweden. Moreover, unlike the *bloc de constitutionnalité* (constitutionality block) developed by France's Constitutional Council under the Fifth Republic,[4]

[1] R Albert, 'Multi-Textual Constitutions' (2023) 109 *Virginia Law Review* 1629.

[2] Constitution of Ukraine [28 June 1996] (with amendments as of 1 January 2020) zakon.rada.gov.ua/laws/show/en/254%D0%BA/96-%D0%B2%D1%80#Text.

[3] (1) Such constitutions consist of more than one document of higher law; (2) The various documents are not necessarily adopted at the same moment; (3) There is more than one higher law at the top of the constitutional pyramid. For more details see Albert (n 1) 1636–40.

[4] See Albert (n 1) 1659; J-S Boda, 'Bloc de Constitutionnalité ou Désordre Constitutionnel? [Constitutionality Block or Constitutional Disorder?]' (2022) 130 *Revue Française de Droit Constitutionnel* 393, 396–405 (in French).

the Constitutional Court of Ukraine (CCU, or the Court) has never established a comparable doctrine.

However, a closer examination of the Constitution and its connection with certain other legal instruments reveals multi-textual tendencies embedded within Ukraine's constitutional design. In this chapter, I argue that the interactions between the Constitution and, at minimum, the Act of Declaration of Independence of Ukraine (Independence Act),[5] Law of Ukraine 'On Adoption of the Constitution of Ukraine and Its Entry into Force' (Law on Adoption of Constitution),[6] and the Rules of Procedure of the Verkhovna Rada of Ukraine (Parliament's Rules of Procedure)[7] demonstrate an implicit form of multi-textual constitutionalism, despite the formal appearance of the 1996 Constitution as a classic uni-textual instrument.

First, Ukraine's Independence Act and the Constitution are closely interconnected and share co-equal legal and symbolic significance for the nation (see Section II). The Constitution explicitly references the Independence Act, affirming and elaborating the foundational values articulated in that document. The relationship between the two is mutually constitutive. Without the Independence Act, there would have been no basis for adopting a constitution as the *lex fundamentalis* of a sovereign Ukraine. Without the new Constitution, the Independence Act would have remained largely symbolic, lacking the institutional and legal framework necessary for effective state-building.

Second, the Law on Adoption of Constitution, enacted on the same day as the Constitution itself but as a separate legal instrument, effectively functions as an operational addendum to the main constitutional text (see Section III). It contains provisions that could have been incorporated into the Constitution but were, by deliberate choice of the drafters, set apart. This instrument also bears all the official signatures absent from the published Constitution. Moreover, the Constitution shares the legal identification number assigned to this law, even though the Constitution was formally adopted first.

Third, the CCU[8] has at times interpreted the Constitution through the lens of ordinary statutes, specifically the Parliament's Rules of Procedure (see Section IV). This form of judicial engagement has contributed to a de facto expansion of the material scope of the Constitution. In my view, such jurisprudence does not represent the best model of constitutional adjudication, but it remains valid and operative

[5] Act of Declaration of Independence of Ukraine [24 August 1991].

[6] Law of Ukraine No. 254/96-VR 'On Adoption of the Constitution of Ukraine and Its Entry into Force' [28 June 1996].

[7] Law of Ukraine No. 1861-VI 'On the Rules of Procedure of the Verkhovna Rada of Ukraine' [10 February 2010].

[8] In Ukraine, the CCU is the only body of judicial review, which (1) assesses the constitutionality of the laws of Ukraine, international treaties, proposed national referendum questions, presidential impeachment procedures, and other legal instruments; (2) provides the official interpretation of the Constitution. The Court conducts an abstract judicial review, evaluating the conformity of an instrument with the Constitution, either by assessing the constitutionality of its provisions or by examining the constitutionality of legislative procedural aspects.

within the Ukrainian legal system. I refer to this phenomenon as a 'macro-constitutional reality,' in which the Court treats both the Constitution and selected pieces of legislation as integral components of a broader constitutional mosaic. While the Constitution remains formally the sole supreme law of the land, its practical applicability has at times been contingent on the norms of ordinary legislation.

These dynamics not only reflect the multi-textual nature of Ukraine's constitutional practice but also demonstrate that the theory of multi-textuality can be reconceptualised across different jurisdictions in diverse, and sometimes unorthodox, ways.

II. Links between the Independence Act and the Constitution of Ukraine

Given that the Ukrainian nation was subjected to foreign colonial powers for a significant part of its history, it is understandable that the notion of independence was widely celebrated and deeply valued during the constitutional drafting process. The ongoing Russian military aggression against Ukraine – accompanied by political rhetoric denying Ukraine's statehood and identity[9] – further underscores the significance of independence as a constitutional value. Adopted by 346 out of 450 members of Parliament on 24 August 1991, the Independence Act[10] not only proclaimed the country's sovereignty but also provided a guiding framework for its future, paving the way for the development of Ukrainian statehood.

The Independence Act was grounded in four key rationales: (a) the existential threat posed to Ukraine by the 19 August 1991 *coup d'état* in the Soviet Union; (b) the continuity of Ukraine's millennia-long tradition of statehood; (c) the right to self-determination under the UN Charter and other international legal instruments; and (d) implementation of the Declaration on State Sovereignty of Ukraine, adopted on 16 July 1990.[11] By adopting the Act, the Verkhovna Rada of the Ukrainian Soviet Socialist Republic solemnly declared the independence of Ukraine and the creation of an independent Ukrainian state, affirmed the indivisibility and inviolability of its territory, and proclaimed that, from that day forward, only the Constitution[12] and laws of Ukraine shall be valid on its territory.

[9] For instance, C Apt, 'Russia's Eliminationist Rhetoric Against Ukraine: A Collection' (*Just Security*, 16 May 2025) www.justsecurity.org/81789/russias-eliminationist-rhetoric-against-ukraine-a-collection/.

[10] First, the Parliament adopted a short Resolution No. 1427-XII *'On the Declaration of the Independence of Ukraine'* (321 votes), which provided for a republican referendum to be held on 1 December 1991 to confirm the Independence Act. Immediately after this, the Independence Act was put to a vote and adopted.

[11] The 1990 Declaration–the 1991 Act transition demonstrates the step-by-step evolution of Ukraine's status from a republic of the Soviet Union to a sovereign and independent state. See Declaration of State Sovereignty of Ukraine [16 July 1990].

[12] The Independence Act referenced the 1978 Constitution of the Ukrainian SSR, which Parliament renamed the 'Constitution of Ukraine' in September 1991. It remained de jure in force until the adoption of the 1996 Constitution, which marked the next stage of Ukraine's national state-building.

The Preamble of the 1996 Constitution,[13] adopted by Parliament, explicitly invokes the Independence Act as its foundational legal and ideological basis. It states that the Verkhovna Rada of Ukraine adopted the Constitution on behalf of the Ukrainian people and was guided by the Independence Act, which had been approved by national referendum on 1 December 1991.[14] Although the Constitution quotes the Independence Act directly only once, it contains many implicit references to the principles enshrined in the Act, particularly the values of sovereignty, independence, and territorial integrity. These references include:

> Article 1: Ukraine is a sovereign and independent, democratic, social, and law-based state.
>
> Article 2(3): The territory of Ukraine within its present borders is indivisible and inviolable.
>
> Article 17(1): Protection of the sovereignty and territorial indivisibility of Ukraine is the most important function of the State and a matter of concern for all the Ukrainian people.
>
> Article 37(1): Prohibition of the establishment and activities of political parties and public associations if their programmatic goals or actions are aimed, *inter alia*, at undermining the independence of Ukraine or violating the sovereignty and territorial integrity of the State.
>
> Article 65(1): Defence of the Motherland, of the independence and territorial indivisibility of Ukraine, is the duty of the citizens of Ukraine.
>
> Article 73: Issues of altering the territory of Ukraine are resolved exclusively by the national referendum.
>
> Articles 79(1) and 104(3): Devotion to the independence of Ukraine in oaths of members of Parliament and the President-elect.
>
> Article 106(1)(1): The President of Ukraine ensures national independence, national security, and the legal succession of the state.
>
> Article 157(1): The Constitution of Ukraine shall not be amended if the amendments foresee the abolition or restriction of human and citizens' rights and freedoms or if they are aimed at the liquidation of the independence or violation of the territorial indivisibility of Ukraine.

It is evident that the ideas articulated in the Independence Act were further developed to form the ideological core of the 1996 Constitution. The responsibility for ensuring that the pro-independence character of Ukraine's Constitution is never amended or undermined rests with the CCU, which conducts a preliminary (*a priori*) review of any proposed constitutional amendment under

[13] Since 2019, the Preamble of the Constitution has also affirmed the European identity of the Ukrainian people and the irreversibility of Ukraine's European and Euro-Atlantic course.

[14] On 1 December 1991, 90.32% of voters confirmed the Independence Act. Following this decisive endorsement, other foreign nations began to recognise Ukraine as an independent state. See also S Plokhy, *The Last Empire: The Final Days of the Soviet Union* (Basic Books, 2015) 152–70, 275–94; Ch Lalpychak, 'Over 90% Vote Yes in Referendum; Kravchuk Elected President of Ukraine' (*The Ukrainian Weekly*, 8 December 1991).

Article 159 of the Constitution.[15] In its ordinary adjudication, however, the CCU has rarely referred to the Independence Act. It has explicitly cited the Act in only two decisions, No. 20-rp/2001[16] and No. 1-r/2021,[17] as well as in a few separate opinions authored by individual judges.[18] By contrast, Article 1 of the Constitution is one of the most frequently quoted constitutional provisions in the Court's practice.

In comparison, Ukrainian legal academia has engaged more extensively with the Independence Act. The authors of the latest academic commentary on the Constitution emphasise that the Preamble underscores the historical, political, and legal foundations for the Ukraine's restoration as an independent state. These foundations include the centuries-old history of Ukrainian statehood and the inalienable right of the Ukrainian nation to self-determination, exercised by the entire Ukrainian people. Together, they form the legal basis for adopting the Constitution as the Basic Law of an independent state. The commentary further recognises the Independence Act as 'the direct legal source that guided the Verkhovna Rada of Ukraine in adopting the Constitution.'[19]

More cautious scholarly approaches also exist. For instance, Hryhorii Berchenko argues that it is premature to recognise either the Independence Act or the Declaration of State Sovereignty as possessing constitutional status. While he opposes including the Declaration in any hypothetical *bloc de constitutionnalité* of Ukraine, Berchenko nonetheless acknowledges a clear and direct connection between the Independence Act and the Constitution.[20]

Is a single reference to the Independence Act in the Constitution sufficient to support a claim of constitutional multi-textuality or extra-constitutionality? Given the unique constitutional significance of the Independence Act in Ukraine's emergence as an independent state in 1991 – together with subsequent domestic political developments and the ongoing existential threats to Ukraine's independence and territorial integrity – I believe such a claim is both reasonable and well-justified. The links between the Independence Act and the Constitution are indeed conceptual and legal. The Independence Act provided the foundational legitimacy and

[15] In Ukraine, the CCU, along with Parliament, is actively engaged in the political process of constitutional revision. See M Hein, 'Do Constitutional Entrenchment Clauses Matter? Constitutional Review of Constitutional Amendments in Europe' (2020) 18(1) *International Journal of Constitutional Law* 78, doi.org/10.1093/icon/moaa002.

[16] Constitutional Court of Ukraine. Decision No. 20-rp/2001 [27 December 2001].

[17] Constitutional Court of Ukraine. Decision No. 1-r/2021 [14 July 2021].

[18] Constitutional Court of Ukraine. Decision No. 2-r/2017 (*Separate Opinion of Judge Moisyk*) [20 December 2017]; Opinion No. 3-v/2018 (*Separate Opinion of Judge Lytvynov; Separate Opinion of Judge Tupytskyi*) [22 November 2018]; Decision No. 2-r/2020 (*Dissenting Opinion of Judge Holovatyi*) [18 February 2020].

[19] RO Stefanchuk and OV Petryshyn (eds), *Konstytutsiya Ukrainy. Nauko-praktychnyi komentar [Constitution of Ukraine: Academic and Practical Commentary]* with a foreword by V Zelenskyi, President of Ukraine (Pravo, 2024) 14.

[20] H Berchenko, *Konstytutsiia yak akt ustanovchoi vlady* [The Constitution as an Act of Constituent Power] (Doctor of Juridical Science dissertation, Yaroslav Mudryi National Law University, 2024) 371 (in Ukrainian).

ideological impetus for Ukraine's sovereignty, while the Constitution translated these aspirations into a consolidated legal framework. The Independence Act may thus be perceived as the historical prologue to the 1996 Constitution. Only jointly do these documents define the essence of Ukraine's statehood and form the cornerstone of its constitutional order. Without the Independence Act, the Constitution of an independent Ukraine would not have been possible; without the Constitution, the Independence Act would have remained merely a symbolic declaration with no binding legal significance.

III. Law on Adoption of Constitution – Enactment Anomaly?

A. Enactment of the 1996 Constitution of Ukraine

At 9:20 a.m. (local time) on 28 June 1996, after almost 24 hours of uninterrupted work, 315 of the 450 members of the *Verkhovna Rada* (Parliament) voted in favour of the Constitution of independent Ukraine. A little later, at 9:33 a.m. during the same session, the Parliament, by an even higher majority of 338 votes, additionally enacted the Law of Ukraine No. 254/96-VR 'On Adoption of Constitution of Ukraine and Its Entry into Force' (Law on Adoption of Constitution) – a technical document that was not required by the new Constitution at all.[21] This instrument formally declared the adoption of the 1996 Constitution of Ukraine, repealed the 1978 Constitution (Basic Law),[22] and terminated the 1995 temporary quasi-constitution,[23] which had operated concurrently with the 1978 Constitution.

On 12 July 1996, the Chairperson of the Verkhovna Rada of Ukraine, Oleksandr Moroz, and the President of Ukraine, Leonid Kuchma, ceremoniously signed the Law on Adoption of Constitution. This law, together with the text of the 1996 Constitution (No. 254k/96-VR), was officially published in the newspaper

[21] O Marusiak, 'Konstytutsiya Ukrainy ta Zakon Ukrainy 'Pro pryynyattya Konstytutsiyi Ukrainy i vvedennya yiyi v diiu': dialektychna yednist chy yurydychne protystavlennia? ['The Constitution of Ukraine and the Law of Ukraine '*On Adoption of the Constitution of Ukraine and Its Enactment into Effect*': Dialectical Unity or Legal Contrast?']' (2019) 4(69) *Pravovyi Chasopys Donbasu* 18–19 doi.org/10.32366/2523-4269-2019-69-4-17-24.

[22] Constitution of the Ukrainian Soviet Socialistic Republic [20 April 1978].

[23] At this stage of the constitutional development of Ukraine, multi-textual tendencies were more apparent than after 1996. The 1995 Agreement states that until the adoption of the new Constitution, the provisions of the 1978 Constitution shall be effective only insofar as they are consistent with the Agreement. See The Constitutional Agreement between the Verkhovna Rada of Ukraine and the President of Ukraine on the basic principles of the organisation and functioning of state power and local self-government in Ukraine for the period before the adoption of the new Constitution of Ukraine [8 June 1995].

Holos Ukrainy.[24] A few weeks later, on 23 July, another official source, *Vidomosti Verkhovnoi Rady Ukrainy*, published the same texts.[25]

A scrupulous reader might note some peculiarities regarding the published documents. First, under Article 160, the Constitution entered into force on the day of its adoption, meaning it became effective even before its official publication. The Law on Adoption of Constitution, meanwhile, contained no operative clauses of its own. Second, the published text of the Constitution has no signatures; the reference to the signatures appears only in the Law on Adoption of Constitution.[26] Third, the Constitution itself lacks a distinct numeric identifier as a standalone legal instrument; instead, it carries the number assigned to the Law on Adoption of Constitution, with the sole addition of a lowercase 'k' (signifying 'Constitution' in Ukrainian). Fourth, Article 1 of the Law on Adoption of Constitution states, 'To enact the Constitution of Ukraine,' although the Constitution had technically already been enacted thirteen minutes before the adoption of this law.

These details raise several puzzling questions. Was the Constitution officially enacted at the time of the final vote, or only upon the subsequent enactment of the Law on Adoption of Constitution? Could the Constitution take effect before the date of its official publication? Is the Law on Adoption of Constitution a separate instrument, or does it constitute an integral part of the Constitution itself? Ukrainian legal scholarship has not provided clear or consistent answers to these questions to this day. However, the theory of multi-textual constitutions provides a plausible framework for understanding and explaining this legislative anomaly.

B. Law on Adoption of Constitution as an Operative Addendum to the 1996 Constitution

Despite the apparent simplicity of these questions, even the Supreme Court of Ukraine lacked a clear legal position on whether the 1996 Constitution entered into force before its official publication. In some cases, the Supreme Court denied it any legal effect until the date of its publication. This uncertainty ultimately

[24] *Holos Ukrainy* [*Voice of Ukraine*], No. 128 (13 July 1996) www.golos.com.ua/edition_archive/ 1996-07.

[25] *Vidomosti Verkhovnoi Rady Ukrainy* [*Bulleting of the Verkhovna Rada of Ukraine*], No. 30 (23 July 1996), Item 141.

[26] The last page of an original copy of the Constitution, available in the State Archive of Ukraine, is signed (see *Central State Archive of Supreme Bodies of Power and Administration*, Collection 1, Inventory 16, File 5466, Page 55). Nonetheless, the official text of the Constitution published in *Holos Ukrainy* and *Vidomosti Verkhovnoi Rady Ukrainy*, as well as demonstrated on the Parliament's website (see zakon.rada.gov.ua/laws/show/254%D0%BA/96-%D0%B2%D1%80#Text lacks any signatures reference. As for text for the *Law on Adoption of Constitution*, its original copy bearing signatures is bound into and attached to the Constitution as a last page (see a scanned version of file 5466 record from the State Archive of Ukraine here: archives.gov.ua/?uniq=1&s=&r=437&a=2).

prompted Oleksandr Barabash to submit a constitutional petition to the newly created CCU, requesting an official interpretation.[27]

The confusion likely stemmed from contradictory provisions within the Constitution itself. First, the Constitution does not distinguish between types of parliamentary statutes – such as constitutional amendments, ordinary laws, or laws ratifying international treaties – but groups them all under the umbrella term 'Law of Ukraine' (*Zakon Ukrainy*).[28] It even refers to the Constitution itself as the 'Basic Law of Ukraine.' However, if an instrument is labeled as a 'Law of Ukraine,' must all the procedural requirements established by the Constitution apply to it uniformly, regardless of the actual content and scope of the act?[29]

Second, Article 94(5) of the Constitution stipulates that any law takes effect ten days after its official publication, unless otherwise specified, but never before publication. Article 57 further mandates that laws defining human rights must be published, and that unpublished laws are invalid. But the Constitution itself diverges from these principles: Article 160 declares the Constitution effective immediately upon its adoption, and Article 161 designates the day of adoption as a national holiday, Constitution Day. Which rule, then, governs the Law on Adoption of Constitution?

In response to Barabash's petition, the CCU delivered Decision No. 4-zp/1997, providing an official clarification on the interpretation of Articles 94(5) and 160 of the Constitution.[30] The Court stated that the Constitution is an act of the constituent power of the people of Ukraine, while the Laws of Ukraine are merely legislative acts passed by Parliament in its capacity as a representative and legislative body. Hence, the procedural rule in Article 94(5) regarding the entry into force of laws does not apply to the Constitution itself. The Court also confirmed that the Constitution entered into force at the moment the Verkhovna Rada announced the final voting results on its adoption during the plenary session, meaning that the Constitution became effective on 28 June 1996, the day

[27] The CCU became fully operational on 1 January 1997. Before the 2016 constitutional reform, it had jurisdiction to provide official interpretations of the Constitution and laws of Ukraine upon a constitutional appeal of a natural or legal persons. In 1996, Oleksandr Barabash, citing ambiguity in the application of certain constitutional provisions by the Supreme Court of Ukraine – particularly the inconsistent judicial approaches regarding the Constitution's entry into force in cases affecting his private interests – sought relief through an official and final interpretation of the Constitution by the CCU.

[28] This term corresponds to the statute or 'Act of Parliament' in the UK and other countries of the Westminster system, '*Gesetz*' in Germany, or '*loi*' in France.

[29] This issue has always been a matter of political challenge. For instance, in the 2000s, there were debates over whether the President could apply veto powers toward the law on constitutional amendment. Using formal approach, the CCU ruled that, since a constitutional amendment is adopted in the form of a Law of Ukraine, the President is required to either sign or veto it. The 2004 constitutional amendment explicitly prohibited the President's veto toward such laws. See Constitutional Court of Ukraine. Decision No. 6-rp/2003 [11 March 2003].

[30] Constitutional Court of Ukraine. Decision No. 4-zp/1997 [4 October 1997].

of its adoption. As for the Law on Adoption of Constitution, the Court briefly mentioned that the Constitution's entry into force was independent of the adoption of this law, but it did not explain the law's legal nature or status.

At least two questions remained unresolved. First, when did the Law on Adoption of Constitution enter into force – upon its adoption, upon its signing, or ten days after its official publication, as required by Article 94? Second, what is the legal significance of the phrase 'To enact the Constitution of Ukraine' in that Law, given the Court's clarification that the Constitution was already enacted at the time of the final vote?

Since the Constitution entered into effect immediately after the final vote – before the Law on Adoption of Constitution was passed – I interpret the Law as an operative epilogue that completed the enactment process of the new Basic Law. In adopting it, Parliament continued to exercise its constituent power, just as it had during the adoption of the Constitution itself. This Law is functionally integral to the Constitution yet remains formally a distinct document. Like the Constitution, it evidently entered into force immediately and fell outside the scope of Article 94. Accordingly, the phrase 'To enact the Constitution of Ukraine' in Article 1 of this Law is best interpreted not as constitutive, but as a confirmatory statement, more accurately rendered as, 'To proclaim the official enactment of the Constitution of Ukraine.'

Why, then, did Parliament adopt this extra-constitutional instrument? One possible explanation is that members of Parliament, for ideological reasons, sought to avoid referencing the Soviet-era Constitution or the interim Constitutional Agreement, both associated with a period of acute political crisis, in the 1996 Constitution. Alternatively, Parliament may have followed the established practice of double adoption,[31] a common law-drafting technique during the 1990s. In either case, the enactment of the Law on Adoption of Constitution as an operational addendum or epilogue to the Constitution serves as evidence of the multi-textual nature of Ukraine's Basic Law from the very date of its adoption.

If Ukraine's constitutional multi-textuality consisted solely of the Independence Act and/or the Law on Adoption of Constitution, this chapter would be considerably shorter, and the concept itself would remain largely theoretical, with no real practical relevance for Ukraine's constitutional design. Fortunately (or unfortunately), judicial activism has since introduced another phenomenon in Ukraine's constitutional law, adding not only a practical dimension but also new challenges.

[31] The 1978 Constitution of Ukrainian SSR also was supplemented with a separate Law 'On the Procedure for Enactment into Force the Constitution (Fundamental Law) of the Ukrainian Soviet Socialist Republic.' During the 1990s, such practice continued; laws of Ukraine were often formally reaffirmed by additional instruments.

IV. The Phenomenon of the Parliament's Rules of Procedure in Ukraine

The Constitutional Court has developed a practice of occasionally (re)interpreting certain constitutional provisions through the lens of ordinary legislation. This has led to situations in which a legal instrument of lower hierarchical status has effectively modified the meaning of constitutional clauses. While this practice has historically been exceptional, its recurrence in the future cannot be ruled out. When the CCU develops a form of jurisprudence in which the Constitution and ordinary legislation become functionally interconnected and mutually dependent components of a broader constitutional framework, I refer to this phenomenon as a *macro-constitutional reality*. The Court's jurisprudence on the Rules of Procedure of the Verkhovna Rada of Ukraine (the Parliament's Rules of Procedure, or '*Rehlament*' in Ukrainian) offers the clearest illustration of this dynamic.

A. Legal Nature and Material Scope of Parliament's Rules of Procedure

The Parliament's Rules of Procedure is another legal instrument explicitly mentioned in the 1996 Constitution, intended to regulate all aspects of parliamentary procedure. Initially, it was marked as a 'Law of Ukraine.' Nevertheless, the Rules of Procedure was never formally enacted as a law under the 1996 version of Constitution. Instead, Parliament continued to operate under the 1994 Rules of Procedure, an ordinary by-law act that had been granted '*the effect of a law*.'[32] This practice persisted despite clear constitutional requirements. Article 82(5) states that the operational procedure of the Verkhovna Rada of Ukraine shall be established by the Constitution and the Law on the Rules of Procedure. Similarly, Article 92(1)(21) provides that the organisation and operational procedure of the Verkhovna Rada, as well as the status of members of Parliament, shall be determined exclusively by the Laws of Ukraine. In December 1998, the CCU reaffirmed this constitutional requirement, emphasising that Parliament must adopt the Rules of Procedure in the form of a law.[33]

During the Orange Revolution, on 8 December 2004, Parliament amended the 1996 Constitution, shifting the system of government from a president-parliamentary to a premier-presidential model, effective after the parliamentary elections of March 2006.[34] The 2004 version of the Constitution did not overlook the issue

[32] Article 1.0.2 of the Rules of Procedure of the Verkhovna Rada of Ukraine No. 130/94-VR [27 June 1994].

[33] Constitutional Court of Ukraine. Decision No. 17-rp/1998 [3 December 1998].

[34] Law of Ukraine No. 2222-IV '*On Introducing Amendments to the Constitution of Ukraine*' [8 December 2004].

of the Rules of Procedure either. First, it omitted all explicit references to the 'Law of Ukraine' in the relevant clauses, but left the wording of Article 92(1)(21) unchanged. Second, it introduced additional references to the Rules of Procedure within the text of the Constitution itself, including Article 85(1)(15), which singled out the adoption of Rules of Procedure as a distinct power of Parliament.

However, since the amended Constitution did not explicitly specify whether the Rules of Procedure should be enacted as a law or merely as an internal by-law act, the Verkhovna Rada adopted a new and significantly updated version of the Rules of Procedure during its final session in March 2006 in the form of a simple resolution. This approach, nevertheless, did not resolve the constitutional ambiguity. Over the next two years, Parliament and the CCU became entangled in a recurring cycle of adopting and invalidating the Rules of Procedure. The CCU declared three different by-law versions unconstitutional, consistently prioritising Article 92(1)(21) of the Constitution over other relevant provisions.[35] Yet, some CCU judges dissented, stressing in their separate opinions the need for an evolutionary interpretation of the amended provisions of the Constitution concerning the Rules of Procedure.[36]

In February 2010, Parliament finally adopted the Rules of Procedure in the form of a law, which President Yushchenko (2005–2010) signed during his final month in office. This version, despite undergoing more than 60 amendments, remains valid and in force.

Why was the form of the Rules of Procedure such a crucial issue for political stakeholders? The answer lies in the material scope of the document and the President's desire to intervene in this area. Under Article 83(5) of the 2004 version of the Constitution, the operational procedure of the Verkhovna Rada of Ukraine is to be established by both the Constitution and the Rules of Procedure. Consequently, the material scope of the Rules of Procedure scrutinises and, at times, complements provisions of the Constitution – for instance, with respect to the organisation of parliamentary sessions, legislative and budgetary procedures, the exercise of Parliament's appointing powers, quorum requirements and voting procedures, and so on.

Also, since 2006, the Rules of Procedure has regulated not only the routine parliamentary operations but also several highly politicised matters. These include: (1) the process for introducing, considering, and adopting constitutional amendments, as well as the procedural parameters governing interaction between Parliament and the CCU during the a priori review of proposed amendments;[37] (2)

[35] See Constitutional Court of Ukraine. Decision No. 4-rp/2008 [1 April 2008]; Decision No. 16-rp/2008 [17 September 2008]; Decision No. 30-rp/2009 [19 November 2009].

[36] See eg Constitutional Court of Ukraine. Decision No. 4-rp/2008 (*Separate Opinion of Judge Markush*) [1 April 2008].

[37] For example, only the Rules of Procedure establish a synchronisation mechanism for the simultaneous adoption of amendments that are subject to different procedures under Articles 155 and 156 of the Constitution. It also addresses the issue of the CCU's legal reservations in the process of the *a priori* review of constitutional amendments.

the formation and functioning of the parliamentary coalition and opposition (until October 2010); (3) the impeachment of the President (until September 2019);[38] (4) the early termination of presidential powers due to health-related incapacity; and (5) the granting of consent for the criminal prosecution, detention, or arrest of a member of Parliament (until January 2020),[39] as well as the detention or arrest of a CCU judge or a judge of general jurisdiction (until September 2016).

The CCU, in its constitutional adjudication, has consistently faced challenges in addressing matters jointly regulated by the Constitution and the Parliament's Rules of Procedure. To what extent can the Rules of Procedure supplement existing constitutional norms? Should the CCU rely solely on an autonomous interpretation of the Constitution in matters of parliamentary procedure, or should it treat the Constitution and the Rules of Procedure as co-equal sources of law? When reviewing the constitutionality of the legislative process, should the Court also examine procedural compliance with the Rules of Procedure? The selected cases below illustrate the Court's inconsistent approach to these questions.

B. Constitutional Court's Ambiguous Approach towards the Parliament's Rules of Procedure

In general, the CCU has repeatedly emphasised that a parliamentary instrument may be declared unconstitutional only if Parliament violated procedural requirements established directly by the Constitution, rather than by the Rules of Procedure.[40] For example, in Decisions No. 2-r/2018 and No. 4-r/2018, the Court invalidated the Law of Ukraine No. 5029-VI '*On the Principles of State Language Policy*' [3 July 2012] and the Law of Ukraine No. 5475-VI '*On the All-Ukrainian Referendum*' [6 November 2012], respectively, on the basis of gross violations of the constitutional procedure for their adoption. In both cases, the Court made no reference to the Rules of Procedure at all.[41]

Nonetheless, some judges have disagreed with this limited approach. For example, in a separate opinion to Decision No. 2-r/2018, Judge Horodovenko argued that, in determining whether the constitutional procedure for the adoption, consideration, and entry into force of a law has been violated, the Court should also consider non-compliance with the Rules of Procedure, particularly if such non-compliance compromised the genuine expression of the will of Parliament as

[38] In 2019, almost all provisions of the Rules of Procedure regarding the impeachment process were transferred to the Law of Ukraine No. 39-IX 'On the Special Procedure for Removing the President of Ukraine from Office (Impeachment)' [10 September 2019].

[39] Since 1 January 2020, parliamentary immunity in Ukraine was completely abolished.

[40] See Constitutional Court. Decision No. 9-rp/2000 [12 July 2000], as well as different Constitutional Court's procedural rulings like No. 15-u/2004 [19 February 2004], No. 35-u/2011 [14 July 2011], No. 65-u/2011 [27 December 2011], No. 37-u/2015 [7 September 2015], No. 12-u/2017 [6 July 2017] and others.

[41] See Constitutional Court of Ukraine. Decision No. 2-r/2018 [28 February 2018] and Decision No. 4-r/2018 [26 April 2018].

a representative body.[42] Judge Sas, likewise, in a separate opinion to Decision No. 4-r/2018, pointed out that the Verkhovna Rada's failure to comply with the Rules of Procedure when adopting laws and other acts may also indicate a violation of relevant provisions of the Constitution.[43]

In Decision No. 2-r/2022, concerning the *a posteriori* review of the Law of Ukraine No. 27-IX 'On Amendments to Article 80 of the Constitution of Ukraine (Regarding the Immunity of Members of Parliament of Ukraine)' [3 September 2019], the CCU adopted an even more sophisticated approach.[44] First, it analysed the constitutional procedure for adopting constitutional amendments, and then examined the provisions of the Rules of Procedure in detail, referencing the document 15 times. However, ultimately, the Court found no violations of the Constitution in the amendment process. In a dissenting opinion, Judge Pervomaiskyi criticised the CCU's distinction between procedures established by the Constitution and those outlined in the Rules of Procedure, arguing that both documents jointly regulate constitutional amendment process. Therefore, any violation of the Rules of Procedure in this context, he contended, should also be deemed a violation of the Constitution itself.[45]

There have also been situations where the CCU invalidated certain norms of the Rules of Procedure as unconstitutional. For example, in Decision No. 12-rp/2012, the Court considered whether members of Parliament have the right to introduce draft laws on the *denunciation* of international treaties.[46] The CCU emphasised that the Constitution explicitly identifies the subjects entitled to legislative initiative, which include members of Parliament, and that the Rules of Procedure cannot impose additional restrictions beyond those outlined in the Constitution. Despite the Court's decision, however, the current version of the Rules of Procedure still imposes limits on members of Parliament in introducing draft laws on the *ratification* of international treaties – an issue not directly addressed in the 2012 decision. It appears that Parliament does not intend to lift the restriction it created itself – even though it is clearly unconstitutional – which further blurs the hierarchical distinction between the Constitution and the Rules of Procedure on the matters of parliamentary business.

In certain highly politicised cases, however, the Constitutional Court has treated the Constitution and the Rules of Procedure as equally authoritative – and, perhaps, co-equal – sources of law. In Decision No. 11-rp/2010, the Court addressed whether individual members of Parliament – including those unaffiliated with any parliamentary group – may participate in forming a parliamentary

[42] Constitutional Court of Ukraine. Decision No. 2-r/2018 (*Separate Opinion of Judge Viktor Horodovenko*) [28 February 2018].
[43] Constitutional Court of Ukraine. Decision No. 4-r/2018 (*Separate Opinion of Judge Serhii Sas*) [26 April 2018].
[44] Constitutional Court of Ukraine. Decision No. 2-r/2022 [1 November 2022].
[45] Constitutional Court of Ukraine. Decision No. 2-r/2022 (*Separate Opinion of Judge Oleh Pervomaiskyi*) [1 November 2022].
[46] Constitutional Court of Ukraine. Decision No. 12-rp/2012 [30 May 2012].

coalition.[47] This question arose in March 2010 when individual members tried to form a new coalition to support President Viktor Yanukovych (2010–2014). Under Article 83(6) of the Constitution, a parliamentary coalition is constituted solely by groups, not by groups together with individual members. Nonetheless, Parliament amended Article 61 of the Rules of Procedure, allowing individual members to join the coalition. Following this amendment, a formal request was submitted to the CCU for an official interpretation of relevant provisions of both the Constitution and the Rules of Procedure.

The CCU noted that Article 83 of the Constitution stipulates that the principles governing the formation, organisation, and termination of a parliamentary coalition are established by both the Constitution and the Rules of Procedure. Accordingly, it held that the relevant constitutional provisions must be interpreted in systemic connection with the Rules of Procedure. Hence, the Court issued an official interpretation of the constitutional provisions through the prism of the newly updated norms of the Rules of Procedure. This interpretation enabled the formation of a pro-presidential coalition and the appointment of a new government, marking the initial steps in the consolidation of power by Yanukovych.

A similar dynamic occurred in Decision No. 1-rp/2016, where the Court again modified the meaning of the constitutional text by validating amendments to the Rules of Procedure.[48] On 31 August 2015, the final day of its second regular session, Parliament preliminarily approved the controversial Draft Law No. 2217a, which introduced decentralisation reforms and, among other provisions, granted special constitutional status to certain Ukrainian territories occupied by the Russian Federation.[49] Under Article 155 of the Constitution, the draft law had to be adopted during the next regular session. In the case of Draft Law No. 2217a, it was the third regular session – starting on 1 September 2015 and scheduled to conclude before 2 February 2016, the first day of the fourth regular session. Yet, procedural delays and political tension in Parliament regarding this draft law raised concerns that it might not be adopted within this constitutional timeframe.

To address this, on 28 January 2016, just days before the constitutional deadline, Parliament amended Article 149 of the Rules of Procedure to provide that if a draft constitutional amendment under Article 155 of the Constitution is preliminarily approved but not considered at the next regular session, it may instead be addressed during any subsequent regular session. Concurrently, members of Parliament requested an official interpretation from the CCU of the phrase 'at the next regular session of the Verkhovna Rada of Ukraine' in Article 155. The CCU interpreted this phrase to mean any subsequent regular session following the one in which the draft law was preliminarily approved, rather than strictly the immediate next session. Additionally, the Court emphasised that Parliament has the

[47] Constitutional Court of Ukraine. Decision No. 11-rp/2010 [6 April 2010].

[48] Constitutional Court of Ukraine. Decision No. 1-rp/2016 [15 March 2016].

[49] See TA Olszański, 'Ukraine is divided over constitutional reform' (2015) *Centre for Eastern Studies* (OSW), www.osw.waw.pl/en/publikacje/analyses/2015-09-02/ukraine-divided-over-constitutional-reform.

discretion to modify its Rules of Procedure to accommodate constitutional amendment procedures across later sessions. This interpretation created legal uncertainty and disrupted the established consensus among key political stakeholders, which had been based on the actual wording of the Constitution. While Decision No. 1-rp/2016 had no immediate effect on the political system of Ukraine,[50] its long-term political and legal consequences remain uncertain.

Decision No. 6-r/2019 further demonstrates how the wording – or indeed the absence of wording – in the Rules of Procedure can significantly influence the interpretation of relevant provisions of the Constitution.[51] When Parliament removed regulations on parliamentary coalition from the Rules of Procedure in October 2010, it failed to establish a coherent framework to govern coalition formation after 2014. This regulatory gap enabled President Volodymyr Zelenskyi to declare early parliamentary elections in 2019, citing the absence of a parliamentary coalition under Article 90(2)(1) of the Constitution as the legal basis for dissolution. The CCU noted that the existence or absence of a parliamentary coalition could not be established as a legal fact due to the regulatory gap in the Rules of Procedure. Ultimately, the Court ruled that the President's decree to dissolve Parliament was constitutional. In doing so, the CCU again linked the Constitution and the Rules of Procedure: the normative gap in the latter shaped the Court's interpretation of the constitutionality of the President's decree.

The above-mentioned decisions were severely criticised by dissenting judges. For instance, Judge Stetsiuk argued that the provisions of the Rules of Procedure cannot, under any circumstances, be considered equal in legal force to constitutional provisions.[52] Similarly, Judge Melnyk contended that the CCU unreasonably elevated the Parliament's Rules of Procedure to the same legal level as the Constitution and, in some instances, even gave it precedence.[53] As for the coalition case, Melnyk noted that, if the Rules of Procedure lacks the necessary provisions, the issue shall be addressed on the basis of the Constitution only, which sets out the basic principles for the formation of a parliamentary coalition.[54]

The Rules of Procedure is not the only instrument to which the CCU has applied this 'macro-constitutional' approach. Similar reasoning, though rare, has also been applied to other laws. As an example, in Decision No. 21-rp/2003, the Court interpreted constitutional provisions on local self-government in Kyiv City

[50] Draft Law No. 2217 was not adopted. But, if, hypothetically, it had been adopted, the Law of Ukraine No. 1680-VII '*On the Special Order for Local Self-Government in Certain Districts of Donetsk and Luhansk Oblasts*' [16 September 2014], which was adopted in advance, would have immediately officially become a part of constitutional framework.

[51] Constitutional Court of Ukraine. Decision No. 6-r/2019 [20 June 2019].

[52] Constitutional Court of Ukraine. Decision No. 11-rp/2010 (*Separate Opinion of Judge Petro Stetiuk*) [6 April 2010].

[53] Constitutional Court of Ukraine. Decision No. 1-rp/2016 (*Separate Opinion of Judge Mykola Melnyk*) [15 March 2016].

[54] Constitutional Court of Ukraine. Decision No. 6-r/2019 (*Separate Opinion of Judge Mykola Melnyk*) [20 June 2019].

through the lens of the Law of Ukraine No. 401-XIV 'On the Capital of Ukraine–Hero-City Kyiv' [15 January 1999].[55]

Regardless of how controversial or politically motivated these decisions may be, they remain valid and binding within Ukraine's legal system, as they have not yet been overturned by the Court. This line of jurisprudence by the CCU indeed reflects some multi-textual tendencies within Ukraine's constitutional order, suggesting that the constitutional text can be interpreted and applied in conjunction with other instruments that are inferior in the legal hierarchy. Perhaps in the future, the Court will adopt a more cautious interpretive approach that avoids linking constitutional provisions to extra-constitutional sources.

V. Conclusion

The analysis of Ukraine's constitutional framework – including the Independence Act, the Constitution, the Law on Adoption of Constitution, and, at a minimum, Parliament's Rules of Procedure – alongside relevant CCU decisions, reveals the existence of a hidden multi-textuality within Ukraine's constitutional framework. Although the Constitution stands as a single codified document, these supplementary instruments, while formally subordinate, play a crucial role in shaping a *macro-constitutional reality* in Ukraine. What does this reality entail? It is a constitutional order in which the codified Constitution does not operate in isolation; instead, it is complemented and shaped by auxiliary instruments that together form a broader and unified constitutional mosaic.

Ukraine's constitutional landscape presents a compelling yet underexplored subject of research. This chapter provides only a starting point in the exploration of the multi-textual elements of Ukraine's constitutional order, challenging the conventional understanding of the country's legal framework and constitutional identity. I do not doubt that future jurisprudence of the CCU may confirm, redefine, or even challenge the hypothesis presented in this chapter. Still, the CCU's interpretive activism, particularly in its engagement with the Constitution, not only highlights the possibilities for interplay between the formal text of the Constitution of Ukraine and other legal instruments but also represents a valid and exciting area for further study of constitutionalism in the country.

[55] Constitutional Court of Ukraine. Decision No. 21-rp/2003 [25 December 2003].

10

Multi-Textuality in China: Revisions and Revolutions

LEIGHA C CROUT*

I. Introduction: China's Changing Constitutions[1]

In the People's Republic of China (PRC), constitutional identification remains an ongoing conversation. The nation has adopted four Constitutions since its founding in 1949, each representative of a distinct political era. The first, promulgated in 1954, signaled the end of a civil war, the defeat of the Nationalist Party (Taiwan's Kuomintang, or KMT) by the Communist Party (CCP) forces, and the consolidation of early CCP leadership.[2] The next, adopted in 1975, facilitated the legal entrenchment of the Cultural Revolution, a violent sociopolitical movement with Communist Party Chairman Mao Zedong at its centre,[3] which decimated the nation's legal system with the aim of 'purging' any non-Communist elements that might threaten the Party's leadership. Following Mao's death, more moderate Party members introduced a transitional constitutional text in 1978 that led to the adoption of its most recent draft.[4]

China's current Constitution, first promulgated in 1982, is a product of these significant moments and has likewise been influenced by subsequent sociopolitical transformations.[5] The text has been amended five times. Its first four amendments were close in step with what might be expected in a liberal

* This chapter has benefitted from the comments received during the Spring 2025 Colloquium on Comparative Constitutional Law and Politics at the University of Texas at Austin School of Law and at the Cornell Law School Cornell Clarke Program in East Asian Law & Culture.

[1] The title of this section is an allusion to Jerome Cohen's early and groundbreaking work on China's initial three constitutions. Jerome Cohen, 'China's Changing Constitution' (1979) 1 Northwestern Journal of International Law & Business 57.

[2] PRC Constitution 1954.

[3] For a compelling firsthand account of the Cultural Revolution and its impact on Chinese law and society, see J Chang, *Wild Swans: Three Daughters of China* (First Touchstone edition, Touchstone, 2003). PRC Constitution 1975.

[4] PRC Constitution 1978.

[5] PRC Constitution 1982.

constitutional order (and indeed, a capitalist economy) – granting, first, permission for the privatisation of businesses in 1988; introducing the rule of law in 1999; then constitutionalising the government's obligation to respect and protect human rights in 2004.[6] These developments generated speculation that the nation was perhaps on a 'long march towards the rule of law,' or on a path of progressive democratisation.[7]

This cautious optimism was staunched with the amendments of 2018. These revisions eliminated term limits for the nation's highest offices, created a political supervisory body over state institutions, and constitutionalised the Communist Party's leadership.[8] These were arguably the first set of amendments enacted without conferring real, tangible public benefits or creating new rights. With these changes, China's constitutional order became very different. Led by a Party-state intolerant of dissent, the nation's formerly robust civil society and avenues for public participation have been suppressed.[9]

Some features of China's current Constitution, like its promise of the freedoms of speech and association, are now dormant.[10] Simultaneously, other areas including the structure of the legal system and citizens' obligations to the state remain binding.[11] Whether the present Constitution might truly be considered as such has been the subject of debate given its inconsistent enforcement.[12] In the absence of its judicialisation and meaningful checks on legislative overreach, China's Constitution has even been referred to as a 'dead letter,' or a Constitution that 'does not in fact constitute.'[13]

Despite this grim assessment, there is still much that can be learned through engagement with the constitutional text, its influences, and its application. The concept of multi-textuality provides a promising framework for such an inquiry. It rests on the premise that while some constitutional systems are anchored in a singular constitutional text (like that of the United States), others distribute

[6] PRC Constitution 1982 (1988 Amendment); PRC Constitution 1982 (1999 Amendment); PRC Constitution 1982 (2004 Amendment).

[7] R Peerenboom, *China's Long March toward Rule of Law*, 1st edn (Cambridge University Press, 2002) www.cambridge.org/core/product/identifier/9780511493737/type/book.

[8] PRC Constitution 1982 (2018 Amendment).

[9] Over the past decade, China's human rights record has progressively declined. See eg 'Variable Graph – V-Dem' v-dem.net/data_analysis/VariableGraph/ (evaluating the civil liberties indicator from 2014–2024). E Pils, *Human Rights in China: A Social Practice in the Shadows of Authoritarianism* (Polity, 2018)."plainCitation":"Eva Pils, Human Rights in China: A Social Practice in the Shadows of Authoritarianism (Polity 2018

[10] 'Variable Graph – V-Dem' (n 9).

[11] PRC Constitution 1982, Ch III; PRC Constitution 1982, art 54.

[12] C Minzner, *End of an Era: How China's Authoritarian Revival Is Undermining Its Rise* (Oxford University Press, 2020) (discussing how China's political leadership is 'cannibalising' institutional norms and practices in favour of political leadership).

[13] Qianfan Zhang, 'A Constitution without Constitutionalism? The Paths of Constitutional Development in China' (2010) 8 *International Journal of Constitutional Law* 950. D Clarke, 'Puzzling Observations in Chinese Law: When Is a Riddle Just a Mistake?' in S Hsu (ed), *Understanding China's Legal System: Essays in Honor of Jerome A. Cohen* 93 (New York University Press, 2003).

constitutional meaning across multiple texts of equal legal force.[14] Multi-textual constitutionality may invigorate this otherwise dormant field by expanding the scope of what might be considered part of China's Constitution, though the challenges of this approach are incidental to the opportunities it presents.

For example, there exists in the PRC a body of 'Constitution-related laws' (宪法相关法, *xianfa xiangguan fa*) that build upon the main constitutional text. These laws are not only related to constitutional guarantees; they are also contemplated and anticipated by the text of the Constitution. These laws relate to key aspects of governance, including legislation, courtroom administration, and the management of Special Administrative Regions (SARs) like Hong Kong and Macau.[15] The Basic Laws of these SARs are sometimes considered important features of constitutional law in China.[16]

Building on this understanding, some scholars have put forward a different and more politicised version of multi-textuality, one that includes the Constitution's Preamble, which has historically been considered non-binding. Left-leaning (that is, pro-government) scholars argue that the Preamble offers a reflection of China's history and instantiates the importance of the Communist Party.[17] Other scholars take this argument further, proposing that the Charter of the Communist Party must also be treated as a binding part of the Constitution; and furthermore, that certain unwritten features (like political authority) must take precedence over formal legal provisions.[18]

In the converse, reformist scholars reject this Party-centric approach, offering different proposals of what they consider to be China's 'true Constitution' – one with rights, checks on government power, and the rule of law.[19] Influential grassroots proposals reflecting these values have been regularly proposed over the last two decades, including one co-drafted by Nobel Peace Prize laureate Liu Xiaobo.[20] These

[14] Professor Albert indicates in his Article that in practice the United States Constitution may in fact be considered a multi-textual one; however, its other documents have not received the requisite public recognition as sources of constitutional law. R Albert, 'Multi-Textual Constitutions' (2023) 109 *Virginia Law Review* 1629.

[15] PRC Constitution 1982, art 89; PRC Constitution 1982, art 131; PRC Constitution 1982, art 31.

[16] Given these are themselves the organising laws of virtually autonomous areas, this is a controversial perspective. The resource provided is a translation of an article that is no longer available at its original source. The piece discusses Hong Kong's Basic Law as 'an important part of the constitutional system of the country.' Jiang Shigong, 'Probing the Imaginary World' (*Reading the China Dream*) www.readingthechinadream.com/jiang-shigong-probing-the-imaginary-world.html.

[17] Xie Weiyan (谢维雁), 'Lun xianfa xuyan (论宪法序言) [Discussing the Constitution's Preamble]' (2004) 5 *Social Sciences Research* (社会科学研究).

[18] Chen Duanhong (陈端洪), 'Chen Duanhong: lun xianfa zuowei guojia de genbenfa yu gaojifa,' (陈端洪：论宪法作为国家的根本法与高级法) [Chen Duanhong: The Constitution as the Fundamental Law and Highest Law of the Country] Public Law Research Center of Renmin University (2008), www.calaw.cn/article/default.asp?id=1210.

[19] Qianfan Zhang, *The Constitution of China: A Contextual Analysis* (Hart Publishing, 2012); Zhangrun Xu, 'Viral Alarm: When Fury Overcomes Fear' (2019) 31 *Journal of Democracy* 5.

[20] I refer here to Charter 08, a political manifesto calling for a democratic transition in China and challenging one-party rule. For an English translation, see P Link, 'China's Charter 08 | Perry Link' www.nybooks.com/articles/2009/01/15/chinas-charter-08/.

texts and the broad public acclimation they have inspired raise different and intriguing questions about the status and future of China's constitutional whereabouts.

The following section discusses how multi-textuality might act as a conceptual binding agent in this dormant and highly politicised field and investigate the question of China's constitutional identification. It begins with an analysis of the major jurisprudential arguments regarding the nature of the Constitution in China, providing a foundation for understanding how these perspectives may interact with multi-textual constitutionality. This chapter then turns to the question of whether China's Constitution can be meaningfully understood as multi-textual and founded upon multiple instantiations of higher law, and considers the implications and challenges that would arise from this characterisation.

II. Perspectives on Multi-Textuality in China

The nature and scope of the Constitution are controversial subjects in the People's Republic of China. Since 2013, the Constitution and related terminology have become increasingly politically sensitive (敏感, *mingan*) on and offline, to the point that scholarship that contradicts or criticises Party-state orthodoxy is often subject to censorship.[21] Authors of such work risk professional demotion, confrontations with law enforcement, or even enforced disappearances, creating a chilling effect on domestic academic contributions to the field.[22]

Prior to the current administration, pro-government scholars with more extreme viewpoints were largely considered outliers and disruptors that delegitimised meaningful discussions of reform.[23] Today, however, it is considerably more challenging for reformist perspectives to enter constitutional discourse.[24]

Because of the topic's political sensitivity, the range of scholarly contributions has dramatically waned. Questions of constitutional identification tend to be addressed by those on either end of the political spectrum who are more willing or more able to take on the subject.[25] This includes liberal scholars, who adopt a 'Western' or thick understanding of constitutionalism and the rule of law, and pro-government scholars who are generally supportive of Party leadership.

[21] There are many individual examples of resources becoming inaccessible or otherwise unavailable. Zhang Qianfan's textbook on constitutional law was pulled from the shelves in 2019 as part of a campaign against Western influences in education. C Shepherd, 'Disappearing Textbook Highlights Debate in China over Academic Freedom' *Reuters* (24 July 2019) web.archive.org/web/20190724081338/https://ca.reuters.com/article/topNews/idCAKCN1PQ45T-OCATP.

[22] 'China: Free Rights Defenders for Lunar New Year | Human Rights Watch' (24 January 2020) www.hrw.org/news/2020/01/24/china-free-rights-defenders-lunar-new-year.

[23] TE Kellogg, 'Arguing Chinese Constitutionalism: The 2013 Constitutional Debate and the "Urgency" of Political Reform' (2016) 11 *University of Pennsylvania Asian Law Review* 337, 399.

[24] See T Phillips, '"It's Getting Worse": China's Liberal Academics Fear Growing Censorship' *The Guardian* (6 August 2015) www.theguardian.com/world/2015/aug/06/china-xi-jinping-crackdown-liberal-academics-minor-cultural-revolution.

[25] Kellogg (n 23) 399.

Prior to considering the relationship of these theorists and their proposals with the concept of multi-textuality in this text, this Part will first offer an abbreviated critical summary of the main arguments submitted by the proponents of these core approaches to the question of constitutional identification in the Chinese context.

A. The New Left

A contingent of pro-government constitutional law theorists has become known as the 'New Left' in China. The moniker represents an ideological shift from the 'Old Left' guard that preceded them during Mao's leadership, whose shared traditions fell out of favour following the nation's transition out of the Cultural Revolution in the late 1970s and 1980s.[26] There are significant distinctions between the Old and New that will not be addressed here, but it must be said that the New Left is a more diverse group than that of its predecessor. This group adopts a broad range of approaches to constitutional law and theory, both critical and supportive of state action.

This analysis incorporates works within this camp that are united by a belief in the centrality of the nation's political leadership – specifically, that the Communist Party's right to rule is an inseparable aspect of China's constitutional governance.[27] These scholars recognise 'socialism with Chinese characteristics' (中国特色社会主义, *zhongguo tese shehui zhuyi*), as referenced in the Constitution's Preamble, as the correct model of governance for a modern, socialist China.[28]

The New Left's understanding of China's Constitution is that it is realistic, contextual, and organic.[29] Setting aside for a moment the nature of these arguments, New Left proponents hold, first, that the text is realistic in that it is descriptive of the actual realities of constitutional governance in China.[30] The Constitution is contextual in that it is divorced from the idealism inherent in much of Western or liberal constitutional theory and is instead based on China's own theoretical traditions.[31]

[26] Li He, 'China's New Left' in *Political Thought and China's Transformation: Ideas Shaping Reform in Post-Mao China* (Palgrave Macmillan, 2015).

[27] This group is sometimes referred to as Political Constitutionalists, as a smaller subset of New Left theorists. The broader term is used here to widen the pool of theorists whose work touches on this point. L Crout, 'Present Trends of Authoritarian Legality in China: The Operational Constitution' (2023) 8 *Asian Law Bulletin* 39.

[28] PRC Constitution 1982 Preamble.

[29] Gao Quanxi (高全喜), '政治宪法学的兴起于嬗变' ['Emergence and Evolution of Political Constitutionalism'] in idem, 政治宪法学纲要 [Outline of Political Constitutionalism] (Central Compilation and Translation Press, Beijing, 2014) 1, 6; L Brang, 'Carl Schmitt and the Evolution of Chinese Constitutional Theory: Conceptual Transfer and the Unexpected Paths of Legal Globalisation' (2020) 9 *Global Constitutionalism* 117, 134.

[30] Crout (n 27).

[31] Su Li, *The Constitution of Ancient China* (Zhang Yongle and Daniel A Bell eds, Princeton University Press, 2018) www.degruyter.com/document/doi/10.23943/9781400889778/html.

Finally, the Constitution is organic in that it represents a form of governance that is consistent with the nation's history and is representative of a natural construction based on the development trajectory of the legal system. Consistent with this idea, much of the new left draws from the work of Carl Schmitt, including his understanding of a constitution as inherently political in both form and nature.[32]

Consistent with this framework, the New Left embraces the idea that China's Constitution can be identified only through reference to a variety of sources. Although there are minor disagreements within the group about which sources precisely are among this number, there is prominent alignment on the constitutional relevance of the Constitution's Preamble and the Charter of the Communist Party of China.[33] The emphasis on the legality of the Preamble can also be traced back to Schmitt.[34] Whether China's constitution-related laws are a natural part of China's Constitution is not a settled matter among the group.

The New Left also holds that certain political norms possess the same legal force as the main constitutional text. These include the Party's leadership, the principle of democratic centralism (as an alternative to the separation of powers), and the forms of political thought introduced by China's influential political leaders, like 'Xi Jinping Thought on Socialism with Chinese Characteristics for a New Era,' now codified in the Preamble.[35]

Certain aspects of these arguments at best implicate the values of democracy and constitutionalism, and at worst directly undermine them. As a result, liberal reformist constitutional scholars have condemned the approach of the New Left as antithetical to both. For example, the elevation of the Charter of the Communist Party and the Preamble to constitutional status does raise serious concerns regarding equal political participation.

Alongside the elimination of term limits, the 2018 constitutional amendments mentioned earlier in this chapter also altered the Preamble. It was modified to explicitly codify the CCP's exclusive legal and political leadership.[36] The Party's own organisational Charter affirms this point, stating that:

> [The CCP] shall lead the people in developing socialist democracy, … preserve the organic unity of Party leadership, the running of the country by the people, and law-based governance, [and] follow the Chinese socialist path of political development and the path of socialist rule of law with Chinese characteristics.[37]

[32] C Schmitt, *Constitutional Theory* (J Seitzer tr, Duke University Press, 2008) 78–79. E Pils, 'China's Dual State Revival' (2022) 46 *Fordham International Law Journal.*

[33] Some scholars liken China's current orientation towards law to that of Nazi Germany – a dual state structure that holds space for both a formal legal system and the prerogatives of the nation's political leadership. See Brang (n 29); Pils (n 32).

[34] Schmitt (n 32) 78–79.

[35] Chen (n 18).

[36] PRC Constitution 1982 Preamble (2018 Amendments).

[37] '中国共产党章程 (Zhongguo Gongchandang Zhangcheng) [Charter of the Communist Party of China]' www.12371.cn/2017/10/28/ARTI1509191507150883.shtml.

The concentration of complete legal and political power in the Communist Party raises serious questions regarding the New Left's perspective on constitutional identification. The following section will consider this theory from the opposing end and present the perspectives of their intellectual adversaries – the liberal reformist scholars working within and outside China.

B. Liberal Reformers

Scholastic dialogue on constitutional law and theory is closely regulated by China's political leadership. This control is observable not only in the filtering and censorship of certain publications, but also in explicit statements within internal Party documents on at least one occasion. In 2013, a document called the 'Communique on the Current State of the Ideological Sphere' (hereinafter the Communique) was leaked by journalist Gao Yu.[38] In this document, the Party paints constitutionalism and Party leadership as diametrically opposed:

> Western Constitutional Democracy has distinct political properties and aims. Among these are the separation of powers, the multi-party system, general elections, independent judiciaries, nationalized armies, and other characteristics. … The concept of constitutional democracy originated a long time ago, and recently the idea has been hyped ever more frequently. … In commemorating the thirtieth anniversary of the enactment of the [Chinese] Constitution, [some people] hold up the banners of 'defending the constitution' and 'rule of law.' They attack the Party's leaders for placing themselves above the constitution, saying China 'has a constitution but no constitutional government.
>
> The point of publicly proclaiming Western constitutional democracy's key points is to oppose the party's leadership and implementation of its constitution and laws. Their goal is to use Western constitutional democracy to undermine the Party's leadership, abolish the People's Democracy, negate our country's constitution as well as our established system and principles, and bring about a change of allegiance by bringing Western political systems to China.[39]

The Communique was drafted and leaked at the very start of Xi Jinping's term in office. It references the percolating discussions on liberal constitutionality and the rule of law that were quite wide-ranging at that time.[40] Consistent with the sentiments in the Communique, it has since become even more challenging to publicly

[38] This exposé was exceptional. Internal Party memoranda like this Communique almost never appear in public media. Gao Yu was 73 years old at the time of the leak, and was later sentenced to 7 years in prison for the 'release of state secrets.' Her sentence was subsequently reduced to 5 years in light of health concerns, most of which she was able to serve under house arrest. C Buckley, 'Chinese Journalist Sentenced to 7 Years on Charges of Leaking State Secrets' *The New York Times* (17 April 2015) www.nytimes.com/2015/04/17/world/asia/china-journalist-gao-yu-gets-7-year-sentence.html.

[39] 'Document 9: A ChinaFile Translation' (*ChinaFile*, 8 November 2013) www.chinafile.com/document-9-chinafile-translation.

[40] Kellogg (n 23).

articulate support for Western or liberal-style constitutionalism in China.[41] One consequence is that official journals are less likely to accept such pieces, since their publishers may face political repercussions if the piece gains traction as an anti-Party text.[42]

As a result, equally qualified liberal scholars who oppose New Left-style constitutionality are often forced to publish their works in the online public sphere as open letters, or in international journals that are more receptive to these perspectives. Of course, sometimes this is done strategically to generate broad public support or to appeal to international audiences.[43] However, it does not change the fact that liberal scholars are more limited in their opportunities to publish, share, and discuss their contributions to the field of constitutional law in China.

Liberal scholars themselves are a diverse group, even more so than the New Left. There are many, for example, who identify as quasi-libertarian or populist strands of thought and have voiced support for figures like Donald Trump.[44] Despite these internal divisions, there are some features that unite these liberal perspectives, many of which relate to the question of constitutional identification.

Contrary to the New Left's positioning of the Constitution as a document reflecting the realities of China and supplemented by political texts, liberal scholars argue that this approach does not reflect a 'legitimate' constitutional order.[45] Legitimacy, in this context, refers to the values imputed to constitutionalism by traditional liberal theory – specifically, the rule of law, the separation of powers, and human rights, among others.[46]

[41] See eg A Jacobs, 'Chinese Professor Who Advocated Free Speech Is Fired' *The New York Times* (10 December 2013) www.nytimes.com/2013/12/11/world/asia/chinese-professor-who-advocated-free-speech-is-fired.html.

[42] See eg Kiki Zhao, 'Liberal Chinese Journal, Claiming Interference by Overseers, Files Lawsuit' *The New York Times* (15 July 2016) www.nytimes.com/2016/07/16/world/asia/yanhuang-chunqiu-china-du-daozheng.html.

[43] Prior to his enforced disappearance, Xu Zhiyong was a prolific author of open letters calling for constitutionalism and criticising leader Xi Jinping. Zhiyong Xu, 'Dear Chairman Xi, It's Time for You to Go' (Geremie Barmé tr, *ChinaFile*, 26 February 2020) www.chinafile.com/reporting-opinion/viewpoint/dear-chairman-xi-its-time-you-go.

[44] The sharp division on support for Trump has driven a wedge within liberal scholars. Those in support are sometimes referred to as the 'conservative liberals,' who accuse their white liberals (白左, *bai zuo*) counterparts as being overly politically correct. For a fascinating discussion in English on the acclimation of Chinese liberal scholars and activists to Trumpian politics, see Ling Li and Teng Biao, 'An Anatomy of Trump's Appeal to Chinese Liberals: A Conversation with Teng Biao' (*Made in China Journal*, 1 February 2021) madeinchinajournal.com/2021/02/01/an-anatomy-of-trumps-appeal-to-chinese-liberals-a-conversation-with-teng-biao/; Qianfan Zhang, 'Zhang Qianfan, "Left and Right"' (David Ownsby tr, *Reading the China Dream*) www.readingthechinadream.com/zhang-qianfan-left-and-right.html.

[45] Xu Zhangrun (许章润), 'Xu Zhangrun: guodu zhengti xia de linshi xianfa (许章润｜过渡政体下的临时宪法) [An Interim Constitution Under a Transitional Regime]' (中国数字时代 [*China Digital Times*], 28 May 2012) chinadigitaltimes.net/chinese/227641.html; Zhang, *The Constitution of China* (n 19).

[46] Some scholars refer to this as a 'thick' as opposed to a 'thin'-style constitutionalism. See FI Michelman, *Constitutional Essentials: On the Constitutional Theory of Political Liberalism* (Oxford University Press, 2022); M Tushnet and B Bugarič, 'What Is Constitutionalism?' in *Power to the People* (Oxford University Press, 2022) academic.oup.com/book/38889/chapter/338031927.

This sentiment is reflected in liberal scholars' assessment of the Constitution itself. While there are some elements of China's written Constitution that appear quite similar to constitutions in liberal democracies, it also incorporates certain principles and ideas that reinforce authoritarian governance.[47] Along with the political principles emphasised by the New Left, the Constitution imposes obligations on citizens to respect the motherland and keep state secrets, among other responsibilities.[48] Thus, contrary to New Left approaches, only some portions of China's Constitution are regarded as binding constitutional norms by liberals. These include articles preserving judicial independence and checks and balances on state power. However, these are also the same provisions most systematically violated by the Party-state government.

This division between text and practice – and other motivating factors – has sparked several grassroots efforts to draft alternative constitutional texts and petition for the revival of constitutional rights over the past few decades.[49] The most internationally prominent of these was led in part by Liu Xiaobo, the Nobel Peace Prize laureate who passed away in prison in 2017 for his involvement in this and other efforts to advance liberal constitutionalism in China.[50] He and several other scholars took part in drafting Charter 08, a manifesto that proposed an alternative constitutional vision for China:

> [T]he ruling elite continues with impunity to crush and to strip away the rights of citizens to freedom, to property, and to the pursuit of happiness, we see the powerless in our society – the vulnerable groups, the people who have been suppressed and monitored, who have suffered cruelty and even torture, and who have had no adequate avenues for their protests, no courts to hear their pleas – becoming more militant and raising the possibility of a violent conflict of disastrous proportions. The decline of the current system has reached the point where change is no longer optional. …
>
> The time is arriving everywhere for citizens to be masters of states. For China the path that leads out of our current predicament is to divest ourselves of the authoritarian notion of reliance on an 'enlightened overlord' or an 'honest official' and to turn instead toward a system of liberties, democracy, and the rule of law, and toward fostering the consciousness of modern citizens who see rights as fundamental and participation as a duty. Accordingly, and in a spirit of this duty as responsible and constructive citizens,

[47] Crout (n 27).

[48] PRC Constitution 1982, arts 53–54.

[49] One recent open letter was drafted by long-time members of the Communist Party. See Editorial, '三名中共老党员董洪义、马贵会、田奇庄发联名发表公开信反对'党领导一切', 呼吁坚决抵制'个人崇拜', 避免文革的悲剧重演 (San Ming Zhonggong Lao Dangyuan, Dong Hongyi, Ma Guihui, Tian Qizhuang Fa Lianming Fabiao Gongkaixin Fandui 'Dang Lingdao Yiqie', Huyu Jianjue Dizhi 'Geren Chongbai', Bimian Wenge de Beiju Chongyan) [Three Veteran Members of the Communist Party of China, Dong Hongyi, Ma Guihui, and Tian Qizhuang, Jointly Issued an Open Letter Opposing 'the Party's Leadership of Everything' and Called for a Resolute Boycott of the 'Personality Cult' to Avoid a Recurrence of the Tragedy of the Cultural Revolution]' 维权网 (*Weiquan Wang* [*Rights Protection Network*]) (25 August 2022) wqw2010.blogspot.com/2022/08/blog-post_31.html.

[50] Liu Xiaobo was denied timely medical care and passed away from complications arising from liver cancer. Chris Buckley, 'Liu Xiaobo, Chinese Dissident Who Won Nobel While Jailed, Dies at 61' *The New York Times* (13 July 2017) www.nytimes.com/2017/07/13/world/asia/liu-xiaobo-dead.html.

> we offer the following recommendations on national governance, citizens' rights, and social development.[51]

Charter 08 proceeds to offer both a set of core values and specific recommendations for building a new constitutional state. Among its 19 proposals, the first five call for the adoption of a new constitution, the separation of powers, legislative democracy, an independent judiciary, and public control of public servants.[52] To these liberal scholars, a constitution is not a 'true' constitution in the absence of these core ideals. From their perspective, the question of constitutional identification is necessarily tied to the question of constitutional legitimacy.

Other notable grassroots attempts at constitutional drafting emerged during the COVID-19 pandemic, when the central government implemented punishingly long-term and poorly managed lockdowns.[53] These efforts include the Freedom of Speech Petition, issued in response to the death of COVID-19 whistleblower Dr. Li Wenliang; Professor Xu Zhangrun's essay *When Fury Overcomes Fear* against oppressive authoritarian governance; and 'Bridge Man' Peng Lifa's manifesto advocating for political freedoms, inspired by Charter 08.[54] All three of these publications, like Charter 08, offer new constitutional designs and call for the revival of constitutional rights and principles that have grown dormant over the past decade.

On one side of the political divide, the New Left argues that China's Constitution is drawn from a variety of sources. It derives its content not only from the main constitutional text, but also from supplementary political documents and the principle of Party leadership. On the other end of the spectrum, liberal scholars maintain that this style of multi-textuality is dangerous – and that the only valid Constitution is one aligned with classic ideals of liberal constitutionalism and the values that entails.

[51] Link (n 20).

[52] ibid.

[53] The lockdowns began in November 2019 and continued until December 2022. From the beginning, problems were reported regarding mismanaged resource distribution and a lack of access to healthcare services. One of the key problems was the absence of communication between relevant government agencies and representatives. Zhongjie Li and others, 'Comprehensive Large-Scale Nucleic Acid–Testing Strategies Support China's Sustained Containment of COVID-19' (2021) 27 *Nature Medicine* 740; 'Dissenting Voices Speak out against Ongoing Zero-COVID Restrictions in China' (*Radio Free Asia*) www.rfa.org/english/news/china/dissent-08292022203026.html.

[54] Editorial, 'CDS档案 | 言论自由从今天开始 – – 中国民众纪念李文亮医生（持续更新）(CDS Dang'an | Yanlun Ziyou Cong Jintian Kaishi – Zhongguo Minzhong Jinian Li Wenliang Yisheng [Chixu Gengxin]) [CDS Archives | Freedom of Speech Starts Today – Chinese People Commemorate Dr Li Wenliang]' *Chinese Digital Times* (7 February 2020) chinadigitaltimes.net/chinese/634788.html; Zhangrun Xu, 'Viral Alarm: When Fury Overcomes Fear (An Essay by Xu Zhangrun, Translated and Annotated by Geremie R. Barmé)' *ChinaFile* (10 February 2020) www.chinafile.com/reporting-opinion/viewpoint/viral-alarm-when-fury-overcomes-fear; 许章润 (Xu Zhangrun), '【404文库】许章润：愤怒的人民已不再恐惧 (404 Wenku: Xu Zhangrun: Fennu de renmin yi bu zai kongju) [404 Library: Xu Zhangrun: The Angry People Are No Longer Afraid]' 中国数字时代 (*ZHONGGUO SHUZI SHIDAI*) [*CHINA DIGITAL TIMES*] (4 February 2020) chinadigitaltimes.net/chinese/634216.html; Editorial, '"Bridge Man" Peng Zaizhou's Mission Impossible and His "Toolkit for the Removal of Xi Jinping"' *China Change* (20 October 2022) chinachange.org/2022/10/19/bridge-man-peng-zaizhous-mission-impossible-and-his-toolkit-for-the-removal-of-xi-jinping/.

Meaningful dialogue between these camps is frustrated by their mutual refusal to recognise the legitimacy of one another's perspectives. Given their divergent understandings of constitutionality, it is unlikely that these approaches could ever be truly reconciled. In this context, Richard Albert's concept of multi-textual constitutionality may provide a new analytical platform for these discussions – though, like the above positions, it cannot be entirely divorced from questions of constitutional legitimacy.

The following section will discuss how this style of multi-textuality might fit in China's legal system. First, it begins with how multi-textual constitutionality may contribute to an ongoing constitutional debate. It then turns to how this concept interacts with existing perspectives on China's constitutional identification question, and the challenges and opportunities this approach presents.

C. Multi-Textual Constitutionality

Multi-textual constitutions, in Albert's view, possess three essential characteristics. The first is *multiplicity*, meaning that constitutional rules can be found through reference to multiple written texts, primarily legislation but not excluding other texts. The second is *asynchrony*, meaning that the different components of the constitution are adopted *asynchronously* in response to the 'needs and forces of the time.'[55] The third is *shared supremacy*, whereby these texts, like a constitution, trump any inconsistent laws or rules.

Another condition of shared supremacy is that a constitutional document must be either legally or politically entrenched. Put simply, legal entrenchment indicates that the document cannot be repealed by ordinary legislative measures. Political entrenchment, by contrast, exists under the limited circumstances where certain texts are regarded as 'constitutionally special but nonetheless technically remain revisable or replaceable by ordinary legislative means.'[56]

Finally – and quite significantly – Albert identifies a sociological test of public recognition that distinguishes a 'uni-textual constitution' from a multi-textual one. Even if the aforementioned formal criteria are met, a constitution may still not be considered multi-textual if public recognition fails to meet a certain threshold in law and society.[57] The parameters of this test are limited, though Albert uses the US Constitution as a compelling illustration of this point. He specifically remarks that, although the US Constitution is likely multi-textual in practice, public veneration of the text's controlling uni-textual status means that it is not likely to cross the threshold into a multi-textual type.[58]

[55] Albert (n 14) 1629, 1637.
[56] ibid 1639–40.
[57] ibid.
[58] ibid 1697.

In China, multi-textuality may provide an answer to an ongoing and controversial constitutional debate. In explaining the drafting process, one author of China's 1982 Constitution described it as 'unfinished,' and the sum result of political compromise amid Party divisions.[59] The generality of several mandates demanded further development, which was subsequently addressed by the introduction of a unique set of laws.

These are the so-called 'Constitution-related laws,' also known as China's basic laws – legislation that supplements and complements the constitutional text. They are a clearer (and perhaps slightly less controversial) source of constitutional rules. They build upon the Constitution's foundational mandates to construct a practical implementation programme.

These laws address topics that are central to national governance procedures and inform the operation of China's legal system. These areas include:

> (1) the creation, organization, functions, and operations of state institutions; (2) the systems of ethnic regional autonomy and grassroots-level self-governance; (3) special administrative regions; (4) state sovereignty and territory, national security, and national symbols; and (5) citizens' fundamental political rights.[60]

There is no set number of laws, but legislation addressing these subjects is generally recognised as part of this greater constitutional body.

These laws would meet the multi-textual constitutionality metrics. They were adopted at different points in China's history, often in response to the legal challenges of the time, and they trump any other laws or regulations on their subjects of focus.[61] Moreover, the amendment procedures for several of these laws (if not all) are distinct from those governing ordinary laws.[62]

Ordinary legislation in China can be amended at will by the Standing Committee of the National People's Congress (NPCSC), the highest organ of the legislative

[59] Peng Zhen (彭真), Guanyu Zhonghua Renmin Gongheguo Xianfa Xiugai Caoan De Baogao (中华人民共和国宪法修改草案的报告) [The Report on the Draft of the Constitutional Amendments of the People's Republic of China], Nov. 26, 1982. Yan Lin, 'Constitutional Evolution through Legislation: The Quiet Transformation of China's Constitution' (2015) 13 *International Journal of Constitutional Law* 61, 63.

[60] This is a summary adapted from a political speech and translated by the NPC Observer, an online platform run in part by Yale's Tsai China Center meant to provide accessible information on the NPC to English speakers. Li Fei (李飞), 'Lifa Fa Yu Quanguo Renmin Daibiao Dahui Changweihui de Lifa Gongzuo (立法法与全国人大常委会的立法工作: 中国人大网) [The Legislation Law and the Legislative Work of the Standing Committee of the National People's Congress]' (*Quanguo renmin daibiao dahui (全国人民代表大会) [The National People's Congress of the People's Republic of China]*, 29 June 2018) www.npc.gov.cn/npc/c12434/c541/201905/t20190521_268462.html. Changhao Wei, 'Legislation: China's National Laws' (*NPC Observer*) npcobserver.com/legislation/statutes/; Changhao Wei, 'About Us' (*NPC Observer*) npcobserver.com/about/.

[61] For example, the Law of the People's Republic of China on Regional Ethnic Autonomy stipulates that any ethnic autonomous areas shall govern themselves 'according to the authority invested in them as prescribed by the Constitution and by this Law.' Law of the People's Republic of China on Regional Ethnic Autonomy, adopted by the National People's Congress on 31 May 1984, revised 28 February 2001, translation available at en.npc.gov.cn.cdurl.cn/2024-01/10/c_954912.htm.

[62] Legislation Law of the People's Republic of China, adopted by the National People's Congress on 15 March 2000, revised 15 March 2015, art 10, translation available at www.chinalawtranslate.com/en/legislation-law-2023/.

branch.[63] However, Constitution-related laws cannot be altered by the NPCSC in ways that interfere with their 'basic principles' without convening the full National People's Congress. From a multi-textual constitutional perspective, this legal entrenchment confers on these laws constitutional supremacy.[64] Depending on the content of these laws, some consensus could exist on their necessity as natural constitutional developments.

While this may not seem controversial, problematic aspects become clear when remembering the dualistic nature of China's Constitution and its inconsistent enforcement. Certain laws that are typically considered Constitution-related laws by state actors perpetuate the suppression of civil and political rights. For example, the Law on Assemblies, Processions, and Demonstrations imposes severe restrictions on freedom of assembly; the Heroes and Martyrs Protections Law likewise limits the freedom of speech by prohibiting the defamation of national heroes; and the Supervision Law establishes a constitutionally ordained political body tasked with monitoring the ethics of public officials, further entrenching Party oversight.[65] The acknowledgement of these anti-liberal laws as part of China's constitutional framework inevitably forces arguments on legitimacy back to the fore.

A comparison with the New Left's interpretation of constitutionality further strains the boundaries of multi-textuality, presenting new concerns about how the concept might apply within an authoritarian state. From a New Left perspective, an argument for recognising China's multi-textual constitutionality might proceed as follows.

First, the Constitution may clearly be found in multiple textual sources, like the Preamble and the Charter of the Communist Party of China. The Charter, adopted asynchronously with the Constitution, certainly satisfies the second requirement of multi-textuality. While the Preamble was originally adopted along with the main text in 1982, its subsequent revisions and elevated political status would not disqualify it as a distinct constitutional text. Finally, these texts are the object of shared supremacy as a matter of course – the Preamble is only modifiable under the same conditions as the Constitution itself, and the Charter has arguably achieved political entrenchment, granting it the status of a constitutionally special text.[66]

[63] ibid art 10.

[64] ibid art 20.

[65] Law of the People's Republic of China on Assemblies, Processions, and Demonstrations, adopted by the Standing Committee of the National People's Congress on 31 October 1989, effective 1 October 1990, translation available at www.npc.gov.cn/zgrdw/englishnpc/Law/2007-12/12/content_1383911.htm. Heroes and Martyrs Protection Law of the People's Republic of China, adopted by the Standing Committee of the National People's Congress on 27 April 2018, effective 1 May 2018, translation available at www.chinalawtranslate.com/en/peoples-republic-of-china-law-on-protection-of-heroes-and-martyrs/. Supervision Law of the People's Republic of China, adopted by the National People's Congress on 20 March 2018, effective 20 March 2018, translation available at www.chinalawtranslate.com/en/supervision-law-2025/.

[66] For a similar argument from a New Left scholar, see Jiang Shigong, 'Written and Unwritten Constitutions: A New Approach to the Study of Constitutional Government in China' (2010) 36 *Modern China* 12.

If we accept this New Left interpretation, multi-textuality appears to incorporate documents that grant supreme legal and political authority to one entity – the Communist Party. Given the Party's rights record and the sharp decline of the rule of law under its current leadership, it is difficult to lend credence to these claims without also legitimising or 'constitutionalising' the Party's authoritarian governance.

Liberal scholars of Chinese constitutional law may paint an opposite portrait, one that highlights the opportunities presented by multi-textuality. In lieu of viewing political texts as the multiple sources from which China's Constitution draws, they may, first, indicate that the New Left's interpretation would fail the sociological test of legitimacy; and second, point to different grassroots constitutional proposals as the more likely recipients of broad social approval.

On this first point regarding the sociological recognition of China's Constitution, the liberal perspective holds water. Neil Damant, for example, has conducted a pertinent and comprehensive historical analysis of China's 1954 Constitution and the way in which the state, independent entities, and civil society interacted with the document.[67] On the whole, what he observed is consistent with core principles of legal mobilisation.[68] While many citizens did not believe all the promises included in the constitutional text, they were able to use its contents in a sophisticated and useful way that improved their status as citizens. Observing the Constitution's mandates, in turn, granted the Constitution credence and legitimacy in the eyes of the people.[69]

By contrast, it is not difficult to imagine that the New Left's vision of multi-textual constitutionality, rooted in unfulfilled political promises and Party supremacy, would fail such a public legitimacy test. However, it is important to acknowledge here that it is virtually impossible to prove either argument on the basis of sociological legitimacy given the difficulties in acquiring data on authentic public opinions in China.

Liberal scholars may also argue that China's 'real' Constitution is best represented by grassroots texts like Charter 08, or other proposals that seek to preserve the people's political authority. From this perspective, the multiple texts that would facilitate a transition into a constitutional democracy would meet the parameters that multi-textual constitutionality sets.

The debates surrounding constitutional identification inexorably involve existential discussions for the current regime – which is why this topic is considered politically sensitive. Constitutional legitimacy is a challenging topic at the best of

[67] NJ Diamant, *Useful Bullshit: Constitutions in Chinese Politics and Society* (Cornell University Press, 2021).

[68] MW McCann, *Rights at Work: Pay Equity Reform and the Politics of Legal Mobilization* (Reprint, University of Chicago Press, 1997); M McCann and J Dudas, 'Retrenchment … and Resurgence? Mapping the Changing Context of Movement Lawyering in the United States' in A Sarat and SA Scheingold (eds), *Cause Lawyers and Social Movements* (Stanford University Press, 2006) www.degruyter.com/document/doi/10.1515/9780804767965-004/html.

[69] Diamant (n 67) 2–4.

times, and is a special consideration when equal political participation is threatened or suppressed. At present, it is difficult to apply multi-textual constitutionality in an authoritarian context like China without tangling with these considerations.

However, certain adaptations or clarifications related to multi-textual constitutionality could encourage future discussion. One way forward would be to limit multi-textual constitutionality to liberal democracies, where there may be fewer concerns about granting certain political documents constitutional status. In doing so, this would entirely avoid questions of legality and legitimacy under an authoritarian order, though it is perhaps a disappointing limitation for those interested in how multi-textual constitutionality might shape comparative constitutional studies in authoritarian contexts.

Another method of adapting multi-textuality to an authoritarian context would be to limit its application to textual sources that do not consolidate or reinforce authoritarian governance. For example, while the Patriotic Education Law would be excluded from constitutional status, the National Emblem Law could be brought into the fold.

There are many paths forward from here. In sum, multi-textuality may offer an exciting framework for ongoing discussions regarding China's Constitutional identification. However, it is ultimately not immune from some of the main challenges that have long frustrated internal discussions on constitutional identification. These key questions must be addressed to fully explore the true potential of multi-constitutionality.

III. Conclusion

This chapter discusses multi-textuality as a concept and how it interacts with constitutional law and theory in the People's Republic of China. It began with a brief introduction of China's recent constitutional history and the heightened political sensitivity of the topic under the current administration. It then introduced some of the main arguments related to constitutional identification within China, which are then organised along the political spectrum.

The following proceeded to discuss two prominent jurisprudential approaches to constitutional theory, including those advocated by the New Left, a group of pro-government aligned scholars, and liberal theorists, who adopt a 'Western' approach to constitutionalism and whose works are heavily censored by state authorities. Questions of legal and political legitimacy are central to both camps of theorists, yet both respectively challenge the validity of the other's approach.

The final section of this chapter discussed how multi-textual constitutionality might be received in China. It stipulated that while there is potential for multi-textual constitutionality to resolve controversial debates and encourage further engagement among theorists, it is unfortunately not immune from some of the challenges that frustrate dialogue between the two main camps. Moreover, these considerations are likely endemic to authoritarian contexts in which the law is utilised as a tool to entrench absolute political authority.

For multi-textuality to reach its full analytical potential, its characteristics must be reassessed. Can multi-textuality be divorced from democracies with independent institutions and 'thick' constitutionalism? If so, are there boundaries to what might be considered a source of constitutional law? What – and perhaps, whose – values are necessary to those assessments?

In encouraging these questions, multi-textuality redirects attention back to this topic of law and legitimacy in authoritarian states. It returns us to the foundational question of what, exactly, we mean when we refer to our Constitution, and what that may entail.

11

Multi-Textuality and the Question of Constitutional Authorship

DOLUNAY BULUT

I. Introduction

'Are there … uni-textual constitutions functionally operating as multi-textual, or multi-textual constitutions functionally operating as uni-textual, and does this reveal something important about the permeability, malleability, or fusion of formally distinguishable constitutional forms?'[1] Contemporary Turkish constitutionalism, particularly the eventful life of the current 1982 Constitution, offers one answer to this question, epitomising how functional multiplicity can persist beneath the surface of formal singularity of the constitutional text. The constitutional history of modern Turkey has been shaped by recurring legal and extralegal encounters between the state bureaucracy, which represents the founding constitutional principles and authorship, and the people, who represent both the source and embodiment of constitutional power and identity. Historically, these tensions not only shaped the constitutional text but also defined what legitimate constitutional authorship and identity ought to be. Since the founding of the Republic in 1923, Turkey has adopted three constitutions,[2] two of which (1961 and 1982) were drafted at the behest of the *junta* governments, in the aftermath of the 1960 and 1980 coups d'état. Although these constitutional texts appeared singular in form, the constitutional order has recurrently appealed to extraconstitutional, secondary legal resources that in practice enjoyed the status of constitutional supremacy.

Every constitution operates alongside secondary sources, written or unwritten, that co-constitute its content, structure, and purposes, shaping the foundations of

[1] R Albert, 'Multi-Textual Constitutions' (2023) 109 *Virginia Law Review* 1629, 1698.

[2] For the purposes of this article, I am not concerned with the late Ottoman experiments on constitutional monarchy in the 19th century, or the 1921 revolutionary constitution, which was drafted by the constituent assembly of the Independence War and, in terms of its structure, purposes, and operations, it was a different, transitionary constitutional framework, designed for the conditions of emergency. For more, see B Tanör, *Osmanlı-Türk Anayasal Gelişmeleri* (Yapi Kredi Yayinlari, 1998).

state authority. In other words, the apparent multiplicity or singularity of a constitution as a legal and political framework conceals a complexity far beyond the parchment barrier.[3] When it comes to society's collective self-understanding as a constitutionally entrenched and territorially defined entity, textuality is only the tip of the iceberg. As a script that encodes both prescriptive and descriptive knowledge of societal organisation, a constitution is inherently multidimensional; its legal and textual character accounts for only one layer. Constitutionalism, in turn, comprises at least three core dimensions essential to a critical understanding of the multiplicity of ordering forces in any constitutional setting:

- Text (written or unwritten; framing ideas, ideals, and values).
- Author (creator/designer – elected, delegated, or self-appointed).
- Identity (of the people, the constitutional order, and its interpretation).

Building on this postulate, this chapter explores multi-textualism's potential as a conceptual framework for illuminating the dynamics of constitutional degeneration and evolution in hybrid[4] political systems such as Turkey. Multi-textuality offers a promising lens for better understanding how and for what purpose constitutional systems operate both within and beyond textually defined boundaries. Among its obvious advantages are flexibility in constitutional design and evolution, plowing the soil for smooth and gradual regime change, and challenging constitutional veneration[5] that puts the constitutional text on a pedestal. It also helps unravel the three-dimensional nature of the modern constitution and illustrate the multiplicity of ordering forces that, though asynchronous, may hold equal claims to supremacy without delegitimising the constitutional text. As such, multi-textualism serves as a useful conceptual tool for understanding not only positive transformations towards constitutional democracy or regime change, but also democratic regress, constitutional degeneration, and regime preservation in hybrid contexts, as well as for distinguishing different forms of constitutional and political hybridisation.

The case of Turkish constitutionalism epitomises how a seemingly uni-textual constitution could operate with functional multiplicity, serving the ends for regime preservation as much as for regime change. Turkey's current Constitution, drafted and ratified in 1982 by the *junta* government, is widely considered an imposed charter[6] due to the undemocratic conditions of its adoption and the questionable legitimacy of its authorship. The 1982 text stands on the written, uni-textual, rigid

[3] J Madison, *The Federalist Papers* (Penguin Random House, 2012) No. 48 and 51.

[4] Hybrid regimes combine democratic and authoritarian features. Many adjectivised democracies of the past decades are hybrids that are situated in a potentially transitionary grey area between consolidated democracy and full-fledged authoritarianism. For more on the concept, see L Diamond, 'Elections Without Democracy: Thinking About Hybrid Regimes' (2002) 13(2) *Journal of Democracy* 21; P Norris, 'Is Western Democracy Backsliding? Diagnosing the Risks' (2017) Harvard Kennedy School Faculty Research Working Paper Series RWP17-012, www.hks.harvard.edu/publications/western-democracy-backsliding-diagnosing-risks.

[5] Albert (n 1) 1685.

[6] A Arato, *Post-Sovereign Constitution Making: Learning and Legitimacy* (Oxford University Press, 2016).

side of the spectrum and has been heavily criticised for its authoritarian origins, as well as the obvious anti-democratic qualities inherent to it.[7] Following the reinstatement of multiparty parliamentary politics in the late 1980s,[8] constitutional debates in the Turkish parliament – Turkish Grand National Assembly (TGNA) – addressed not only the constitutional text, but also other laws, precedents, and institutions that hindered democratic consolidation and transition. These included military and state security courts, the Turkish Criminal Code specifically on the definition of national treason, National Security Policy Document,[9] and the Internal Service Law of the military – often invoked to legally justify military coups. In terms of content, critiques addressed the Preamble, freedoms of speech and association (Articles 26, 28, 33, and 34), the death penalty (Articles 15 and 17), emergency powers (Articles 119, 120, 121, and 122), and procedural rigidity (Article 4, Article 175) – all viewed as major impediments to the country's European Union (EU) accession and broader democratisation goals.[10]

Under AKP rule, debates on constitutional change and the legacy of the 1982 Constitution took a different direction, focusing more and more on the legitimacy and representativeness of its military authorship and the secular, republican identity it was designed to safeguard. Although the AKP has not succeeded in drafting and enacting a new constitution after two decades in power, it has – by expanding the battleground over the legal-institutional configuration of the secular, republican *raison d'état* – nonetheless transformed the regime, as well as the nature of multi-textual operations of the longstanding 1982 Constitution to serve its own regime-preserving goals. Predictably, the outcome has been neither a more democratic nor a more constitutional order, at least in terms of textual integrity and normative coherency. In other words, the AKP has neither formalised nor dissolved the functional multiplicity of the Turkish constitutional system. Instead, it has simply replaced the legal and institutional practices of the secular *ancien régime* with its own, redefining legitimate constitutional authorship and identity

[7] E Özbudun, 'Judicial Review of Constitutional Amendments in Turkey: The Question of Unamendability' (2019) 21 *European Journal of Law Reform* 278; E Tombuş, 'The People and Its Embodiment: Authoritarian Foundations of Constitutions in Turkey' in F Petersen and Z Yanaşmayan (eds), *The Failure of Popular Constitution Making in Turkey* (Cambridge University Press, 2020).

[8] After the transition to civilian politics in 1983, 1987 amendments (Law No.3361) revised Articles 67, 75, and 175, which are respectively concerned with the right to universal suffrage, structure of parliamentary elections, and regulations on constitutional amendment procedures. Law No.3361 (*The Official Gazette*, 15 May 1987) www.tbmm.gov.tr/files/anayasa/docs/1982/1982-1/1-degisiklik.pdf.

[9] National Security Policy Document (Milli Güvenlik Siyaseti Belgesi, MGSB) is produced for five year periods by the National Security Council, known as the hidden constitution or red book. For the historical evolution of the Document's role, see Ministry of National Defense, www.mgk.gov.tr/index.php/25-kasim-2021-tarih-.

[10] From 1995 to 2001, TGNA passed several critical constitutional amendments with multi-party parliamentary reconciliation. The amendments of 1995, 1999, and 2001 revised and expanded the scope and protection of basic and civic rights, freedom of speech, and reformed the judiciary to meet the standards of EU accession. On this period of constitutional change, see E Özbudun, 'Democratization Reforms in Turkey, 1993–2004' (2007) 8 *Turkish Studies* 179.

in line with its theologically informed ideological programme, and tearing down the secular republican constitutional fabric.

Next, following brief remarks on Turkey's modern constitutional development and the secular republican regime's multi-textual constitutional operations, I will discuss how the constitutional order under AKP rule has evolved along with the 1982 text to facilitate regime change. I distinguish between two patterns of functional constitutional multiplicity that have manifested under the 1982 Constitution: a secular multi-textuality employed by the republican regime to preserve its core characteristics, and a *de facto* Islamist legal pluralism under the AKP government, which compartmentalises constitutionally entrenched social, political, and moral functions to consolidate its authoritarian rule. While secular multi-textuality may have had questionable legitimacy, it nevertheless maintained internal normative coherency aligned with the *raison d'état* and core principles of the Constitution. The AKP's Islamist legal pluralism, by contrast, fragments authority by empowering religious sources and authorities and challenging the secular republican *raison d'état.*[11]

II. Constitutional Development in Turkey: A Rocky Road

The history of constitution-making and constitutional change in Turkey has been unilateral, rigid, textual, and representative rather than participatory. As the driving force behind the republican foundation and particularly the last two constitutions (1961 and 1982), the military – the Turkish Armed Forces (TAF) – certainly held on to a claim of constitutional authorship. Its guardian role extended beyond direct involvement in constitutional revision, transition, or abrogation; rather, its conception of the constitutional order encompassed the protecting and steering of the constitutional identity as the embodiment of founding values, including, but not limited to, republicanism, nationalism, and secularism.[12]

Constitutional identities come into existence through the lived experience[13] of managing tensions between a society's future aspirations and its historical foundations. In Turkey's case, although the textual identity of 'the People' did not radically change from 1924 to 1982, the broader constitutional identity was far from static. Amid social and political fluctuations, both the meaning of the constitutional identity and the claims to legitimate, representative constitutional authorship evolved.

[11] On the increasing Islamic influence on positive law and secular constitutional order in Turkey, see Z Çitak, 'The Transformation of the State-Religion Relationship Under the AKP: The Case of Diyanet' in P Bedirhanoğlu and others (eds), *Turkey's New State in the Making: Transformations in Legality, Economy, and Coercion* (Zed Books, 2020); I Yilmaz, *Authoritarianism, Informal Law, and Legal Hybridity: The Islamisation of the State in Turkey* (Palgrave, 2022).

[12] The founding values of the Turkish republic under the Republican People's Party single-party government are republicanism, populism, nationalism, statism, secularism, reformism. The Six Arrows were added to Article 2 of the 1924 Constitution with 1937 amendments and discarded in the 1961 Constitution.

[13] G Jacobsohn, *Constitutional Identity* (Harvard University Press, 2010) 7.

The secular, republican constitutional authorship responded to these fluctuations in two ways. First, the evolution of constitutional texts from 1924 to 1982 illustrates a guardianship model defined by a militant, self-protective approach to the aforementioned foundational principles and values of the republic. This approach long motivated constitutional authors to control and contain the shifts and developments in the nation's sociopolitical fabric and its constitutional self-identification, as seen in the entrenchment of the Six Arrows in 1937, the establishment of the Constitutional Court in 1961, and the introduction of the eternity clause in 1982 to protect the secular and nationalist character of the Turkish state.

The 1982 text clearly articulates amendment procedures and delineates constitutional red lines,[14] which raises the issue of irrevocable clauses.[15] Its first three articles define the Republic's constitutional identity and vision of political unity: a democratic and secular republic governed by the rule of law, grounded in the nationalist and republican principles of the founding elite, indivisible in its territory and nation, with Turkish as its official language. Article 4 reinforces this framework, stating that 'the provision of Article 1 regarding the form of the State being a Republic, the characteristics of the Republic in Article 2, and the provisions of Article 3 shall not be amended, nor shall their amendment be proposed.'[16] This clause codifies the founding vision of the Republic, while putting a vague reservation on the boundaries of constitutional identity and authorship as embodiments of constituent power.

All these provisions were incorporated into the constitutional text as formal revisions. At the same time, secular republican authors established constitution-adjacent mechanisms – laws that could outlive individual constitutional texts and serve as supreme safety valves for the secular nationalist order. This approach reflects a more complex understanding of the Constitution that extends beyond the mere written text. For the architects of the republican order, the Constitution embodied a material political and social entity, co-constitutive with the text itself. One canonical example of this broader constitutional infrastructures is Article 35 of the Internal Service Law of the Turkish Armed Forces. Enacted asynchronously as a constitutional safety valve, the law positioned the military at the heart of the constitutional order, granting it self-authorising power to decide on when and how to intervene in defence of constitutional values and identity – including the authority to suspend, revise, or entirely abrogate constitutional texts and procedures.

While the unamendable first four articles have attracted most scholarly interest,[17] other laws that historically enjoyed a form of supremacy – enabling them to enforce, protect, and rectify the principles enshrined in those articles – have not

[14] O Yeğen, 'Debating Unamendability: Deadlock in Turkey's Constitution-Making Process' in R Albert and B Emrah Oder (eds), *An Unamendable Constitution? Unamendability in Constitutional Democracies* (Springer, 2018).

[15] O Yeğen, 'Constitutional Changes under the AKP Government of Turkey' (2017) *Bij de Buren* 70, 72.

[16] Constitute Project, *Turkey 1982 (rev. 2017)* constituteproject.org/countries/Asia/Turkey?lang=en.

[17] On unamendability problem in Turkey, see Yaniv Roznai and Serkan Yolcu, 'An Unconstitutional Constitutional Amendment – The Turkish Perspective: A Comment on the Turkish Constitutional

been equally examined. The next section addresses this gap by focusing on one of the most notorious and controversial legal provisions in Turkish constitutional history. Let us see how Article 35 of the Internal Service Law of the Turkish Armed Forces functioned for decades as a hidden eternity clause aimed at preserving the republican and secular regime.

A. Internal Service Law: Hidden Eternity Clause

Constitutions come and go. But how and when does a constitutional order become something new? Does constitutional change consist in adopting a new regime type (such as parliamentary democracy or hyper-presidentialism), enacting a different constitutional text (as in 1961 or 1982; or through major amendments to the latter), articulating a novel constitutional identity (from Turkish nationalism to the Muslim *ummah*), or transferring authorship (from military to civilian actors or deliberative roundtables)? Regime preservation in Turkey has been tied as much to the continuity of constitutional identity and authorship as the content of the constitutional text. The text could be suspended or amended, as long as identity and authorship remain intact. Conversely, the constitutional text could be formally preserved, if it continued to control and tame the fluctuations in identity and contesting authorship claims that challenge the foundational values of the republic. In such a multilayered topography, constitutional change acquires a broader and more complex meaning. Article 35 of the Internal Service Law of the Turkish Armed Forces comes to the forefront in this context as a supreme law that spelled out the process of constitutional change beyond the regulations entrenched in the constitutional text.

The Internal Service Law of the Turkish Armed Forces outlived numerous constitutions as a hidden component of the supreme law, determining when and how to dissolve and rewrite a constitutional text. The first version of the law (*Ordu Dahilî Hizmet Kanunu*, Law No. 2771) was enacted in 1935. Article 34 of that law stated that:

> The duty of the army is to protect and safeguard the Turkish homeland and the Turkish Republic, which has been established by the fundamental organization law. The army is tasked with learning and teaching the art of warfare. The necessary institutions and organizations are established, and measures are taken for the fulfillment of this duty.[18]

Article 34 practically justified the military intervention and subsequent constitutional transitions of 1960, functioning as a form of supreme law setting out the conditions for both constitutional change and inertia.[19] Following the 1960 coup,

Court's Headscarf Decision' (2012) 10(1) International Journal of Constitutional Law 175; Albert and Oder (n 14).

[18] *Ordu Dahili Hizmet Kanunu* No. 2771 (18 June 1935), TGNA Archives, www5.tbmm.gov.tr/tutanaklar/KANUNLAR_KARARLAR/kanuntbmmc015/kanuntbmmc015/kanuntbmmc01502771.pdf.

[19] *1924 Tarih ve 491 Sayılı Teşkilâtı Esasiye Kanununun Bâzı Hükümlerinin Kaldırılması ve Bâzı Hükümlerinin Değiştirilmesi Hakkında Geçici Kanun* (June 12, 1960) stated that 'The Turkish Army,

the *junta* government revised this law alongside the drafting of a new constitution. While Article 4 of the 1961 Constitution highlighted the role of constitutionally entrenched institutions and agencies in protecting and exercising the popular sovereignty of the Turkish nation, Article 35 of the new Internal Service Law (Law No.211) stated in a complementary fashion that 'The duty of the Armed Forces is to protect and safeguard the Turkish homeland and the Republic of Turkey as defined by the Constitution.'[20] This wording subtly expanded the military's guardian role to include internal as well as external enemies and threats. Moreover, it effectively positioned the military as a latent fourth branch of the government, capable, when necessary, of overseeing or entirely assuming the functions of the executive and legislative branches.

Until 1982, there were no formal eternity clause in the country's constitutions. The Internal Service Law filled this space in practice, guaranteeing the maintenance of constitutional values and identity later codified in the unamendability clause of the 1982 text, and functioning as a hidden eternity clause for the secular, nationalist, republican regime. Formally, Article 35 was not a constitutional law. It was not drafted and ratified through the procedures required for constitutional amendments. However, it certainly enjoyed constitutional supremacy, as it was interpreted and implemented as an authoritative mechanism for identifying and overcoming constitutional crises, with the *de facto* power to suspend, nullify, and rewrite the constitutional text. The peculiar character of military interventions in Turkey and the continuity of political legitimacy in their aftermaths prove the functional supremacy and asynchrony of Article 35. The military governments in Turkey had remarkably shorter life spans than their Latin American or African counterparts. Each intervention resulted in massive constitutional change and institutional reform,[21] and each ended with the military voluntarily stepping down. In a way, the military approached these interventions as instances of constitutional maintenance, a system reset or a software update of the constitutional script, calibrated to meet evolving social, political, or economic circumstances. Although there is no democratic justification for these intervals of military rule, they nonetheless illustrate the military's self-appointed yet somehow legally entrenched role as guardian of the constitutional order in Turkey. Article 35 stood still for nearly eight decades as a hidden eternity clause of the republic, not only witnessing but

which has been entrusted with the duty of 'protecting and safeguarding the Turkish homeland and the Turkish Republic as established by the Constitution' under Article 34 of the Internal Service Law of the Army, has undertaken this sacred and lawful duty. … Acting on behalf of the Turkish Nation to reestablish the rule of law, the Army dissolved the Parliament, which had lost its capacity to represent the nation, and temporarily entrusted power to the National Unity Committee.' TGNA Archives, www5.tbmm.gov.tr/tutanaklar/KANUNLAR_KARARLAR/kanuntbmmc043/kanunmbkc043/kanunmbkc04300001.pdf.

[20] *Türk Silahlı Kuvvetleri Iç Hizmet Kanunu* No.211 (*The Official Gazette*, 1 January 1961) www.mevzuat.gov.tr/mevzuat?MevzuatNo=211&MevzuatTur=1&MevzuatTertip=4.

[21] For critical comparative perspectives on Turkish military as a political actor, see T Demirel, 'Lessons of Military Regimes and Democracy' (2005) 31(2) *Armed Forces & Society* 245; D Pion-Berlin, 'Turkish Civil-Military Relations: A Latin American Comparison' (2011) 12(2) *Turkish Studies* 293.

also enabling the rise and fall of constitutions, the transformation of constitutional governments, and fluctuations in constitutional identity. As the flagship law of the republican, secular, nationalist *raison d'état*, it not only preserved but more importantly represented the regime and legitimised the military's constitutional authorship claims. It embodied the veneration of what were considered to be core, unamendable, and indisputable principles and features of the constitutional republic, while at the same time it worked to defetishise and dismantle the authority of the constitutional text itself.

However, everything comes to an end. Now, let us move on to the demise of Article 35, together with several constitutional and institutional changes during the same time period, the sum of which led to a subtle regime change. We will examine the ways in which the AKP disjointed and redesigned the functional multiplicity of the 1982 Constitution to consolidate a new presidential, authoritarian regime with an Islamist flavour.

III. AKP and Legacy of 1982: New Regime, Same Old Constitution?

The AKP has always placed constitutional change at the centre of its agenda. In its early years, the party appeared to be addressing pressing constitutional issues that had posed major obstacles to democratisation and EU integration – concerns already debated in the parliament in the 1990s.[22] From 2002 to 2007, proposed amendments passed with broad parliamentary consensus. At that time, the AKP government presented itself as a conservative democratic actor aligned with international law and liberal constitutional principles, working to dissolve the military's self-proclaimed constitutional guardianship and to reclaim authorship in the name of the historically oppressed, excluded, alienated conservative masses of the periphery.

In the 2000s, the AKP's political rhetoric around drafting and enacting a 'civilian' constitution[23] to democratise Turkish politics received positive responses from various ethnic, religious, and socioeconomic segments of society. The party advertised its constitution-making project as the only democratic solution to dissolving the military's constitutional guardianship, which had, for decades, obstructed the development of representative politics and civil society. In the AKP's narrative, a new civilian constitution would resolve the country's deeply rooted social,

[22] A Arato, 'Democratic Constitution-Making and Unfreezing the Turkish Process' (2010) 36(1) *Philosophy & Social Criticism* 473, 476. For more, see L Gönenc, 'The 2001 Amendments to the 1982 Constitution of Turkey' (2004) 1(1) *Ankara Law Review* 94; E Özbudun, 'Democratization Reforms in Turkey, 1993–2004' (2007) 8 *Turkish Studies* 179; Ö Faruk Genckaya, 'Politics of Constitutional Amendment in Turkey 1987–2002' in GH Flanz (ed), *Constitutions of the Countries of the World: Turkey* (Oceana, 2003).

[23] M Tokatlı, 'A Turkish Fairy Tale About a New, Civilian Constitution' (*Verfassungsblog*, 19 February 2021) verfassungsblog.de/turkey-civ-constitution.

religious, ethnic, and ideological divisions. However, although the goal was noble and public demand for a new constitution strong, the outcome of massive constitutional amendments and complementary legal and institutional reforms revealed that a new constitution, even with 'civilian' authorship, would not necessarily cure the chronic diseases of Turkish democracy.

A. AKP and 1982 Text: A Constitutional Patchwork

The year 2007 marked a milestone in the AKP's ambitious constitutional push towards regime change. Beginning with the presidential elections in April, tensions with the secular, republican opposition started to escalate. After failing to block the candidacy and parliamentary election of Abdullah Gül, a prominent AKP member, the Republican People's Party (*Cumhuriyet Halk Partisi*, CHP) – the stronghold of Kemalism and the main opposition party – challenged the election results before the Constitutional Court. The Court declared the election unconstitutional,[24] prompting the TGNA to call for re-elections. The military also weighed in. The TAF released a statement on its official website on 27 April 2007,[25] highlighting the constitutional principles of secularism and nationalism and reasserting its role as the absolute defender of those values.[26] The statement was widely criticised and interpreted as a resurgence of the military's traditional guardianship reflex, insinuating the constitutional entrenchment of that role. The AKP responded by proposing a constitutional amendment package. In the ensuing referendum, the power to elect the president of the republic was transferred from the TGNA to the people. This victory bolstered the AKP's confidence to intensify the frequency and intensity of its constitutional strikes.

From 2002 to 2017, the AKP amended the 1982 Constitution twelve times, rewriting 134 of its 177 articles.[27] Among these, the 2010 and 2017 amendments are particularly significant for understanding how the constitutional machinery was deployed to effect regime change. First, in a well-orchestrated attempt to dissolve constitutional checks and balances, the notorious 2010 amendments restructured the Constitutional Court by altering its membership, jurisdiction, and voting rules, increasing the number of judges, and revising appointment procedures. Overall, the amendments shattered judicial independence by placing the judiciary under the influence of the Ministry of Justice, hence the executive.[28]

[24] *Constitutional Court Ruling No. 2007/56,* 29 November 2007. normkararlarbilgibankasi.anayasa.gov.tr/Dosyalar/Kararlar/KararPDF/2007-56-nrm.pdf 5.

[25] Full text of the memorandum is no longer available at TAF's website. For excerpts, see 'Excerpts of Turkish army statement' *BBC News* (28 April 2007) news.bbc.co.uk/2/hi/europe/6602775.stm.

[26] C Balkir, 'The July 2007 Elections in Turkey: A Test for Democracy' (2007) 12(3) *Mediterranean Politics* 415; A Göl, 'The Identity of Turkey: Muslim and Secular' (2009) 30(4) *Third World Quarterly* 795.

[27] F Petersen and Z Yanaşmayan (eds), *The Failure of Popular Constitution Making in Turkey* (Cambridge University Press, 2020); Yeğen, 'Constitutional Changes' (n 15).

[28] *Türkiye Cumhuriyeti Anayasasinin Bazi Maddelerinde Degisiklik Yapilmasi Hakkinda Kanun* No.5982 (7 May 2010) www.anayasa.gen.tr/5982.htm.

The reallocation of the means of governance through constitutional change was not limited to crippling the judiciary and diluting the power of the legislature. Gradually, these amendments paved the way for regime change. Following the thwarted military coup in 2016,[29] which led to the declaration of a nationwide state of emergency, the AKP introduced another set of constitutional amendments in April 2017, finally replacing the parliamentary democratic system with hyper-presidentialism.[30] The amendments transferred executive power from the parliament to a largely unchecked presidency (Article 8); redefined the state of emergency and disproportionately expanded the limit and content of emergency powers of the president (Article 119); empowered the presidency to monopolise decision-making authority (Articles 106, 116), further weakening parliament and blurring the crucial line between the legislative and executive branches in favour of the executive. In an oddly similar fashion to the 1982 constitutional referendum, the vote was held under the post-2016 state of emergency. Altogether, the amendments formalised the new presidential regime and rewired the functional operations of the constitutional system to serve a new, Islamist *raison d'état*.

Eventually, the 1982 Constitution has become a patchwork, a pale replica of its original form. The AKP's amendments have neither acknowledged and validated the functional multiplicity of constitutional operations in the country nor have they defied and dissolved them. Rather, the AKP government has simply appropriated existing practices to serve new ideological agendas. More importantly, the constitutional order stemming from the 1982 text has lost its internal normative coherence, which is crucial to maintaining both the legality and legitimacy of a constitutional system. What remains is a loosely woven patchwork with contrasting colours and patterns that distort the overall image and give it a sense of incompleteness.

The main contrast that bothers the eye in this constitutional patchwork lies between secularism, upheld as an unamendable principle of the Kemalist *ancien régime*, and Islamic law and morality, which have become key signifiers of the AKP's political identity. These two centrepieces are made of fundamentally different constitutional fabrics and represent two structurally and epistemologically distinct actors: the military, long positioned as the constitutional guardian, and the Directorate of Religious Affairs (Diyanet), now acting as the state-approved gatekeeper of Sunni Muslim faith, tradition, and customs within a formally secular constitutional system. While the former preserved regime continuity for decades

[29] Ş Gümüşçü and B Esen, 'Turkey: How the Coup Failed' (2017) 28(1) *Journal of Democracy* 59; A Zarakol, 'Turkey Through the Looking Glass' (*London Review of Books Blog*, 3 August 2016) www.lrb.co.uk/blog/2016/august/turkey-through-the-looking-glass; N Christofis (ed), *Erdoğan's 'New' Turkey Attempted Coup d'état and the Acceleration of Political Crisis* (Routledge, 2020).

[30] For the original discussion on hyper-presidentialism, see S Rose-Ackerman, DA Desierto and N Volosin, 'Hyper-Presidentialism: Separation of Powers without Checks and Balances in Argentina and the Philippines' (2011) 29 *Berkeley Journal of International Law* 246. On hyper-presidentialism and the AKP government, see E Tombuş and A Arato, 'Learning from Success, Learning from Failure: South Africa, Hungary, Turkey and Egypt' (2013) 39(4–5) *Philosophy and Social Criticism* 427.

through multiple legal instruments such as the Internal Service Law, constitutional amendments, and emergency regulations, the latter, under the AKP government, has been used to assert and normalise informal Islamist legal pluralism. The Diyanet has safeguarded the core values of the AKP's vision of 'moderate' Islamism[31] and facilitated regime change. By orchestrating the tensions between these two deeply contested frameworks, the AKP has managed to amend the unamendable, at the expense of constitutional coherence and regime continuity. However, this certainly reflects a different pattern of functional multiplicity.

B. Amending the Unamendable

How does the AKP's appeal to functional multiplicity of constitutional order relate to and differ from its secular antagonist? Has the AKP merely established a new regime that operates within the framework of the same old 1982 Constitution, or has it brought about a brand new political and constitutional order that departs from and effectively reconfigures that framework? If the latter, by what means has the AKP managed to conduct such a profound change in Turkey's constitutional and political fabric?

The AKP has utilised constitutional operations in ways analogous to those of its antagonist, the secular republican constitutional designers. It has not only deployed formal, procedural, and legal-institutional means, but also appropriated and repurposed the once highly condemned multi-textual functionality and self-protective guardianship practices of the 1982 constitutional order.[32] However, there are also fundamental differences that place the AKP's constitutional experiments on a distinct trajectory, marked by authoritarian consolidation, legal fragmentation – if not outright extralegal maneuvering. In its first decade, the AKP did not openly promote *sharia* rule. For the consolidation and preservation of its own regime, it instead gradually embraced a broader legal catalogue extending beyond formal amendments to the Constitution. This included the informal operations of Islamic law, the use of presidential decrees, and the reconstruction of key state apparatuses such as the TAF, the Diyanet, and the judiciary. Through its discourse and policy- and law-making priorities, the AKP has compartmentalised the social, economic, private, public, political, and moral dimensions of life,

[31] On the AKP's moderate Islam, see E Özbudun, 'From Political Islam to Conservative Democracy: The Case of the Justice and Development Party in Turkey' (2006) 11(3) *South European Society and Politics* 543; J Schwedler, 'Can Islamists Become Moderates? Rethinking the Inclusion-Moderation Hypothesis' (2011) 63(2) *World Politics* 347.

[32] A Kars Kaynar, 'Post-2016 Military Restructuring in Turkey from the Perspective of Coup-Proofing' (2022) 23(3) *Turkish Studies* 383; A Kutay, 'Civilian and Military Relations in Turkey: A Historical Survey' (2016) 11 *Chr. Michelsen Institute Working Paper* 1; T Korkut, 'Hükümet Genelkurmay'ı Savunma Bakanlığı'na Bağlamalı!' *Bianet* (9 November 2009) bianet.org/haber/hukumet-genelkurmay-i-savunma-bakanligi-na-baglamali-118143; Editorial, 'Darbe Dayanağı 35. Madde Yeni Akıllarına Geldi' *Bianet* (22 July 2010) bianet.org/haber/darbe-dayanagi-35-madde-yeni-akillarina-geldi-123629; A Insel, 'Vesayet Rejiminin Sonu ve Sonrasi' (2010) 251–252 *Birikim*.

reallocating constitutional functions that regulate these dimensions between the constitutional text and Islamic law and custom.

This reallocation of constitutional functions and the subsequent transfer of power between the TAF and the Diyanet as critical state apparatuses have become particularly visible over the past decade. The 2010 amendments marked a pivotal moment, enabling the AKP to expand its agenda by targeting other critical legislative instruments that had historically functioned as safety valves for the secular republican constitutional order, such as the ill-famed Internal Service Law. Following the 2007 military memorandum, the AKP increasingly identified Article 35 as a major obstacle to democratic consolidation and EU accession,[33] along with the 1982 Constitution and its assertive secularism. On July 31, 2013, the TGNA passed Law No.6496, revising and reframing Article 35 to eliminate ambiguity and clarify the scope of the military's guardian role.[34] While the 2013 revisions shut the doors on the Internal Service Law's constitutional interpretative authority and supremacy attribution and formally ended the military's constitutional guardianship,[35] at the same time, they opened space for the AKP government to circumvent – if not outright violate – the unamendable constitutional principles, specifically secularism. This was achieved by paving the way for introducing new legal frameworks and mobilising alternative ordering forces to take over multi-textual constitutional operations, this time directed towards AKP's regime consolidation and preservation. The functional multiplicity of the 1982 Constitution was ideologically appropriated, obviously not to advance democratisation, but to sustain a different form of authoritarian hybridity. However, the actual constitutional change lies beyond the text: the dissolution of Article 35 marked the formal transfer of legitimate constitutional authorship from the secular republican authoritarian *ancien régime* to an Islamist authoritarian order. In other words, although authoritarianism stands still, Turkey now certainly operates under a distinctly new constitutional and political regime.

Now there is a new constitutional author, representing a new constitutional identity and a reconfigured structure of political and constitutional power. There is no longer a hidden eternity clause that once interrupted democratic politics in order to preserve the secular regime. Does the new regime need a guardian – a gatekeeper or safety valve – to manage fluctuations in constitutional identity and to maintain its authorship claims, and, if yes, who should this guardian be? Since 2016, AKP members have vocalised their commitments to Islamic law, asserting

[33] Editorial, 'Darbe Dayanağı 35. Madde Yeni Akıllarına Geldi' *Bianet* (22 July 2010) bianet.org/haber/darbe-dayanagi-35-madde-yeni-akillarina-geldi-123629.

[34] The law clarified that the duty of the army is to protect the Turkish nation and land from *external* threats. *Sözleşmeli Erbaş ve Er Kanunu ile Bazi Kanunlarda Degisiklik Yapilmasina Dair Kanun* No.6496 (*The Official Gazette*, 13 July 2013) www.resmigazete.gov.tr/eskiler/2013/07/20130731-10.htm.

[35] S Sokollu, 'A Coup Against Coups in Turkey' *Deutsche Welle* (7 March 2013) www.dw.com/en/turkey-plans-legal-reform-to-prevent-coups/a-16927618.

in parliament sessions, public statements,[36] and social media posts that *sharia* stands above general law and modern constitutionalism.[37] Especially after the 2017 amendments, with the apex courts packed and the military's guardian role dissolved, Sunni Islamic norms and Diyanet *fatwa*s (religious edicts) and sermons have become legitimate resources in areas regulated by positive law under the 1982 Constitution, which in its singularity remains indisputably secular. References to religious resources such as Quranic verses or Islamic legal precedents have noticeably increased not only in government discourse but also in parliamentary sessions, court proceedings, and policy domains such as education and family law.[38] This growing invocation of religious authority signals fluctuations in constitutional identity as well as mounting contestations over legitimate authorship. In this period, political discourse radically shifted from the modern concept of the nation to the Muslim concept of *ummah* – a transnational Muslim community. The Diyanet has been instrumental in spreading this message, routinely replacing 'nation' with '*ummah*' in its official communications.[39] Although the constitutional text remained secular on the surface, constitutional identity and authorship have increasingly tilted in favour of a more religiously and theologically informed Sunni Muslim identity. Meanwhile, the Diyanet has become a *de facto* extension of the government and the messenger and gatekeeper of its regime and ideology, operating well beyond the scope of its constitutionally defined duties.

After the 2010 amendments, the Diyanet has gradually become a critical state apparatus representing Islamic rules and values in social, political, cultural, and moral matters.[40] As early as 2012, its rank in the state protocol was raised to 10th from 51st, outranking even the high commanders of the military. [41] Through a

[36] Editorial, 'Erdoğan: Şeriata düşmanlık, esasında dininin bizatihi kendisine husumettir!' *Birgun* (2 January 2024) www.birgun.net/haber/erdogan-seriata-dusmanlik-esasinda-dininin-bizatihi-kendisine-husumettir-503189; H Simsek, "Şeriat hükümleri' Meclis'te' *Birgun* (13 March 2020) www.birgun.net/haber/seriat-hukumleri-meclis-te-291577; Editorial, 'AKP'li vekilden Meclis'te 'şeriat' çıkışı: Şeriat bizim hukukumuzdur' (*Haber Sol*, 10 December 2020) haber.sol.org.tr/haber/akpli-vekilden-mecliste-seriat-cikisi-seriat-bizim-hukukumuzdur-21211.

[37] A Temel, 'Between State Law and Religious Law: Islamic Family Law in Turkey' (2020) 8(1) *Electronic Journal of Islamic and Middle Eastern Law* 68; R Powell, 'Evolving Views of Islamic Law in Turkey' (2013) 28(2) *Journal of Law and Religion* 467; Yilmaz (n 11).

[38] C Tecimer, 'Rethinking Turkish Secularism: Towards 'Unofficial' Islamic Constitutionalism?' (*Verfassungsblog*, 27 September 2017) verfassungsblog.de/rethinking-turkish-secularism-towards-unofficial-islamic-constitutionalism/; A Uludağ, 'Besmele ile Duruşma Açan Hakimler Var' (*Deutsche Welle*, 19 August 2021) www.dw.com/tr/besmele-ile-duru%C5%9Fma-a%C3%A7an-hakimler-var/a-58907132.

[39] N Mutluer, 'Diyanet's Role in Building the 'Yeni (New) Milli' in the AKP Era' (2018) 27 *European Journal of Turkish Studies* http://journals.openedition.org/ejts/5953.

[40] On various social, political, and legal aspects of the rise of Diyanet under the AKP rule, see S Adak, 'Expansion of the Diyanet and the Politics of Family in Turkey under AKP Rule' (2021) 22(2) *Turkish Studies* 200; S Cevik, 'Erdoğan's Comprehensive Religious Policy: Management of the Religious Realm in Turkey' (*Stiftung Wissenschaft und Politik*, 5 March 2019) www.swp-berlin.org/10.18449/2019C12/; I Yilmaz and I Albayrak, *Populist and Pro-Violence State Religion: The Diyanet's Construction of Erdoğanist Islam in Turkey* (Palgrave, 2022).

[41] Mutluer (n 39) 5; A Uludağ, 'Diyanet, Protokolde Genelkurmay' in Önüne Geçti' *Deutsche Welle* (31 August 2021) www.dw.com/tr/diyanet-protokolde-genelkurmay%C4%B1n-%C3%B6n%C3%BCne-ge%C3%A7ti/a-59038711.

series of inter-ministerial cooperation protocols, the Diyanet obtained a distinct role in overviewing, providing feedback to, and collaborating with the operations of other state apparatuses. In 2017, the changes to the Civil Registry Law authorised *muftis* (chief religious officials) to administer religious marriage ceremonies and register them as legally binding civil unions.

The increasing appeal to religious practices and references soon extended beyond the private sphere. *Fatwas* on gender, family, inheritance, social media, and political economy[42] repeatedly challenged constitutional regulations, without facing any institutional checks and balances to assess the constitutionality of this state body's operations. Through its official website, weekly sermons in mosques across the country, door-to-door outreach, and hotlines, the Diyanet issued edicts and invoked religious texts that conveyed government-approved social and moral codes, effectively compartmentalising the constitutional order by claiming an adjacent, equally supreme, yet profoundly different jurisdiction.

In 2017, a series of highly controversial *fatwa*s on incest, child marriage, polygamy, and adoption, published on the Diyanet's official website, sparked massive public backlash and raised questions about the constitutional boundaries of its operations as a state institution.[43] In parliamentary debates, AKP MP Fikri Işık stated that the government judges Diyanet *fatwa*s by their compatibility with the Holy Quran and Islamic law, not the standards of modern constitutionalism.[44] This was one of several instances when the government openly acknowledged its *de facto* compartmentalisation of the prescriptive and descriptive knowledge of social and political organisation, legitimising Islamic legal practices in domains traditionally considered private, while relegating the constitutional text and its unamendable principles to the domain of formality and proceduralism. Since then, judges have increasingly opened court hearings with Muslim prayers and cited religious sources in legal reasoning.[45] On one occasion, even the Director of the Diyanet appeared at the judicial year's opening ceremony to pray and bless the courts,[46] right next to President Erdoğan.

[42] A Erdi Öztürk, 'Turkey's Diyanet Under AKP Rule: From Protector to Imposer of State Ideology?' (2016) 16(4) *Southeast European and Black Sea Studies* 619 https://doi.org/10.1080/14683857.2016.1233663; Yilmaz (n 11) 53.

[43] Editorial, 'Diyanet'in 'Evlatlık çocukla evlenebilirsiniz' Açıklamasına Tepkiler: Anayasaya ve Medeni Kanuna Aykiri' *Bianet* (18 February 2023) bianet.org/haber/diyanet-in-evlatlik-cocukla-evlenebilirsiniz-aciklamasina-tepkiler-274455; Editorial, 'Evrensel Hukuk Yerine Dini Referans Temel Alındı' *Birgün* (21 August 2021) www.birgun.net/haber/evrensel-hukuk-yerine-dini-referans-temel-alindi-355936.

[44] Editorial, 'Diyanet'in Fetvasına 'Anayasaya Uygun mu?' Diye Bakılmaz' *Yeni Şafak* (13 December 2017) www.yenisafak.com/gundem/diyanetin-fetvasina-anayasaya-uygun-mu-diye-bakilmaz-2936918; Editorial, 'Yargı, Diyanet'in Skandal Fetvasına Takipsizlik Verdi' *Birgun* (31 March 2023) www.birgun.net/haber/yargi-diyanet-in-skandal-fetvasina-takipsizlik-verdi-426855.

[45] Tecimer (n 38).

[46] Editorial, 'Yeni Yargitay Binasina Duali Acilis' *Birgun* (2 September 2021) www.birgun.net/haber/yeni-yargitay-binasina-duali-acilis-357296; A Uludağ, 'Laiklik Anlayışına Aykırı Bir Görüntü' *Deutsche Welle* (2 September 2021) www.dw.com/tr/laiklik-anlay%C4%B1%C5%9F%C4%B1na-ayk%C4%B1r%C4%B1-bir-g%C3%B6r%C3%BCnt%C3%BC/a-59069026; F Öztürk, 'Diyanet fetvaları ve açıklamaları: Sonra 10 yılda hangileri tartışma yarattı?' *BBC* (3 January 2018) www.bbc.com/turkce/haberler-turkiye-42552621.

In line with the government-sponsored and Diyanet-led project of promoting a more conservative, Islamist identity, in 2021, Turkey withdrew from the Istanbul Convention on preventing violence against women and domestic violence by presidential decree. Since then, Diyanet personnel have assumed the duty of domestic conflict arbitration, highlighting the importance of family and motherhood.[47] The effectiveness of these interventions remains unclear. They do not offer legal protection to victims but instead aim to prevent formal legal action from being taken. In this sense, it is another example of multiplication of functions; however, it also exposes an obvious challenge of legitimacy and normative coherence, making the fragmentation and partial Islamisation of the constitutional order under the AKP an example of informal legal pluralism with a pragmatic more than normative orientation.

What would have been considered unconstitutional under the secular *ancien régime* has been normalised and internalised through the AKP's Islamist hybridisation of constitutional functions. The AKP transformed the regime without writing a new constitution from scratch or even practically altering the unamendable articles, but instead by appropriating the functional multiplicity of the secular constitutional *raison d'état* and dissolving its safety valves for regime preservation, such as Article 35 and judicial independence. Although the Diyanet's role was not codified in a fashion similar to the military's, it is obvious that it now represents and protects a supreme (Islamic) law and set of customs, embracing gatekeeping duties across moral, private, social, constitutional, and political domains. The result is an uneasy amalgamation of fundamentally incompatible constitutional and political forms: a constitutional, representative democracy layered with authoritarian guardianship and Islamic law–inflected autocracy.

This peculiar amalgamation has produced a paradoxical juxtaposition of secular and Islamic Law and thus the establishment of a *de facto* legal pluralism. The Diyanet has served to compartmentalise and redistribute state authority once anchored in the Constitution. What empowered this Diyanet-led rise of legal pluralism was not a single constitutional change but a loosely legalised transfer of authority through a series of laws and inter-ministry protocols. Although the Diyanet's expanded powers are partially grounded in law, in practice it draws its power from Islamic religious authority and the Holy Quran. On that account, the functional multiplicity of the constitutional order under the AKP is fundamentally different from that of its secular antagonist. The AKP fragments state authority and reallocates it between the constitutional text (positive law) and the Diyanet (the Holy Quran and Islamic law). There is no shared constitutional framework that both sources acknowledge and abide by. In other words, this simultaneous claim to supremacy renders Islamist legal pluralism inherently paradoxical and poses a challenge to Turkey's constitutional – if not political – legitimacy. This is what makes this constitutional patchwork particularly difficult to suture.

[47] Diyanet Family and Religious Guidance Services https://dinhizmetleri.diyanet.gov.tr/kategoriler/hizmetlerimiz/aile-ve-dini-rehberlik-daire-ba%C5%9Fkanl%C4%B1%C4%9F%C4%B1.

IV. Conclusion

For what purposes does multi-textuality serve? As Albert articulates, there are at least three potential advantages:

> they make possible the incremental development of a constitutional state as it transitions from one regime to another, they make available multiple options for constitutional reform and may therefore offer more flexibility in managing higher law, and they may help forestall the rise of a popular obsession with the constitution, what scholars have diagnosed as 'constitutional veneration.'[48]

In the case of Turkey, we see how multi-textuality has served as much for regime preservation as for regime change, as much for constitutional veneration as for its dethronement. Interestingly, these opposing outcomes under the secular regime proved advantageous for preserving constitutional democracy, at least at a procedural level. Yet constitutional disentanglement, followed by the extralegal appropriation of multi-textual functions, accelerated democratic regress and authoritarian upheaval. The 2013 revision of Article 35 marked a turning point in the functional multiplicity of constitutional operations. Obviously, it was not the only cause of constitutional disintegration in Turkey; however, abolishing this hidden eternity clause clearly affected the trajectory of constitutional identity and authorship.

Multi-textuality is a helpful framework for comparing and contrasting secular and Islamist hybrid regimes in Turkey. Although both have authoritarian qualities inherent to them, this lens highlights critical differences between them. The secular regime's functional multiplicity had internal coherence (rooted in a shared *raison d'état*, consistent sources of multi-textual authority, and recognition of the rule of law) and retained some legitimacy despite limited democratic credentials. In contrast, the AKP's recycled and repatched functional multiplicity is desynchronised, irregular, normatively incoherent, and overtly instrumental, raising serious concerns about constitutional and democratic legitimacy.

Is the AKP the new constitutional author, or does the current Constitution still represent its original authorship, identity, and regime? Four decades and dozens of amendments since its promulgation, the 1982 Constitution has become a legal patchwork. The AKP has certainly emerged as the new constitutional author, who has managed to amend even the unamendable and effect regime change. By deploying and repurposing the multi-textual functions embedded in the constitutional order, it has largely succeeded in advancing its constitutional agenda. In contradistinction to its secular predecessors, the AKP's multi-textual operations have not centralised but reallocated state authority. Through compartmentalisation across public and private, social and political, moral and cultural spheres, it has established a form of informal legal pluralism, weaving two conflicting constitutional

[48] Albert (n 1) 1634.

forms into a hybrid. What enabled this radical shift in the political and legal topography of Turkey's constitutional system was not formal amendments alone, but rather a more comprehensive effort to restructure the legal-institutional power configuration of the secular, republican *raison d'état*. However, the outcome has been neither a more democratic nor a more constitutional order. While the secular regime's practices of constitutional guardianship and regime preservation through controlled constitutional change could be considered multi-textual strategies within a seemingly uni-textual constitution, the AKP's approach would be better understood as a constitutional patchwork, which fragments state authority and constitutionally entrenched domains of life between the secular constitutional text and Islamic law, falling short of constitutional legitimacy and legal normative coherence. However, the AKP has transformed the constitutional order, changing the ideological orientation of hidden multi-textual practices and, subsequently, the identity and authorship of Turkish constitutionalism.

12

The Taliban's Multi-Textual Constitution: Cultivated Ambiguity as Authoritarian Technique

AMAL SETHI

I. Introduction: Ruling Without Writing

Few countries have experienced as many constitutional experiments and as many constitutional failures as Afghanistan. Across the last century, charters were repeatedly introduced to centralise authority and project modern statehood, only to collapse under the weight of elite division, clerical opposition, and rural mistrust. When the Taliban returned to power in August 2021, the question arose once more whether a new constitution would be promulgated. The answer was no.

Instead of drafting a single charter, the Taliban govern through a mosaic of texts: scripture, insurgency codes, doctrinal tracts, relic constitutions, and a steady stream of decrees. This is not a legal vacuum but a structural shift. What emerges is not the absence of constitutional authority, but its reconstitution through dispersed sources. Existing scholarship has not yet treated this phenomenon as a constitutional system[1] in its own right[2] and one that differs from uncodified constitutions such as the UK or New Zealand.[3]

[1] It is a common assumption in constitutional theory that constitutions must limit power or guarantee rights. While this chapter does not dismiss these normative ideals, it adopts a functional perspective, treating constitutions as frameworks, whether codified or not, through which authority is structured, justified, and exercised. This lens enables the study of constitutional ordering in regimes that do not conform to liberal constitutional assumptions.

[2] Few early blog posts have described the Taliban's system as either anti-constitutional or an unwritten one. See W Maley, 'Taliban Rule and Anti-Constitutionalism' (*Australian Outlook*, Australian Institute of International Affairs, 23 August 2023) www.internationalaffairs.org.au/australianoutlook/taliban-rule-and-anti-constitutionalism/; S Pasarlay, 'Afghanistan's Unwritten Constitution under the Taliban' (*I.CONnect: Blog of the International Journal of Constitutional Law*, 17 May 2022) www.iconnectblog.com/2022/05/afghanistans-unwritten-constitution-under-the-taliban/.

[3] This approach differs from uncodified constitutional systems such as those in the United Kingdom or New Zealand, which, despite lacking a single written charter, maintain identifiable foundational

Using a doctrinal and interpretive approach,[4] this chapter argues that the Taliban sustain their constitutional order – built from a dispersed set of textual sources – through what this chapter terms *cultivated ambiguity*: the deliberate maintenance of uncertainty about which legal sources apply, how they interrelate, who may interpret them, and when each may be invoked. Cultivated ambiguity allows the regime to perform the classic functions of constitutions, such as facilitating change, resolving conflicts, legitimating authority, and establishing foundational order. Yet it does so not by stabilising a clear hierarchy but by preserving conditions of uncertainty that prevent closure and insulate authority from challenge. Recognising cultivated ambiguity as a constitutional technique expands the conceptual horizons of constitutional theory, showing that authority can rest on uncertainty just as much as on hierarchy or text.

To theorise this order, the chapter draws on Richard Albert's concept of the multi-textual constitution, a framework in which constitutional authority is dispersed across multiple textual sources rather than confined to a single document.[5] Coined primarily with liberal democracies in mind, Albert's idea can surprisingly be extended to authoritarian contexts as well. In doing so, the chapter contributes to the growing literature on authoritarian constitutionalism by showing how authoritarian regimes can strategically use multi-textual constitutions to consolidate control, mute dissent, and evade constraint. Whereas most studies on modern-day authoritarianism focus on how rulers manipulate or hollow out constitutional texts,[6] this chapter demonstrates that authoritarian functions can also be performed more subtly, and at times more effectively, through a multi-textual legal repertoire deployed with cultivated ambiguity.

The phenomenon above is not confined to Afghanistan. The chapter also draws on a mini comparison with three other authoritarian regimes, Iran, Saudi Arabia, and China, each of which sustains a multi-textual constitutional grounded in cultivated ambiguity to serve authoritarian ends. The comparison shows that cultivated ambiguity is not unique to the Taliban but part of a more expansive repertoire

norms, stable institutional hierarchies, and recognised principles of interpretive pluralism. In the UK, for example, parliamentary sovereignty is publicly acknowledged as a constitutional doctrine and guided by established conventions. The Taliban model, by contrast, rejects not only codification but also the public articulation of constitutional authority. While invoking Sharia as its source, the regime neither specifies its content nor designates an interpretive body. Refer to Section III for an explanation of how constitutional authority is structured under the Taliban.

[4] The chapter adopts an interpretive and doctrinal approach, treating Taliban legal instruments, public edicts, and doctrinal texts as constitutional in function. It draws on comparative constitutional analysis and secondary reporting to reconstruct institutional practice. Given the opacity of internal Taliban decision-making, the analysis necessarily infers from patterns of practice, publicly released texts, verified social media statements, and reports by journalists and local observers. These very constraints illuminate how ambiguity is operationalised in authoritarian legal orders.

[5] See R Albert, 'Multi-Textual Constitutions' (2023) 109 *Virginia Law Review* 1629, 1629–31.

[6] See for an overview of tactics, eg, K Lane Scheppele, 'Autocratic Legalism' (2018) 85 *University of Chicago Law Review* 545; D Landau, 'Abusive Constitutionalism' (2013) 47 *UC Davis Law Review* 189; S Levitsky and LA Way, *Competitive Authoritarianism: Hybrid Regimes after the Cold War* (Cambridge University Press, 2010); DS Law and M Versteeg, 'Sham Constitutions' (2013) 101 *California Law Review* 863; OO Varol, 'Stealth Authoritarianism' (2015) 100 *Iowa Law Review* 1673.

of autocratic governance. Recognising this tactic is vital, since authoritarian regimes increasingly borrow from one another's practices,[7] and multi-textual constitutions sustained through cultivated ambiguity can very easily emerge as a transferable constitutional strategy. Understanding its operation not only clarifies the Taliban's order but illuminates wider patterns of authoritarian resilience in an era of democratic decline.

The rest of the chapter proceeds in five parts. Section II traces Afghanistan's repeated but failed experiments with codified constitutionalism, setting the stage for the Taliban's rejection of written frameworks. Section III examines the regime's multi-textual architecture. Section IV shows how cultivated ambiguity operates in practice and the functions it serves. Section V situates the Taliban within broader authoritarian patterns to highlight both generalisable strategies and their exceptional features. Section VI concludes by drawing out the theoretical and practical implications for the study of authoritarian constitutionalism and for this volume's inquiry into constitutional authority beyond the single text.

II. The Collapse of Codified Form in Afghanistan

Over the past century, Afghan rulers repeatedly turned to constitutions to consolidate authority and present themselves as modern statesmen. Yet each experiment collapsed under pressure, producing rupture rather than stability. The problem was not simply poor design or foreign interference, but recurring structural divides: tensions between Islamic authority and reformist modernisation, between Kabul's urban elites and rural communities, and between rival factions within the political elite. Each constitution was introduced with the promise of stability, only to aggravate one or more of these divides.

The first attempt came in 1923 under King Amanullah Khan. Inspired by regional reformers in Turkey and Iran,[8] the charter created a legislative assembly, recognised rights such as access to secular education, and reformed personal status laws touching on marriage and veiling.[9] These measures collided with tribal and clerical authority.[10] The reforms were denounced as foreign impositions, revolts spread, and Amanullah was forced to abdicate power in 1929.[11] This episode showed that ambitious constitutional modernisation could trigger immediate backlash from clerical and rural forces.

[7] See eg R Dixon and D Landau, *Abusive Constitutional Borrowing: Legal Globalization and the Subversion of Liberal Democracy* (Oxford University Press, 2021).

[8] S Amir Arjomand, 'Constitutional Developments in Afghanistan: A Comparative and Historical Perspective' (2005) 53 *Drake Law Review* 943, 945.

[9] See Constitution of the Kingdom of Afghanistan (adopted 9 April 1923) arts 1, 8–24, 39, 68.

[10] International Crisis Group, 'Afghanistan's Flawed Constitutional Process' (ICG Asia Report No 56, Kabul/Brussels, 12 June 2003) 3.

[11] ibid 3–4.

Nadir Shah's 1931 Constitution marked a conservative recalibration. It reaffirmed the monarchy, declared Islam the state religion, and gave Sharia primacy over statutory law.[12] The text endured for over three decades, the longest-lived Afghan constitution, but did so by avoiding substantive reform. Rather than building consensus, it placated clerics and tribal elites through legal ambiguity and deference to custom.[13] When liberalising pressures mounted in the 1960s, the 1931 framework offered no path forward, prompting its replacement with the 1964 constitution.

The 1964 Constitution represented the high-water mark of Afghan liberalism. It created a constitutional monarchy, recognised civil liberties, and established a bicameral legislature.[14] It sought to synthesise Islamic identity with rights and institutions borrowed from democratic models.[15] Urban elites in Kabul welcomed these reforms, but rural communities remained anchored in customary and religious norms.[16] The urban–rural divide, compounded by intensifying elite factionalism, soon eroded the charter's legitimacy. In 1973 Mohammed Daoud Khan staged a coup, abolishing the monarchy and ending the constitution.[17] Once again, codification cracked along the lines of rural resistance and elite fragmentation.

Daoud's 1977 Constitution was designed to consolidate his new republic. It established a strong presidency, declared Afghanistan a one-party state, and centralised authority in Daoud's hands.[18] The effect was to sideline Islamists, alienate leftist factions, and even strain ties with the Soviet Union.[19] The charter never gained broad legitimacy and lasted barely fifteen months before the Saur Revolution of 1978 swept Daoud from power. Instead of stabilising his rule, codification deepened ideological polarisation and hastened collapse.

During the communist era, Afghanistan cycled through three constitutions – in 1980, 1987, and 1990 – within just over a decade.[20] Each reflected regime survival tactics under Soviet occupation and civil war rather than genuine consensus.[21] They gestured alternately toward socialism, Islam, or pluralism, but carried little practical weight.[22] Constitution-making became political theatre: ceremonies of drafting substituted for effective governance.[23]

[12] PL Kakar and J Schiwal, 'Lessons from the 1931 Constitution of Nadir Khan: Religious Inclusion and Reform' (Afghan Peace Process Issues Paper, United States Institute of Peace, March 2021) 5.

[13] ibid 4–7.

[14] See Constitution of Afghanistan 1964 (adopted 1 October 1964), arts 2, 28–40, 41–51.

[15] See ibid arts 2, 28–40, 41–51, 64, 74–81.

[16] M Hassan Kakar, 'Constitutional History of Afghanistan' *Encyclopedia Iranica* (15 December 1992) www.iranicaonline.org/articles/constitutional-history-of-afghanistan.

[17] B Rubin, *The Fragmentation of Afghanistan: State Formation and Collapse in the International System*, 2nd edn (Yale University Press, 2002) 76–77, 79.

[18] Library of Congress, *Afghanistan: A Country Study* (Library of Congress, 2012) 9.

[19] ibid 9–10.

[20] See S Amir Arjomand, 'Constitutional Developments in Afghanistan: A Comparative and Historical Perspective' (2005) 53 *Drake Law Review* 943, 954–55.

[21] Library of Congress (n 18) 9–14.

[22] ibid.

[23] ibid.

The Taliban's first rule from 1996 to 2001 broke decisively with this pattern. Rejecting republican frameworks, they governed without a constitution, relying instead on decrees and religious edicts issued by the then Amir (Supreme Leader) Mullah Omar.[24] This lack of recognised structures complicated fiscal management and foreign relations,[25] but it also revealed that governance could function through dispersed authority rather than codification. The experience provided a template: decree-based governance could sustain order in place of a charter, a lesson the movement would later refine after 2021.[26]

After the US-led intervention, the 2004 Constitution was the most ambitious effort to reconstruct Afghan statehood. Drafted under international auspices, it defined Afghanistan as an Islamic republic, enshrined gender equality, free expression, and judicial independence, and created a strong presidency.[27] Yet power centralisation enabled patronage networks,[28] while large parts of the countryside operated outside its framework under warlords or Taliban shadow governance.[29] The Taliban rejected the 2004 Constitution from the start as foreign-imposed, establishing parallel legal and administrative structures in an expanding belt of districts under their control,[30] which, by mid-2021, had increased to almost half of Afghanistan's 419 districts.[31] The 2004 charter thus produced a façade of order in Kabul but little authority beyond it.

Given the Taliban's longstanding denunciation of the 2004 Constitution, when the Taliban regained power in 2021, annulment of the 2004 Constitution was widely expected.[32] At first, officials suggested elements of the 1964[33] or 2004[34] texts might be provisionally applied. But in August 2022, reports surfaced from

[24] M Bashir Mobasher, Mohammad Qadam Shah, and Shamshad Pasarlay, *The Constitution and Laws of the Taliban 1994–2001: Hints from the Past and Options for the Future* (International IDEA, 14 December 2022) 20–21.

[25] See A Suhrke and S Schmeidl, 'Working with the Taliban: From the First to the Second Emirate' (2023) 42(3) *Central Asian Survey* 518, 520–21.

[26] See A Wright, R Sexton and D Grasse, 'Courting Civilians During Conflict: Evidence from Taliban Judges in Afghanistan' (2024) 78(1) *International Organization* 134, 144–46. See also W Mehran, S Habib and Z Riedel, 'Rebel Governance: an analysis of the Taliban's Governance from 2001–2021' (Small Wars & Insurgencies, first published online 27 November 2023).

[27] See Constitution of the Islamic Republic of Afghanistan (adopted 4 January 2004) arts 1, 22, 34, 116.

[28] A Sethi, 'Book Review: Afghanistan Legal Education Project, *An Introduction to the Constitutional Law of Afghanistan* (Stanford Law School, Rule of Law Program, 2nd Edition, 2015)' (2021) 5 *Indian Law Review* 250, 251.

[29] ibid.

[30] See generally Mehran, Habib, and Riedel (n 26).

[31] Special Inspector General for Afghanistan Reconstruction, *Quarterly Report to the United States Congress* (Special Inspector General for Afghanistan Reconstruction, 30 July 2021) 55.

[32] H Rahimi, 'Afghanistan's Laws And Legal Institutions Under The Taliban' (*Melbourne Asia Review*, 6 June 2022) melbourneasiareview.edu.au/afghanistans-laws-and-legal-institutions-under-the-taliban/.

[33] AFP, 'Taliban To 'Temporarily' Adopt 1964 Monarchy Constitution' *The Hindu* (18 November 2021) www.thehindu.com/news/international/taliban-to-temporarily-adopt-monarchy-constitution-with-caveats/article36713113.ece.

[34] S Pasarlay, 'Dead or Alive?: The Taliban and the Conundrum of Afghanistan's 2004 Constitution' (*I.CONnect: Blog of the International Journal of Constitutional Law*, 23 March 2022) www.iconnectblog.com/2022/03/dead-or-alive-the-taliban-and-the-conundrum-of-afghanistans-2004-constitution/.

an internal meeting where the Amir orally declared both annulled to provincial governors.[35] No decree was published, and the Ministry of Justice continued to display the 2004 text online as 'Enforced.'[36] Outsiders only learned of the annulment through provincial leaks and media reports.[37] This contradiction was not an oversight but a deliberate technique. By communicating annulment orally while retaining the text publicly, the Taliban turned ambiguity itself into a legal tool.

Across a century of Afghan history, then, constitutions repeatedly collapsed along the same structural divides. Instead of producing stability, codification invited contestation and exposed rulers to new challenges. The Taliban's rejection of codification must be read against this backdrop. By refusing to anchor authority in a single text, they avoid the cycle of constitutional promise and constitutional collapse. What follows is not the absence of constitutional order, but its substitution: a multi-textual system designed to govern through cultivated ambiguity.

III. The Architecture of the Taliban's Multi-Textual Constitutional Order

Against a century of failed charters, the Taliban have assembled an alternative constitutional order that rests not on a single text but on a dispersed repertoire of sources.[38] Authority is concentrated in the Amir, whose decrees are binding and unappealable.[39] A Rahbari Shura, or leadership council, formally advises the Amir; however, its influence has waned as power has concentrated in his hands.[40] Ministries inherited from the previous republic continue to manage finance, education, and health under Taliban oversight.[41] At the same time, governors appointed from within the movement are supervised by Ulema Councils empowered to veto decisions deemed un-Islamic.[42] Courts staffed by loyal clerics reinforce this framework.[43] The design is not anarchic but deliberately structured to channel all

[35] A Ghafoor Saboori, 'Parwan Governor, Citing Supreme Leader, Says Previous Constitution Invalid' *TOLOnews* (4 August 2022) tolonews.com/afghanistan-179259.

[36] See Ministry of Justice, Islamic Republic of Afghanistan, 'Enforced Constitution of Afghanistan' (Ministry of Justice) moj.gov.af/en/enforced-constitution-afghanistan.

[37] Saboori (n 35).

[38] S Pasarlay, 'Afghanistan's Unwritten Constitution under the Taliban' (*I.CONnect: Blog of the International Journal of Constitutional Law*, 17 May 2022) www.iconnectblog.com/2022/05/afghanistans-unwritten-constitution-under-the-taliban/#more-11897.

[39] L Maizland, 'The Taliban in Afghanistan' (*Council on Foreign Relations*, 15 September 2021) www.cfr.org/backgrounder/taliban-afghanistan#chapter-title-0-5.

[40] See H Rahimi and A Watkins, 'Taliban Rule At 2.5 Years' (2024) 17(1) *CTC Sentinel* 1–2.

[41] Maizland (n 39).

[42] A Watkins, 'What's Next for the Taliban's Leadership Amid Rising Dissent?' (*USIP*, 11 April 2023) www.usip.org/publications/2023/04/whats-next-talibans-leadership-amid-rising-dissent.

[43] A Sethi and others, 'Afghanistan' in L Roberto Barrosa and R Albert (eds), *International Review of Constitutional Reform* 2021 (Constitutional Studies at the University of Texas at Austin and the International Forum on the Future of Constitutionalism, 2022) 8.

authority upward and deny any realistic institutional routes for managing dissent and legal contestation.

The Taliban present their rule as based on Sharia, but this functions more as a legitimising tool than as a determinate legal code. References to Islamic law are broad, doctrinally vague, and interpreted exclusively by clerics close to the Amir.[44] Sharia thus serves as an umbrella, under which multiple and often contradictory sources can be invoked without the need to reconcile them. This formula preserves maximum flexibility while cloaking the rule in divine legitimacy.

Five sources form the multi-textual order. The first are foundational Islamic texts, including the Qur'an and hadith.[45] These are interpreted through Hanafi jurisprudence (one of the schools of Islamic jurisprudence) but coloured by South Asian Deobandi theology and Pashtun tribal custom.[46] These texts provide ultimate religious authority, but as they were developed between the seventh and eleventh centuries, they offer little guidance for modern statecraft, such as on corporate law or public administration.[47] That gap between classical texts and contemporary governance creates space for other sources to assume constitutional roles.[48]

The second source is internally authored doctrinal writings. Most prominent is *Al-Imārat al-Islāmiyyah wa-Manẓumatuha* (*The Islamic Emirate and Its System*),[49] published in 2022 by Abdul Hakim Ishaqzai – then Chief Justice and the regime's highest religious authority – and endorsed by the Amir.[50] It outlines institutional structures and ideological principles, but is never formally enacted.[51] Earlier texts, including the unratified 1998 draft constitution[52] and successive editions of the *Layha*,[53] an insurgency code also shapes practice. The *Layha*, first issued in 2006 and revised in 2009 and 2010, expanded from fighter discipline to cover taxation, education, and local administration, making it one of the movement's most operationally influential texts.[54] Circulating through sermons, judicial training, and

[44] Oxford Analytica, 'Senior Afghan Taliban Figures Move to Curb Leader' (*Emerald Expert Briefings*, 10 March 2023) doi.org/10.1108/OXAN-DB276639.

[45] See generally, CB Lombardi and AF March, 'Afghan Taliban Views on Legitimate Islamic Governance: Certainties, Ambiguities, and Areas for Compromise' (USIP Peaceworks No 182, February 2022).

[46] S Mahmoud Hanifi, 'Sifting Facts from Fiction: The Underpinnings of the Taliban's Islamic Emirate' (15 February 2024) SAIS Review of International Affairs, saisreview.sais.jhu.edu/sifting-facts-from-fiction-the-underpinnings-of-the-talibans-islamic-emirate/.

[47] See eg Z Keskin and M Ozalp, 'Explainer: what is shariah law and what version of it is the Taliban likely to implement?' *The Conversation* (24 August 2021) theconversation.com/explainer-what-is-shariah-law-and-what-version-of-it-is-the-taliban-likely-to-implement-166490.

[48] K Robinson, 'Understanding Sharia: The Intersection of Islam and the Law' (*Council on Foreign Relations*, 17 November 2021) www.cfr.org/backgrounder/understanding-sharia-intersection-islam-and-law.

[49] See generally, A Hakim Ishaqzai, *al-Imārat al-Islāmiyyah wa-Manẓumatuha* [*The Islamic Emirate and its System*] (Darul Uloom al-Sharia, 2022).

[50] See C Bunzel, 'The Taliban's Political Theory: 'Abd al-Hakim al-Haqqani's Vision for the Islamic Emirate' (*Hudson Institute*, 29 July 2024) www.hudson.org/terrorism/talibans-political-theory-abd-al-hakim-al-haqqanis-vision-islamic-emirate-cole-bunzel.

[51] ibid.

[52] Pasarlay, 'Dead or Alive?' (n 34).

[53] See K Clark, 'The Layha: Calling the Taleban to Account' (*Afghanistan Analysts Network*, July 2011) www.afghanistan-analysts.org/en/special-reports/the-layha-calling-the-taleban-to-account/.

[54] ibid.

bureaucratic guidance, these writings embed ideology in governance while carefully avoiding the binding force of a charter.

The third source is executive instruments: decrees, rulings, and farmans issued by the Amir.[55] These are the most authoritative in practice, but can be revoked or replaced by the Amir at any time. They establish institutions, set national policies, and regulate morality.[56] Some are short directives or simply oral commands, whereas others are detailed codes drafted by ministries and ratified by decree.[57] Although they may be published in the official gazette, their authority flows not from legislative procedure but from executive command of the Amir.[58]

The fourth source is administrative instruments, ranging from ministerial circulars and public statements to fatwas and handwritten memos.[59] These regulate day-to-day governance, enforce morality, and coordinate ministries.[60] Between 2021 and 2023, over eighty morality-related directives were issued, many curbing women's education, employment, and movement.[61] Their forms range from informal notes to gazetted notices, yet they shape social and political life as decisively as constitutional provisions, constitutionalising governance through routine paperwork.[62]

Finally, remnants of the 2004 Constitution persist. Fiscal procedures, customs collection, and budget preparation continue largely unchanged unless overridden by decree.[63] For example, public financial management procedures remain essentially unchanged, and the Ministry of Finance continues to use the former regime's systems for revenue collection, customs duties, and budget preparation.[64] This continuity supports basic state operations. Some original procedures have been integrated into executive instruments, diminishing the original text's relevance. Nonetheless, as discussed in the next section, the Taliban sometimes invoke the 2004 Constitution to signal continuity to international audiences.

[55] See eg US Department of State, *2022 Country Reports on Human Rights Practices: Afghanistan* (Bureau of Democracy, Human Rights and Labor, US Department of State 2023) www.state.gov/reports/2022-country-reports-on-human-rights-practices/afghanistan/.

[56] See eg ibid; M Yunus Yawar and C Greenfield, 'Taliban Codify Morality Laws Requiring Afghan Women to Cover Faces, Men to Grow Beards' *Reuters* (23 August 2024) www.reuters.com/world/asia-pacific/taliban-codify-morality-laws-requiring-afghan-women-cover-faces-men-grow-beards-2024-08-23/; A Azizi, 'Taliban Near Completion of Legal Code Rooted in Religious Law' *Amu TV* (18 June 2025) amu.tv/181259/.

[57] ibid.

[58] A Dawi, 'Unseen Taliban Leader Wields Godlike Powers in Afghanistan' *Voice of America* (28 March 2023) www.voanews.com/a/unseen-taliban-leader-wields-godlike-powers-in-afghanistan-/7026112.html.

[59] US Department of State (n 55).

[60] See eg Yawar and Greenfield, 'Taliban Codify Morality Laws' (n 56); Editorial, 'Taliban Warns NGOs to Comply with Ban on Women's Employment or Face Closure' *Kabul Now* (29 December 2024) kabulnow.com/2024/12/taliban-warns-ngos-to-comply-with-ban-on-womens-employment-or-face-closure/.

[61] S Hasan, 'Issue Update: Religious Freedom and Women's Rights in Afghanistan' (United States Commission on International Religious Freedom, August 2023) 1.

[62] ibid.

[63] Rahimi (n 32) .

[64] See W Hamoon and A Tawakkoli, 'National Budgeting and Revenue Collection under the Taliban' (2024) 7(1) *Journal of Social and Political Sciences* 122, 126.

These five sources are sustained not by a clear hierarchy but by cultivated ambiguity. No institution has authority to decide which prevails, and contradictions are left unresolved. The Amir's decrees can, in practice, override any text, yet even this power is exercised without codified finality. Supremacy is asserted episodically, invoked when useful, and set aside when inconvenient. By refusing closure, the Taliban preserve maximum discretion while projecting just enough coherence for governance. This deliberate maintenance of uncertainty – authority claimed but never definitively settled – is what allows the multi-textual order to function as a constitutional system without a constitution.

IV. Constitutional Practice: Cultivated Ambiguity in Action

The Taliban's constitutional order operates without a single text, codified hierarchy, or formal interpretive procedure. This is not oversight but deliberate design. Their governing technique can be called cultivated ambiguity: the deliberate maintenance of uncertainty about which legal sources apply, how they interrelate, who may interpret them, and when each may be invoked. Through this technique the regime secures four dividends that correspond to classic constitutional tasks: policy flexibility, elite containment, tactical legitimacy, and foundational evasion. These correspond to the functions of constitutions such as enabling change, managing elite conflict, legitimating authority, and establishing foundational order. However, they do so through indeterminacy rather than clarity, and without a singular constitutional document.

Cultivated ambiguity should also be distinguished from neighboring concepts. Unlike 'rule by law,' which entails the instrumental use of determinate rules,[65] cultivated ambiguity depends on leaving the rules unsettled. Unlike 'fragmented authoritarianism,' where overlap arises from bureaucratic competition,[66] here indeterminacy is engineered from above as a constitutional technique. And unlike classical legal pluralism, where multiple normative orders interact organically,[67] ambiguity is deliberately structured to preserve discretion at the centre. Its novelty lies in transforming uncertainty itself into a governing resource.

The dividends of this technique are evident in practice. The ban on opium cultivation in 2022 illustrates policy flexibility. After the takeover in 2021, the Taliban initially taxed the vast poppy economy, which supplied over 80 per cent of the global heroin market and provided a vital source of revenue under financial

[65] See eg M Lavička, 'Rule of Law with Chinese Characteristics: A Contested Landscape' (2025) 17 *Hague Journal on the Rule of Law* 277 link.springer.com/content/pdf/10.1007/s40803-025-00247-6.pdf.

[66] See AC Mertha, '"Fragmented Authoritarianism 2.0": Political Pluralization in the Chinese Policy Process' (2009) 200 *The China Quarterly* 995.

[67] See S Engle Merry, 'Legal Pluralism' (1988) 22 *Law & Society Review* 869.

isolation.[68] In April 2022, however, the Amir issued a farman banning all narcotics cultivation, production, and trade, citing religious duty.[69] No statute was amended, no procedures followed, and enforcement began immediately, with poppy fields razed and taxation halted in most districts.[70] By 2023, UN and NGO reports estimated that cultivation had collapsed by over 90 per cent.[71] Because no legal hierarchy gave past practice binding force, the regime could reverse policy without contradiction, contestation or institutional rupture. Religious authority supplied justification, while ambiguity erased the need for procedural closure.

Elite management reveals the second function, containment. In early 2023, senior figures such as Sirajuddin Haqqani (Interior Minister) and Mullah Yaqoob (Defense Minister) publicly criticised the concentration of authority in the Amir's hands and warned against international isolation – a striking departure from past practice, when questioning the Amir was unthinkable.[72] Yet no institutional process was invoked, no formal sanction imposed, and no explicit boundary set between tolerable and intolerable dissent. Instead, both figures were quietly weakened: loyalists were installed around them, deputies absorbed their responsibilities, and their operational scope narrowed without acknowledgement of conflict. [73] With no settled procedures for contestation, rivals could not know whether dissent would be tolerated or punished, nor whether an institutional channel for redress existed at all. Ambiguity disciplines precisely by keeping rivals uncertain of the boundaries: dissent may be tolerated or punished, sidelined quietly or ignored entirely, with no predictable rule. This lack of clarity forces elites to self-censor and restrain their actions, allowing the Amir to neutralise challengers without overt repression.

The regime's treatment of the 2004 Constitution shows how ambiguity sustains tactical legitimacy. In August 2022, the Amir reportedly annulled the charter orally in a closed meeting with provincial governors. No decree was published. Yet the Ministry of Justice continued to display the text online as the 'Enforced Constitution of Afghanistan,' and bureaucratic routines in finance and customs still relied on its procedures.[74] When engaging international actors, Taliban officials cite constitutional provisions to suggest legal continuity deserving recognition.[75]

[68] United Nations Office on Drugs and Crime, 'Opium Cultivation in Afghanistan: Latest Findings and Emerging Threats' (UNODC Research Brief, November 2022) www.unodc.org/documents/crop-monitoring/Afghanistan/Opium_cultivation_Afghanistan_2022.pdf.

[69] ibid.

[70] Editorial, 'Taliban say order restored after Afghan opium poppy protests' *Reuters* (7 May 2024) www.reuters.com/world/asia-pacific/taliban-say-order-restored-after-afghan-opium-poppy-protests-2024-05-07/.

[71] C Greenfield, 'Afghanistan opium poppy supply plummets 95% after Taliban ban, U.N. says' *Reuters* (5 November 2023) www.reuters.com/world/asia-pacific/afghanistan-opium-poppy-supply-plummets-95-after-taliban-ban-un-2023-11-05/.

[72] O Baheer, 'The Taliban Rift' (*South Asian* Voices, Stimson Center, 21 March 2023) southasianvoices.org/the-taliban-rift/.

[73] ibid.

[74] See nn 63–64 and accompanying text.

[75] Pasarlay, 'Dead or Alive?' (n 34).

However, when confronted with liberal provisions such as rights guarantees or electoral mandates, they dismiss these as incompatible with Islamic governance.[76] Without recognised supremacy for any single text, the Constitution can be simultaneously enforced and annulled, cited and dismissed, depending on audience and purpose.[77] Ambiguity allows one document to serve contradictory political functions at once.

Foundational evasion is the final function. Afghanistan's earlier constitutions became lightning rods for opposition: Amanullah's 1923 charter provoked clerical revolt, the 1964 framework fractured amid elite pluralism, and the 2004 text symbolised foreign imposition. The Taliban avoid this trap by dispersing authority across scripture, doctrinal tracts, decrees, and administrative notices, while refusing to declare any single text supreme. Authority is exercised but never anchored. This deprives not only domestic actors but also international organisations of stable targets for constitutional mobilisation or rights-based pressure. No document acquires symbolic weight, and therefore none can serve as a rallying point for challenge. It is the cultivated uncertainty over which source, if any, is ultimate that prevents opposition from crystallising: ambiguity dissolves potential rallying points before they can form.

Taken together, these strategies reveal cultivated ambiguity as a way of doing what constitutions do – enabling change, legitimating power, organising elites – while avoiding what constitutions normally impose: hierarchy, clarity, and constraint. Moreover, unlike familiar authoritarian tools such as constitutional manipulation or emergency decrees, which depend on formal procedures and leave legal precedents, ambiguity operates through indeterminacy that is harder to challenge legally or politically.

Before proceeding to the next section, it is important to address two points. First, critics might reasonably argue that what this analysis identifies as 'cultivated ambiguity' simply reflects institutional incapacity or transitional disorder, given their brief tenure since 2021. Perhaps the Taliban lack the technical expertise or political consensus to draft a constitution, and their multi-textual approach represents makeshift governance rather than strategic design. This interpretation would view the retention of 2004 constitutional procedures not as a tactical legitimacy, but as a bureaucratic necessity, and the lack of hierarchy among sources not as deliberate indeterminacy, but as unresolved confusion.

While these objections merit consideration, several factors suggest strategic choice rather than mere contingency. First, the Taliban's systematic deployment of ambiguity across multiple policy domains demonstrates consistent patterns rather than ad hoc responses. Second, their 20-year insurgency experience included developing sophisticated parallel governance structures, suggesting institutional capacity beyond what critics assume. Third, the selective and strategic nature of their ambiguity, such as maintaining clarity in revenue collection while cultivating

[76] See Sethi and others (n 43) 7–10.
[77] ibid.

uncertainty in political authority, indicates a deliberate calibration rather than uniform confusion. Finally, the regime's refusal to draft a constitution (or formally retain an older one), despite historical precedent and international expectations,[78] suggests a principled opposition rather than a technical inability. Nevertheless, distinguishing strategic ambiguity from institutional weakness remains methodologically challenging given limited access to internal decision-making processes.

Second, the sustainability of cultivated ambiguity remains an open question. While the Taliban have maintained this system for over three years, pressures for some degree of codification or formalisation can certainly emerge over time. Economic actors, particularly those seeking foreign investment or trade relationships, typically demand predictable legal frameworks. Within the bureaucracy, mid-level administrators managing routine functions may push for clearer guidelines to reduce decision-making burdens. However, the Taliban's experience differs from conventional state-building trajectories. Having governed territories through informal legal orders during their insurgency years, they have developed institutional practices that function without setting things in stone. Moreover, Afghanistan's economic isolation reduces pressure from international capital that might otherwise demand legal predictability. Crucially, the regime's primary economic partners, particularly China and Russia, have shown willingness to engage without demanding constitutional clarity or legal reforms.[79] The regime's ability to sustain ambiguity likely depends on maintaining sufficient economic autonomy and preventing the emergence of powerful bureaucratic constituencies demanding procedural clarity.

V. Multi-Textual Constitutionalism in Authoritarian Practice

Are the Taliban's governance techniques sui generis, or do they reflect broader authoritarian patterns? This section widens the perspective to show how other regimes, namely, Iran, Saudi Arabia, and China, also construct constitutional orders sustained through multi-textualism. In each case, constitutional authority is dispersed across multiple sources and sustained not by hierarchy but by cultivated ambiguity. Supremacy among sources is left unresolved in practice, allowing rulers to consolidate control and mute opposition. The result is not legal chaos but

[78] A Sethi, 'The Rule Of Law In Afghanistan: Prospects Under The Taliban Rule' in M Safjan (ed), *The Revival of the Rule of Law Issue* (Intersentia, 2024) 75–78.

[79] See eg M Yunus Yawar and C Greenfield, '*Afghan Taliban sign deal for Russian oil products, gas and wheat*' *Reuters* (28 September 2022) www.reuters.com/markets/commodities/exclusive-afghan-taliban-sign-deal-russian-oil-products-gas-wheat-2022-09-27/; M Yunus Yawar and C Greenfield, 'China becomes first to name new Afghan ambassador under Taliban' *Reuters* (13 September 2023) www.reuters.com/world/asia-pacific/taliban-say-chinese-envoy-appointed-kabul-first-ambassadorial-appointment-since-2023-09-13/.

a deliberately maintained uncertainty, as regimes exploit the suspension of hierarchy to preserve discretion and flexibility.

Iran, Saudi Arabia, and China are selected intentionally for this mini comparison. They exemplify three distinct constitutional traditions: a theocratic republic, a dynastic monarchy, and a party-state socialist system, each illustrating that a multi-textual constitutional order sustained through cultivated ambiguity is not limited to any specific ideology or institutional model. Other regimes, from Egypt to Russia to Vietnam to North Korea, could have been included, but these three provide the clearest contrasts. They are not intended to cover the entire spectrum of authoritarian regimes with a multi-textual order sustained through cultivated ambiguity, but to highlight their adaptability across jurisdiction.

Iran's political system is structured by the 1979 Constitution, which establishes ordinary republican institutions such as elections, a legislature, and a president, but embeds within them powerful clerical bodies. At the top stands the Supreme Leader, who issues binding decrees and appoints key officials (similar to the Amir in Afghanistan).[80] When Parliament passes legislation, the Guardian Council – a panel of six clerics and six jurists – can veto it for inconsistency with either the Constitution or Islamic law.[81] If Parliament resists, the matter can be referred to the Expediency Council (whose members are generally clerics and appointed by the Supreme Leader), which arbitrates and whose decision prevails.[82] Iran's multi-textual constitution thus rests on three overlapping sources: the written Constitution, Islamic law as interpreted by clerical councils, and political expediency as determined by the Expediency Council. On paper, this looks like a system of checks and balances. In practice, there is no court or institution empowered to decide definitively whether Islamic principle, constitutional provision, or political expediency governs.[83] This structural absence is precisely what generates cultivated ambiguity, enabling actors to shift disputes across religious, constitutional, and political registers and reframing rights without ever altering the text.

This dynamic was evident during the 2020 parliamentary elections, when the Guardian Council disqualified over 7,000 candidates, including many reformists, citing ideological criteria and vague grounds that were never spelt out in law.[84] Reformists appealed to constitutional guarantees of equal participation,[85] but the Council chose to override them.[86] The effect is that rights remain on paper,

[80] Constitution of the Islamic Republic of Iran (adopted 24 October 1979, amended 28 July 1989), art 110.

[81] ibid arts 4, 91, 94, 96, 98 and 99.

[82] ibid art 112.

[83] ibid (noting absence of any constitutional court or definitive arbiter beyond the Guardian and Expediency Councils).

[84] See Editorial, 'Questions loom in Iran as reformist factions lose hope in elections' *Radio Farda* (23 January 2020) en.radiofarda.com/a/questions-loom-in-iran-as-reformist-faction-loses-hope-in-elections/30393458.html. See also A Azizi, 'Factbox: Iran's 2020 parliamentary elections' (*IranSource*, Atlantic Council, 14 February 2020) www.atlanticcouncil.org/blogs/iransource/factbox-irans-2020-parliamentary-elections/.

[85] Constitution of the Islamic Republic of Iran (n 80), arts 19, 20, 23 and 62.

[86] *Radio Farda* (n 84).

but their enforcement depends entirely on clerical interpretation, and ambiguity makes them contingent rather than secure.[87] Here, multi-textualism exercised with cultivated ambiguity provided policy flexibility (through shifting interpretive registers), elite containment (through exclusionary vetting), tactical legitimacy (by citing constitutional rights even as they are denied), and foundational evasion (since Islamic law and republicanism are never reconciled in a single hierarchy).

Saudi Arabia's constitutional system rests on the 1992 Basic Law, which declares the Qur'an and Sunna to be the state's constitution.[88] Alongside this religious foundation, the Basic Law empowers the monarch to rule by royal decree,[89] authorises ministries to issue binding regulations,[90] and allows the Council of Senior Scholars to issue religious rulings (fatwas).[91] Saudi Arabia's multi-textual order, therefore, combines scripture (Qur'an and Sunna), the Basic Law, royal decrees, ministerial regulations, and fatwas, none of which are arranged in a binding hierarchy. Although formally all sources must conform to Sharia, in practice, no court or agency is authorised to assess whether a royal decree violates Sharia or the Basic Law.[92] Authority rests in whichever source the Crown chooses to invoke.[93] Supremacy is thus proclaimed in scripture and the Basic Law but never enforced against the monarch, leaving royal decrees effectively unreviewable. This refusal of enforcement is what sustains cultivated ambiguity, giving the Crown maximum flexibility.

This ambiguity was exploited during the 2017–19 Ritz-Carlton detentions, when more than 300 princes, officials, and business leaders were confined under the banner of anti-corruption reform.[94] A royal decree created a special committee with the power to detain and seize assets 'without judicial review.'[95] Statutory procedures were bypassed, courts sidelined, and the Basic Law silent.[96] Yet the decree carried full legal force, and no forum could test its conformity with constitutional or religious standards. The episode shows how deliberately undefined relationships among legal sources allowed royal authority to override every other norm while still cloaking itself in legality. Here too, multi-textualism delivered

[87] In the context of elections, see eg M Bizaer and Z Rasheed, 'Mass disqualification of candidates add to discontent in Iran' *Al Jazeera* (27 January 2020) www.aljazeera.com/news/2020/1/27/mass-disqualification-of-candidates-add-to-discontent-in-iran.

[88] Basic Law of Governance (Royal Order No A/90 of 1 March 1992) art 1.

[89] ibid arts 67 and 70.

[90] ibid art 67.

[91] ibid art 45.

[92] A Ansary, 'An Overview of the Saudi Arabian Legal System' (*GlobaLex*, July/August 2020) www.nyulawglobal.org/globalex/saudi_arabia1.html.

[93] ibid.

[94] S Kalin and K Paul, 'Future Saudi king tightens grip on power with arrests including Prince Alwaleed' *Reuters* (5 November 2017) www.reuters.com/article/world/future-saudi-king-tightens-grip-on-power-with-arrests-including-prince-alwaleed-idUSKBN1D5070/.

[95] Human Rights Watch, 'Saudi Arabia: Corruption Arrests Raise Due Process Concerns' (News Release, 8 November 2017) www.hrw.org/news/2017/11/08/saudi-arabia-corruption-arrests-raise-due-process-concerns.

[96] ibid.

policy flexibility (emergency economic crisis management), elite containment (neutralising rival elites), tactical legitimacy (the rhetoric of anti-corruption), and foundational evasion (no reconciliation between Sharia and royal command).

China's constitutional system combines the 1982 Constitution with the supremacy of the Communist Party.[97] The Constitution proclaims itself the 'fundamental law,' and a 2018 amendment explicitly affirmed Party leadership.[98] Yet ordinary citizens cannot invoke constitutional rights in court.[99] Since 2008, the Supreme People's Court has barred judges from using the Constitution as a direct legal basis, and subsequent doctrine has reinforced its non-justiciability.[100] In practice, governance proceeds through a dense web of Party directives, disciplinary codes, and ideological circulars, which sit outside the legislative hierarchy but routinely prevail over it. China's multi-textual constitution is therefore made up of the 1982 Constitution, formal legislation, and an extensive repertoire of Party directives and disciplinary instruments that in practice can override the constitutional text. The system builds in ambiguity: the Constitution and the Party both proclaim ultimate authority, yet it is always the Party that decides which prevails. By never reconciling this contradiction, the regime keeps authority permanently dependent on Party discretion.

A notable example is Document No. 9, a confidential Party circular issued in 2013 that warned against 'Western constitutional democracy' and 'civil society.'[101] Though never published as law, it triggered a national campaign: universities purged curricula, NGOs faced new restrictions, and rights lawyers were arrested or disbarred.[102] No court could review these actions for constitutionality. The effect is that constitutional rights exist textually but can be nullified interpretively whenever Party priorities shift. In this model, multi-textualism enables the Party to retain policy flexibility, neutralise alternative elites, sustain legitimacy through the formal symbolism of the Constitution, and avoid ever resolving the foundational contradiction between Party leadership and constitutional supremacy.

Taken together, these cases show that Afghanistan is not an anomaly but part of a broader authoritarian repertoire. Despite their differences, all exploit cultivated ambiguity for the same dividends: policy flexibility, elite control, tactical legitimacy, and foundational evasion.

[97] Constitution of the People's Republic of China (adopted 4 December 1982, amended 11 March 2018) Preamble.

[98] L Zhang, 'China: 2018 Constitutional Amendment Adopted' (*Global Legal Monitor*, Library of Congress, 18 May 2018) www.loc.gov/item/global-legal-monitor/2018-05-18/china-2018-constitutional-amendment-adopted/.

[99] S Lubman, 'Citizens' Rights, the Constitution and the Courts' *UC Berkeley Law* (26 September 2011) www.law.berkeley.edu/article/citizens-rights-the-constitution-and-the-courts/.

[100] ibid.

[101] See DW Drezner, 'The political economy of Document Number Nine' *Foreign Policy* (20 August 2013) foreignpolicy.com/2013/08/20/the-political-economy-of-document-number-nine/. See also Editorial, 'Document 9: A ChinaFile Translation' *ChinaFile* (8 November 2013) www.chinafile.com/document-9-chinafile-translation.

[102] ibid.

VI. Conclusion

This chapter has argued that the Taliban's multi-textual constitutional order is neither a legal vacuum nor institutional chaos. It is instead an example of cultivated ambiguity: a deliberate strategy of maintaining uncertainty about which sources apply, who may interpret them, and when. By dispersing authority across diverse instruments, the Taliban achieve the core functions of constitutionalism without maintaining a single constitutional document.

Three main insights emerge. First, maintaining multi-textual constitutions in authoritarian contexts is a designed technique, not an improvised arrangement. The Taliban's consistent deployment of ambiguity across different domains reveals a patterned strategy. It is also selectively calibrated: clarity is maintained where it sustains routine governance, such as fiscal procedures, but ambiguity is cultivated where it insulates political authority from challenge. The comparative cases of Iran, Saudi Arabia, and China confirm that this is not an Afghan anomaly but a wider authoritarian practice, embedded in different institutional traditions.

Second, constitutional functions can be performed through indeterminacy. Conventional theory assumes governance requires fixed hierarchies and predictable rules. Yet these regimes govern by deliberately keeping authority unsettled. The effect is that constitutional functions persist even when constitutional form is abandoned. This suggests that indeterminacy itself must be theorised as a constitutional technique in its own right, rather than dismissed as dysfunction or transitional weakness. Existing typologies emphasise manipulation, suspension, or sham constitutions; cultivated ambiguity should be understood as an additional modality, one that sustains authority through uncertainty rather than clarity.

Third, multi-textual constitutionalism represents an evolution in authoritarian governance. Earlier strategies – hollowing out constitutions, declaring emergencies, or suspending texts – relied on visible acts of exception. These tactics are increasingly costly, exposing rulers to domestic resistance and international censure. Cultivated ambiguity, by contrast, avoids creating clear targets. Power is preserved not by suspending law but by multiplying it, ensuring that no single text can constrain authority. This marks a broader shift in authoritarian technique: from rule through suspension to rule through uncertainty.

These findings open new directions for research. Conceptual work could explore how far cultivated ambiguity through the use of a multi-textual constitution can travel across different legal traditions before breaking down. Empirical studies might examine its long-term effects on bureaucratic effectiveness and regime legitimacy. Methodologically, fieldwork and archival research could map the informal networks through which interpretive discretion operates. Comparative work might identify further cases, testing whether multi-textualism is a transitional strategy or a stable authoritarian model. More broadly, the study of cultivated ambiguity raises questions for constitutional theory itself. Can indeterminacy function as a stabilising principle in hybrid or even democratic systems, or is it unique to outright authoritarian contexts? And under what conditions does ambiguity lose its resilience, giving way to pressures for hierarchical closure? Exploring these questions extends the analysis beyond Afghanistan and into the foundations of comparative constitutionalism.

The analysis also carries practical implications in transitional regimes and authoritarian states. International actors should not interpret the absence of a settled constitutional framework as weakness or transition. Authority may be deliberately dispersed, and effective engagement requires identifying the pressure points where ambiguity is operationalised: decrees that carry shifting authority, administrative discretion that blurs responsibility, and legal signals tailored to different audiences. Focusing narrowly on the search for a settled constitutional framework risks obscuring the more diffuse sites where authority actually operates.

Ultimately, the contribution of this chapter is threefold: it reconceptualises Afghanistan under the Taliban as a constitutional order in its own right, extends the idea of multi-textual constitutions into authoritarian contexts, and theorises cultivated ambiguity as a constitutional technique. Taken together, these insights expand the horizons of constitutional theory, showing that authority can rest on uncertainty just as much as on hierarchy or text.

INDEX

www.ingramcontent.com/pod-product-compliance
Ingram Content Group UK Ltd.
Pitfield, Milton Keynes, MK11 3LW, UK
UKHW021019260926
475984UK00003B/724

9 781509 980697